# Riches, Rivals, and Radicals

## AMERICAN ALLIANCE OF MUSEUMS

The American Alliance of Museums has been bringing museums together since 1906, helping to develop standards and best practices, gathering and sharing knowledge, and providing advocacy on issues of concern to the entire museum community. Representing more than 35,000 individual museum professionals and volunteers, institutions, and corporate partners serving the museum field, the Alliance stands for the broad scope of the museum community.

The American Alliance of Museums' mission is to champion museums and nurture excellence in partnership with its members and allies.

Books published by AAM further the Alliance's mission to make standards and best practices for the broad museum community widely available.

# Riches, Rivals, and Radicals

## A History of Museums in the United States

## Third Edition

MARJORIE SCHWARZER

ROWMAN & LITTLEFIELD

*Lanham • Boulder • New York • London*

Executive Editor: Charles Harmon
Editorial Assistant: Erinn Slanina
Interior Designer: Rhonda Baker

Credits and acknowledgments for material borrowed from other sources, and reproduced with permission, appear on the appropriate pages within the text.

Published by Rowman & Littlefield
An imprint of The Rowman & Littlefield Publishing Group, Inc.
4501 Forbes Boulevard, Suite 200, Lanham, Maryland 20706
www.rowman.com

6 Tinworth Street, London SE11 5AL, United Kingdom

British Library Cataloguing in Publication Information Available

**Library of Congress Cataloging-in-Publication Data Available**

ISBN: 978-1-5381-2806-0 (cloth: alk. paper)
ISBN: 978-1-5381-2807-7 (pbk.: alk. paper)
ISBN: 978-1-5381-2808-4 (electronic)

♾™ The paper used in this publication meets the minimum requirements of American National Standard for Information Sciences—Permanence of Paper for Printed Library Materials, ANSI/NISO Z39.48-1992.

# Contents

# *Foreword*

WHEN I JOINED THE STAFF OF THE AMERICAN ALLI-ance of Museums (AAM) in 2010, one of the first things I was handed was a copy of *Riches, Rivals, and Radicals.* Eager to soak up everything I could about the mysterious museum field, I read it cover to cover. And in the 10 years since that first reading, I have referred to and quoted from the text many times. It is still required reading for AAM new hires—and should be for anyone passionate about museums.

In 1939, AAM president Laurence Vail Coleman authored the first book on modern museum history, titled *The Museum in America: A Critical Study.* In the intervening decades, AAM published many other widely read studies, manuals, and books. They galvanized the field to make important changes in museums' approaches to fulfilling their missions and articulating their values. So much had transformed within the museum field since Coleman's original study that as part of its 100th anniversary celebration in 2006, AAM commissioned the first edition of *Riches, Rivals, and Radicals.* Marjorie Schwarzer's robust research, deep knowledge, and accessible writing style have made this seminal text a must-have on many reference shelves.

For this third edition, we are fortunate that the author has updated *Riches, Rivals, and Radicals* with important new research, contemporary analysis, and emergent voices, making it required reading for any leader who is looking to change—or simply understand—their institution within the context of the larger story of the museum field. As the pace of change in our field and our society accelerates, it is important to appreciate the pivotal points of museum history

described in this book and to acknowledge that many of today's progressive movements have roots in previous generations' efforts to lead museums toward better serving a broad and diverse public.

As any museum leader understands, the first step to making change is to understand the history of the challenges we face today. The last several decades of museology have seen a growing emphasis on education and accessibility, in all its forms. Progressive and successful leaders are moving beyond compliance related to the physical environment toward providing equitable access to everyone along the continuum of human ability and experience. There's a concerted effort to "decolonize" museums, tell previously untold stories, and broaden museums' funding sources.

Museums exist to make the world a better, more beautiful, more enlightened place. As storehouses of knowledge and protectors of history and culture, museums have long sought to house, preserve, and share the most important parts of our world—for current and future generations.

Rowman & Littlefield, in cooperation with AAM Press, is pleased to bring this inspiring third edition of *Riches, Rivals, and Radicals: A History of Museums in the United States* to you as its part of the Alliance's mission to champion museums and nurture excellence. Working together as part of a global Alliance, our future is filled with institutions that are relevant, sustainable, and vital in our changing world.

Laura L. Lott
President and CEO, American Alliance of Museums

The great force of history comes from the fact that we carry it within us, are unconsciously controlled by it in many ways, and history is literally present in all that we do.

—JAMES BALDWIN[1]

Extraordinary events shape generations. In turn, those generations shape events into museums. Nowhere has this been truer than in the United States of America where, since 1773, women and men have constructed museums that are as diverse as the nation itself. The country's museums have risen and changed alongside a growing and diversifying population. Their founders have come from all walks of life: from business tycoons to political activists, from the children of immigrants to the ancestors of the enslaved and displaced, from civil servants to social entrepreneurs, from gatherers to seekers, from pragmatists to poets. Museums might seem like mere repositories for each generation's vast accumulations of stuff. But at their heart they are so much more. Museums are tellers of stories and keepers of memory, places built to speak to present as well as future generations.

Over the past 250 years, the United States has weathered wars, economic swings, political strife, technological innovation, epidemics, and pandemics, amid changing ideas about education, democracy, and citizenship. So have its museums, some of them collecting and exhibiting artifacts of social and cultural revolution even as it was occurring. Singular

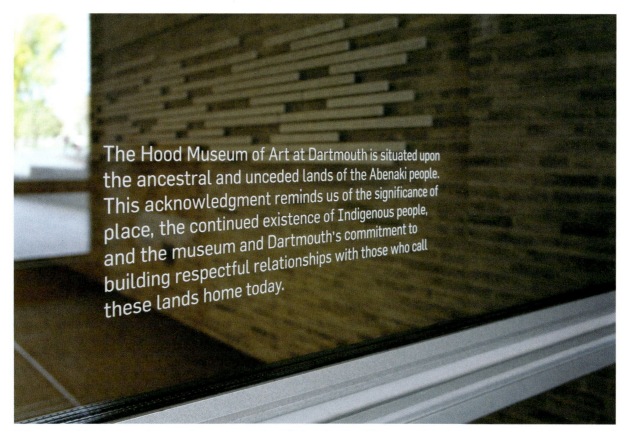

The Hood Museum of Art at Dartmouth is situated upon the ancestral and unceded lands of the Abenaki people. This acknowledgment reminds us of the significance of place, the continued existence of Indigenous people, and the museum and Dartmouth's commitment to building respectful relationships with those who call these lands home today.

This ancestral land acknowledgment permanently installed at the Hood Museum of Art's front entrance on the campus of Dartmouth College in New Hampshire honors the history and spirit of the region's Native American communities.
Courtesy of Hood Museum of Art. Photo by Alison Palizzolo, 2019

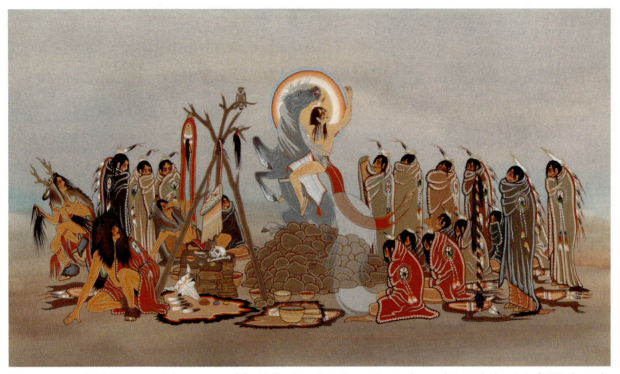

**Many museums initially opposed the passage of the Native American Graves Protection and Repatriation Act of 1990, but others were at the forefront of supporting contemporary Native American artists. This work (watercolor and tempura on paper) is titled** *Burial Ceremony—Spirit Ascending.* **It was created around 1945 by Woodrow (Woody) Wilson Crumbo (Potawatomi) for the Gilcrease Museum in Tulsa, OK.**
Courtesy of Gilcrease Museum, Tulsa

economic events in the United States have greatly influenced museums, at least in terms of building spurts. These include post–Civil War industrialization; post–World War I prosperity; the federal Works Progress Administration during the Great Depression; the establishment of the National Endowments for the Arts and Humanities during the 1960s; and the start-up Internet economy of the late 1990s. But if we look at the institution's staying power through subsequent financial downturns; technological rupture; societal transformation; and even, most recently, the COVID-19 pandemic, it is clear that something larger and more profound is going on here.

Perhaps it is that the museum is a fundamentally optimistic institution, even in difficult times. Museums build and preserve some of the nation's most extraordinary architecture. They showcase the beauty and promise of new scientific discoveries, historical breakthroughs, and artistic creation. They provide places of inspiration and repose. At the same time, museums have exposed some of the nation's most painful legacies—racism, inequity, violence. They strive to be places for healing and reckoning. This too, one could argue, is an act of optimism, for it expresses the hope that museum visitors will gain empathy and understanding from the evidence of others' struggles.

Americans have always longed for secular community spaces that connect them to deeper experiences, to each other, and to resonant things and ideas. Museums have sought to fill this role and to help us find meaning and inspiration in a chaotic world. Even though they are mindful of legacy and the weight of the past, museums—even the most traditional ones—are always focused on the future. Like the nation, they are constantly changing and adjusting to new ways of perceiving the world. They have done this throughout their history.

Museums in the United States have a history of struggles of their own. Tied to the egos of collectors, beholden to wealthy benefactors, bound up with artifacts that may have been stolen or looted, perpetuators of stereotypes to the detriment of some people and the aggrandizement of others, museums are associated with those seeking status, control, territory, and dominance. However, especially in the past few decades, many people have worked hard to confront that history and open museums' doors to a wider number of interpretations and ideas. And new kinds of museums have come into being along the way.

Artist Kenneth R. Bunn created this dramatic bronze sculpture of deer running through a pond for the opening of the Eiteljorg Museum of the American Indians and Western Art in Indianapolis in 1989. Today the museum houses one of the finest collections of Native American art in the world.
© Michael Ventura

Montgomery, Alabama's The Legacy Museum: From Enslavement to Mass Incarceration opened in 2018. It occupies the site of a former slave warehouse and pays tribute to the thousands of victims of lynching in the nation's history.
© Michael Ventura

**Stereograph showing a display of animal skeletons in glass cases and hanging from the ceiling at the Smithsonian National Museum, ca. 1900.**

Prints and Photographics Division, Library of Congress, https://www. loc.gov/pictures/item/2002695422/

Museums are no longer the dusty, exclusive enclaves of yore. The array of activities one might find in museums across the nation would undoubtedly have shocked their earliest founders. On one floor, visitors might encounter someone taking a selfie with a toddler and mock dinosaur; on another, older strangers sharing memories in a history exhibition about underground Queer culture. One might stumble upon a masterpiece or a makerspace. A dance performance, naturalization ceremony, or avant-garde film screening. A program devoted to the design of computer games, the art of hip-hop, the science of mixing a great cocktail. Some might decry 21st-century museums as being too "woke," so hyped on the caffeine of the moment that they are in danger of losing their way. But people have been accusing museums of all kinds of

**At the Field Museum in Chicago, visitors gaze at SUE's fearsome skull. SUE's head is detached from the rest of the mount because it's the most frequently researched part of the *T. rex*.**

Copyright Field Museum of Chicago. Photo by Martin Baumgaertner

**Taking selfies with a friendly dinosaur at the Perot Museum of Nature and Science DinoFest.**
Courtesy of Perot Museum of Nature and Science, Dallas, TX.

digressions for decades. If one follows the history of museums in the United States, it becomes apparent that for a long time, they have bent a few rules and ruffled some feathers as they have aspired to appeal to wider audiences across generations and, most importantly, contribute to society.

Americans have been described as a myopic people, prone to ignoring the past in order to plow into the next big thing. Why then have they continually put so much faith in museums? Even when one considers the nation's museums that have downsized or folded as well as the people who rarely—if ever—visit them, museums have outperformed other public destinations. Consider, for example, that, as of 2019, annual museum visitation well exceeded attendance to all major-league sporting events and theme parks combined. Or look at the decline or repurposing of places such as movie theaters in the past decades. As different kinds of cultural venues have risen and fallen, the number of museums has steadily increased—by over twentyfold. In 1928 the American Association (now Alliance) of Museums estimated that the country had

**Phillip Lindsay Mason. *Rainbow Dream*, 1970. Acrylic on canvas, 48 in. × 33 in. Part of the Black Power exhibition at the Oakland Museum of California. Gift of Michael J. Learned.**
Courtesy of the Oakland Museum of California

Entrance panel from *All Power to the People: The Black Panthers at 50* at the Oakland Museum of California (2016).
Courtesy of the Oakland Museum of California

*The Black Panthers at 50* at the Oakland Museum of California (2016) or retrospectives of popular artists at art museums throughout the nation? Why have other museums become important pilgrimage sites: for example, the National Museum of African American History and Culture in Washington, D.C., and Montgomery, Alabama's The Legacy Museum: From Enslavement to Mass Incarceration, which occupies the site of a former slave warehouse and is credited with helping to revive that small city's tourism economy. Why has a new generation emerged that is working hard to reclaim and retell their forebearers' stories through the vehicle of the museum? What is it about museums of all kinds that has made them so compelling to so many people, and for so many reasons?

There are no easy answers to the mystery of what makes the nation's museums tick. As their numbers, scale, and complexity have increased, U.S. museums have had to embrace some apparent contradictions. They have struggled to define themselves for their many publics: being charitable nonprofit organizations in a marketplace culture, being places of memory and reflection in a nation that stresses action and immediacy, being respectful of tradition in a land of ceaseless innovation, being leisure-time destinations

Claude Monet. *Spring Flowers*, 1864.
Cleveland Museum of Art; gift of the Hanna Fund 1953.155; Cleveland Museum of Art Creative Commons

1,400 museums; by the end of 2019 more than 30,000 were in business. For a country accused of being short-sighted and ahistorical, that sure is a lot of museums![2]

Perhaps there is an easy explanation for this astonishing rate of growth. One could argue that the museum is a concrete (or steel-cladded, as it were) display of the excess wealth of a few dominant collectors for a devoted class of supporters, members, and visitors. But what about the success of museums with a different genesis: children's museums, community museums, those on American Indian reservations, in public libraries, on college campuses, and in municipal airports? Why do public school teachers and parents from all walks of life value museums as field trip sites, even when the logistics of arranging those trips can be so onerous? If museums only speak to an elite class of users, why do studies consistently show the long-term positive impact of visits on people from all backgrounds?[3] And beyond the field trip, what compels the buzz around exhibitions like *All Power to the People:*

**Nick Cave. "Soundsuit, "2007, fabricated, beaded, and sequined body suit, metal armature, metal Victorian flowers. Cave's first Soundsuit was created in 1992 as a direct response to the brutal beating of Rodney King by 4 Los Angeles police officers and the riots that followed their acquittal.**
Photo by James Prinz Photography; courtesy of the artist and Jack Shainman Gallery, New York; collection of the Mint Museum, Charlotte, N.C.; Museum Purchase: Founders' Circle Annual Cause; 2009.19.1A-00000

in a purposeful country where people are always on the go, being places of learning when ideas about what it means to educate are constantly changing, being spiritual and secular at the same time, functioning as businesses that need to meet a bottom line while knowing that the real bottom line is being of service to humanity.

These struggles only lead to more questions. What happens when museums attempt to bridge relevancy with legacy? Can they be both pragmatic and aspirational? Can museums blend academic scholarship with popular culture? Can they bridge education with entertainment? Can they afford to experiment? Can they afford not to?

Questions like these have persisted throughout the history of museums in the United States. What have changed are the answers. Museums are not static institutions and never have been. Even the smallest among

them is a complicated enterprise. Their buildings, collections, exhibitions, and programs have continually changed in light of social, cultural, and technological transformation. *Riches, Rivals, and Radicals: A History of Museums in the United States* tells that story.

This book is structured into five thematic chapters. Along the way, we meet some notorious characters who were integral to the nation's earliest museums—prominent Americans like P. T. Barnum, J. P. Morgan, John D. Rockefeller, Jr., and Henry Ford. Without them and other ambitious, wealthy patrons, the nation's museum culture would probably never have come to fruition. The book also recognizes forgotten figures—people like Anna Billings Gallup, John Cotton Dana, Grace McCann Morley, and Clemency Coggins. We take for granted some of their radical innovations—programs that brought children into museums, shared artifacts with disenfranchised communities, revolutionized the museum's standing in society, and confronted the legacy of looting and pillage. As workplaces mired in both internal and external politics and persistent financial woes, our museums have been blessed with tenacious individuals who have always found a way to either keep the institution afloat or take some risks to change it up. It has taken a large, collective effort waged by people from all backgrounds, genders, and perspectives to stand up to entrenched systems and inch the institution forward in service to future generations.

Since the late 19th century, philosophers, philanthropists, and educators have clashed over how museums should relate to society. This lively debate is threaded into *Riches, Rivals, and Radicals'* opening chapter, titled "Museums and Society." The chapter lays out key moments in U.S. museums in the 20th century that we return to in the chapters that follow. "Museums and Society" focuses on two ongoing debates that impelled the development of museums from the post–Civil War years through the early decades of the 21st century. First, the role of education in society. Second, how to respond to technological innovation. The chapter opens with the nation's first museums, where the tensions between scholarly pursuits and entertainment were already brewing. As museums developed, they gradually came to embrace progressive education, that is, education grounded in the principles of democracy and social consciousness. For example, in 1905, during the tuberculosis epidemic, the American Museum of Natural History in New York sponsored exhibitions created by public health agencies. The idea was to communicate essential information to as large an audience as possible. At the same time, Harvard University opened a "Social Museum," designed to help its privileged students develop empathy for others, including child laborers, so they could help bring about a more equitable society. The lack of resources for children prompted the founding of the nation's (and world's) first children's museum in Brooklyn, N.Y. Opening the doors to schoolchildren was a radical and enduring innovation; this began in the 1880s in Connecticut. Museum educators' ideas about how their institutions should relate to society often diverged with collectors and others. The chapter documents how the institution tried to balance many different interests and needs through the Great Depression, two world wars, the Cold War, civil rights activism, and conservative backlash into the early years of the Internet and social media.

*Riches, Rivals, and Radicals'* second chapter is about architecture. In "The Building: From Ionic to Iconic," we look at how architects' ideas about the museum's role in society play out in bricks and mortar. Museums occupy a stunning array of building types: from classical marble palaces to ornate mansions, from undulating titanium containers to repurposed textile warehouses. Yet as architectural critic Ada Louise Huxtable reminds us, museum architecture "has been an uneasy, ambivalent, consistently controversial, and passionately debated subject since the first portrait . . . was transferred from a palace or church for the purpose of collection or display."[4] How do the nation's diverse museum building types reflect changing technologies, streetscapes, and attitudes about education, design, and public space? What happens when an architect's ego gets in the way? In this chapter we look at iconic (and a few controversial) architectural masterpieces to understand why, despite the fact that museums never seem to have enough money to build and maintain the perfect structure, so many architects have coveted the opportunity to design a new one at any given moment in time.

Chapter 3, "The Collection: From Stockpiling to Taking Stock," is the longest section of this book. And no wonder: America's museums have amassed astonishingly large collections of stuff. These objects—which, as of this writing, total 4.7 billion—range from the beautiful to the sublime, from the fabled to the superfluous. Looked at together, they are telling evidence of Americans' materialism, our penchant for expressing power through the act of acquisition. The stories behind the nation's foundational collections give us insight into the distribution of wealth and power in America as well as changing values about culture. The

stories that later unfolded when the outside world began to rummage through museums' bulging closets show us how hard it is to let go. What happened in the 1970s when insider practices emerged from the mothballs and into the headlines? How did museums respond in the 1990s to successful legal challenges by indigenous communities and the heirs of Holocaust victims for the return of stolen items? What about today's increased concerns about antiquities looted from other countries and continued calls for decolonizing collections? Which objects belong in a museum and which don't? Who decides what kinds of objects, artifacts, and artworks tell the story of our nation? These questions—as well as a few legendary escapades—are explored in this chapter.

Chapter 4, "The Exhibition: From Cases to Spaces," describes how museums have attempted to transform their galleries from monotonous halls filled with dusty wooden cases and crude taxidermy to the polished and multifaceted spaces we find across the nation today. Which technological, educational, social, and mass-media innovations have museums responded to? How has social activism pushed museums to change the way they interpreted their collections? Which museums began to invite more perspectives to the table, why, and what happened when they did? What are some of the most influential exhibitions of all time?

The concluding chapter of *Riches, Rivals, and Radicals* loops back to events introduced in chapter 1 through the lens of politics, money, and the sheer force of personality. This chapter is about the ongoing struggle to transform museums from private playgrounds into professional organizations with mission-driven values. "People, Politics, and Money: Making Sense of Museums" discusses cases of ethical lapses, censorship, political fallout, workplace inequities, and battles both lost and victorious that impact how museums have functioned in the American marketplace. The chapter opens in 1920s Charleston, S.C., with the story of museum director Laura Bragg who stared down the local city council in the face of Jim Crow laws. It continues through dramatic confrontations in the boardroom, halls of Congress, on picket lines, and even at professional conferences. It culminates with the experiences of 21st-century professionals who understand that the struggle for equity, both within museums and in the nation, continues today, and much work remains to be done. We can take inspiration from the strategies and strength of those who have come before us, as well as those whose voices end this chapter.

The art historian Rosalind Krauss, born in 1941 and herself part of a generation that transformed its profession, has written about how in an expanded field, cultural terms can be "kneaded and stretched and twisted."[5] And so a word about terms used in this book. Museums reflect the times in which they operate, and thus, vocabulary used in one era can sound outdated in the next. This includes language used in the past to discuss race, ethnicity, gender, technology, and national identity (including the term *American*). I have retained original terms, especially when quoting sources, although I have taken some license for the sake of flow. As they update their missions (and funding sources), museums often change their names. I have done my best to keep up with new institutional names and acronyms when discussing different organizations. Even the AAM changed its name since the last edition of this book; the organization's original name was American Association of Museums; in 2012, it rebranded itself as the American *Alliance* of Museums. (My stylistic solution is to call it "AAM.") More problematic are multiple meanings associated with the key word in this book's title: *museum*. In recent years, different parties, from professional organizations like the International Council of Museums to franchises like the Museum of Ice Cream, have attempted to define (and at times, some would argue, co-opt) the term *museum*.[6] For this book, I use the broad definition published by the Institute for Museum and Library Services: the museum that is the subject of this book is a not-for-profit organization organized on a permanent basis for essentially educational or aesthetic purposes, that owns or uses tangible objects, either animate or inanimate, and cares for and exhibits these objects to the general public on a regular basis through facilities that it owns or operates.[7] This book synthesizes key events that have helped to define museums in the United States. It is not a definitive or comprehensive history. Fortunately, AAM's Museum Studies, Media & Technology, and Education Professional Networks as well as other professional groups and researchers actively blog and post resources. The citations in the endnotes are meant to be a treasure chest of sources, authors, and perspectives that might inspire the collecting and documentation of even more stories.

**Self Made**, Exploratorium, San Francisco, 2019.
Copyright Exploratorium, www.exploratorium.edu

The geographic scope of this book is also limited. I tell the unique story of museums in one nation: the United States of America. This book went to press in summer 2020, during the first wave of the COVID-19 pandemic, a trauma that will surely shape the next generation, as well as future institutions.

My hope is that the stories in the pages that follow will illuminate how museums have truly wrestled with terms, meanings, their histories, and events that shape people's lives in order to stake a place in the United States and indeed the world.

## NOTES

1. James Baldwin, *The Price of the Ticket: Collected Nonfiction, 1948-1985*, quote copied by the author from the wall of the Levine of Museum of the South, Charlotte, N.C., in April 2019.

2. About Museums, http://ww2.aam-us.org/about-museums/museum-facts, accessed October 30, 2019; Christopher Ingraham, "There Are More Museums in the U.S. Than Starbucks and McDonald's Combined," *Washington Post*, June 13, 2014, n.p.; Institute for Museum and Library Services, Museum Data File (November 2018), accessed August 25, 2019, https://www.imls.gov/sites/default/files/museum_data_file_documentation_and_users_guide.pdf; Matt Lambros, *After the Final Curtain: The Fall of the American Movie Theatre* (Lanham, MD: Jonglez, 2016); and Jonathan Merritt, "America's Epidemic of Empty Churches," *Atlantic* (November 25, 2018).

3. John H. Falk, "Recollections of Visits to Museums," in *Research on Families in Museums*, eds. Minda Borun and A. Cleghorn (Washington, D.C.: American Association of Museums, 1997), 56–93. See also John H. Falk and Lynne D. Dierking's considerable body of work and studies of museum visitation on https://johnhfalk.com/about//.

4. Ada Louise Huxtable, "Review of *Towards a New Museum*," *New York Review of Books* 46 (April 22, 1999): 10.

5. Rosalind Krauss, "Sculpture in the Expanded Field," *October* 8 (Spring 1979): 30.

6. For a useful discussion of different museum definitions, see "Is It a Museum? Does It Matter?" *Exhibitionist* 30, no. 1 (Spring 2010).

7. See Institute for Museum and Library Services, "Eligibility Criteria," https://www.imls.gov/grants/apply-grant/eligibility-criteria, accessed November 30, 2019.

# CHAPTER 1

# Museums and Society

FROM THEIR VERY BEGINNINGS, MUSEUMS IN THE United States have envisioned themselves as vital participants in an emerging democracy. Their quest to be useful to the nation and beneficial to society began before there was even a nation. In 1773, in the midst of the war for independence, the Charleston Library Society gathered samples of animals, plants, and minerals from the South Carolina low country. This collection, considered to be the first in the nation, was assembled for the purpose of study and scientific research. In 1786 artist Charles Willson Peale opened his Philadelphia home as a cabinet of curiosities. This display, designed "to please, improve and cultivate the mind," is regarded as the nation's first museum open to the public.[2]

Part of the Peale family's collection was purchased by Connecticut businessman Phineas T. (P. T.) Barnum. Prized items like several hundred stuffed fish and a badly preserved Angora cat became part of Barnum's American Museum, which opened in lower Manhattan in 1841. Barnum lived by the motto that the "American people have an intense love of the ludicrous . . . and like to be humbugged."[3] To that end, his museum featured a "Cosmoramic Room," replete with oddities: a Malaysian cigar the size of a walking stick, a whistle fashioned out of a pig's tail, a "genuine" Feegee mermaid skeleton. "My museum was not so refined or classic or scientifically arranged as the foreign governmental institutions, for mine had to support my family . . . hence I was obliged to popularize it," the famous huckster once confessed. At the same time, he

**Interior of the Charleston Museum, ca. 1920s.**
Courtesy of Charleston Museum

*The Artist in His Museum* is an 1822 self-portrait by the American painter Charles Willson Peale (1741–1827). It depicts the 81-year-old artist posed in Peale's Museum, then occupying the second floor of Independence Hall in Philadelphia, PA. The nearly life-size painting is in the collection of the Pennsylvania Academy of the Fine Arts.

Courtesy of Pennsylvania Academy of the Fine Arts, Philadelphia. Gift of Mrs. Sarah Harrison (The Joseph Harrison Jr. Collection) reminded his critics that his museum provided wholesome entertainment suitable for families.[4] Barnum's museum burned to the ground twice, forcing him to abandon the museum world for the more profitable business of traveling circuses.

Most mid-19th-century museums were far less showy. They existed mainly in the basements of libraries, colleges, or antiquarian societies. Collections consisted of plaster casts and copies of Greek, Roman, and Renaissance masterworks. The random plant, seashell, or rock that appealed to an explorer or a missionary laid out in a few wooden cases. Medical instruments. Military records of English immigrants. These were largely private repositories dedicated to scholarship and research. They were often available only to members, usually male adults who were admitted by secret vote.

The first truly public museum in the United States was envisioned by a British chemist who never set foot on American soil. Born in Paris and witness to the French Revolution, James Smithson was inspired by the idea of democracy being sown on the other side of the Atlantic Ocean. He saw the United States as a place where the spread of modern scientific ideas about the "rights of man" could advance society. Smithson bequeathed the U.S. government ample funds for an institution "for the increase and diffusion of knowledge among men." After decades of haggling about what to do with the money, in 1846 Congress established the Smithsonian Institution, signed into law by President James K. Polk. The institution's first task was to construct a castle-like building on the National Mall in Washington, D.C., where Smithson's remains are enshrined today. The Castle was dedicated as a national museum in 1857. It proved to be of immediate use to President Abraham Lincoln. He ascended into the building's highest tower to study the Confederate troops massing across the Potomac River in Virginia.[5]

The Civil War radically changed the nation; its impact still reverberates in many parts of the country. Reconstructing the South, conquering "virgin" Western territories, and dealing with the rapid growth of Northern industrial cities were foremost on the government's agenda. This transformational era resulted in a daunting list of societal challenges that will sound familiar to today's readers: disease epidemics, business scandal, labor disputes, an influx of non-English-speaking immigrants, corruption of the

Barnum's American Museum. Gleason's Pictorial 4, no. 5 (January 29, 1853):72. Drawn by Chapin. Engraved by Avery.

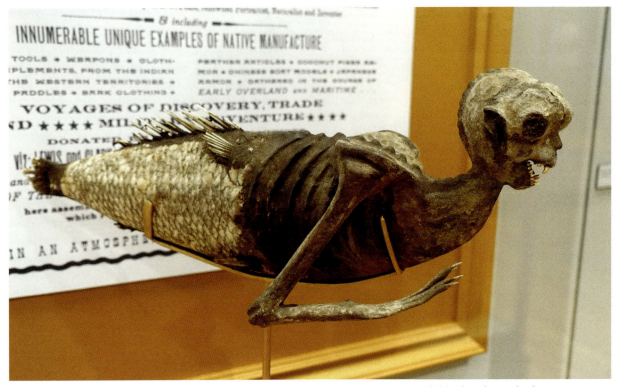

A papier-mâché mermaid modeled on the Feejee Mermaid exhibited by P. T. Barnum. Exhibited at the Peabody Museum, Harvard University, 2017.
Photo by Daderot, Wikimedia Commons

clergy, political graft, and poverty. Perhaps what was needed was not Smithson's vision of a "diffusion of knowledge" but a cohesive set of aesthetic and intellectual standards to unify and guide the nation. During the Ulysses S. Grant presidency, politicians and other movers and shakers began to float ideas for a centralized cultural institution modeled on the French École des Beaux-Arts. But no one could agree on what the standards should be, who would make decisions, or even where such an academy would be located. Meetings devolved into jealousies, grandstanding, or just plain disagreement.[6] After all, this was the United States of America, land of business opportunity and individualism. Naturally, U.S. cultural institutions would assume a variety of forms, some of which would compete with each other.

Civic leaders in communities around the nation did agree on one solution for "civilizing" a diverse nation and promoting social harmony and economic growth: education. They saw two pragmatic ways to deliver it. The first was opening public schools for children, to be administered by local boards of education. The second was building public institutions for all, chiefly libraries and museums. These would be created and run by wealthy citizens, part of their moral responsibility to secure a community's future. Industrial titans who were in the process of amassing great fortunes agreed. Prominent among them was Pittsburgh millionaire Andrew Carnegie. In his influential essay "The Gospel of Wealth," Carnegie called upon the most prosperous members of society to create "ladders upon which the aspiring can rise" and use their "superior wisdom" to better the world for their "poorer brethren."[7] Thus began the public library movement as well as such

Opening reception in the picture gallery at the Metropolitan Museum of Art, 681 Fifth Avenue, N.Y., February 20, 1872. Wood-engraving published in *Frank Leslie's Weekly*, March 9, 1872.

pioneering museums as New York City's American Museum of Natural History (1869) and Metropolitan Museum of Art (1870), Boston's Museum of Fine Arts (1870), the Art Institute of Chicago (1879), and the Carnegie Museums in Pittsburgh (1895).

Other kinds of museums also took shape during these decades. Settlement workers felt that viewing and creating art could help ease immigrant families into their new surroundings. In 1889, Chicago-based social activists Jane Addams and Ellen Starr Gates instigated the Hull House Labor Museum. Its galleries featured art from abroad that had been collected by its founders. It was supplemented with contemporary art and everyday objects created by "neighborhood immigrants from various countries actively demonstrating their craft skills, an exercise implicitly aimed at

**Art class at Hampton Institute in Virginia, ca. 1899. Hampton Institute established the nation's first African American museum as part of its curriculum to develop an educated class of African American citizens after the Civil War.**
Francis Benjamin Johnston collection, Library of Congress

improving self-esteem and relationships within families," explains museologist Lois Silverman in her book *The Social Work of Museums*.[8]

In the western territories, settlers established museums to document their own achievements. The Minnesota Historical Society, for example, was founded in 1849, nine years before the state was admitted to the Union. In the south, emerging black colleges recognized that art education could help form an educated class in post–Civil War society. In 1868 the Hampton Institute in Virginia created the nation's the first African American museum. Concurrently in the south, societies like Daughters of the Confederacy felt that public displays of Civil War relics could promote "how a brave people and their descendants hold the name and fame of their heroes and martyrs with admiration undiminished by disaster or defeat."[9] They founded museums celebrating the Confederacy in cities like New Orleans (1891) and Richmond (1896).

"It is difficult to overemphasize the stress [museums] placed upon their pedagogical functions [during the 19th century] . . . and the benefits they promised for industrial production, scientific curiosity and historical consciousness," writes University of Chicago history professor Neil Harris.[10] Educational programming was museums' top priority, especially free evening lectures where, before the days of broadcast radio, TV, and the Internet, audiences gathered in museums to learn about topics of the day. The American Museum of Natural History's offerings illustrate the range of topics that fascinated urbanites. They included "Where Lumber Comes From," "Ants and Bees," "In the Land of the Red Men: As They Were and Are," and programs about Arctic expeditions, an exploit that captivated American imaginations during the 1900s.[11] Taken together, these programs not only aimed to civilize and educate, but to demonstrate a young nation's material and intellectual progress.

Many lectures were geared to schoolteachers. They were eager to use museums as new sources of knowledge for their pupils. In the 1880s librarian Henry Watson Kent began the tradition of bringing schoolchildren to public exhibitions when he invited classes to visit the Norwich Museum and Library in Connecticut. In 1899, concerned that almost one-third of the children living in Brooklyn worked as day laborers and received no formal school instruction, a curator named William H. Goodyear founded the world's first museum dedicated to youth education, the Brooklyn Children's Museum.

**Connecticut-based librarian Henry Watson Kent (1866–1948) is credited with two important late-19th-century museum innovations: the public school field trip and the first collections cataloging system.**

Courtesy of Grolier Club, New York City

**John Dewey (1859–1952) was one of the most influential progressive philosophers and educators in American history. His teachings about experiential learning and accessibility influence museums to this day.**

**Schoolchildren on a field trip in the early decades of the 20th century.**
Courtesy of Boston Children's Museum, ca. 1930s

Two public intellectuals, the British poet Matthew Arnold and the American educator John Dewey, profoundly influenced the direction of the nation's cultural organizations. Their divergent ideologies—Arnold was an elitist and Dewey was a progressive educator—would set the stage for philosophical tensions that still tug at museums today. Should museums enshrine the values of an elite strata of society? Or should they reflect more pluralistic values? Should they be aspirational or pragmatic? Arnold and Dewey made forceful arguments to support their perspectives on these questions.

In the 1880s, Arnold sailed to the United States to lecture at churches, universities, and social clubs. Wealthy museum founders like Andrew Carnegie, the Met's Joseph H. Choate, and even P. T. Barnum hosted the English gentleman with sumptuous accommodations and meals. Arnold would later write that he was shocked by Americans' materialism, amused by their eating habits (ice! huge slabs of beef!), and considered most of the people he met to be "philistines." He went

on to warn that without institutions that fed superior Anglo and European values to the minds of the crème de la crème of American society, America would surely descend into anarchy.[12] Some younger academics complained that the older English gent was not only a boring speaker, but "snobbish" and "old-fashioned." His ideas, however, enthralled his monied followers and motivated them to found museums modeled on the values of the European aristocracy. To fill these museums with artistic treasures, Choate called on his fellow millionaires to "convert pork into porcelain . . . railroad shares and mining stocks . . . into the glorified canvas of the world's masters . . . to humanize, to educate and refine a practical and laborious people."[13] A collective investment in the finer things in life would result in monumental museums that would rival those in Europe and serve as showcases for an emerging American sophistication.

The educational reformer John Dewey was a college student in Vermont when Arnold toured the nation, but already he was developing a very different vision for the nation's cultural institutions. In 1896 he and his wife, Harriet Chipman, moved to Chicago, where, at the University of Chicago, they founded an experimental school, appropriately named the Lab School. Students spent one and a half hours per week at a museum, engaging in experiments and adventures. Dewey consulted with Jane Addams on the founding of the Hull House Museum, but his influence extended well beyond Chicago's social activists. Dewey lectured widely on the failures of public schooling. Dubbing desks, blackboards, and rote recitation "dull drudgery," he called on teachers to look beyond the schoolyard and create real-life experiences for students who could "learn by doing." Dewey firmly believed that museums should be central to everyone's lives. Rather than a "secluded monopoly of belief and intellectual authority," he preached that the nation's moral obligation was to "make the sharing of the cream of human experience as nearly universal as possible."[14]

In reality, museums' practices fell somewhere in the middle of these debates, usually with founding board members and collectors on one side, staff and public opinion on the other. While uplifting the nation and educating the populace were always the stated goals of late-19th-century museums, collectors also had more egotistical aims. Wealthy industrialists were beginning to amass their own private collections of art and scientific specimens. Museums were logical places to house those objects. Cities often donated parcels of land, but otherwise the buildings were financed by their founders. For collectors, building a museum represented not only a favorable real estate deal, but a great increase in social stature. For cities, museum building projects represented not only a way to curry favor with the business elite, but a great increase in cultural and economic stature, "as necessary an adornment and advertisement for a city . . . as pavements and bank clearances."[15]

Museums tried to keep both their benefactors and the public happy. Most charged no admission fee, and

**Museum educator Frank DuMond, ca. 1925, with students arriving for a Saturday class in Grand Rapids, MI.**
Courtesy of Grand Rapids Public Museum, Grand Rapids, MI.

their doors were open every day of the week and often at night.[16] However, they sent "coded" messages about who was welcome to visit. The architecture was often imposing, implying who belonged and who did not. So too the location of choice: public parks, most of which were off-limits to people of color. Other museums opened their doors to "colored" visitors one day a week, as long as they were well-behaved schoolchildren or nannies accompanying white children under their care. Even so, they refused access to basic amenities, like restrooms. Even in northern museums that did not overtly abide by segregation laws, some museum guards took it upon themselves to refuse entrance to black visitors.

Museums of this era promised to uplift humanity, even if they looked down on much of it. Becoming cultured, many insiders believed, was a serious endeavor and not a "mere pastime" for the masses.[17] Directors frequently complained not only of visitors touching the objects but also of whistling, singing, nose-blowing, the spitting of tobacco juice on gallery floors, and disruptions by unruly children. Many museum directors held definite attitudes about how visitors should look and behave. As if in church, visitors should be properly attired and reverent. As if in a stranger's house, they should be exceedingly polite and not handle anything that didn't belong to them.[18] "We do not want," stated the director of the Metropolitan Museum of Art in the 1890s, "nor will we permit a person who has been digging in a filthy sewer or working among grease and oil to come in here, and by offensive odors emitted from the dirt on their apparel, make the surroundings uncomfortable for others."[19] Some directors were especially wary of children. Watching the "mob of . . . pushing, pulling" youngsters arrive for Saturday classes at the Public Museum of Grand Rapids, its director exclaimed, "The whole thing is wrong; unbecoming a city department; inimical to gentlemanly and ladylike deportment; dangerous to health and to life and limb."[20]

## FROM PROGRESSIVE EDUCATION TO OBSESSIVE COLLECTING

Even though some directors were overtly hostile toward the uneducated masses, turn-of-the-20th-century U.S. museums distinguished themselves through their educational programs. It was common to offer free on-site classes in drawing, taxidermy, music appreciation, and even cooking. Museums worked closely with local boards of education to lend specimens to schools as teaching aids. The City of Saint Louis was a pioneer in this regard, setting up an Educational Museum that used horse-drawn wagons to deliver hundreds of objects weekly to the city's schools. Museums also regularly offered tours through their galleries. Around 1905 Benjamin Ives Gilman of Boston's Museum of Fine Arts (MFA) coined the verb "to docent." He adapted it from the Latin *docere* as used by a 16th-century British archbishop: "to help us read works of art as we would read books."[21] Gilman's idea was to "radically distinguish" museum instructors from schoolteachers. MFA's docents wouldn't follow a strict curriculum. Rather, they would use objects to arouse visitors' feelings, a philosophy that is still applied today. That same year, just across the river from the MFA, a Harvard University theology professor recognized another educational role for museums: to motivate the nation's future elites to find solutions to urban poverty and other social ills. Francis Greenwood Peabody founded a Social Museum at Harvard filled with documentary photos about factory work, substandard living conditions, and child labor. The aim was to help arouse in his privileged students empathy for the poor.[22]

Museums were beginning to see that their societal purpose extended beyond the school classroom and lectern. As historian Julie K. Brown explains, "a new generation . . . argued that if the museum was to remain a bastion of cultural and intellectual authority . . . it had to . . . respond to the pressing issues of the day."[23] Thus, in the early 1900s, public health workers and museum curators worked together to confront one of the most frightening crises of its day: the tuberculosis epidemic. Since those most vulnerable to the disease distrusted the information hospitals and medical clinics were communicating about its spread, public health workers turned to museums. Between 1905 and 1909, the American Museum of Natural History (AMNH) and Smithsonian hosted two exhibitions about the disease. Supported by pamphlets in Yiddish, Italian, and Chinese—targeted to immigrant families—the shows illustrated TB's dreadful consequences and taught visitors how to minimize their risks. *Tuberculosis* was the most popular exhibition of its time, attended by almost one million people. It was so crowded that AMNH extended its hours, built a special entrance area, and displayed a sign that admonished visitors: "Do Not Spit."[24] This exhibition was a forerunner to public health and safety programs about issues like drug addiction, AIDS, and pandemics undertaken by science museums later in the 20th and early 21st centuries.

This 1910 photo by social reformer and photographer Lewis Hine, titled *Child Labor*, is the kind of documentary photo that was on exhibit at Harvard University's Social Museum. A goal of the museum was to inspire empathy for the poor on the part of the privileged college students.

John Dewey's belief that public education and museums advance democracy was becoming more widely accepted. In 1915 the Cleveland Museum of Art inaugurated one of the nation's first internal departments devoted to instructional programs, eventually hiring one of Dewey's protégés, the progressive educator Thomas Munro, to run it. Like his mentor, Munro was interested in the psychology of art: that is, how people experienced it. He focused not on delivering dry lectures but on developing lively ways for museum visitors to see how art related to their own lives. This energetic and forward-looking approach to museum education caught on quickly. By 1917, nearly every major museum in the nation offered a variety of free-of-charge educational services. They lent objects and specimens not only to schools, but to factories and army bases. They hosted children's story hours and lantern-slide "lectures for the deaf who are able to read lips." They organized "hobby" clubs and nature outings, sponsored concerts and music recitals, and gave college extension courses for credit.[25] The idea was that museum programs could promote a set of shared values in educators' vision of America as a great new cultural and social "melting pot."

Public education, however, was not without its skeptics, in museums and other parts of society. Education was an expensive undertaking, opponents pointed out. Worse, it was potentially counterproductive. What was to be gained by developing a nation filled with overeducated citizens? Did the lower classes even have the ability to understand high culture? Perhaps museums weren't for everyone. About a decade after he coined the term *docent*, the MFA's Benjamin Ives Gilman mused, "We are misled into thinking educational effort is the panacea for all the ills of society . . . a museum of art is primarily an institution of culture and only secondarily a seat of learning."[26] Gilman began to float the idea that the museum's true role was to display the finest paintings and sculptures from Europe for the benefit of the upper classes. Yet even within the walls of the same museum, individuals worked toward different ends. Around the same time as Gilman was narrowing his horizons, the MFA inaugurated the nation's first "Oriental" art department. Its curator, Ernest Francisco Fenollosa, had his own educational mission: to break down a "barrier of mental stupidity and prejudice" on the part of Americans who thought of Asia as "backward."[27] The MFA also opened a gallery of art from India, hiring the Tamil scholar Ananda K. Coomaraswamy to guide acquisitions.

As the nation began to experience post–World War I economic prosperity, museums concentrated less on educational programs and more on building up their collections. For natural science museum benefactors, this meant sponsoring expeditions to gather specimens from around the world, and especially from the western reaches of North America. This included sacred items and remains of Native American people. Art museums took advantage of the conflicts in Europe and Russia. War and revolution led governments and desperate aristocrats to sell art in order to raise cash, often for the purchase of weaponry from U.S. manufacturers or safe passage over the Atlantic. Americans became active buyers of formerly priceless paintings now suddenly not so priceless. Collectors had "no qualms whatsoever about stealing away Europe's art treasures at bargain prices," wrote the biographer of newspaper tycoon William Randolph Hearst, justifying the "wholesale transmigration of art and antiquities" as a moral imperative and act of "creative rescue."[28]

An example of a work acquired in Europe by wealthy collectors after World War I. Jean-Baptiste Pater's late-18th-century oil painting *Dancers in a Pavilion* was donated to the Cleveland Museum of Art by Commodore and Mrs. Louis Dudley Beaumont in 1938. Dudley was a businessman and philanthropist who helped to organize aviators in France during World War I and also donated to hospitals for people suffering from tuberculosis.
Courtesy of Cleveland Museum of Art

Buying European masterworks became a point of pride for newly minted millionaires in the United States as they ruthlessly competed to outdo, outclass, and outbid each other. By 1923, the American Art Dealers' Association estimated that Americans spent $250 million (the equivalent of almost $3.8 billion today) on art purchases. Progressives decried such spending in the face of looming societal problems. As if to prove their point, journalists ran headlines whenever a prominent robber baron—be he banker J. P. Morgan or railroad mogul H. E. Huntington—overpaid for a work that turned out to be fake.

One museum founder who bristled at the mad dash to buy up European oil paintings was Newark, N.J., librarian John Cotton Dana. He suggested a more prudent way to build museum collections: "Get an insect, a bird, an animal, a plant, a lithograph, a plaster cast, a spinning wheel, a teacup, a bit of rock, a mineral, a dozen of the things made commercially in your community . . . and in a few weeks you can open a museum which every intelligent person will rejoice to see."[29] Dana's Newark Museum opened in 1926, with the goal of serving the families of the factory

**Pioneering Newark Museum director John Cotton Dana, ca. 1925.**
Courtesy of Newark Museum Archives

**Schoolchildren in a weaving workshop taught by Newark Museum educators, ca. 1926.**
Courtesy of Newark Museum Archives

workers who were building America. In one of its many educational innovations, the museum invited schoolchildren to help design its inaugural displays using merchandise from five-and-dime stores. One result was a scale model of New Jersey's river systems, surely a crowd-pleaser in its time.[30]

Experiments like Newark's were the antithesis of the extravagant collections buildup in wealthier cities like New York. Progressive educators argued that the nation's museums should "reject the European notion of art as masterpiece . . . in favor of an art created for society."[31] This idea harkened to Smithson's original hope that a new society would create a model institution of learning that would not be entrenched in the past. Rather it would celebrate the creativity of the present day. As their bosses competed for European masterworks at the world's leading auction houses, progressive educators, through the auspices of AAM, organized a series of symposia. The result was a report that accused institutions of being "isolated segments of European culture, disdainful of the vast majority of Americans."[32] One of these symposia was coordinated by none other than Cleveland Art Museum's Thomas Munro, an early advocate within the United States for the collecting and display of African art.

It is safe to say that America's megacollectors ignored the rumblings of progressive educators. During the 1920s connoisseurship and acquisition supplanted public education within the museum. Institutions relegated instructional activities to the basement. A well-dressed public was invited to climb the sweeping staircases of ornate public palaces—the Albright-Knox Museum in Buffalo, N.Y., is one example among many—and view new acquisitions of masterpieces.

The nation was becoming an economic colossus. Signs of its wealth abounded. Ford Model-T automobiles streamed down newly paved avenues, skyscrapers towered above the rapidly growing cities, and ornate movie palaces sprang up in towns large and small. Perhaps the largest and most prestigious symbol of this new prosperity was a new museum. As Alfred C. Parker, director of what is now the Rochester Museum and Science Center, declared: "Unimportant cities have no museums; great cities have flourishing museums."[33] And flourish they did. During the 1920s a museum building was christened every 11.4 days.[34] Businesses like Wells Fargo Bank and Crane & Crane Paper Company founded museums to preserve their contributions to American progress and society. By 1933 President Herbert Hoover's administration could proudly report: "Today a museum is found in every city in the United States of over 250,000 inhabitants."[35] Among the influential museums founded during this roaring decade were Colonial Williamsburg in Virginia (1926), the Henry Ford Museum and Greenfield Village in Dearborn, Michigan (1926), the Museum of Science and Industry in Chicago (1926), and New York's Museum of Modern Art, whose first gallery was christened 10 days after the stock market crash of 1929.

## THE GREAT DEPRESSION AND THE RESURGENCE OF EDUCATION

With the stock market collapse and the onset of the Great Depression, the nation's post–World War I era of prosperity ended almost overnight. By 1933, three-fifths of the nation's banks had failed. Nearly one-quarter of the population was out of work. Local governments endured deep budget cuts that impacted schools and other public services. The result was that people were "hungry, desperate and angry."[36] Around the country, museum educators saw an opportunity to step up to the moment. They organized free classes and activities for children, filling gaps in public education. Many of these services were called "Carnegie courses," named after the foundation that financed them. Museums also developed training courses for unemployed adults, teaching marketable skills like typesetting, graphic design, and lettering. Not surprisingly, museum attendance surged by 50 percent. Even so, at the height of the Great Depression, Philip Youtz, director of the Brooklyn Museum, accused wealthy museum founders and collectors of not understanding what was going on outside their walls. Museums, he declared, were oriented to the "wealthy collector . . . not the common man on the street . . . who enters its great halls with an initial inferiority complex that leaves him cowed from the start."[37]

Three developments during this era sought to build bridges between museums and the "common man." The first was a movement among followers of John Dewey to connect the philosophies of contemporary art and progressive child-centered education. The second was a new communications technology called broadcast radio. The third was one of the most consequential government programs in U.S. history: Franklin Delano Roosevelt's Works Progress Administration. Because of these three movements, the calamity of the Great Depression expanded the role of museums in society.

Grace McCann Morley, an educator at the Cincinnati Art Museum, would play a large role in this expansion. Morley was part of a circle of progressive art

Grace McCann Morley, founding director of what is now the San Francisco Museum of Modern Art, and Delmar Gray, artist and shipyard engineer, in front of Gray's painting *Shift's End* (1941) at the opening of the exhibition *Marinship Artists: Work by Bay Area Artists in the Shipyards, 1943.*
Courtesy of SFMOMA Archives

educators in Ohio that included Cleveland's Thomas Munro. In Cincinnati, she had been charged with creating and implementing the museum's Carnegie courses. Through these connections, she learned to advocate for programs that would bring the museum's resources to wider audiences. Morley moved back to her home state of California, bringing her leadership skills and progressive educational ideals to the West Coast. In 1935, she become founding director of the San Francisco Museum of Art, now known as San Francisco Museum of Modern Art or SFMOMA. She worked to create ties between the city's adventurous collectors, avant-garde artists, local laborers, and public schools. "During the early 1930s, the battle between curators [and] popularizers of scholarly information . . . who were fighting very hard for recognition as part of the museum hierarchy [was] won. . . . Education

departments began to enjoy a certain amount of prestige," she later recalled.[38]

The same kinds of conversations were occurring at New York's Museum of Modern Art (MoMA). In the early 1930s, its founders hired another one of John Dewey's disciples—art educator Victor d'Amico—as MoMA's first director of education. One of d'Amico's signature programs was a Young People's Gallery with exhibitions designed and created by high schoolers, destined to become the museum's future audiences. This commitment to using educational programs to appeal to new generations of audiences would pay off handsomely not just for MoMA but, as we will see shortly, for the field at large.

Educators also sought to broaden museums' reach through the revolutionary new communication medium of broadcast radio. In 1932, the Buffalo Museum

Broadcast radio revolutionized world communication in the 1920s and 1930s. The legendary Clarksdale Mississippi Radio Studio WROX has been re-created at the B. B. King Museum and Delta Interpretive Center in Indianola, MS.
© Michael Ventura

of Science conceived of a program called "roto-radio," which was adopted across the nation. On roto-radio day, the local newspaper published a photo spread of objects from a local museum. That evening, the museum broadcast a talk by a curator that was linked to the pictures. As families huddled around their radios, they learned about strange and wonderful things: mastodons, natural gas, Australian topography, even the science of falling in love. In a later report, AAM admitted that most roto-radio programs were pretty bad because the curators weren't professional broadcasters. Nonetheless, the roto-radio multimedia experiment represented an early attempt on the part of museums to deliver educational objectives via a new communications technology, many decades before more ambitious experiments with television, video, the Internet, and social media.[39]

With programs ranging from the Young People's Gallery to roto-radio, the stage was now set for educators and artists to become more influential in museums around the nation. Their timing was fortunate. In 1935, in response to the Great Depression and

the need for job creation, Franklin Delano Roosevelt created the Works Progress Administration (WPA). This government program ushered in another era of growth for museums, as significant as the museum booms that followed the social upheaval of the Civil War and post–World War I prosperity. Roosevelt believed that museums, at their best, should be "woven into the very warp and woof of democracy."[40] In addition to upgrading existing museums and developing traveling shows around the nation, the WPA opened 53 art centers nationwide. Many later became permanent museums, such as the Walker Art Center in Minneapolis, the Roswell Museum and Art Center in New Mexico, and the North Carolina Museum of Art in Raleigh. The art centers went beyond the WPA's immediate goal of providing employment to artists and teachers and programs for citizens. WPA classes were racially integrated, an idea so controversial at the time that it contributed to the program's demise.[41]

WPA folded in 1943. However, it had a lasting museum legacy, building a cultural infrastructure across the country. The reverberations of this landmark federal

**Works Progress Administration artist Augusta Savage, founder of the Harlem Community Art Center. Today her sculptures are in many museum collections. None were included in the Met's controversial 1969** *Harlem on My Mind* **exhibition.**
Photo by Andrew Herman, ca. 1938. Federal Art Project, Photographic Division collection, Archives of American Art

Augusta Savage. *Gamin*, ca. 1930, painted plaster. Museum purchase with funds provided by the Mint Museum Auxiliary. 2008.58.
Courtesy of the Mint Museum, Charlotte, N.C.

program are still felt in the vibrant murals, meticulous dioramas, and modern architectural forms that stand to this day. Most importantly, however, many Americans entered museums for the first time in their lives and discovered that art and culture can nurture the spirit during difficult times.

### WARS AT MIDCENTURY: THE CALL TO PATRIOTISM

Museums could not and did not ignore the impact of the two world wars on society. During the First World War, AAM beseeched its member institutions to "seriously consider [their] value to the community" and to render the "greatest service at this time of the world's direct need."[42] In response, museums sent free newsletters to "homesick soldiers in the trenches," displayed troops' letters on bulletin boards so stateside citizens could follow the war's progress, and offered free tours for soldiers and classical music concerts for all. With the onset of World War II, museums, now greater in number and influence, responded with an even more vigorous patriotism.

Even before the United States entered the war, museums were participating in programs that encouraged military recruitment and supported national security. In the Minneapolis area, for example, the Walker Art Center displayed modern Marine equipment. Across the river in Saint Paul, the Science Museum of Minnesota hosted an exhibition about stateside safety titled *Can America Be Bombed?* Prophetically, it was featured on the front page of AAM's national newsletter just one week before the bombing of Pearl Harbor.[43]

In January 1942, just weeks after the attack, a group of museum directors issued a resolution: "If, in time of peace, our museums and art galleries are important to the community, in time of war they are doubly valuable." Museums must "fortify the spirit on which Victory depends" through continuous exhibitions and programs. Art museums converted their regal flowerbeds into patriotic victory gardens, and botanical gardens offered classes that taught citizens how to do the same at home. Museums near military training facilities presented lectures for the troops on the value of democracy. Others opened members' lounges to off-duty GIs, serving free refreshments and showing movies. Still others showed locals how to prepare food economically in light of the limitations of rationing. Under Grace Morley's leadership, the SFMOMA stayed open to the public until 10 p.m. every night, dutifully blacking out windows as a defense against potential bombing raids. In Hawaii the Honolulu Academy of Arts and Bishop Museum reopened only days after their city's harbor was bombed. With area schools still closed, they sponsored classes for children and organized a morale-boosting Christmas carol sing-along for the community.[44]

In some cases, patriotic zealousness went too far. To aid the U.S. Army, the American Museum of Natural History produced 162 portable exhibits on racial identification to be used by soldiers to distinguish enemy troops from allies. MoMA's exhibition *Road to Victory* showed a giant photo of bombs blowing up a ship in Pearl Harbor. Pasted below was a photo of two Japanese diplomats, their eyes positioned to look directly at the explosion, their mouths laughing with glee. The caption read "Two Faces." While the government was rounding up Japanese American citizens and interring them in harsh desert conditions, other museums removed all Japanese items from display, sequestering them in storage and replacing them with art and objects produced by American allies.[45] Some museums were even allied with Nazi sympathizers, as we will see in coming chapters.

During World War II, museums around the nation hosted educational and patriotic exhibitions related to the war effort. Shown here is the 1943 *Ordnance Show* at the Gibbes Museum in Charleston, S.C.
Courtesy of Gibbes Museum

Elsewhere museums worked to prove that they were truly "doubly valuable" to the nation by serving as hospitals, Red Cross stations, training and research centers, manufacturers, and offices. New York's Hayden Planetarium trained 45,000 sailors in celestial navigation. Curators at the Franklin Institute in Philadelphia conducted research on camouflage. The California Academy of Sciences manufactured naval optical equipment. A museum even played a central role in the postwar peace process. In 1945, again under Morley's leadership, SFMOMA's galleries served as offices for international delegates convened to discuss the formation of the United Nations.

In the postwar years, museum visits exceeded the nation's total population for the first time.[46] Growing prosperity and programs like the GI Bill led to unprecedented interest in education and culture. Refugees from war-shattered Europe streamed into American cities, profoundly influencing the nation's cultural life, sparking new movements in art, science, and scholarship. Museums benefited too. Middle-class women increased their involvement in collecting and volunteerism. Stunned by the damage they had witnessed in Europe, veterans devoted themselves to rescuing and researching overseas treasures. Teachers looked to museums as field-trip destinations for their classrooms, which were filling rapidly with the first baby boomers.

But with victory came a sobering aftershock: the emergence of the Cold War. Like much of the nation, museums became obsessed with protecting themselves from atomic attack, something that many Americans considered imminent. The focus turned now to the precious items that hung upon museum walls or lay within their vaults. Museum charters of the time spoke less of uplifting the citizenry and more about the obligation to protect and preserve art and artifacts. Conservators, many trained as scientists, aided the cause.

**Naval officers learn celestial navigation at the Hayden Planetarium during World War II.**
Courtesy of American Museum of Natural History

**Col. Paul W. Tibbets Jr. with the Boeing B-29, the *Enola Gay* (named for his mother), the plane he piloted when his bombardier dropped the first atomic bomb over Hiroshima. A planned Smithsonian exhibition of this plane in 1995 was a controversial and defining moment in the late-20th-century culture wars.**

Photo by J. L. Hussey, USAAF. Courtesy of National Air and Space Museum, NASM-USAF-31181AC

Workmen uncrating Caravaggio's *The Madonna of the Rosaries* at the Metropolitan Museum of Art on loan from Austria in 1950.

So did architects. Museum construction projects were increasingly linked not to aspirations of grandeur but to the more concrete concerns of storage, ventilation, and security.

The generous educational programs of previous decades received less attention. In the era of Cold War paranoia and McCarthyism, museums came under pressure to blacklist progressive artists and educators. Fortunately, most resisted. At the same time, in keeping with the ethos of the Cold War, they produced "patriotic" exhibitions about the promise of the "friendly atom," the universal goodness of the human family, and the value of hard work in assuring economic progress. These "feel-good" exhibitions, as well as attempts to censor more "subversive" ones, are discussed in more detail in chapter 4.

During the early years of the Cold War, schools widely discredited John Dewey's ideas about education as "communistic, atheistic and un-American."

**Grand Rapids Public Museum educator Norma Ruby with a set of her famous slides near the WPA map of Michigan in 1951.**
Courtesy of Grand Rapids Public Museum, Grand Rapids, MI

They shifted toward teaching "fundamentals" according to "standards." Museums also disavowed Dewey's ideas. He was too closely associated with the eccentric Philadelphia art collector Albert Barnes, who had hired Dewey to help him formulate his eponymous museum. The two had become good friends. Barnes was controversial in museum circles; he believed in "negro" education, was hostile toward academic art historians and other connoisseurs, and felt that experiencing art was more about viewers' feelings than their intellectual knowledge.[47]

Another jolt to the nation's sense of security came with the 1957 launch of Sputnik, the world's first artificial satellite, by the Soviets. The space race was on, and museums quickly joined in. As part of the push to interest a new generation in science, communities founded science museums and planetariums, among them the Oregon Museum of Science and Industry in Portland (1957), the Pacific Science Center in Seattle (1962), and the Miami Planetarium and Museum of Science (1966). The impetus for these new institutions came not from wealthy industrialists as had often been the case with museums earlier in the century, but from the federal government and university educators. Upgraded planetariums were immediately put to use. The seven original Mercury astronauts learned star navigation at the Morehead Planetarium and Science Center at the University of North Carolina in Chapel Hill.[48] Museums also trained teachers and developed groundbreaking science exhibits with the goal of enticing more children into careers in science. In 1961 the California Museum of Science and Industry in Los Angeles (now the California Science Center) unveiled *Mathematica*, famed modern designers Ray and

**Astronauts Ed White and James McDivitt learn about star navigation at the Morehead Planetarium and Science Center, University of North Carolina, Chapel Hill, during the early 1960s.**
Courtesy of Morehead Planetarium and Science Center

Charles Eames's eye-popping show about the abstract world of mathematics. Designed to be fun, a radical concept in museums at that time, *Mathematica* was one of the country's first interactive exhibitions.

John Dewey's ideas about "learning by doing" came back into fashion. They dovetailed with the scientific method. The hands-on laboratory became the model for a new kind of science museum. Foremost was the Exploratorium in San Francisco, founded in 1969 by Frank Oppenheimer, an atomic physicist who had been blacklisted during the McCarthy era. (His brother J. Robert headed the federal laboratories in Los Alamos, N.M., that developed the first atomic bomb.) In the same spirit, the Boston Children's Museum, founded in 1913 by natural science teachers, introduced hands-on exhibits for children. The visionary behind this new kind of exhibition was Michael Spock, son of the era's most famous pediatrician, prominent social activist Benjamin Spock. Both Oppenheimer and Spock had frequented Victor d'Amico's programs at MoMA when they were youngsters growing up in New York City. The early progressive education museum programs of

**Under the leadership of Michael Spock (seated on the left), the Boston Children's Museum was one of the nation's first client-centered museums. To Spock's left is Elaine Gurian, who would go on to become a noted museum theorist and writer. Standing behind them are Patricia Steuert and Geraldine Robinson.**
Photo by Richard Howard, 1984. Image courtesy of Boston Children's Museum and Marjorie Schwarzer

the 1930s had inspired a new generation of 1960s activists who understood museums' power to transform people's lives and attitudes about the world.

A new challenge was emerging during these years, one that few museums recognized. The mass entertainments of television, the suburban shopping mall, and such theme parks as Disney's Magic Kingdom soon would compete with museums for the attention and leisure-time decisions of the public. Most mainstream museums harkened to the earlier philosophies that had birthed them. They viewed themselves as sanctuaries of highbrow culture, unaffected by mass culture. They were content to remain conservative enclaves, preserving Old World values. In 1957, while documenting the vibrant community life of Pittsburgh, photographer W. Eugene Smith wandered inside the Carnegie Museum and remarked: "Educational television is more imaginative than ... dusty but sound museums. Museums are stale; they need fresh injections of money, spirit and ideas."[49]

**Frank Oppenheimer, founding visionary of San Francisco's Exploratorium.**
© Exploratorium, www.exploratorium.edu

In 1971, San Francisco's Exploratorium pioneered the intersection between art and science in this exhibition called *Cybernetic Serendipity*.

© Exploratorium, www.exploratorium.edu

## FROM CIVIL RIGHTS TO THE BICENTENNIAL: GROWTH AND TUMULT

Museums were taken aback by the sweeping social changes and generational divide that began to take hold in the 1960s. Even bastions of conservative collections and values could not avoid being affected. The public would see to that. American citizens were fighting for civil rights, on the streets and in the courts. On college campuses students demonstrated for free speech and rallied against the war in Vietnam. New academic disciplines like ethnic studies, people's history, and Asian American studies arose. In galleries and artists' studios new movements in experimental art began to bloom. Yet despite some experimentation in the areas of science and children's education, most museums clung to the notion that their primary duty was to defend traditional values, including the Western canon. Ignoring the pioneering educational work of his own institution, Sherman Lee, director of the Cleveland Museum of Art, beseeched his colleagues not to let art museums become "whipping boy[s] for a host of extraneous social issues. . . . It is time for art museums and for those genuinely interested in their survival and proper development to resist actively the

chaotic demands forced upon them . . . [by] moralizing Maoists."[50]

Yet some large institutions did choose to engage with social issues, especially African American empowerment. In 1967, the Smithsonian established a branch facility in a disadvantaged African American neighborhood in Washington, D.C., hiring local pastor John R. Kinard to run it. Kinard and his colleague, the educator Zora Martin Felton, became the first African Americans to be hired by the Smithsonian Institution in directorial roles. They envisioned, in Kinard's words, a museum that would "restore a sense of place among [neighborhood] residents" and serve as a "catalyst for social change."[51] Families flocked to the Anacostia Neighborhood Museum. They came not only to visit a life-size model of a *Triceratops* affectionately named "Uncle Beazley" but also for exhibitions about public health problems that impacted residents. The exhibition *Rats* provided important information about the neighborhood's vermin infestation and, as we will learn in chapter 4, a model for other museums interested in tackling serious and relevant issues.

Museums did not always succeed in empowering disenfranchised communities. The Metropolitan

In the 1960s, the Smithsonian Institution opened a branch in Anacostia, led by pastor and community activist John Kinard, shown here at the left presiding over opening events.
Courtesy of the Smithsonian Institution Archives, image # 91-518

Museum's exhibition *Harlem on My Mind: The Cultural Capital of Black America* (1969), for example, featured not a single work created by a black artist. Political activists began to rally against museum paternalism and racism. "Take me into the museum and show me myself, show me my people, show me Soul America. If you cannot show me myself, if you cannot teach my children what they need to know—and they need to know the truth, and they need to know that nothing is more important than human life—if you cannot show and teach these things, then why shouldn't I attack the temples of America and blow them up?" wrote Harlem-based poet June Jordan.[52]

The rebelliousness and idealism that defined the 1960s inspired a generation, not to blow museums up, but to found new and innovative ones. The period saw vigorous growth characterized by new kinds of institutions, new sources of money, new building projects, and new crowds of visitors. The same im-pulse that wealthy industrialists and civic leaders had felt in prior decades was now taken up by community activists and educators. They wanted museums to build community pride and lift up marginalized communities and founded neighborhood museums based on the principles of social change, civil rights, and ethnic pride. These included the Wing Luke Asian Museum (International District, Seattle, 1966, now the Wing Luke Museum of the Asian Pacific American Experience) and El Museo del Barrio (East Harlem, New York City, 1969). Ironically, museums like these would eventually contribute to the gentri-fication of former poorer ethnic neighborhoods. But at the same time, they have largely remained true to their foundational missions: to offer programs and exhibitions about social activism.

During the late 1960s, the nation's new community-oriented museums were buoyed not only by civil rights activists, but by the founding of government agencies

Wing Luke, the first person of color elected to the Seattle City Council in the 1960s, was an activist who died tragically in a plane crash. The Wing Luke Museum of the Asian Pacific American Experience was founded in his honor in 1967 and, to this day, uses vivid storytelling and inspiring experiences to advance racial and social equity. This exhibition, currently on display in the museum, honors Luke's legacy and vision for social justice.
Photo by Dean Wong. Courtesy of Wing Luke Museum of the Asian Pacific American Experience, 2019

that were devoted to financially supporting museums. By 1971 the National Endowments for the Arts and Humanities, signed into legislation six years earlier by President Lyndon B. Johnson, had designated funds for museums. Government support enabled a plethora of exhibitions, festivals, and educational programs linked to the nation's 1976 bicentennial celebration. Even though these federal agency budgets were modest, their impact was powerful, inspiring a generation of idealistic teachers, artists, and activists to devote their energies to museums.

Ironically, it was influential trustees from major metropolitan museums—the same institutions that initially had resisted change—who lobbied to create the federal agencies that helped bring about that change. A few generations removed from the original founders, many of these trustees began to scrutinize the cost of maintaining collections. They realized that their institutions could not survive financially with the dual mandate of collections care and public education. They turned to the federal government for help. During the 1970s federal funding gave rise to hundreds of

community outreach projects—partnerships between museums and senior centers, hospitals, prisons, and juvenile justice halls; artist-in-residence programs; art vans; and film festivals. Museums furthered their visibility by designing exhibits for neighborhood festivals, YMCAs, local libraries, and shopping malls. They also reinvigorated their presence in public schools. Federal insurance indemnity programs provided the means for importing and insuring valuable artifacts and artworks, ultimately making possible such shows as *Treasures of Tutankhamen* (1976–1979), often called America's first blockbuster art exhibition.

By the end of the decade, museum visits had climbed to over 500 million, double the U.S. population. This growth was fueled not only by school field trips but also by visits from college-age and older adults. During the late 1970s, the affordability of commercial flights and popularity of study abroad programs sparked a boom in cultural tourism. More and more middle-class Americans were able to visit the sites and monuments of the world, whetting their appetites for even more cultural experiences. Young backpackers tripped around Europe, staying in youth hostels and visiting famous national museums. They came back enamored with the majesty of these institutions and desirous of similar experiences at U.S. museums; hence the attraction of blockbusters.

At the same time, retirees were healthier, wealthier, and more educated than ever. In 1975, two young backpackers founded Elderhostel (now Road Scholar) to offer weeklong educational programs for those 60-plus. Many of these programs included museum visits. The American Association for Retired Persons estimated that between 1976 and 1979, the number of people over the age of 65 going to museums more than doubled.[53] To further cultivate the growing legions of frequent flyers, in 1977 the Fine Arts Museums of San Francisco became the nation's first museum to design exhibitions for airport terminals.

For seniors who were less mobile, museums began to create specialized programs, a practice that would grow in the coming decades. Groundbreaking programs for elderly people with severe dementia—such as New England Aquarium's EldeReach program, which was launched during the 1980s—used objects and even live animals to harness memories and, it is hypothesized, improve brain circulation and mental acuity.[54] These programs were forerunners to today's museum programs targeted to seniors, which range from specialized activities for people afflicted with Alzheimer's to classes designed for healthy seniors interested in creative aging.

Benefiting from a confluence of professional creativity, increased research in the efficacy of museum education, federal largesse, and affluence, the number of museums grew at an unprecedented rate during the 1970s and 1980s. More than 3,200 were founded, the equivalent of almost one every other day. Nearly three-fifths of existing museums expanded or undertook major renovations. All told, nearly two million acres—the equivalent of the Florida Everglades—were upgraded and added to the museum landscape.[55] Many projects were linked to urban revitalization plans, with museums serving as catalysts to help revive sagging urban neighborhoods. In rural communities and college towns, citizens were inspired by the 1976 bicentennial celebration and its attention to America's history. They banded together to turn lighthouses, old prisons, courthouses, and other abandoned structures into historical societies. This occurred in locales as diverse as Newland, NC; Duvall, WA; Kutztown, PA; and Bozeman, MT, to name just a few.

Likewise, children's museums began to pop up everywhere. In the late 1970s, affluent and community-savvy parent groups were increasingly disenchanted with public schools. At the same time, the number of divorced, blended, and single-parent households was growing. So were crime rates. "Parental fears for children's safety and physical and psychological well-being soared," notes University of Texas researcher Steven Mintz. Gone were the days when children were "free" to roam the neighborhood and "play in nearby woods or vacant lots."[56] Public television shows like *Mister Rogers' Neighborhood* and *Sesame Street* took up some of the slack, tendering positive messages about friendship and community. Parent groups, including the Junior League, wanted to create safe learning environments that went beyond the television screen. Exhibitions at the Exploratorium and Boston Children's Museum attracted their attention, and suddenly it seemed like every community was founding a youth museum.

In 1984 the Capital Children's Museum in Washington, D.C. (now the National Children's Museum), documented 531 requests from 47 states for guidance in how to start a children's museum. By 2019, more than 280 children's museums were up and running, with 60 more in the start-up stages and in all 50 states.[57] As the *Sesame Street* generation came of age, a new museum culture also took hold, one that valued play as a building block of education and learning for children of all abilities and needs. Museums even embraced the once radical idea of encouraging people to have "fun" in a museum. At the same time, because they were so attuned to their audiences' needs, children's museums tended to be on the forefront of pressing social issues. For example, well before the Centers for Disease Control had identified autism as the nation's fastest growing developmental disability, children's museums in exurban communities, like Naperville, IL; Stevens Point, WI; and Cherry Hill, NJ, had initiated programs for children on the autism spectrum.[58]

Despite their good work in rescuing historic buildings, forwarding educational initiatives, and supporting families, the local history movement and children's museums had their share of detractors. Professional scholars, who had fought so hard to ensure museums' integrity and quality, saw these new kinds of institutions as amateurish. They abhorred the idea of hobbyists interpreting historic events and stretching facts. Turning a historical house into a Halloween haunted house was just wrong. The shift away from viewing masterpieces of art and important historical artifacts and toward making an emotional and physical connection with any kind of object questioned the very nature of what it meant to be a museum. To these critics, children's museums in particular had no business calling themselves museums. By encouraging touching and handling of objects, they were neglecting the museum's primary role as caretakers of collections. Nonetheless, while the arguments that pitted traditionalists against those wanting to experiment still rumbled, museums were more popular than ever. The field's priority had once again changed, as the museum scholar Stephen E. Weil observed, from "being about something to being for somebody."[59]

During the energetic 1960s and 1970s, educators gained more say over the direction of their institutions. Training programs for museum staff increased in number. A national network of professionals revised codes of ethics and established standards for earning accreditation. And despite some curators' worries that educational techniques and programs "dumbed down" content, the scope and depth of scholarship and exhibitions improved, fortified by the involvement of academic experts supported through grants from the National Endowments for the Arts and Humanities.

## 1980s AND 1990s: DIVERSITY AND BACKLASH

As the 1980s approached, the country's priorities changed. Americans worried about gas shortages, high inflation, and government integrity, thanks to the Watergate scandal. Many also voiced fears about the recent waves of refugees arriving from Southeast Asia and the Caribbean. Promising to restore America's "traditional values," Ronald Reagan was elected president in 1980. His "trickle-down" ideology was a throwback to the "gospel of wealth" of prior eras. The idea was that tax breaks for businesses and wealthy individuals would benefit everyone, as American society became more oriented to the marketplace and less focused on government-run programs. Museums were thrown into turmoil. They were serving larger audiences than ever. But they were unprepared for the new economic and demographic realities they would soon face, as well as the backlash from both progressives and conservatives as the institution tried to figure out where it stood in a society that seemed to be coming apart.

At the most basic level, the Reagan administration's budget cuts to federal agencies threatened museums' finances. How could they fulfill their promises to the public without the federal funds that had jump-started so many costly new programs? The question of service to society morphed into one of economic survival. As museums looked for additional ways to pay the bills, business schemes supplanted the traditional focus on scholarship, exhibitions, and programs. Museums became entrepreneurial, a catchphrase in Reagan-era America. Aggressive marketing and effective fundraising were widely seen as essential to a museum's success. Museums expanded their development and marketing staffs, as well as their merchandising. They created appealing programs like lunchtime tours for downtown workers. They implemented fees for programs that had previously been free of charge. And perhaps most controversially, they mounted attention-grabbing exhibitions, such as *The Art of the Muppets* (1982) and *Ramses II* (1988), aimed more at attracting paying customers than exploring new scholarly terrain. The ages-old arguments about pandering to the masses resurfaced. Were museums going back to the days of P. T. Barnum's hucksterism? Or was something even worse brewing? As critic Herbert Muschamp wrote, "the collection of objects gave way to the collection of crowds."[60]

Analyzing the demographics of those crowds and other kinds of market research now received greater attention from directors and boards of trustees conscious of the bottom line. Audience evaluators emerged as important players, conducting surveys and focus groups, observing and interviewing visitors, and gathering statistics. Study after study confirmed the profile of the typical museumgoer. She was white, in her mid- to late-30s, college educated, more likely to be female than male, and more likely to go to museums if she had visited them as a child.[61]

Yet this composite portrait of the museum visitor did not align with the nation's demographics. During Reagan's presidency, America's Asian population doubled, while the Hispanic population grew by 66 percent. As these populations grew, the percentage of whites shrank. In 1986 Reagan signed the Immigration Reform and Control Act, which granted amnesty to more than three million immigrants, mostly of Mexican origin. Thus, while Reagan's policies encouraged a growth in consumer-oriented business practices that some say compromised museum scholarship, they also paved the way for a more diverse audience, which, of course, represented a large opportunity. What role, in the post–civil rights era, could museums play in integrating new immigrant groups into American society? The answer to this question was complex, especially in light of a third concurrent development.

Native Americans and blacks were gaining power in America's public institutions.

Across the nation, the makeup of students in public schools was changing. In response, educators, from kindergarten teachers to dissertation advisors, began to incorporate a much wider view of culture into their teaching, what came to be called "multiculturalism." Whereas prior curricula painted the nation as a "melting pot," a new metaphor emerged: a "salad bowl," a place where different entities were tossed together, each retaining its own shape and flavor and contributing to the whole. The point here was to respect a multitude of cultures and not just privilege the dominant ones. This concept was shocking at the time. Conservatives lashed out. They viewed multiculturalism as "identity politics" and "political correctness." One influential voice came from University of Chicago philosopher Allan Bloom, who, perhaps summoning the ghost of Matthew Arnold, proclaimed that abandoning a singular viewpoint and classical Western learning would result in the nation's moral degradation.[62] Bloom's best-selling book *The Closing of the American Mind* (1987) is often credited with launching what would come to be called America's "culture wars." It was followed a year later by a more mainstream phenomenon: Rush Limbaugh's nationally syndicated right-wing talk radio show. Across the airwaves, Limbaugh hurled insults at a variety of institutions, including "politically correct" museums.[63] Thus began a time of bitter contention over the role of education, the media, and museums in shaping and defining the nation.[64]

These simultaneous developments during the 1980s—economic pressures, the new immigration, the political empowerment of previously marginalized groups, and an immediate conservative backlash—challenged museums to their core. In 1990, for example, after decades of lobbying, the Native American Graves Protection and Repatriation Act (NAGPRA) became federal law. It requires museums that receive federal funds to inventory their collections of Native American sacred objects, human remains, and objects of cultural patrimony and repatriate items if tribes with appropriate cultural affiliation to the objects request it. Many museums, the AAM, archaeologists, and other researchers openly resisted. They clung to paternalistic ideas of how Native American culture was part of the telling of a larger "American" narrative of how the nation had advanced; museums' role was to preserve this story. But Native American communities and progressive anthropologists supported

the law. The door had cracked open to expose other entrenched museum practices.

This was a time when "postmodern" scholars launched stinging attacks against museums, "deconstructing" their historic biases toward the arts and civilization of Western Europe. U.S. museums' past collections and exhibitions practices exemplified the "dread disease of imperialist, capitalist and white culture," wrote University of California, Santa Cruz, professor Donna Haraway, one of the first academics to directly challenge the institution.[65] "Colonial," once used to conjure up quaint images of rocking chairs and butter churns, was now linked to theft, racism, and violence. Public exhibitions showed a preponderance of images and cultural bias that favored white America, especially men. If museums really wanted to reflect the nation, it was time to tell, honestly and fully, the stories of those who had been ignored or oppressed by the majority culture. It was time to acknowledge that the museums into which civic leaders had put so much stock in the early decades of the 20th century were painful places for people whose cultures had been trivialized and looted. "What a great irony that places linked inextricably to the colonization process [became] the sites where the difficult aspects of our history can and must be most clearly and forcibly told," Amy Lonetree, also affiliated with U.C. Santa Cruz, later reflected.[66]

Postmodern and anticolonialist arguments were popular in universities. But they fell on deaf ears in the museum boardroom. More than 97 percent of museum trustees were white. Sixty percent were over the age of 60. Not only had they come of age during an era that emphasized different values, but their profile reeked of privilege. More than a third were Episcopalian and Ivy League (or equivalent) graduates.[67] Yet, even if they did not listen to the "radical elements" in universities, the media, and politics, they did pay attention to data.

In 1993, the researcher John H. Falk published the first comprehensive data on African Americans' attitudes about museums. Museums' prior thinking was that black Americans would "acculturate" to the nation's cultural institutions "as racial barriers to socioeconomic equality diminished."[68] Falk's research proved that this theory, to put it politely, was upside down. A majority of African Americans, the data confirmed, perceived "of museums as racist institutions." And no wonder, given the legacy of guards refusing entrance to black visitors or denying access to restrooms! Falk predicted that it would take at least a generation for museums to break down these barriers.[69] It was becoming increasingly clear that museums were the ones who needed to "acculturate"; if they didn't do something to address past practices in order to become relevant to new generations, they would not survive in the post-Reagan economy.

Working with artists and curators of color who had come of age during the civil rights era, museums began to mount exhibitions and programs that directly challenged the nation's legacy of institutional racism. Influential during this period were *Field to Factory: Afro-American Migration 1915–1940* at the National Museum of American History (1987), *Mining the Museum* at the Maryland Historical Society (1992), and an educational program that reenacted a slave auction at Colonial Williamsburg (1994), all of which are discussed later in this book. Museums also developed exhibitions that confronted conventional ideas about gender identity, art historical scholarship, military history, and American "heroes," from Christopher Columbus to Thomas Jefferson. Some of these programs never came to fruition because of political controversies, but others did, provoking significant backlash. What a curator might have intended as a thought-provoking challenge, politicians and media personalities saw as a direct attack on society's core values. Yet despite a good deal of negative press coverage, some barbed commentary by conservative politicians, and accusations that museum directors were pornographers, traitors, ingrates, lightweights, or worse, museums continued to attract large numbers of people. Visitors waited patiently in line to see what all the fuss was about, and membership and attendance numbers continued to grow. Museums emerged from the 1990s strengthened in their resolve to be a part of the marketplace economy as well as the larger national dialogue about cultural and social issues. The noted museum theorist Elaine Gurian, who had launched her museum career during the 1960s as an educator at the Boston Children's Museum, put the matter simply: "Different people bring different interpretations to a subject. Museums have a responsibility to show that there can be two or more different views of the same subject."[70] Yet, another development emanating out of college campuses and laboratories would soon open up infinite dialogues and bring even more questions about the museum's role in society to the forefront.

## MUSEUMS AND THE DIGITAL WORLD

On a bright spring morning in 1994, two graduate students hovered over the computer server housed within the concrete walls of the curatorial room at the Museum of Paleontology at the University of California, Berkeley. They high-fived as high-resolution images of a *Dilophosaurus* flashed onto the workstation. Months earlier, the museum's director had been dubious about their technological experiment, thinking that no one would care about it or even notice. Now, none other than Vice President Al Gore had scheduled an appointment to dial into the project via Berkeley's barely utilized Internet backbone. At the last minute, Gore was called away due to pressing negotiations in the Middle East. The two budding archaeologists never got the chance to guide the vice president through online images of ancient crocodile teeth, mastodon jaws, and other antediluvian delights. But Rob Guralnick and David Polly had achieved a milestone on the nascent information superhighway: they had created the world's first museum website.

Natural science museums were a perfect laboratory for online experimentation. Like museums, websites could intertwine scholarship, specimens, and public education. "The field of paleontology was geared toward sharing data for free. We wanted it to be available and intellectually interesting to everybody; there was no concept of selling anything or making a profit on the Internet back then," recalls Polly, now a professor at Indiana University. "The goal was the democratization of information."[71]

Most museums, however, were timid, if not overtly hostile to the Internet. They were still reeling from the culture wars and repatriation laws like NAGPRA. Now another forceful wave was upon them. "Museum professionals worried about the role of the 'virtual' museum online," explains multimedia expert Selma Thomas. "Would it compete with brick-and-mortar museums for visitors, funds and programs? . . . Would it demean the value of the collections by circulating tiny pixilated images? Could museums, with their commitment to 'real' objects, protect the authenticity of those objects while developing Web-based programming? And what about visitors? Would they want to see the real thing if they could see digital versions of the collections online?"[72] Museums felt it necessary to defend intellectually and protect financially their foundational legacy of buildings, collections, and exhibitions. Despite the passionate arguments of a few visionary directors and technologists that museums needed to experiment with new forms of communication, most could not yet see the Internet's potential for furthering democracy in museums, and in society as a whole.[73]

In the late 1990s, as society was merging online, museums had moved in the opposite direction. Energized by an upward cycle in the economy, they had experienced another building frenzy. Over the decade almost every redevelopment zone in a U.S. city or exurb had added a museum. A new building or expansion had opened every 15 days.[74] These buildings were bolder, flashier, and costlier projects than their predecessors. They contained more spaces for large gatherings, retail opportunities, and ambitious public programs. They were more accessible than ever, with a few surpassing the requirements of the Americans with Disabilities Act, which mandated features like wheelchair ramps. Attendance was continuing to grow, climbing to 845 million, or three times the nation's population. But would emerging technologies erode the public's desire to venture to museums in the future? How could museums compete with the stream of information and images emanating from screens that were getting tinier, more portable, and more ubiquitous?

By the turn of the millennium, it was clear that digital technology was transforming not only American culture, but communication around the globe. Museums could no longer ignore it. As Leonard Steinbach of the Cleveland Museum of Art reminded his colleagues at the turn of the millennium, "We have an entire generation coming up speaking digital as a first language."[75] Generations Y (the millennials) and Z (those born post-1995) were not only increasingly seeing the world through digital screens, but they also were growing up in an educational system that encouraged them to use computer technology to learn about the world.

By the mid-1990s, some institutions (notably the Getty) had already experimented with loading information about artwork into computer kiosks in their galleries. Now at the dawn of the new century, others—from smaller institutions like the Dayton Art Institute in Ohio to the larger Philadelphia Museum of Art—launched more ambitious projects. Nascent technologies like MP3 and "personal data assistants" (a precursor to the smartphone) allowed them to enter large audio files onto handheld devices. Visitors could now stand in front of artwork and listen to different perspectives and ideas, in different languages, all at their own pace. By 2001, 60 percent of American art museums were using some kind of digital technology to enhance exhibitions.[76] That number would grow over the years as museums of all disciplines prototyped wearable devices, video walls, holograms, and other digital enhancements to the museum visiting experience. This engendered a new world of interpretation and the ability to bring new stories into the cultural sphere.

Not everyone working inside museums embraced these new educational methods. Computer kiosks turned museums into video-game arcades; would they scare away visitors who came to museums for peace and quiet? Walking around with gadgets could be more distracting than helpful to visitors; would they lose the ability to concentrate on what lay before them? And what would become of the museum's most dedicated educators, volunteer docents, many of whom were used to delivering formal, classroom-style instruction? Even though touring methods had evolved considerably from the days of dry docent lectures, would museumgoers still want to be led around the galleries by a human?[77] Most visitors, however, approved of technologies and methods that offered new perspectives and more information. Museums began to invest in staff who worked to model the responsible yet engaging use of new technologies to fulfill new societal needs. Educational programs went not only digital, but online. As teachers sought more resources for integrating STEM and STEAM into the classroom and adjusting to other curricular demands, museums posted resources like live data feeds of zoo animals, weather satellites, artists at work, lesson plans, and other materials to their websites. They even hosted "field trips" via videoconference and produced apps and podcasts.

Communication around the world continued to change radically and rapidly, transforming from a one-way, top-down channel to the interactive, content-sharing platforms that comprise what we now call social media.[78] In April 2005, the elephant exhibit at the San Diego Zoo was the site of the world's first-ever YouTube video, uploaded as an experiment by engineer Jawed Karim. A year and a half later, the Exploratorium became the nation's first museum to add its own video to YouTube: two scientists somewhat humorously demonstrating infrared heat cameras. Within three months, San Jose Museum of Art began a series of clips related to contemporary art exhibitions, eventually reaching YouTube's "top favorites" with "Road Trip," a chronicle of two educators promoting the lost art of purchasing, inscribing, stamping, and snail-mailing a travel postcard.[79] Museums found that sharing content in virtual space expanded their reach beyond what they had ever experienced. The American Museum of Natural History's 2009 YouTube hit "Known Universe," a soaring journey

Video and audio technology are part of the experience at the B. B. King Museum and Delta Interpretive Center in Indianola, MS
© Michael Ventura

through stars and quasars created in collaboration with the Rubin Museum of Art, attracted almost nine million views in its first year, twice as many as annual visits to both museums.[80]

In December 2007, the Brooklyn Museum inaugurated the nation's first museum Facebook page; a few months later, museums entered the "Twitterverse" when Brooklyn-based @MuseumNerd began to tweet from various New York City exhibits, circumventing official museum rhetoric and established critics. Highly visible online dialogues challenged the museum establishment to relinquish its authoritative voice once and for all and let others add ideas and interpretations of its work that could build on each other and spin off even more content.[81] @MuseumNerd was followed by other museum thought leaders on Twitter, Instagram, and additional platforms. They commented freely on matters both serious and playful. Museum-related posts, likes, tweets, retweets, uploads, and comments soon reached well into the millions and extended to marketing sites like TripAdvisor and Yelp. Amelia Wong, digital content strategist for the J. Paul Getty Trust, noted that this advance was an important step in helping the mu-

seum fulfill its democratizing promise, advancing "notions that all people are equal and should have equal access to participate in public discourse"[82]

By the 2010s, the Internet and social media had unlocked a new spirit of creativity, especially on the part of younger staff members. P. T. Barnum may have once turned heads (and possibly stomachs) by displaying the carcass of a frayed Angora cat, but the Walker Art Center in Minneapolis made housecat history when it tapped into the couch potato phenomenon of online cat videos. In 2012, it organized the world's first outdoor Internet Cat Video Festival. More than 10,000 people (and a fair number of felines) showed up. The festival became an annual program for four years, expanding into the Minnesota State Fair and then venues around the world. It raised funds for animal rescue organizations and, in the words of beloved mascot Henri le Chat, established the "cultural sovereignty of cats." Social media birthed other of-the-moment, playful events at museums: flash mobs, Pokémon GO, Minecraft days, and more. Museums changed their restrictive policies on social media and cell phone use in the galleries to encourage even more social media as a way to build buzz, belonging, and community.

**The Walker Art Center's Internet Cat Video Festival was so popular in the 2010s that it filled the bleachers at the Minnesota State Fair.**
Gene Pittman for Walker Art Center

**Cutout of Walker Art Center's handsome Internet Cat Video star, Henri le Chat, in 2013.**
Gene Pittman for Walker Art Center

**Older adults enjoying the digital touchtables in the History Galleries at the Oakland Museum of California.**
Photographer: Greg Habibi. Image courtesy of the Oakland Museum of California

The high volume of traffic across different platforms may have called on museums to stay up with social and cultural trends, but it also inserted them into serious conversations. For example, in the wake of the August 2014 police shooting of a young black man named Michael Brown in Ferguson, MO, a group of activists created #MuseumsRespondtoFerguson, a site for dialogue among museum workers, as movements like #BlackLivesMatter gathered visibility. "Where do museums fit in?" the bloggers wrote in a jointly authored statement. "What should be our role—as institutions that claim to conduct their activities for the public benefit—in the face of ongoing struggles for greater social justice both at the local and national level?"[83] The passionate online commentary and exchanges provided more evidence of the public's belief that museums should be involved in, and even lead the way for, addressing pressing social issues.

The rise of social media coincided with the beginning of an age of anxiety. Suddenly it seemed like news became more instantaneous, sensationalized, and scattered. Who could be trusted, especially after such apocryphal events as the terror attacks of September 11, 2001? It seemed impossible to ignore the reality of the early decades of the 21st century: wars in the Middle East; a global upswell in hurricanes, fires, and other events linked to climate change; and an epidemic of domestic gun violence, among other crises.

During these decades, concerns for safety have tested the role of civic gathering spaces as never before. Schools now mandate active-shooter trainings for teachers and students. The market for surveillance devices has boomed. Museums have been forced to invest in security measures, especially after such tragedies as the 2009 murder of guard Stephen Tyrone Johns by a white supremacist shooter at the United States Holocaust Memorial Museum, and public health and sanitization measures, especially in light of the COVID-19 pandemic. During these trying times, as we will see in the coming chapters, museums have continued to work hard to come to a deeper understanding of their unique role in society.

From the first school field trips in late-1800s Connecticut to the digital field trip of today, from roto-radio to Instagram, from droning lectures about ants and bees to outdoor Internet video festivals featuring housecats,

**Young Tinkerers at the Fleet Science Center take apart an old computer keyboard on their way to making new discoveries about the world.**
Courtesy of Fleet Science Center

from exhibitions about public health to contemporary Native American resilience, museums can still harken to the progressive educators of the 1930s who called on them to "modify . . . their ideas to fit the changing world conditions."[84] In this changing world, the public thirsts for meaning and places they can trust. Museums, as SF-MOMA educational technologist and researcher Peter Samis has noted in his thoughtful analysis of the early years of the museum digital revolution, increasingly understand that no matter how exciting developments in technology are, their biggest strength is their belief in humanity and people.[85] This is the quality they will need in order to do their part in society as the nation lurches forward into the 21st century.

### NOTES

1. Jane Addams, "Jane Addams's Own Story of Her Work: The First Five Years at Hull-House," *Ladies' Home Journal* (March 1906): 13.
2. Robert Scholfield, "The Science Education of an Enlightened Entrepreneur: Charles Willson Peale and His Philadelphia Museum, 1784–1827," *American Studies* 30 (1989): 21–40.
3. P. T. Barnum, quoted in James Parker, "The Original Huckster," *Atlantic* (August 2019): 32.
4. P. T. Barnum, "Letter to the Editor," *Nation*, August 10, 1865, https://lostmuseum.cuny.edu/archive/mr-barnum -on-museums-the-nation-august-10.
5. Heather Ewing, *The Lost World of James Smithson: Science, Revolution and the Birth of the Smithsonian* (New York: Bloomsbury, 2007), 4.
6. National Academy of Sciences, *The National Academy of Sciences: The First Hundred Years 1863–1963* (Washington, D.C.: National Academies Press, 1978).
7. Andrew Carnegie, *The Gospel of Wealth* (1889; New York: Carnegie Corporation of New York, 2017).
8. Lois H. Silverman, *The Social Work of Museums* (London: Routledge, 2010), 9. See also Jennifer Lynne Bosch, "The Life of Ellen Gates Starr, 1859–1940" (PhD dissertation, Miami University, 1990). For a discussion of the settlement museum movement, see Cynthia F. Heider, "Sympathy and Science: Social Settlements and Museums Forging the Future through a Usable Past" (master's thesis, Temple University, August 2018).

9. Promotional brochure, Confederate Memorial Hall Civil War Museum, acquired by the author on visit to the site in May 2019.

10. Neil Harris, "A Historical Perspective on Museum Advocacy," *Museum News* (November/December 1980): 75.

11. *American Museum of Natural History Annual Report* (1902).

12. Desire Goldsmith, "Matthew Arnold's Visit to America" (master's thesis, Boston University, 1940), https://open .bu.edu/ds2/stream/?#/documents/26781/page/98. The author wishes to acknowledge many conversations with her father, Allan B. Lefcowitz, a scholar of the work of Matthew Arnold and former editor of the *Arnoldian*.

13. Joseph Choate, quoted in John Brewer, *The American Leonardo: A Tale of Obsession, Arts and Money* (Oxford, U.K.: Oxford University Press, 2009), 13.

14. John Dewey, *Experience and Education: The 60th Anniversary Edition* (West Lafayette, IN: Kappa Delta Pi, 1998); George E. Hein, "John Dewey and Museum Education," *Curator* 47, no. 4 (October 2004): 413–27; M. D. Dietz, "An Awkward Echo: Matthew Arnold and John Dewey" (dissertation, University of Texas, Austin, 2008); and Robert L. Duffus's review of John Dewey's *Experience and Nature*, *New York Times*, May 3, 1925.

15. Sinclair Lewis, quoted in Joan Shelley Rubin, *The Making of Middle Brow Culture* (Chapel Hill: University of North Carolina Press, 1992), 30.

16. Initially, Sunday openings were controversial. Museums were not concerned that they were infringing on churchgoing. Rather, they feared an influx of the "laboring classes" and immigrants. In 1891 a group called the Working People's Petition Committee presented 80,000 signatures to the Metropolitan Museum of Art requesting Sunday hours. Although the experiment worked in terms of opening the Met's doors to larger audiences, the Sunday opening "offended some of the Museum's best friends and supporters" and resulted in the loss of a $50,000 bequest. See Lillian D. Wald, *The House on Henry Street* (1915; New York: Dover, 1971), 79–81.

17. Lawrence Levine, *The Opening of the American Mind* (New York: Beacon Press, 1997).

18. Carol Duncan analyzes the ritual of the museum visit in *Civilizing Rituals: In Public Art Museums* (New York: Routledge, 1995).

19. Calvin Tompkins, *Merchants and Masterpieces: The Story of the Metropolitan Museum of* Art (New York: E. P. Dutton & Co., 1970), 85.

20. Julie Christianson Stivers, *The Presence of the Past: The Public Museum of Grand Rapids at 150* (Grand Rapids, MI: Public Museum of Grand Rapids, 2004), 19.

21. Benjamin Ives Gilman, "The Museum Docent" (first published in 1915), reprinted in *Museum Education Anthology*, ed. Susan K. Nicholls (Washington, D.C.: Museum Education Roundtable, 1984), 148–62.

22. Harvard Art Museums, "Classified Documents: The Social Museum of Harvard University, 1903–1931," https:// www.harvardartmuseums.org/visit/exhibitions/3371/ classified-documents-the-social-museum-of-harvard -university-1903-1931.

23. Julie K. Brown, "Connecting Health and Natural History: A Failed Initiative at the American Museum of Natural History, 1909–1922," *American Journal of Public Health* 104, no. 10 (2014): 1877–88, doi:10.2105/ AJPH.2013.301384.

24. Geraldine Santoro, "'To Stamp Out the Plague Consumption,' 1908–1909," *Curator* 36, no. 1 (1993): 13–28. For more on public health initiatives undertaken at the Smithsonian during the 1920s, see Julie K. Brown, "Connecting Health and the Museum: An Exhibition Initiative by the National Health Council at the Smithsonian Institution's United States National Museum, 1922–1924," *Museum History Journal* 12, no. 2 (2019): 111–28.

25. American Association of Museums, *Museum News Letter* (December 1917): 3.

26. Benjamin Ives Gilman, *Museum Ideals* (Cambridge, MA: Harvard University Press, 1923), 51; and Gilman, quoted in Lisa Roberts, *From Knowledge to Narrative: Educators and the Changing Museum* (Washington, D.C.: Smithsonian Institution Press, 1997), 22.

27. Ernest Fenollosa, quoted in Akiko Murakata, "Ernest F. Fenollosa's 'Notes for a History of the Influence of China upon the Western World': A Link between the Houghton and the Beinecke Library Manuscripts," Kyoto University, 1982, https://repository.kulib.kyoto-u.ac.jp/ dspace/bitstream/2433/135160/1/ebk00047_033b.pdf.

28. David Nasaw, *The Chief: The Life of William Randolph Hearst* (Boston: Houghton Mifflin, 2000), 296–97.

29. John Cotton Dana, *The New Museum* (Woodstock, VT: Elm Street Press, 1917).

30. "School Classes Help the Museum," *Newark Museum Association Monthly Journal* (January 1927): 124.

31. David Beasley, *Douglas Macagy and the Foundation of Modern Art Curatorship* (Simcoe, ON: Davus, 1997), 7.

32. Beasley, *Douglas Macagy*, 7.

33. Arthur C. Parker, quoted in Terry Zeller, "Arthur C. Parker: A Pioneer in American Museums," *Curator* 30, no. 1 (1987): 46.

34. Ellen C. Hicks, "AAM after 72 Years," *Museum News* (May/June 1978): 47; and *A Statistical Survey of Museums in the United States and Canada* (Washington, D.C.: American Association of Museums, 1965). See also Laurence Vail Coleman, *Handbook of American Museums* (Washington, D.C.: American Association of Museums, 1932).

35. Paul J. DiMaggio, "Constructing an Organizational Field," in *The New Institutionalism in Organizational Analysis*, eds. Paul J. DiMaggio and Walter W. Powell (Chicago: University of Chicago Press, 1991), 272.

36. Howard Zinn, *A People's History of the United States* (New York: New Press, 1997), 284.

37. Philip Youtz, quoted in DiMaggio, "Constructing an Organizational Field," 285.

38. Grace McCann Morley, Oral History, San Francisco Museum of Modern Art archives.

39. Marjorie Schwarzer, "Bringing It to the People: Lessons from the First Great Depression," *Museum* (May/June 2009): 49–54.

40. Franklin D. Roosevelt, at the 1932 inauguration of the Museum of Modern Art's new building, quoted in *Art in Our Time: A Chronicle of the Museum of Modern Art*, eds. Harriet S. Bee and Michele Eliot (New York: Museum of Modern Art, 2004).

41. John Franklin White, ed., *Art in Action: American Art Centers and the New Deal* (Metuchen, N.J.: Scarecrow Press, 1987).

42. American Association of Museums, *Museum News Letter* (April 1918): 3.

43. "Eastern Museums Circuit Saint Paul National Security Exhibit," *Museum News* (December 1, 1941): 1.

44. "Art Museum Directors Hold New York Meeting on War Emergency," *Museum News* (January 1, 1942); "Museums of Honolulu Go through Japanese Air Raids Unharmed," *Museum News* (January 15, 1942): 1; "Wartime Activities in Two NYC Museums," *Museum News* (March 1, 1944).

45. Mary Anne Staniszewski, *The Power of Display: A History of Exhibition Installations at the Museum of Modern Art* (Cambridge, MA: MIT Press, 1998), 212–21.

46. *Statistical Survey of Museums*, 16.

47. Working with Dewey in the 1920s, Barnes had created a series of classes about his prized Impressionist paintings. Open only to those without formal education, including "negroes," the classes focused on a viewer's feelings (instead of intellectual knowledge) about a picture. As MoMA educator Carol Morgan explains, "Barnes's unique application of Dewey's theories became legendary in the art world, and perhaps has done more to undermine a serious reading of the uses of progressive educational theories in art education." See Carol Morgan, "From Modernist Utopia to Cold War Realty: A Critical Moment in Museum Education," in *The Museum of Modern Art at Mid-Century: Continuity and Change*, ed. John Elderfield (New York: Museum of Modern Art, 1995), 172–73. Morgan cites Howard Greenfield's *The Devil and Dr. Barnes: Portrait of an American Art Collector* (New York: Viking Press, 1989). See also Myra Pollack Sadker and David Miller Sadker, "The History of American Education," in *Teachers, Schools and Society* (New York: McGraw Hill, 1991), 291.

48. Rose Bennett Gilbert, "Space Age Education," *Museum News* (November 1965): 25.

49. W. Eugene Smith, *Popular Photography*, 1959, n.p.

50. Sherman Lee, "The Art Museum as Wilderness Act," reprinted in *Museum News* (February 1984): 59.

51. John R. Kinard, "The Neighborhood Museum as a Catalyst for Social Change," *Museum* 37, no. 4 (1985): 217–22.

52. June Jordan, quoted in Barry Schwartz, "Museums: Art for Who's Sake," *Ramparts* 9, no. 11 (1971): 38.

53. *Attracting Older Visitors to Museums* (Washington, D.C.: American Association of Retired Persons, 1985), 1. This report cites a 1981 Louis Harris poll published by the American Council for the Arts.

54. Silverman, *Social Work of Museums*, 117.

55. *Museums Count* (Washington, D.C.: American Association of Museums, 1994), 35, 78.

56. Steven Mintz, "Where Kids Come First: Children's Museums as Spaces Where Children and Families Can Play and Grow," *Hand to Hand* 31, nos. 2 and 3 (Summer/Fall 2017): 3.

57. The 1984 statistic comes from A. Lewin, "Children's Museums: A Structure for Family Learning," *Hand to Hand* 3 (1989): 16. The more recent statistic comes from Jen Rehkamp (director of field services, Association of Youth Museums), email exchange, June 3, 2019.

58. Source for autism statistics: Autism Society, "Facts and Statistics," https://www.autism-society.org/what-is/facts-and-statistics/. See also Kathryn S. Williams, "Programming for Children and Teens with Asperger's Syndrome in Museums" (master's capstone, John F. Kennedy University, June 2008), library2.jfku.edu/capstone/Museum_Studies/Programming_for_children.pdf.

59. Stephen Weil, "From Being about Something to Being for Somebody: The Ongoing Transformation of the American Museum," *Daedalus* 128, no. 3 (1999): 229.

60. Herbert Muschamp, "Crowds and Power," *New Republic* (April 12, 1993): 38.

61. Paul DiMaggio and Francie Ostrower, "Participation in the Arts by Black and White Americans," *Social Forces* (March 1990): 753–78.

62. Allan Bloom, *The Closing of the American Mind: How Higher Education Has Failed Democracy and Impoverished the Souls of Today's Students* (New York: Simon & Shuster, 1987).

63. Rush Limbaugh, "*Enola Gay* commentary," January 31, 1995, http://digital.lib.lehigh.edu/trial/enola/r3/january/.

64. Camille Paglia, "Ask Camille," *Salon*, (July 22, 1997): 2.

65. Donna Haraway, "Teddy Bear Patriarchy: Taxidermy in the Garden of Eden, 1908–1936," *Social Text* 11 (Winter 1984).

66. Amy Lonetree, *Decolonizing Museums: Representing Native America in National and Tribal Museums* (Chapel Hill: University of North Carolina Press, 2012), 9.

67. Grace Glueck, "Power and Aesthetics," *Art in America* (July 1971): 81.

68. DiMaggio and Ostrower, "Participation in the Arts," 753.

69. John H. Falk, "Leisure Decisions Influencing African-American Use of Museums," *Visitor Behavior* (Summer 1993), https://www.informalscience.org/sites/default/files/VSA-a0a1u2-a_5730.pdf.

70. Elaine Gurian, quoted in Jay Pridmore, "Museums Exhibit Fears for Their Future Finances," *Chicago Tribune*, May 13, 1990, https://www.chicagotribune.com/news/ct-xpm-1990-05-13-9002080342-story.html.

71. David Polly, personal correspondence, October 11, 2011.

72. Selma Thomas, introduction, in *The Digital Museum: A Think Guide*, eds. Herminia Din and Phyllis Hecht (Washington, D.C.: American Association of Museums, 2007), 3.

73. Joseph Veach Noble, "Controversial Exhibitions and Censorship," *Curator* 38, no. 2 (1995): 75–77.

74. Jane Lusaka and John Strand, "The Boom—And What to Do about It," *Museum News* (November/December 1998): 55–60.

75. Len Steinbach, quoted in Karen Jones, "Technology; New 'Smart' Galleries, Wireless and Web-Friendly," *New York Times*, April 24, 2002.

76. Marjorie Schwarzer, "Art and Gadgetry: The Future of the Museum Visit," *Museum News* 80, no. 4 (July/August 2001).

77. The touring technique Visual Thinking Strategies, created by educators Abigail Housen and Philip Yenawine, gained popularity in the early 1990s. It encouraged docents not to deliver a factual lecture but to engage viewers in a dialogue about an object that allowed them to draw their own conclusions, deepening their observational and critical thinking skills. See Philip Yenawine, *Visual Thinking Strategies: Using Art to Deepen Learning across School Disciplines* (Cambridge, MA: Harvard Education Press, 2013). Other kinds of tours that activated museum spaces were developed by such outside companies as Museum Hack, founded in 2013 by Nick Gray. Its tagline is "Museums Are F***ing Awesome." See "About Museum Hack," Museum Hack, https://museumhack.com/about/.

78. Valerie Wainwright, "Social Media and the Democratization of American Museums" (master's capstone, University of San Francisco, 2019), accessed October 10, 2019, https://repository.usfca.edu/capstone/898.

79. Other early museum YouTube channels were developed by Ontario Science Centre, Hirshhorn Museum, Indianapolis Museum of Art, and Museum of Modern Art. See Chris Alexander et al., "Beyond Launch: Museum Videos on YouTube," in *Museums and the Web 2008: Proceedings*, eds. J. Trant and D. Bearman (Toronto: Archives and Museum Informatics, March 31, 2008), consulted September 28, 2011, http://www.archimuse.com/mw2008/papers/hart/hart.html; and Nina Simon, *The Participatory Museum* (Santa Cruz, CA: Museum 2.0, 2010), 341–42.

80. American Museum of Natural History, "The Known Universe by AMNH," YouTube video, December 15, 2009, accessed August 28, 2019, www.youtube.com/watch?v=17jymDn0W6U.

81. @Museum Nerd, personal correspondence, August 2011.

82. Amelia Wong, cited in Wainwright, "Social Media," 30.

83. "Joint statement from museum bloggers & colleagues on Ferguson & related events," 2014, quoted in Therese Quinn, "The Justice Work of Culture," *New Art Examiner* 33, no. 3 (January/February 2019): 7.

84. Beasley, *Douglas Macagy*, 7.

85. Peter Samis, "Revisiting the Utopian Promise of Interpretive Media: An Autoethnographic Analysis Drawn from Art Museums, 1991–2017," in *The Routledge Handbook of Museums, Media and Communication*, eds. Kirsten Drotner, Vince Dziekan, Ross Parry, and Kim Christian Schroder (Abingdon, U.K.: Routledge, 2018), 47–66.

# CHAPTER 2

# The Building
## From Ionic to Iconic

On one of the many mornings that I visited the museum['s construction site], I saw an elderly African American man staring at the nearly-completed building. When I looked back at him, he was crying, so I rushed over to see if he needed help. He explained that he was simply overcome with emotion by the reality of the museum building and said it should "help us better understand who we are as Americans and point us toward a better tomorrow." . . . [I] hope he is right.

—LONNIE G. BUNCH III, FOUNDING DIRECTOR, NATIONAL MUSEUM OF AFRICAN AMERICAN HISTORY AND CULTURE, 2016[1]

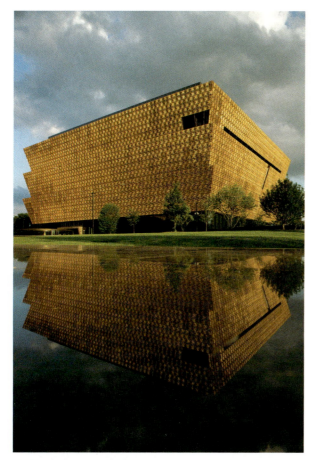

**National Museum of African American History and Culture.**
© Michael Ventura

IT IS 9:00 A.M. THE DOORS DON'T OPEN FOR ANOTHER hour. But already families, children, elderly, and tourists are gathering. Together, they form a line under the overhang of an exquisitely patterned bronze lattice palace. They are keenly aware of the building's power; after all, it permeates five acres of our nation's most symbolic real estate. Yet they are likely unaware of this building's less-than-glamorous beginnings. The National Museum of African American History and Culture on the National Mall spent its early days in a small office so insignificant that on founding director Lonnie Bunch's first day on the job, no one could find the keys. Bunch had to crowbar the door open.

Museums occupy some of the country's most stunning buildings and prominent sites, symbols of permanence and hope. But, as with the National Museum of African American History and Culture, the origins of the museums we visit today are far less glamorous.

The Massachusetts Historical Society once shared quarters with butcher stalls in a market hall. The Metropolitan Museum of Art set up its first exhibit in a defunct dance academy. The Brooklyn Children's Museum operated in a remodeled auto showroom; the Oregon Museum of Science and Industry in a hotel room; the Bellevue Arts Museum in an abandoned funeral parlor. Like each of these venerable institutions, most museums do not start with a grand building and fashionable address. They begin with a grand idea.

For years, often decades, museum founders and staff gather their wares and wander between spaces. The nomadic existence ends when, after much searching and a bit of politicking, they settle on an address. Only then do they begin to realize their largest physical achievement: a building of their own. In some cases, museums settle into historic buildings, turning obsolete structures into vibrant public places. Across the country, we find museums in old mansions, fire stations, and factories; in airplane hangars, railroad depots, and naval vessels. A defunct ice house in Cedar Falls, Iowa. An iron foundry in Birmingham, AL. A storefront shaped like a giant duck in Suffolk County, N.Y. In other cases, museums decide to build from scratch, or add a wing to an existing structure. Whether renovated or new, each museum building is part of an even larger story: the dramatic fruition of a cultural landscape across a changing nation.

Translating dreams into bricks and mortar involves an extensive cast of characters. Civic leaders, boards of trustees, directors, and the patrons who put up the money all have a say. Architects simultaneously play the role of savior and villain, pursued by a Greek chorus of critics and boosters. Behind the scenes, developers, planners, and politicians influence the selection of a site. The buildings wouldn't function without the contributions of engineers. They wouldn't get built at all without construction workers. Scenes play out in ornate palaces in urban parks; modern cubic forms nestled on college campuses or between downtown skyscrapers; renovated warehouses on waterfronts; and shiny edutainment complexes in locales as diverse as urban renewal districts, exurban tracts, and rural American Indian reservations.

The nation's story of museum architecture starts at the end of the Civil War. From the mid-19th century to the beginnings of World War II, architects looked to museums' western European roots. To them, classical and medieval palaces communicated enduring values, antidotes to the fleeting nature of daily life and commerce. Then, with the arrival of modern architecture in the 1930s on into the capital improvement projects of the 1970s and 1980s, builders performed an about-face, linking their projects not to past expressions of power but to present realities. Practical concerns like efficiency and urban economic revitalization dominated their agendas. In the late 1990s, museums veered toward sizzle and spectacle. In this era of themed malls and revitalized downtowns, museums became high-stakes attractions, icons to brand a city or region. In 2000, recognizing the urgent need for more environmentally sustainable building practices, the U.S. Green Building Council developed standards for Leadership in Energy and Environmental Design (LEED). Museums continued to build and renovate their spaces into the 21st century, but now looked at how their buildings could strike the right note between respecting both their publics and the planet.

## THE 19TH-CENTURY ORIGINS OF MUSEUM ARCHITECTURE

Museum architecture began its symphonic grandeur in Europe. The first public building constructed expressly as a museum was Karl Friedrich Schinkel's Altesmuseum in Berlin, Germany (1830). Schinkel felt that a museum needed the towering presence of a cathedral to assert its cultural and societal importance. He created a grand, central domed hall and an Ionic colonnade that spanned the entire front of the building. As visitors ascended through the palatial structure to the second-story galleries, they saw sweeping views of contemporary Berlin. Schinkel's goal was to give people a space where they could contemplate works of aesthetic purity without forgetting their obligation to the everyday world. He was inspired by the ancient Greek muses, nine goddesses who presided over the arts and sciences; the word *museum* derives from them.[2]

U.S. museum architecture began a generation later, on a somewhat lesser note. While Schinkel had studied at the prestigious German Bauakademie, early U.S. architects learned their trade via apprenticeship. All too often, 19th-century American museum architects copied European castles and cathedrals, unconcerned about the relationship of a building to its landscape or the nation's citizens. In 1842, the country's first public art museum, the Wadsworth Atheneum, was completed in Hartford, CT. Its architects, Ithiel Town and Alexander Davis, created a forbidding hybrid of Gothic cathedral and Roman fortress, meant more to project power than inspire contemplation. Another early public museum, the 1849 Smithsonian Institution (a building now known as the Castle) was designed by James Renwick. Its bulky forms harkened to the medieval cathedrals of France and England, another reflection of the prevailing attitude about the role of museum spaces.

In the decades after the eclectic Smithsonian Castle opened, the nation's architects professionalized. The American Institute of Architects was founded in 1857, and academies modeled on the French École des Beaux-Arts soon followed. Beginning with the Massachusetts Institute of Technology in 1863, these schools taught architects to design in the extravagant style that would dominate U.S. museums for the next few decades—Beaux-Arts classicism. Similar to Schinkel's approach, the Beaux-Arts method combined motifs from ancient Greece (Ionic and Doric columns and pediments), Rome (arches and vaults), the Renaissance (elevated domes), and Baroque palaces (endless enfilade corridors filled with rows of treasures). In the post–Civil War urban building boom, the traditions of Europe appealed to museums' industrialist-founders, who were attempting to reinvent themselves as cultivated aristocrats. They envisioned museums as elevated buildings with grand stairways. Sculptures of lions—those ancient symbols of strength—would

**Lithograph of the Smithsonian Castle, 1849.**
William Wade Archive, Library of Congress

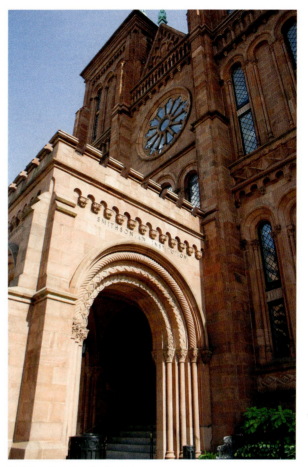

**Smithsonian Castle doorway.**
Photo by David Bjorgen

guard the entrances. Phrases in Latin—the ancient language of Europe's philosophers and statesmen—would adorn the pediments. These early museums were designed more to serve as civic monuments than as places to show objects.[3]

The aristocratic pretensions of late-19th-century museums in the United States were tempered by the real estate adage "location, location, location." Cities were taking over "undesirable" spaces and turning them into parkland. Museum founders saw great potential in these new green parcels and put their energies into lobbying for space; urban parks were the nation's closest approximation to European palace grounds. Set back from busy streets, far from the bustle, sootiness, and dangers of the city, and surrounded by greenery, a museum in a park commanded a powerful presence. Robert Koehler, the first director of what is now the Minneapolis Institute of Art, declared that parks were "ideal and practical at the same time." Land was cheap and available, and the "natural setting" enhanced the beauty of the artworks, while permitting expansion that did not conflict with downtown business interests.[4]

New York's Metropolitan Museum of Art was one of the first museums established in a park. In the 1870s, while the institution was still bouncing between rented spaces, its founders were persuaded to build in the recently completed Central Park. This was a significant decision. Cultural life in New York was divided along lines of class, religion, and race. Downtown was the place of daytime commerce and nighttime entertainment for the lower and immigrant classes. Central Park lay within New York's wealth corridor, between avenues filling up with mansions. Implicit then in the choice of a location was an expectation about whom the museum would serve. Some founders argued vehemently for a site more accessible to the working classes, but political forces—specifically the Central Park commissioners—prevailed. The Met would move to the park and have an entrance on fashionable Fifth Avenue. Luring the Met and, later, the American Museum of Natural History (AMNH) was a triumph in the park commissioners' plan for a bucolic area of refined activity, worlds apart from the sooty commer-

**The Minneapolis Institute of Art's façade is a classic example of a Beaux-Arts museum.**
Photo by Alexius Horatius

cial downtown with its tawdry entertainments and cramped immigrant sweatshops.[5]

The Central Park location allowed the new museums to occupy a top position within the evolving cityscape. But it did not immediately guarantee a top-notch building. According to the *New York Herald*, AMNH's first building was "hideous . . . half convent, half prison in appearance." The Met's first building fared no better. Completed in the 1880s, its barn-like appearance was criticized as a "forcible example of architectural ugliness . . . fit only for a winter garden or a railway depot." Ironically, a century later, some convents, prisons, and railway depots would be converted into museums. But at the time, cheap, awkward structures like the Met's were civic embarrassments. Rather than ascending elegant marble steps, visitors toddled over wooden boards, designed to keep mud off their shoes rather than to elevate their spirits. The glass roof leaked on rainy days, forcing staff to cover art with tarps and patrons to step around pails that caught the dripping water. The Met's patrons certainly deserved a more dignified house for their new museum, a promise that would be realized in the coming years.

Still, situating the Met in Central Park would establish a long-standing pattern of securing grand park locations for art museums. Soon after the Met's decision, the trustees of the Museum of Fine Arts, Boston, selected 12 acres in Boston's Back Bay Fens as a permanent site. The Cincinnati Museum Association chose that city's Eden Park. And the trustees of the Art Institute of Chicago accepted the city's offer of a smaller financial contribution in return for a spot in the newly created Lake Park (now Grant Park) when their museum was planned as part of the World's Columbian Exposition of 1893.[6]

Urban park settings and Beaux-Arts architecture met at that 1893 world's fair. Exposition planners wanted the fair's architecture, built on lakefront landfill, to communicate a vision of European culture. They thought the conservative Beaux-Arts style would counter a new commercial architectural phenomenon: bold, steel-frame skyscrapers being erected in Chicago's downtown. To traditionalists, the skyscraper was an abomination or, as novelist Henry James put it, a "mere economic convenience . . . a huge, continuous fifty-floored conspiracy against the very idea of the ancient graces."[7] Beginning in 1893 and through the 1920s, Chicago built a series of neoclassical museums in harmony with the fair's classicizing objectives. The building that now forms the nucleus of the Art Institute of Chicago was modeled on a Renaissance revival palazzo. At the time, the institute had no original works of art to speak of—only casts and reproductions. The monumental building, with later additions of bronze lions, a statue-lined staircase, and a fountain, expressed the confidence that someday Chicago would accumulate the original masterpieces it deserved.

Chicago's exposition inspired leaders in cities from Buffalo to Saint Louis to San Diego to combine palatial architecture, a park location, and the occasion of a world's fair to establish museums. Buffalo's original Albright Art Gallery (now Albright-Knox Northland) epitomizes the Beaux-Arts museum. Built for the Pan-American Exposition of 1901, it opened as a museum in 1905. Visitors entered by ascending a grand staircase and passing through a portico topped by a pediment. Once inside the spacious foyer, marble staircases led them to two symmetrical wings of galleries. Divided by the art of different nations and periods,

the galleries encouraged a sense of artistic diversity amid architectural harmony. Such architectural poetry was repeated in a variety of ways in several cities. The cool stone exteriors and the hushed halls created a quasi-religious experience. Like churches, Beaux-Arts museums had little place for visitor amenities, save for a few makeshift sales stands near the cloakroom or in the basement, where guards sold leaflets and postcards for a few pennies.[8] Anything more elaborate would have undermined the museum's stature as a place of education and scholarship, far removed from the taint of commerce.

Not everyone rejoiced over these high-minded palaces, which communicated more pomp than circumstance. Some thought they were frozen visions of Old World Europe and did not reflect the nation's vitality. In 1917 John Cotton Dana, visionary director of the Newark Museum in New Jersey, proposed that museum buildings no longer harken to bygone periods. Instead they should represent their times, using contemporary materials such as steel and concrete. Would the Greeks have built with columns of stone in the modern era? Why, then, should contemporary

**World's fairs birthed many of the nation's early museums, including the Albright-Knox in Buffalo, N.Y., which was originally built for the Pan-American Exposition of 1901.**
Library of Congress LC-DIG-ds-02304

museum architects refer to past styles? "To build first an expensive home, a palace, a temple or any grandiose and permanent structure on the conventional lines of so-called museum architecture" is, Dana said, "to do a foolish, wasteful, antiquated thing; a thing possible only to those who [know] little of modern community life."[9]

Dana criticized not only classical architecture but also park locations as inaccessible to most people. In the 1920s, when New Jersey politicians fought to move the downtown museum to an affluent, leafy neighborhood, Dana resigned from several civic committees in protest. He held his ground, and in 1926, in the city's downtown, the Newark Museum opened one of the first museum buildings with modern features. As was typical of the tensions between staff and trustees, Dana's enthusiasm for radical ideas was tempered by the building's patrons, department store magnates Louis and Carrie Bamberger. Fearing that the director would go overboard—Dana originally wanted a 16-story skyscraper—Mr. Bamberger supervised the entire building process and hired his store's architect, Jarvis Hunt, whose uncle, Robert Morris Hunt, had designed the Metropolitan Museum of Art. The result was a compromise between Beaux-Arts and modernism: a stripped-down, classical exterior nestled into a tight urban lot and a conventional interior courtyard that opened onto a floor plan modeled on contemporary office buildings.

### THE 1920s BUILDING BOOM

Newark Museum was part of the museum building boom fueled by the strong post–World War I economy. The rush of museum expansions, however, did not translate into inventive design. Museum architecture paled in comparison to the concurrent dazzling

When it was built in the mid-1920s in Sarasota, FL, the Italianate John and Mable Ringling Museum must have been quite an unusual sight.
Carol M. Highsmith Archive, Library of Congress

experiments of modernism seen in skyscrapers, Art Deco movie houses, suburban bungalows, and parkways. For museums, nostalgic architectural visions would continue in most of the nation for at least the next two decades. To house their European masterworks, museum founders continued to commission Beaux-Arts palaces that, to them, communicated wealth, status, and longevity. The stately John and Mable Ringling Museum of Art in Sarasota, FL, typifies the era's spirit. In 1925, circus impresario John Ringling founded this museum to house his collection of Baroque art and circus memorabilia. Using off-season circus performers as his construction crew, he built a sprawling complex on a former alligator-infested swamp—i.e., a brand-new building pretending to be a centuries-old Italianate villa. No one need be bothered by the fact that Florida's real-estate boom was less than a decade old.[10]

Even museums about technological progress hid their futuristic exhibits behind fluted columns and frumpy garlands. Inspired by the Deutsches Museum during a visit to Munich in the 1920s, Sears and Roebuck department stores President Julius Rosenwald founded the nation's first museum of science and industry. Highlighting industriousness in the technologies of aviation, transportation, and electricity, the Chicago institution often is called the country's first noisy museum, with exhibitions that squeaked, chortled, and immersed visitors in a boisterous, activity-filled environment. However, the container for this push-button ode to innovation was old-fashioned: a restored neo-Grecian palace, leftover from the Columbian Exposition. The Museum of Science and Industry opened to the public in 1933, in time for the city's 100th anniversary and in tandem with the Century of Progress World's Fair.[11]

A few years earlier, Sears trustee and stockholder Max Adler had become entranced with a German optical device that created an indoor illusion of the night sky. In 1928 he announced his quest to build the country's first planetarium. Like Rosenwald, Adler looked to the past for a container for his newfangled idea. He commissioned Beaux-Arts-trained architect Ernest Grunfeld Jr. to design a dressy palace that would display the universe in a classical costume. The resulting Adler Planetarium in Chicago received a gold medal from the American Institute of Architects for resisting the pernicious influence of modern architecture.

**The Adler Planetarium in Chicago, a palace designed during the late 1920s to display the universe.**
Courtesy of the Newberry Library

Walking the harmonious and repetitive corridors of Beaux-Arts museums was a novel experience for Americans, but it soon wore them down. In 1925, Yale University psychologist Edward Robinson described a phenomenon known as "museum fatigue . . . characterized by aching muscles, tired neck and eyes, and by the vague but insistent desire to escape from too many pictures or too much sculpture." To solve this problem, John Cotton Dana created "museum fatigue stools" that visitors could tote throughout the museum. Fiske Kimball, director of the Philadelphia Museum of Art, had bigger ideas. He envisioned a building to counter this fatigue and invited researchers using new techniques for studying visitor behavior to the museum for five months. Holding stopwatches, they timed people looking at artwork, discovering that they spent an average of 2.8 seconds looking at each picture. The problem was the architecture. Or, as the researchers put it, "large galleries, high ceilings, oppressive architectural detail combine to diminish people's attention to the actual things on exhibition."[12]

Kimball conceived of three kinds of interiors to slow visitors down and inspire more contemplation: one for the general public that would show the "evolution" of art history; another for scholars that would classify art by its materials; and the period room, an innovation that would show art in a furnished room. Kimball also envisioned garden courts as "rest-places, offering the public relief not only from the strain of constant looking, but also from the drag of standing and slow walking."[13] Rooms would be of different sizes and shapes (and sometimes reflect the measurements of specific works of art). Instead of straight avenues of movement, frequent turns would create intimacy and a sense of discovery. Electric lighting would combine with outside skylights and windows for brighter viewing spaces.

The new Philadelphia Museum of Art (PMA) opened in 1928. One wonders, however, how Kimball could have possibly felt this building would not overwhelm visitors. Many prominent museums had been built along urban boulevards, but Philadelphia's museum took this practice many steps forward. The building crowns the Benjamin Franklin Parkway, completed just before the institution broke ground. Not until 1997, when the Getty Museum opened in the Los Angeles hills, would a U.S. museum loom over its city, physically and symbolically, the way Philadelphia's did.

Many Philadelphians did not appreciate this stroke of monumentality. Nor did the museum's design slow

**The Philadelphia Museum of Art has crowned the city since 1928 and is still a focal point for celebrations and important community events.**
Courtesy of Philadelphia Museum of Art

The north entrance to the Philadelphia Museum of Art one month before its opening in 1928.
Courtesy of Philadelphia Museum of Art

visitors down the way Kimball had intended. As two critics lamented when the building opened:

> The architects seem to have gone out of their way to produce an exhausting building. The front presents a hillside with steps more forbidding than those of the Capitol in Rome . . . the U-shaped plan . . . also assures the maximum amount of travel . . . one always has to start at the center, go to the end of the wing, and retrace one's steps through the galleries already seen . . . the acuteness of exhaustion [is] produced by the lack of any furniture to sit on.[14]

Psychologists who studied visitors' use of PMA shortly after it opened discovered that people made a beeline for the exit, shortening their visit as much as they possibly could. Perhaps the long flight of stairs leading to PMA's entrance is best known as the site of Sylvester Stallone's victory dance in the hit movie *Rocky* (1976); even the Philadelphia Eagles grasped the significance of the uphill climb when they cel-

ebrated their 2018 Super Bowl victory in that same spot.[15] And art lovers will be grateful that, in 2019, PMA began an ambitious interior renovation designed to "possibly [end] that feeling of being lost amid proliferating galleries of art."[16]

By 1929 the Beaux-Arts formula was growing tired. The Great Depression soon would put it to rest. Museums began to seek new models to communicate their values. Two schools of thought emerged. One, echoing John Cotton Dana's progressive ideas, was a call for European modernism. The second, more popular at the time, looked for design inspiration from America's early colonists.

A keen nostalgia for colonial history arose at the same time the United States was beginning its love affair with the automobile. Descendants of the earliest colonists openly feared that massive numbers of new immigrants—notably Eastern Europeans, Italians, and Greeks—would undermine their "traditional" values. They also believed that with the rise of industrial cities,

**The Philadelphia Museum of Art's monumental interior staircase serves as seating for 21st-century audiences who gathered on a Friday night in 2019 for performances such as this one.**
Courtesy of Philadelphia Museum of Art

the United States was in danger of losing its architectural heritage. To them, reviving examples of colonial architecture could educate the growing nation about how the noble forefathers had civilized the raw continent. Of course, they never bothered to consider the role of enslaved and subjugated laborers.

In the western United States, museums copied motifs of the Spanish missions won over from Mexico half a century earlier. As examples of Spanish colonial revival architecture, the Santa Barbara Museum of Natural History (1923) and the San Diego Museum of Art (1926) boasted red tile roofs and romantic bell towers. In the eastern United States, colonial buildings and homes of American presidents were restored as historic sites, and automobile travel made them accessible to more than just the local residents. In 1923, for example, the Thomas Jefferson Foundation acquired Monticello, the former president's home near the University of Virginia, with plans to restore it and open it up to tourists from all over the world. It would take many decades for archaeologists and social historians to unearth structures occupied by those who had been forced to work the land as well as the tiny indoor room

occupied by Jefferson's slave Sally Hemings, who gave birth to at least four of his children.[17]

An important Colonial Revival project took place 125 miles southeast of Monticello. In 1926, John D. Rockefeller Jr., son of America's first billionaire, was convinced by a religious studies professor at the College of William and Mary to purchase a group of rundown 17th-century buildings in Williamsburg, VA. Although his money came from the mega-industrial destruction of past structures, Rockefeller believed that the values associated with the quaint cobblestone streets and humble homes of preindustrial society were superior and worth resuscitating. Ignoring the fact that the majority of the town's population was African American and that these buildings had originally been built with slave labor, Rockefeller worked with town leaders to re-create an "authentic" colonial village, essentially whitewashing much of its history. Colonial Williamsburg became the nation's first large-scale themed "historic" attraction, an automobile pilgrimage site whose history most visitors "understood but faintly, if at all."[18] As with Monticello and other colonial-era structures in Virginia, it would take until

The Santa Barbara Museum of Natural History in California, ca. 1924, is an example of the Spanish Colonial revival in the western United States.

Thomas Jefferson's Monticello was restored as a historic site in the 1920s, when this photo was taken.

the 1980s for the stories of its enslaved inhabitants to be told. During the 1920s Rockefeller's project inspired other crumbling towns to create historic sites that would serve as tourist destinations. In 1929, on a wooden dock on Connecticut's Mystic River, for example, citizens founded Mystic Seaport, a collection of historic ships, fishing vessels, and repair shops meant to preserve the disappearing remnants of America's maritime past.[19]

Like Rockefeller, industrialist Henry Ford believed that architecture could shape the national consciousness. Ford was infamous for his declaration that "history is more or less bunk" as well as for his virulent anti-Semitism. Thus, he did not look to the past, and he chose his "real" Americans carefully. He was inspired by Henry Mercer, proprietor of the Moravian Tile Works in Doylestown, PA. Mercer's ceramics factory produced handsome tiles for various structures, including, eventually, the Isabella Stewart Gardner Museum in Boston and the Joslyn Art Museum in Omaha. In 1916, Mercer created his own museum, which told an upbeat story of progress by meshing modern technology with nostalgia, highlighted by more than 50,000 preindustrial tools. Though the building borrowed Beaux-Arts decorative elements, structurally it was a six-story skyscraper, one of the nation's first buildings to use reinforced concrete.

Mercer's approach clicked with Ford. In 1929 the legendary industrialist created the Henry Ford Museum and Greenfield Village in Dearborn, MI, the largest history museum of its time. Rather than restoring a site like Rockefeller had or creating an original design in the spirit of Mercer, Ford purchased agricultural and industrial buildings—such as the nation's oldest windmill and all the New Jersey quarters (including soil samples) associated with Thomas Edison's invention of the light bulb—uprooted them from their towns, and rearranged them in "Greenfield Village."[20]

In the 1930s, Henry Ford purchased and relocated the laboratory where Thomas Edison invented the light bulb from New Jersey to Greenfield Village, MI.
By Swampyank—Own work, CC BY-SA 3.0, https://commons.wikimedia.org/w/index.php?curid=11540843

Colonial Williamsburg, Mystic Seaport, and Greenfield Village were milestones in museum history. Architecture was now a collections object and exhibition in its own right, establishing a trend of preserving historic places because of the aesthetic of their architecture. Re-created villages became automobile destinations. After World War II, as more middle-class white families took to the road, the number of outdoor history museums grew. Examples include Massachusetts's Old Sturbridge Village (1946), Indiana's Conner Prairie (1964), and Strawbery Banke in Portsmouth, N.H. (1965).

**Interior of the Mercer Museum, Doylestown, PA.**

**The Mercer Museum, constructed in 1916 by Henry Mercer, was one of the first buildings in the United States to use reinforced concrete.**

Library of Congress open access, http://www.loc.gov/rr/print/res/114_habs.html

## THE ERA OF MODERNISM

There are probably . . . more cubic feet of [museum] architecture per person in the United States than in any country in the world. The growth of our museums has been phenomenal.

—HAROLD STARK, ART HISTORIAN, 1934[21]

Until the Great Depression, cities continued to build ornate museums. Unfortunately, the energies devoted to constructing palatial passageways, sweeping staircases, and towering vaults left little room for the museum's more practical functions. Architects must have assumed that all collections would be on display, because none of the new buildings included sufficient storage. Staff frequently criticized the cramped working conditions, while museumgoers complained about poor ventilation, dreadful odors, and the exhaustion of laboring up multiple flights of stairs and through seemingly endless galleries. Who could appreciate the divine realm of culture with swollen feet and aching knees? Directors began to see Beaux-Arts museums as more of a handicap than an asset.[22] Like Newark's John Cotton Dana, they lobbied their cities for more functional buildings that took advantage of the latest technologies—such as rust-free plumbing and climate control. In 1935, while its architects were out of the country, lest they protest, the Brooklyn Museum eliminated its steep staircase and relocated the entrance to the first floor. Likewise, the country's oldest museum building—the Wadsworth Atheneum—completed what is considered the first modern museum renovation in the country. But most museums weren't so lucky. Conservative aesthetic tastes and shortages of materials during the Depression and World War II stymied most pleas for change.

Modern functional technologies may have appealed to those who worked in the nation's treasure houses, but their industrial aesthetic was not appreciated by those footing the bills. Throughout the Depression years, most museums favored stone materials and Beaux-Arts motifs. Examples include the 1931 Art Deco Joslyn Art Museum in Omaha, faced in 38 kinds of marble and entered through decorated bronze doors; the 1933 classical Beaux-Arts Nelson Gallery in Kansas City; and the 1941 National Gallery of Art (NGA) in Washington, D.C., constructed in pale pink Tennessee marble with Greek columns and an imposing flight of stairs. NGA's one nod to modernism was a functional basement cafeteria, complete with gleaming steam trays from which cafeteria workers spooned up institutional sustenance to fill patrons' stomachs, a trend that soon spread to other museums.[23]

Although these new museums were important additions to their cities, critics continued to sound the calls for modernism. Architectural critic Lewis Mumford dubbed Beaux-Arts museums "imperialist façades" that were "loot-heap[s] . . . for plunder."[24] Several directors agreed, calling them "'me too' Louvres of the New World."[25] Attacks by critics notwithstanding, three related phenomena pushed museums to accept modern architecture. First, classicism—in its purist incarnation—was associated increasingly with the fascist monuments built by Mussolini and Hitler. Second, in the 1930s collectors, artists, and architects fleeing European fascism began to arrive in the United States, where they influenced tastes in art and architecture. And later, due to wartime industrialization, modern materials were more available (and thus cheaper) than older ones.[26]

Three museums in New York City—the Museum of Modern Art, the then-called Guggenheim Museum of Non-Objective Painting, and the Whitney Museum of American Art—seized the moment to develop a new framework for museum architecture. In the late 1920s, as John D. Rockefeller Jr. was reviving colonial architecture in Virginia, his wife Abby and her collector-friends Lillie Bliss and Mary Quinn Sullivan were organizing a new kind of museum that would become a leading tastemaker for modern architectural ideas. In 1929 they founded the Museum of Modern Art (MoMA). While most trustees at traditional museums were hostile to contemporary art and architecture, MoMA's mission was to promote these ideas. As part of this mission, in 1932 MoMA organized and toured an influential exhibition of the work of avant-garde European architects. The curators of this show, Henry Russell Hitchcock and Philip Johnson, coined the term *International Style* to describe a new vision for architecture. To International Style architects, the Beaux-Arts style was more or less bunk. Rejecting applied historical ornament and symmetrical planning, architects like the famed Swiss innovator Le Corbusier favored a fresh style that focused on a building's function and exploited the qualities of industrial materials and technological advances. Concrete, steel, and plate glass were not only more economical than marble and stone, they were "modern" and thus more beautiful.

In 1939 MoMA broke ground for what would become the first building in New York designed in the International Style. Its first director, Alfred H. Barr Jr., convinced MoMA's trustees to build modern, declaring that a conservative building would "betray the very purposes for which the museum was founded."[27] Barr had wanted to hire one of the international architects featured in Johnson and Hitchcock's exhibit. But an American architect, Philip Goodwin, who happened to be on MoMA's board, won the commission.

Breaking a long museum tradition, MoMA moved toward New York's commercial core—that is, away from Central Park. Instead of vistas of park greenery, visitors would have to make do with a small sculpture garden behind the museum, an exercise in landscape abstraction that paralleled the canvases hanging in the galleries. Goodwin and his protégé Edward Durrell Stone fashioned a six-story building with two rows of horizontal strip windows and a slab cornice that featured punched holes open to the sky. The smooth and uniform façade of white Thermolux (a new translucent cladding) was revolutionary, resembling a department store or office building rather than a palace or temple.

In another break with tradition, visitors entered directly from the sidewalk through a set of glass doors. Rather than climbing giant staircases, they boarded elevators that took them to upper-story galleries. The architects took advantage of steel-frame technology, which allowed them to dispense with immovable interior walls. Within MoMA's columnar grid, exhibit designers could move walls and partitions freely and as needed to compose exhibition spaces. The building concluded in a penthouse rooftop—part of it open to the sky and emblazoned with the words "Museum of Modern Art"—which was used for social events.

With its location and architecture allied to commerce, and its opening broadcast on national radio with tributes from the Henry Ford family and Walt Disney, MoMA sent a strong message to collectors and gallery owners. Calling it "Utopia, Ltd. . . . a colonial complex inflated to prodigious dimensions," satirist Tom Wolfe later astutely claimed that the building signaled MoMA's intent to colonize the art market from the postwar spoils of Europe.[28] Indeed, soon after the museum opened its doors, New York became the center of the art world.

MoMA paved the way for an even more radical challenge to museum architecture a few blocks away. In 1943 Frank Lloyd Wright was commissioned to design the Guggenheim, his first and only New York building. Reveling in the freedom given him by collector Solomon Guggenheim and founding director Hilla Rebay, Wright stretched the definition of museum further than it had ever gone, even proposing a new name: "Archeseum." He eventually designed one of the most controversial (and Instagrammed) museum buildings of all time: a daring helix containing a gigantic ramp that rises for three-quarters of a mile toward a concrete dome punctuated by skylights. Visitors to the Guggenheim need make no tiring decisions about which direction to take; they have only one route to follow, either up or down the spiraling ramp. Wright envisioned the museum visit as a literary or cinematic narrative and created a linear path of experience that would forever challenge the ambitions of curators. Completed just after the architect's death in 1959, the museum's exterior was as radical as its interior. The building maximized the possibilities of cast concrete to create a wholly plastic form, a sculptural break in the regular building wall of Fifth Avenue.

On its opening day, October 21, 1959, all eyes were on the Guggenheim. The building garnered tremendous media attention and became a pilgrimage site for architects. Architectural historian Spiro Kostof praised it as a "gift of pure architecture . . . the great swan song of a great architect." But critic Lewis Mumford declared it a "mischievous failure" and even the Guggenheim's director at the time, James Johnson Sweeney, detested the building. Artists protested Wright's scheme almost as soon as it left the drawing board. Leave the art-making to the artists, they begged; give us a workable

In his 1959 design for the iconic Guggenheim Museum in New York City, Frank Lloyd Wright stretched the definition of museum architecture as far as it would go. Solomon R. Guggenheim Museum, New York.
Photo: David Heald. © SRGF ID: SRGM2010_ph004

building. To this day, many artists and critics feel this corkscrew building with its tilted ramp compromises artwork on display. Discussed and debated at length because of the celebrity of its architect and audacity of its design, Wright's Guggenheim foreshadowed the era of star architects creating bold statements that were more about their egos than the art or the visitor.[29]

The last of New York's triad of modern art museum triumphs was the original Whitney Museum of American Art, completed in 1966 by Marcel Breuer, a Hungarian émigré. The museum had been founded in 1930, a year after the Met refused Gertrude Vanderbilt Whitney's offer to donate more than 500 works of American art. Ironically, fifty years later, the Met took over the building that held the collection it had refused; it was known as the Met Breuer until, in 2020, it closed and the building was leased to temporarily house the Frick Collection. Breuer's midcentury building harmonized with the museum's mission to focus on changing exhibitions on the American scene and had a floor plan that resembled MoMA's: an open gallery shaped by movable wall panels and flexible lighting. Its granite-clad façade, however, was sculptural, composed of a series of stepped cantilevers and several oddly shaped windows. At ground level, a dry moat separated Madison Avenue's sidewalk from the lobby. Two decades after MoMA opened, architects were already uncomfortable with museum entrances that too closely met the city street.

With modernism taking hold of New York's museum culture, function dictated form in even the most traditional of buildings. In 1966 the Metropolitan Museum of Art embarked on an architectural experiment of its own that would alter the way Beaux-Arts museums used their classical façades: above its entrance, it hung a massive nylon banner advertising its exhibition of frescoes in a building-as-billboard approach.

In the postwar period, colleges and universities around the nation took advantage of the International Style. Some, like the Cranbrook Art Academy in Michigan, improved the look and feel of interior galleries. The Cranbrook Museum of Art, designed by Eliel Saarinen in 1942, featured state-of-the-art incandescent lighting that became a model for the field.[30] Because of the GI Bill, universities had experienced tremendous postwar growth, and campus planners were willing to test the tenets of modernism. Campus museums expanded to house researchers and growing archives and collections. The museum planners put their faith in young architects, giving them license to make original statements. In 1951 the Yale University Art Gallery became the first major

commission for one of the nation's most important modern architects, Louis Kahn. Distinguished by a hollow concrete floor—which housed mechanical systems—the museum had windowless, brick-and-glass curtain walls that broke with Yale's conservative legacy of collegiate Gothic design. In 1959 at Washington University in Saint Louis, 31-year-old faculty member Fumihiko Maki designed his first building, the Steinberg Art Gallery, a concrete-and-glass structure distinguished by its butterfly roof. Forty-five years later the university gave Maki the rare opportunity to update his youthful modernist vision; the Mildred Lane Kemper Art Museum opened in 2006 in the same spot where the Steinberg Art Gallery once stood.

Other universities commissioned buildings by the architects who had introduced the International Style to the United States. At Harvard, 76-year-old Le Corbusier realized his only U.S. building in 1963: the Carpenter Center for the Visual Arts, with floors raised on a columnar grid, a dominating ramp, and a roof terrace. Philip Johnson's Sheldon Memorial Art Gallery at the University of Nebraska in Lincoln opened that same year. Characterized by symmetry and allusions to historical forms like the arch, the Sheldon was a harbinger for the postmodern epoch that would soon follow.

Science center planners were intrigued by modern materials, such as concrete, and new ideas, such as structuring their spaces as flexible plants. For the most part, their buildings were not aesthetically successful. Between 1951 and 1960, for example, Boston's Museum of Science expanded into a huge, nondescript concrete box overlooking the Charles River.[31] In 1957 Portland's Oregon Museum of Science and Industry moved into a utilitarian concrete building, fashioned mostly by contractors and volunteers from labor unions. Some science centers, however, were inspired works of modern architecture. Built as part of Seattle's 1962 Century 21 Exposition, the Pacific Science Center was fashioned as a graceful, airy structure with stylized arches and a concrete plaza with a fountain. Its young architect, Minoru Yamasaki, would later achieve fame as the designer of New York's fated World Trade Center towers. The space race inspired a spate of modern planetariums at colleges such as St. John's College in Annapolis and the University of Nevada in Reno, and in cities as diverse as Miami and Dayton. As buildings, planetariums had advanced a long way from Max Adler's Chicago treasure. Modern ones were so unique in their design

**Harvard University's Carpenter Center for the Arts was designed in the International Style by famed Swiss architect Le Corbusier.**
Photo by Gunnar Klack

and functioning that the controlled interior settings at the Morehead Planetarium and Science Center at the University of North Carolina in Chapel Hill served as training grounds for astronauts.[32]

Modern architects' ability to manipulate lighting, climate, and other aspects of nature also appealed to institutions with living collections. New possibilities opened up for botanic gardens in 1960 when the Missouri Botanical Garden in Saint Louis opened a Buckminster Fuller geodesic Climatron, the world's first climate-controlled display greenhouse. Zoos entered the "disinfectant era," favoring outdoor concrete and steel, and pale-green glazed tile structures that were thought to be more hygienic for animals.[33]

Museum staff reveled in the joys of hygiene and modernization. Up-to-date technologies for plumbing, atmospheric control, and lighting promised to make their buildings cleaner and more functional. Humming ventilation systems and shinier materials promised to end the era of stuffy and dusty exhibit halls. Even Frank Lloyd Wright took to heart the American obsession with ridding the world of germs. He proposed a suction mat system at the entrance of the Guggenheim that would clean patrons' clothes and shoes of loose dirt, all the better to protect the artwork.[34]

Unfortunately, these visions were far beyond the means of most institutions, especially those housed in antiquated structures never intended to be museums. Many buildings were in dreadful condition, endangering collections. Electrical systems were obsolete. Fire prevention was close to impossible. Many that tried to modernize faced uphill battles and public outcry against the aesthetic of modern architecture. Government agencies and local residents often took issue with innovative ideas that clashed with surrounding buildings.

The Children's Museum of Indianapolis's late-1940s run-in with zoning authorities and citizens over a proposed addition is typical of museums' struggles to modernize. On donated space in a leafy part of Indianapolis, architect Kurt Vonnegut (the famed novelist's father) proposed a "clean modernistic building" with wide bands of glass block to admit natural light into a gallery and highlight a reproduction of a ground sloth skeleton. Yet residents protested that such a design would "ruin the neighborhood." Vonnegut's vision was realized when the museum decided to build in the modern style in a less fussy neighborhood. It would go on to become one of the finest children's museums in the world.[35] Elsewhere, citizens felt that they had to protect parkland from the travesties of modern buildings. In 1962, picketers took to the streets of Chicago, calling the Art Institute's modernist addition ugly and demanding the reinstallation of a Beaux-Arts fountain removed for the expansion.[36] Even artists expressed antipathy toward buildings meant to house their masterpieces. Edward Ruscha's mid-1960s painting *The Los Angeles County Museum on Fire* captured many citizens' fantasies of arson for the cold, modernist 1964 building.[37]

The most pressing problem facing modernization, however, was not public outcry; it was lack of money. Thankfully, relief was in sight. During the 1960s, changes in federal funding policies channeled money into museums. Half a century after the roaring twenties, museums again found themselves in a building frenzy. With new sources of money and a cadre of trained modern architects at their disposal,

**Architect Kurt Vonnegut Sr. admiring the collections at the Indianapolis Children's Museum.**
Courtesy Indianapolis Children's Museum

**Buckminster Fuller's geodesic Climatron at the Missouri Botanical Garden in Saint Louis.**
Library of Congress Prints and Photographics Division, HABS MO,96-SALU,105L—2

museums went on a building spree. The 1970s and 1980s saw the establishment of more than 3,200 new museums and the expansion or renovation of almost three-fifths of existing institutions. Naturally, growth of this magnitude transformed museum buildings as well as their locales. "The museum has become, not only on campus[es] but everywhere, the architectural laboratory of our time," declared *New York Times* architecture critic Paul Goldberger.[38]

Inspired by Wright's Guggenheim and campus museum projects, architects, to borrow a phrase from that era, "did their own thing." Like clothing trends of the 1970s, the resulting museums tended toward the gaudy and clunky, with occasional veers toward brutalism and a few rare nods to elegance. In 1971 Gio Ponti fashioned a 28-sided, gray-tiled structure for the Denver Art Museum. Set in the city's civic center, this fortress-like building was so austere that unsuspecting tourists often mistook it for a prison tower. (It is now part of the museum's north tower and in the process

of being revamped.) Houston, a rising metropolis in the heyday of the oil economy, was the site of Gunnar Birkerts's 1972 airplane-hangar-like Museum of Contemporary Art. The interior space was so vast that artists were asked to work on larger canvases so their work would fit the architecture.[39] Elemental geometries inspired Gordon Bunshaft's 1974 Hirshhorn Museum, part of the Smithsonian Institution in Washington, D.C., and across the Mall from the staid National Gallery of Art. Bunshaft believed he could improve on the Guggenheim, declaring that Wright's creation was "no more a museum than I am Napoleon." He fashioned a cylindrical building that rose on concrete piers and featured an interior courtyard in the round. When it opened, critics called it a "defensive pillbox" that had no business housing an art collection.[40]

As an antidote to the now-commonplace use of artificial light, in 1972 Louis Kahn fashioned the Kimbell Art Museum in Fort Worth, TX—a masterpiece of modern architecture. Its features include a curved

Gordon Bunshaft designed the Hirshhorn Museum and Sculpture Garden on the National Mall in 1974, believing he could improve on Frank Lloyd Wright's Guggenheim.
Courtesy of the Smithsonian Institution Archives, image # 78-6607

concrete vault to filter light through the top of the building and distribute it via stainless steel reflectors. The light streams into small, comfortable galleries creating an intimate, richly lit experience with artwork.

Whether their designs were adored or panned, these early-1970s buildings established that museums outside New York could attract attention through bold modern designs. And people flocked to them. After the ribbon was cut at the Smithsonian's National Museum of Air and Space in Washington, D.C., in 1976, for example, just in time for the nation's bicentennial celebration, more than one million people came through the doors in the first month alone. Crowd control was one logistical problem that architects could not ignore. Philip Johnson, using a somewhat unflattering simile, pleaded for large orientation spaces: "The public, upon entering a museum, and choosing one of six or seven things

to do, requires space, like a dog who upon entering a room, will sniff in one or two circumambulations of the room and will at last coil himself in one particular spot. I assure you, orientation space is not wasted."[41]

Other architects were influenced by a new building type sprouting throughout the country—the indoor shopping mall, whose features could be adapted to museums. Institutions began to add atriums to give a sense of roominess, interior escalators to move crowds efficiently, and large, comfortable eateries to feed the masses. These features were especially attractive to older museums that were expanding. I. M. Pei's 1978 triangular East Wing addition to the National Gallery of Art added an enormous underground shopping and eating concourse. Likewise, César Pelli's 1984 MoMA gallery expansion doubled exhibition space, added an interior escalator, expanded the lobby and cafeterias, and included a light-filled glass atrium.[42]

Large, airy spaces allow museums like the Udvar-Hazy Center branch of the Smithsonian Air and Space Museum at Dulles Airport to accommodate large crowds who come to see even larger objects.
© Michael Ventura

Interior view of Udvar-Hazy branch of the Smithsonian Air and Space Museum at Dulles Airport.
© Michael Ventura

MoMA's 1984 expansion project included another innovation: a neighboring 52-story condominium complex. In an elaborate financial scheme and through the aegis of a trust, MoMA sold its air rights to a developer and generated funds out of the thin air above its building. Three entities profited from the deal. The developer sold the condos. MoMA raised funds for a larger museum. The city gained a private, upscale housing development that would change the tenor (and tax base) of the street. MoMA, a pioneer in seeing the link between a museum's building and the commercial life of a downtown, had cut one of the most savvy real-estate deals ever concocted by a museum.

By the 1980s it was far easier to erect a 52-story building than to plow further into urban parks. With increased environmental consciousness, citizens' groups lobbied against encroaching upon precious green space. Even the powerful Metropolitan Museum of Art faced intense public and legal battles over its 1970s expansions. While the Met was able to grab more parkland to build a wing for the Temple of Dendur, a first-century Roman-Egyptian temple it had acquired, its building plate was fixed forever: no more expansions into Central Park. To gain more room, many museums adopted a solution similar to the one used by the National Gallery of Art; they put new facilities underground. Some, such as the Brooklyn Children's Museum, had no choice but to submerge their entire structures.

Founded in 1899, the world's first children's museum finally built a permanent home in 1977. To provide a large, continuous space that did not destroy its Brower Park location, the architects built an entire museum underground. Visitors enter via an old trolley kiosk and descend a 180-foot ramp through four floors of colorful exhibits. (In 2017, the museum added a rooftop terrace.)

What if a museum couldn't find a park to build on (or under)? In 1969, the Oakland Museum of California devised an innovative solution. Working with local citizens, the city decided to combine its early-20th-century parkland museums of art, history, and the natural sciences into a four-block lot at the edge of downtown. Originally, the museum commissioned Eero Saarinen, known for his space-age airport terminals. But when Saarinen died unexpectedly, his young

During the 1970s, Oakland Museum of California landscape architects Dan Kiley and Geraldine Scott programmed a garden right into the building, which overlooks the Oakland hills.
Photo by Odell Hussey Photography; courtesy of Oakland Museum of California

Retail spaces now occupy considerable square footage in museum buildings. This 2019 photo of the store at the Mint Museum in Charlotte, N.C., shows a particularly attractive museum retail space.
Photo by Heather Gwaltney

magnets, and desk ornaments. When the Guggenheim went so far as to create ceramic teapots and cups shaped like Frank Lloyd Wright's building, it was clear that museums had gone 180 degrees from their earliest days in urban parks, purposefully removed from the temptations of commerce. Even in the era of e-tailing, museum stores have thrived, perhaps because of their unique merchandising, perhaps because the very nature of a museum speaks to acquisition.

After-hours special events also influenced museum architecture; in this case, space demands were not add-ons but integrated into the core design of the building. Of course, museums always have used their grand buildings to host public gatherings. On New Year's Eve 1917, for example, the Minneapolis Institute of Art threw what was perhaps the nation's

first public museum costume ball. Still, it wasn't until 1974 that the Art Institute of Chicago became the first museum to develop a formal program to rent space to other organizations. Around the same time, the Center of Science and Industry (COSI) in Columbus, OH, pioneered overnight "camp-ins," turning its interior into a veritable campground and hotel.[66] By the 1990s museums were "hot" spots for all kinds of one-shot events that stretched the traditional use of their buildings: weddings, bar and bat mitzvahs, birthday parties, festivals, movie shoots, and even raves, meetups, and tequila tastings.

Curators and conservators protested; parties in the galleries put precious objects in grave danger. Reports of damage from caterers and rambunctious revelers were common. The solution was not to put an end to

Girl Scout camp-in at COSI in Columbus, OH. COSI is credited with creating the very first overnight museum camp-in.
Courtesy of COSI and Robb McCormick Photography

this very profitable function, but to design dramatic gathering spaces for special events. Museum spaces now needed to adapt to caterers, bands, performers, and movie crews and yet be special enough to attract such rentals. Some museums configured their entire designs around high-ticket rentals. The sizzle was becoming more important than the beef.

## STARCHITECTURE

The identification of [high-profile art] museums with their most famous [paintings] . . . is being replaced by an association with their high-profile architects.

—VICTORIA NEWHOUSE,
ARCHITECTURE CRITIC, 1999[67]

Another way to add sizzle was to hire a celebrity architect to design a "look-at-me" building. Once a museum in and of itself added to the luster of a city; now a unique structure designed by a famous architect was as important as a workable building, perhaps more so. In 1993 the University of Minnesota gave emerging Los Angeles architect Frank Gehry license to experiment with his design philosophy of decon-

structivism. The result was the shimmering Weisman Art Museum on its Minneapolis campus. Four years later, Gehry's billowing titanium spaceship of a Guggenheim Museum opened on the larger stage of Bilbao, Spain. It was a "wow" of a building, as iconic and recognizable as the Saint Louis Arch or Golden Gate Bridge. Architecturally, Gehry had broken new

The Frederick R. Weisman Art Museum (1993) designed by "starchitect" Frank Gehry for the University of Minnesota, Minneapolis.

Designed by Frank Gehry, the Museum of Pop Culture in Seattle certainly is eye-popping. This photo was taken in 2008.

ground, using a sophisticated computer program to engineer previously unimagined shapes and forms. As they had with Wright's Guggenheim, critics disparaged the showiness of Gehry's creation. But no one could dispute that the building was an economic triumph, generating $500 million for the Spanish city in its first three years. Like Chicago's late-19th-century museums, Guggenheim Bilbao's architecture was more significant than its collections. Like the cathedrals of yore, it became a pilgrimage site for cultural tourists and a harbinger of a phenomenon now called the "Bilbao effect" or "architourism."[68]

Suddenly everyone wanted a "Gehry." Even before Guggenheim Bilbao was finished, Paul Allen, a collector of Jimi Hendrix memorabilia and cofounder of Microsoft, had commissioned the architect to design the Experience Music Project in Seattle (now the Museum of Pop Culture, or MoPOP). In a synergy between celebrity architect, technology guru, and mythic dead rock guitarist, Gehry delivered a striking guitar-like building, which opened in 1999. Its bulging shapes are sheathed in gold, silver, and purple stainless steel and in red and blue aluminum shingles. Critics called it an "upside-down jello mold."[69]

In 1997, after 14 years in the making, the most expensive museum in U.S. history—costing more than $1 billion—opened atop a private hillside overlooking a heavily traveled freeway. The Getty Museum, designed by Richard Meier, borrowed an idea from universities and research centers: the museum as a campus. Not only does the 24-acre complex contain a research center and a state-of-the-art conservation institute, the museum itself is spread over several buildings. The campus affords stunning views and is highly visible from the air, for those aboard planes bound to and from LAX. Indeed, the Getty's viewpoints of Los Angeles are so spectacular that the museum's site rivals its collection.

The 1995 building for San Francisco's Museum of Modern Art epitomized what a striking façade could do for a museum and a city. Previously housed in cramped quarters within a war memorial building, the new museum joined the ranks of the world's top contemporary art museums. Mario Botta created a landmark destination. Because its central tower was an unusual red-brick-faced, sliced cylinder, people readily remembered the building. Architecture became logo. Attendance and collections grew at such a

Richard Meier's design for the sprawling Getty Center campus initially drew protests from neighbors. Completed in 1997, today it is one of Los Angeles's architectural highlights.

Snøhetta expansion of the new SFMOMA, 2016.
Photo © Henrik Kam; courtesy SFMOMA

fast clip that SFMOMA soon decided to commission an expansion to triple its space. A multistory addition by the Norwegian firm Snøhetta opened in 2016. "We could never recreate Mario Botta," lead architect Craig Dykers said. "You don't want to copy your dance partner, you want to be complimentary to it so you don't step on each other's toes."[70]

Known for his expressive bridges, train stations, and more recently the New York Oculus, architect Santiago Calatrava brought "high" design to his 2001 addition to the Milwaukee Art Museum. From a distance, the building looks like a bird alighting, the white concrete-and-glass infrastructure soaring to the sky and establishing a distinctive icon for the Milwaukee skyline. The museum's geometries were even featured in an ad campaign for the Toyota Solara, with the tagline "you can't go anywhere without being noticed."[71] Not every city, however, wants its art museum noticed. The Nelson-Atkins Museum of Art in Kansas City chose Steven Holl to design a low-key addition to its 1933 Beaux-Arts building. It opened to wide acclaim in 2007.

## FIN DE SIÉCLE CONTROVERSIES

In the past, architectural commissions had been debated primarily in boardrooms. But the 1990s saw wider involvement from the public, who battled museums' attempts to make bold statements. Often blaming the "arrogant architect," citizens' groups filed lawsuits against projects they considered outlandish. They battled Richard Meier and the Getty over the white hue of the stone he originally proposed and the possibility that museum visitors could see into their homes from its hilltop location. Eventually, Meier chose beige travertine, and the city planted view-blocking trees and vines around the museum.[72] From 1999 to 2004, citizens' groups in San Francisco filed multiple lawsuits against the de Young Museum to reduce the height of a proposed tower, intended to house educational programs, in a new building to be designed by the Swiss firm Herzog and de Meuron. They worried "that the tower might be seen from afar, forgetting that standing high . . . has defined the meaning of towers for millennia."[73] Eventually, the judge fined the plaintiffs for slowing down the project with one frivolous suit after another. In 2005 the new de Young with its iconic 144-foot copper-skinned tower opened, and today the tower is one of its most popular features, and one wishes that it was even taller.

As museums battled to build, some trustees battled their "starchitects," firing them from commis-

sions—at the Contemporary Jewish Museum in San Francisco; the Blanton Museum at the University of Texas in Austin; the Smithsonian's National Museum of the American Indian in Washington, D.C., to name a few. As if to prove these instincts right, in 2001, the Bellevue Arts Museum opened a swanky, high-tech building designed by starchitect Steven Holl in a suburb of Seattle. The community hated the building. Audiences stayed away in droves, bringing the museum to the brink of financial collapse within two years of the ribbon-cutting ceremony. The museum was forced to revisit Holl's vision and "soften" the building with a new color palette and carpeting to make it more visitor-friendly.[74] Likewise, that same year, in midtown Manhattan, the American Folk Art Museum (AFAM) opened a distinctive 40-foot-wide bronze-and-copper-clad building by architects Billie Tsien and Tod Williams. The community loved the building. But soon AFAM defaulted on the loan it had taken out to finance the expensive project. It had no choice but to sell the building to its wealthy neighbor, the Museum of Modern Art. And in 2014, MoMA argued that it had no choice but to demolish the building. The art and architecture community decried MoMA for thumbing its nose at its own foundational vision by destroying a modern masterpiece.[75]

Classical masterpieces also teetered toward extinction. In 1990, Detroit was hemorrhaging amid severe budgetary woes. Michigan's governor approved massive budget cuts to all "nonessential services," including the Detroit Institute of Arts. The DIA's Founders Society, comprised largely of wealthy citizens, pressured the museum to abandon its 1927 Beaux-Arts building and move to a new building in an affluent suburb. But city leaders felt that "overhauling such a visible symbol" would be too traumatic for the people of Detroit. Through a bond, they raised the money to save the museum. Perhaps the classical building served as a promise that vitality and stability could return someday to that stricken city. DIA's struggles would continue, as we see in the next chapter. But in 2019, DIA proved its worth by leading a design competition for an ambitious cultural district. The French firm Agence Ter and Detroit-based studio Akoaki was commissioned to create "Detroit Square," intended to link DIA and 12 other cultural institutions through landscaping, "to be activated with outdoor cafes, performance spaces, a mobile DJ booth, green spaces, [and] public art."[76]

By the early 21st century, even though the building process had become more expensive and politicized

than ever, museums had become central to the civic fabric of a community. But doubts remained. Were museum projects spiraling out of control? Had the glitz gone too far? With the rise of the Internet, wasn't it more logical to build a new kind of digital architecture for museums as opposed to a brick-and-mortar one? In 2002, Franklin W. Robinson, director of the Herbert F. Johnson Museum of Art at Cornell University, observed that building projects are seductive and "dangerous and there are other ways to serve one's institution and community. . . . I say no more buildings!"[77]

Still, the seduction of building has been hard to resist. Even during the recession of 2008–2009, 70 major building projects, totaling billions of dollars, remained on the books. Cities continued to peg their hopes on matching a high-profile architect with an ambitious fundraising campaign. In Atlanta, the High Museum of Art, citing phenomenal growth of both attendance and collections, raised more than $85 million for a soaring Renzo Piano addition. The Telfair Museum of Art in Savannah, GA, chose Israeli architect Moshe Safdie and commenced the largest fundraising campaign in the city's history.[78] Ohio's Akron Art Museum hired architectural firm Coop Himmelb(l)au to handle its planned $30 million upgrade. The list goes on, as communities invested in the flourishing spirit of museums.

## DEFYING THE ODDS: CASINOS, MUSEUMS, AND GREEN ARCHITECTURE

A discussion of late-20th/early-21st-century museum architecture would not be complete without noting the meeting of two odd bedfellows: museums and casinos. These institutions began to mix, toward different ends, in Las Vegas and on American Indian reservations. During the 1990s, Las Vegas was the nation's fastest growing city, seeking to change its sinful image to appeal to families and cultural tourists. The city and county invested in a children's museum, a history and nature museum, displays of aviation history at its airport, a museum of historical neon signs, and even an elaborate, light-studded museum dedicated to the life of flamboyant entertainer-pianist Liberace. With three incongruous partners—the Hermitage of Russia, the Kunsthistorisches Museum of Austria, and the Venetian Casino Resort—in 2001 the Guggenheim opened a flashy Vegas branch, designed by Rem Koolhaus and displaying everything from Titians to high-tech racing bikes. In flyers distributed all over town, the museum billed itself as the "Guggenheim Experience at the Venetian . . . sensationally sensual."[79] Most of these over-the-top experiments (except for the children's

museum) went bankrupt. This did not stop the city from turning its historic courthouse into the National Museum of Organized Crime and Law Enforcement, otherwise known as the Mob Museum. This being Las Vegas, one can imagine its re-created speakeasy and its menu of "prohibition-era craft cocktails" helping the Mob Museum stay above board.

As Vegas was going museum, American Indian nations were going casino. The 1988 National Gaming Act permitted federally recognized tribes to run casinos on reservation lands. Soon these gaming establishments were generating tens of billions of dollars—providing both a financial boost for one of the country's most economically disadvantaged populations and a means for reinvigorating cultural traditions. American Indians had long been concerned with how they would pass on their living traditions to a younger generation. The Gaming Act mandated that at least 3 percent of gaming proceeds fund cultural and educational programs. Now some serious cash was available to meet this goal. In addition, the Native American Graves Protection and Repatriation Act (NAGPRA) of 1990 mandated that museums return certain sacred objects to their tribes of origin. Tribal leaders, in turn, initiated state-of-the-art museum projects to house and care for these items. With their intensive attention to the natural environment, the tribal museum projects added a new dimension to museum architecture.

One of the first was the Warm Springs Tribal Museum in Oregon, which opened in 1993. Stastny & Burke: Architecture designed a building to harmonize with both the landscape and the native traditions of the region. The architects described their vision:

The visitor's journey begins near water in a rock-strewn stream bed. The water becomes polished green slate and leads the visitor through a circular stone drum and into the lobby. . . . Inside the building, columns resemble trees, finished wood is detailed with rough-hewn juniper . . . forms, materials and details embody traditions evolved over centuries of life in harmony with the earth.

The building won an Award of Excellence from the American Institute of Architects for combining environmental sensitivity with an "emotional wallop all too seldom felt in contemporary public buildings."[80] Fortified with casino revenues, tribal museum projects continued.

In 1998, adjacent to the Wildhorse Casino Resort near Pendleton, OR, the Cayuse, Umatilla, and Walla

The Museum at Warm Springs in Oregon was one of the first designed to harmonize with its surrounding landscape and native traditions. Courtesy of the Museum at Warm Springs, OR.

Walla tribes opened the Tamastslikt Cultural Institute with a display celebrating past and present native life in the region. It aims to "tell the story of Western expansionism from the tribal point of view."[81] That same year, near Mystic, CT, the Mashantucket Pequot tribal nation—perhaps the smallest tribe in the country—opened the Mashantucket Pequot Museum and Research Center, the largest Native American cultural facility in the country at the time. The aegis was the nearby tribal-run Foxwoods Resort Casino. The $193 million museum featured a reconstructed 16th-century Pequot coastal village as well as multisensory displays on eastern woodland and native life.[82] In keeping with Native American beliefs, its building responds to the ecology of its site. By the 2000s, tribal museums were one of the fastest growing segments of the museum community.

Tribal museums introduced enlightened ideas into museums. A movement called "green architecture," gaining popularity in Europe, had garnered little notice in the United States. But to Native American museum planners, studying the ecology of a site, using efficient energy systems and recycled and renewable

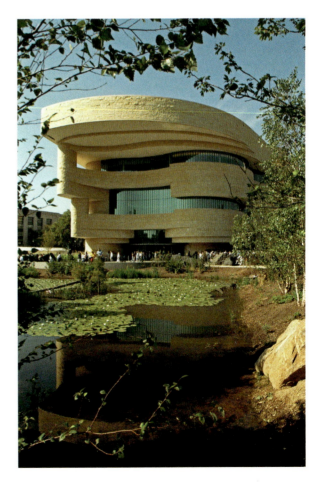

The Smithsonian's National Museum of the American Indian evokes precontact nature.
© Michael Ventura

materials, and other principles of green architecture fit with a spiritual connection to the Earth that was so vital to American Indian religious and cultural traditions. The National Museum of the American Indian, in both its 1997 Cultural Resource Center in Suitland, Md., and its 2004 museum on the National Mall, was perhaps the nation's first large museum to embrace designs that respect the native habitat.

Of course, the philosophies of green architecture stretched beyond Native American tribal communities. In 1998 the Madison Children's Museum in Wisconsin designed *First Feats*, the first wholly "green" exhibition with materials free of pesticide residues, off-gassing particleboard, unstable plastics, and toxic carpeting.[83] In 2000 the Architecture League of New York organized *Ten Shades of Green*, an exhibition about the principles of green architecture that traveled to several museums. While not meeting the myriad requirements needed to be certified as green, the Nevada Museum of Art's 2003 building defied common honky-tonk building convention in Reno and instead responded to its terrain. Designed by Arizona architect Will Bruder, the museum's exterior was inspired by the shape of a bluff in the eastern Sierra Mountain desert basin. Bruder used local black stone and created a rooftop sculpture garden that allows visitors to see over the cacophony of casinos and out onto the deserts and mountains beyond.

In 2003, ECHO at the Leahy Center, a science center in Burlington, VT, became the first new museum building to receive a Leadership in Energy and Environmental Design (LEED) certificate. Built overlooking Vermont's Lake Champlain, it invested in super-efficient windows and insulation. Following this model, in 2008, the California Academy of Sciences in San Francisco completed an even-larger LEED-certified green building in Golden Gate Park. On a "living roof," architect Renzo Piano designed a two-acre roof-top native plant garden that slopes into a glass-enclosed piazza. Inside, the Academy instituted strict processes for reducing its use of plastics, re-using supplies, recycling as much as possible, and, most radically, divesting its investment portfolio from fossil fuels.

## POSTRECESSION MUSEUM ARCHITECTURE: LOCATION, LOCATION, LOCATION

The terrorist attacks on September 11, 2001, altered the United States forever. Like all public buildings, museums found themselves shoring up entrances with security checkpoints and devices. Both were costly and unattractive, but necessary for an increasingly nervous nation. The subsequent real estate bust further challenged museum building practices, as some institutions came dangerously close to defaulting on loans they had taken out to finance capital expansions. Others were forced to shut their doors for good. But the economy reenergized in the 2010s in a lopsided boom that benefited wealthy museum patrons. Some poured their financial gains into contemporary art purchases and museum building projects that once again established museums' prominence on the American landscape.

College campuses, always places of experimentation, took advantage of the donations of grateful alumni. By now, campus museums were no longer isolated outposts for a few faculty and students; they were using their collections and exhibitions as integral parts of university curriculum across the arts and sciences. They could also help universities bridge "town and gown" divisions by offering programs with broad appeal. To that end, in 2012, Michigan State University in East Lansing, one of the oldest land-grant colleges in the nation, cut the ribbon on Iraqi-born architect Zaha Hadid's extraordinary Eli and Edythe Broad Art Museum. Hadid's pleated stainless steel and glass shard structure resembles a light-filled futuristic sea vessel. *Architectural Digest* has called her creation the "best designed building in the state of Michigan."[84]

In 2015, the Broads underwrote another significant public museum: this one a downtown Los Angeles structure for their personal contemporary art collection. Diller Scofidio + Renfro's Broad Museum poses as a gigantic chicken eye, set within a waffle-like concrete surface (the Broad describes the look as "veil and vault"). The building looms over the downtown streetscape and a small plaza of olive trees and entices visitors inside, again an example of innovative architecture playing a role in enlivening a city's central business district in an era of declining retail frontage.

Another "single-donor" museum designed to enliven and even potentially transform an entire community is the Crystal Bridges Museum of American Art (2011). The sprawling campus, designed by Moshe Safdie, was built on family-owned land in a northwest Arkansas company town, far from the nation's traditional art centers. In 1950, entrepreneur Sam Walton purchased a five-and-dime store in Bentonville, AR, an Ozark town of less than 3,000 residents. Walton's investment grew into the multibillion-dollar Walmart

**Crystal Bridges Museum of American Art, Bentonville, AR, by architect Moshe Safdie.**

retail empire, making him one of the richest men in the world. In the 2000s, Sam Walton's daughter Alice spearheaded a museum meant both to serve the local community (especially schoolchildren) and position her hometown as a cultural oasis. Inspired by Denmark's Louisiana Museum of Modern Art, Safdie carved out a grandiose landscape of exhibition that alters its environment almost beyond recognition. The original Crystal Springs, from whence the museum derived its name, was dammed and turned into a trio of ponds. Parts of the museum are positioned above them, two of the pavilions acting as bridges. "We wanted to intertwine the art with nature," said Safdie, "so you are constantly aware of nature. That's an important test for a building: how it cycles with the seasons and over time."[85]

The themes of time and transformation underlie two of the most visited new museum buildings of the 2010s: The National September 11 Museum in Lower Manhattan, New York City, and the National

**Zaha Hadid's soaring design for Michigan State University's Broad Museum in East Lansing is the perfect setting for an aerial performance.**
Photography by Aaron Word. Courtesy of MSU Broad.

Museum of African American History and Culture on the National Mall.

Almost immediately after the collapse of the World Trade Center towers, the public began to debate the future of the eerily vacant site. There was no question that something had to come of the wreckage. But what form should it take? How does one transform what was once a brash center of global enterprise into a respectful place for private mourning and public healing?[86] The Lower Manhattan Development Corporation looked for answers by opening a design competition for a memorial to be built within the footprint of the destroyed towers; 5,201 entrants from 63 nations and 49 states proposed solutions.[87] The winners, Michael Arad, an architect working for the New York City Housing Authority, and Peter Walker, a landscape architect, envisioned the grounds as both a space for memory and a living part of the city with trees forming the green roof of a museum. In May 2014, The National September 11 Museum opened to the public. Its primary artifact is the site itself, but it also contains artifacts, archives, and a private reflection room and columbarium for the families directly impacted. Visitors learn the story of the terrorist attack as they descend into the towers' original 70-foot, steel-studded concrete foundation.[88] As of this writing, the museum attracts millions of visitors annually. But for the museum's staff the question remains: how will the memories and stories of this single day and its aftermath evolve with the passage of time? This question is brought into sharper focus today, as the museum field ponders how museum architecture will change within the context of the COVID-19 pandemic and other worldwide upheavals.

It was 100 years in the making, but in 2016, the National Museum of African American History and Culture finally opened on the National Mall.[89] Architect David Adjaye's dark bronze building stands in contrast to its surrounding white stone monuments, as if to complicate those earlier buildings' smooth and privileged existence. Shaped like the crown of Benin royalty, found beneath the ground and only partially excavated, NMAAHC promises to deepen the his-

torical thinking about our nation. Indeed, like the September 11 Museum, much of NMAAHC's structure lies below grade, and it is there, dozens of feet below the surface, that visitors descend to and begin their upward voyage through the story of African American slavery and subjugation, resilience, and resistance.

All over the country, museum buildings continue to uplift and inspire their growing base of admirers and users. Each building reflects the aspirations of its times as well as a universal desire to celebrate culture, community, landscape, and location. In the Beaux-Arts era, museums strove to look alike. Founders were united in their desire to achieve eternal grandeur in the guise of European stateliness. During the modernist era that followed, museum designers worked from a common set of principles based on functional planning and the use of industrial materials. Directors were united in their desire for workable, practical buildings as sites for collections care, visitor centers, and urban renewal. By the end of the 20th century and into the 21st, the design of the museum became more diverse, mirroring the pluralism of the marketplace. Regardless of style or process, the players or the politics, or the evolving needs of our times, the opening of each museum building is still a momentous event. Moreover, the public's enthusiasm for museum architecture lasts well beyond the ribbon-cutting ceremonies and opening receptions. In fact, even museums that initially were considered eyesores or enigmas have a way of endearing themselves to the public.

Architect Daniel Libeskind claims that he is inspired by the "atmosphere a museum exudes." High-profile projects like his 2006 Denver Art Museum expansion, riffing off the silhouette of the Rocky Mountains, and 2008 Contemporary Jewish Museum in San Francisco, modeled on the Hebrew words for "to life," incorporate the spiritual and emotional. "If a certain care has been taken in building a museum," Libeskind says, "it glows from within. . . . When everything has been authentically placed in relation to everything else, then the building has its own special quality. That's the soul of the building."[90]

Contemporary Jewish Museum in San Francisco by architect Daniel Libeskind. Courtesy of the Contemporary Jewish Museum.

## NOTES

1. Lonnie G. Bunch III, foreword, in *Begin with the Past: Building the National Museum of African American History and Culture*, ed. Mabel O. Wilson (Washington, D.C.: Smithsonian Institution, 2016), 7.

2. Douglas Crimp discusses Schinkel's influence on museum architecture in *On the Museum's Ruins* (Cambridge, MA: MIT Press, 1993), 285–318; and "The End of Art and the Origin of the Museum," *Art Journal* (Winter 1987): 261–66.

3. John Burchard and Albert Bush-Brown, *The Architecture of America: A Social and Cultural History* (Boston: American Institute of Architects, 1966), 218.

4. Daniel M. Fox, *Engines of Culture: Philanthropy and Art Museums* (Madison: State Historical Society of Wisconsin, 1963), 79.

5. For an account of the politics behind the Met's decision, see Calvin Tomkins, *Merchants and Masterpieces: The Story of the Metropolitan Museum of Art* (New York: E. P. Dutton & Co., 1975), 39–42. The New York Historical Society was supposed to occupy this parcel of land, as discussed in Kevin M. Guthrie, *The New York Historical Society: Lessons from One Nonprofit's Long Struggle for Survival* (San Francisco: Jossey Bass, 1996). The NYHS could not raise the funds to move to Central Park in the 1860s and did not purchase a building until 1904. See also Geoffrey Hellman, *Bankers, Bones and Beetles: The First Century of the American Museum of Natural History* (Garden City, N.Y.: Natural History Press, 1969), 77.

6. See Linda S. Phipps, "The 1893 Art Institute Building and the 'Paris of America': Aspirations of Patrons and Architects in Late Nineteenth Century Chicago," *Art Institute of Chicago Museum Studies* 14, no. 1 (1988): 28–45. See also Erik Larson, *The Devil in the White City* (New York: Vintage Books, 2004), for a spellbinding creative nonfiction account of the influence of the 1893 Chicago Exposition on American society.

7. Henry James, "New York, Revisited" (1906), in *The Portable Henry James*, ed. Morton D. Zabel (New York: Viking Press, 1960), 547.

# CHAPTER 3

# *The Collection*
## From Stockpiling to Taking Stock

My [collections] have had eventful lives—pampered by the aristocracy and pillaged by revolution, courted with ardor and cold-bloodedly abandoned. They have been honored by drawing rooms and humbled by attics.... What stories they could tell, what sights they must have seen.

—J. PAUL GETTY, 1955[1]

The most important measure of success will be determined generations from now. Did we collect the right materials? Take care of the things that can teach us? Our way of thinking about the collection—artifacts and documents—is that... they will teach us when we are not here to do it.

—ROBERTA CONNER, TAMÁSTSLIKT CULTURAL INSTITUTE, 2019[2]

GEORGE WASHINGTON'S GRIZZLED DENTURES ARE A strange, one could even say cringe-worthy, sight. But they are one of the most acclaimed museum artifacts in the United States. To some, this object is a mere curiosity. Others might argue that it is a national treasure. At the very least, this crude mouthpiece confirms that the nation's first president suffered from swollen gums. It explains why portraits of Washington—even the one on the dollar bill—always show him square-jawed, with his lips tightly shut. Currently in the collection of George Washington's Mount Vernon in Virginia, the only remaining full set of our first president's false teeth was found in a trunk purchased in 1949 by the Mount Vernon Ladies' Association of the Union. The incisors are fashioned from the teeth of cows, horses, and very likely the enslaved people who worked on his land. Weird and ghoulish, fascinating and strange, this one artifact opens up larger stories about the nation: the health care of our founding fathers, the role of women's committees in establishing some of our nation's iconic museums, and details that Mount Vernon only recently began to reveal about Washington's connection to and exploitation of enslaved labor.

The marble bust *America* was carved between 1850 and 1854 by Hiram Powers as a personification of America.
The Metropolitan Museum of Art; gift of Mrs. William A. M. Burden Jr., 1966 (66.243)

**The only known complete set of George Washington's dentures (1790–1799). Materials: Human teeth, probably horse and cow teeth, ivory (probably elephant), lead, copper, and silver alloy. Object # W1520-A/B, purchased in 1949.**
Courtesy of Mount Vernon Ladies' Association Office of Photo Services

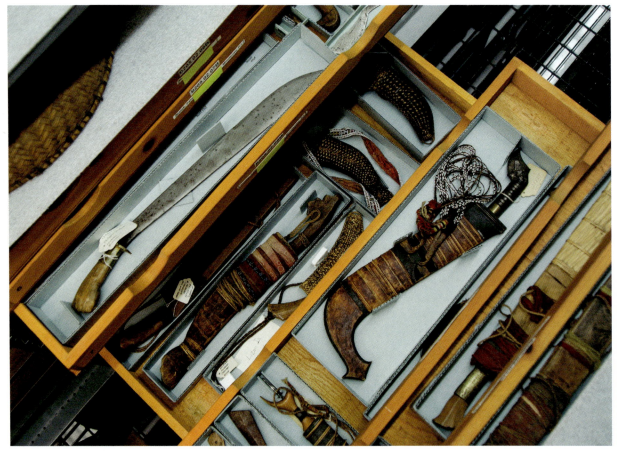

The Field Museum in Chicago is home to more than 10,000 objects from the Philippines, a U.S. colony from 1898 to 1946. A "co-curation" program engages the Filipino American community to participate in the stewardship, documentation, and interpretation of the artifacts.
© The Field Museum; photographer Mikayla Delson

**Rolled textiles in storage, the Field Museum.**
© The Field Museum, photographer Mikayla Delson

The nation's museums possess a universe of fascinating things. Some are beautiful. Others rare. Still others provocative, politically charged, and controversial. But there is one thing we know for sure. Each tells unique stories, as unique as the human fingerprints that first touched it. Like the universe, museum collections are continually expanding. So are the stories we tell about them. With haiku-like elegance, in 1969, Secretary of the Smithsonian S. Dillon Ripley summed up the reason behind this growth: "Culture creates collections; collections create culture."[3] It could be said that this exponential growth speaks loudly, if not always eloquently, to materialism: our desire to gather—even hoard—things and then selectively show them off to others. At last count (and this is a conservative estimate), U.S. museums housed 4.7 billion objects, artifacts, and works of art. Not all museums have collections, but those that do house so much stuff that less than 5 percent can be exhibited at any one time. The rest sits in storage rooms, laboratories, or wherever else there is space for one more marble bust or bolo knife, perhaps waiting to be digitized into a website thumbnail. Yet lack of space doesn't stop museums from acquiring even more things. The estimated aggregate rate of collection growth is 1 to 5 percent annually: millions of additional objects each year.[4] What are museums doing with all this stuff and why should anyone care?[5] Like all good stories, the answers to this question continue to evolve. And all the while collections have continued to grow in size, scope, and meaning.

## 1880s TO 1930s: STOCKPILING ON A GRAND SCALE

> Years ago, I decided that the greatest need in our country was Art . . . we were a very young country and had very few beautiful things . . . so I was determined to make it my life's work.
>
> —ISABELLA STEWART GARDNER, 1903

The nation's earliest millionaires used their fortunes to amass amazing things. Their hard-won treasures form the basis for some of our nation's most beloved museums. In one sense, their goal was noble; they sought to construct a three-dimensional "encyclopedia" of the world to inform, civilize, and define a growing nation. Collections of scientific specimens and anthropology would demonstrate the evolution of life and the belief that, as Harvard University president Charles Eliot Norton put it, the American nation could "advance civilization from good to better."[6] Displays of art would raise the level of Americans' aesthetic tastes and understanding of their proper place in society. But of course their goals were also personal. To these wealthy citizens, the act of collecting was both an adventure and a marathon. Great white hunters stalked and bagged wild prey, spinning tales of narrow escapes from charging rhinos or howling sandstorms. Art collectors sailed the turbulent seas (in luxury, of course) to rifle through galleries in search of paintings of Madonnas, saints, and aristocrats. These elite collectors competed fiercely with each other. Then, intriguingly, they bequeathed their collections to public institutions in service to humanity—and, let's be honest, their egos.

Art buying, as the myth goes, was intuitive, a kind of noblesse oblige for the moneyed classes, a genteel cultural pursuit that offered a welcome break from the rough-and-tumble of the business world. In fact, art buying was always a hard-nosed business, usually conducted with the help of expert advisors and skillful dealers. After all, what successful business tycoon wants to be swindled into overpaying for a shoddy item, or worse, a fake? Two prominent early gatekeepers who earned their clients' trust were Harvard-trained connoisseur Bernard Berenson and British dealer Joseph Duveen.[7]

Berenson was a scholar of Italian Renaissance art who believed fervently in the virtues of pedigree, classical beauty, and the superiority of European aristocratic values. An immigrant to Boston from Lithuania, he was best known to "squillionaire" collectors (to use Berenson's phrase) as an authenticator of masterworks. Berenson claimed that his life's mission was to make sure all paintings were correctly attributed: "We must not stop till we are sure that every Lotto is a Lotto, every Cariani a Cariani, every Santa Croce a Santa Croce." An attribution from Berenson could vastly augment the price of an artwork, much to the delight of the dealers who paid him to study a work with a magnifying glass (later, a flashlight) and then sign a certificate of authenticity.

From 1906 until their public falling out in the 1930s, Berenson worked with the legendary Duveen. Based in London, Sir (and eventually Lord) Duveen was the persuasive voice behind some of the most important (and expensive) American art acquisitions of the early 20th century, including Thomas Gainsborough's *Blue Boy* for the Huntington Library, Art Collections, Botanical Gardens in Pasadena, CA and Botticelli's *The Resurrected Christ* for the Detroit Institute of Arts. To find just the right piece for his eager clients, it is said that Duveen "was at the center of a vast, circular nexus

**Lower interior courtyard of the Isabella Stewart Gardner Museum, ca. 1930s.**
Library of Congress

of corruption that reached from the lowliest employee of the British museum right up to the King." Duveen drove up prices by urging American collectors to bid against each other. Once a sale was final, however, he then talked the collector into giving the work to a museum, all the better to raise Duveen's stature.[8]

Although dealers and connoisseurs courted their powerful clients vigorously and advised them freely, when it came to purchasing art the collectors usually prevailed. As David Finley, founding director of the National Gallery of Art, notes of these early collectors: "To many people the making of a great collection represents only a combination of money and luck . . . [but] there is far more to it than that. To make a really great collection, the collector must have taste, the ability to recognize quality, and perseverance."[9]

One such collector was the eccentric Boston socialite Isabella Stewart Gardner. In the 1890s, a proper

**Early-20th-century collectors augmented their collections with the help of expert advisors like Bernard Berenson.**

The legendary art dealer Joseph Duveen helped to acquire some of the most important works in U.S. museum collections. Among his illustrious clients was railroad tycoon Henry Huntington, who purchased *Jonathan Buttall: The Blue Boy*, ca. 1770, by Thomas Gainsborough (1727–1788) for the Huntington Library, Art Collections, and Botanical Garden.
Courtesy of the Huntington Art Collections, San Marino, Calif.

public in 1903. In her desire for immortality, Gardner forbade any alterations to her building or to the precise arrangements of art. Her lack of foresight would have grave consequences; in March 1990, thieves evaded the outmoded security systems and stole 13 priceless works, the greatest art heist of the 20th century.[10] As of this writing, the works still haven't been recovered, although fortunately the museum has undergone significant upgrades, including a modern addition.

Gardner wasn't the only U.S. collector to establish an eponymous museum mansion. In Washington, D.C., steel scion Duncan Phillips established the Phillips Memorial Gallery to honor relatives who perished during the Spanish influenza epidemic. Philadelphia's pharmaceutical magnate Alfred C. Barnes; Baltimore railway tycoon Henry Walters; New York industrialist Henry Clay Frick; and Los Angeles oilman J. Paul Getty are other well-known early-20th-century collectors who founded art museums that bear their names and stand as public monuments to their private aspirations.[11]

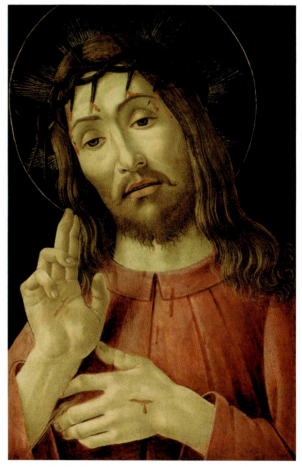

Sandro Botticelli's *The Resurrected Christ* (ca. 1480) is currently in the collection of the Detroit Institute of Arts. The purchase was arranged by Joseph Duveen in 1927.

member of Boston high society would have collected French academic art, a tasteful and safe choice. But Gardner—a native New Yorker who delighted in rattling the powerful families in her adopted city—had other ideas. She teamed up with Berenson, and together they hunted down authentic Italian Renaissance masterpieces, combing Europe for Botticellis and Titians.

Even with Berenson's informed guidance Gardner often made impulsive purchases, driven by what has been described as an ego so "cosmic and insatiable" that the "hint that anyone else was after an object catapulted her into an immediate purchase." She built a Venetian-style palace in Boston to display the magnificent pieces she had acquired. Gardner micromanaged every detail of the construction process; arranged each painting, sculpture, or tapestry as she saw fit; and then named the museum after herself. It opened to the

Not every mansion-museum belonged to an informed collector with impeccable taste and altruistic motives. California newspaper publisher William Randolph Hearst was reputed to "represent the nux vomica of bad collecting on a grand scale." Between the 1890s and 1930s, Hearst traveled regularly to New York auction houses and bought every "modern gewgaw or ancient tchotchke . . . that drew his eye," stuffing his booty of "fourth-rate paintings of Madonnas," Georgian silver, and Grecian urns into railroad cars. Sometimes, it is alleged, he would even reserve works of arts at various auctions and then "forget" to pay for them. The items were crammed into Hearst's castle on the Pacific coast, subject of the semifictional 1941 Hollywood film *Citizen Kane*. In 1942, about $4 million worth of objects from Hearst's collection was sold at Gimbel's Department Store in New York. Many pieces—including a vast amalgamation of lamps, ceramic dogs, and portraits of Hearst's mistress—ended up in private collections, although plenty remains at Hearst's San Simeon estate. Today this "Bastard-Spanish-Moorish-Romanesque-Gothic-Renaissance-Bull-Market-Damn-the-Expense" mansion-as-museum is one of the most popular tourist attractions in California.[12]

Collectors like Hearst felt that for the right price the world could be theirs. This attitude motivated unethical dealers to raise prices and move shoddy goods. In the 1920s Italian forger Alceo Dossena became a local celebrity for creating convincing copies of sculptures in styles from Etruscan to Rococo. Fooling both dealers and collectors, many of Dossena's artistic fakes landed on display in U.S. museums. "You can sell anything to Americans," said convicted French forger Jean Charles Millet in the 1920s. "They know nothing about art. . . . All you have to do is ask a fabulous price."[13]

The collector most credited with paying fabulous prices was J. P. Morgan. Between 1902 and his death in 1913, Morgan spent more than $60 million on art. While some of Morgan's purchases made headlines because they lacked authenticity or quality, others stunned the art world for both their magnificence and provenance. As the legend goes, Morgan "would buy a Louis XVI gold box . . . as casually as a commuter picks up a morning paper, and a few minutes later, with the same aplomb, spend $200,000 for the Cellini cup which had come to Adolphe Rothschild via the King of Naples."[14]

At first Morgan's lavish purchases decorated his homes in London and Paris, a practical solution to the burdensome U.S. customs duties that would have been imposed on his treasures had he attempted to

***The Visitation*, ca. 1310, attributed to Master Heinrich of Constance (German, active in Constance, ca. 1300).**
The Metropolitan Museum of Art, gift of J. Pierpont Morgan, 1917 (17.190.724)

ship them to New York. Art more than 20 years old was subject to a heavy tax when imported into the United States. But in 1909 Congress passed the Payne-Aldrich Tariff Act, cosponsored by Rhode Island Sen. Nelson Aldrich. Imported art was now welcomed into the country duty-free. This legislation was to prove of enormous benefit to the nation's museums and, as some Europeans later bemoaned, equal detriment to Europe's collections. Several art museum trustees testified in support of the act, and Morgan's influence was decisive. Only two years earlier, he had orchestrated a bailout of the U.S. banking system, helping the U.S. Treasury avert financial collapse. Because he had almost single-handedly rescued the nation from the "Panic of 1907," Morgan was perhaps the most powerful man in the country. This was no small factor in the repeal of customs duties that allowed him to import his collection to the United States—including, famously, a fan that had once belonged to Marie Antoinette. Morgan bequeathed more than 7,000 objects to the Metropolitan Museum of Art.

After the Tariff Act, Duveen and other international dealers prospered as never before. Using well-oiled

Portrait engraving of J. Pierpont Morgan, ca. 1918.

connections to museums and royalty, they spirited art out of Europe and into the hands of eager clients—including two of Sen. Aldrich's children, Abby Aldrich Rockefeller, a cofounder of the Museum of Modern Art in New York, and her brother William, a trustee of Boston's Institute of Contemporary Art.

In 1913 Congress softened the Tariff Act to allow contemporary paintings and sculptures, in addition to older ones, to enter the country duty-free. The mechanisms were now in place to stockpile the country's museums with art that would be the envy of any royal court.[15] That same year saw the arrival of a controversial new style of artwork from Europe. Works by avant-garde artists like Henri Matisse and Marcel Duchamp sailed across the Atlantic and premiered at one of the most important exhibits of the early 20th century: the Armory Show. The first large-scale public showing of modern art in the United States, the Armory Show opened collectors' eyes to radical new images. It created a buzz that continued for decades. As critic Calvin Tomkins described it, "Hideous and unspeakable tendencies had been let loose upon the land—blue nudes and nudes that descended staircases, wild beasts and

Armory Show, International Exhibition of Modern Art. The Cubist room, Gallery 53 (northeast view), Art Institute of Chicago, March 24–April 16, 1913.

other Parisian monstrosities ... dangerous breeding grounds for Bolshevism and gross sexuality." It was art as scandal, described by contemporary newspapers as "freakish," "mad," "unadulterated cheek." The public couldn't get enough. A growing group of art collectors and dealers would eagerly advocate for this and later radical movements. In the coming decades, they would found the nation's first museums of modern art.[16]

With the outbreak of World War I, the economic balance tilted further in favor of the United States. War contracts filled bank accounts of industrialists and investors, swelling the ranks of wealthy collectors in the United States. The remnants of European aristocracy, desperate for hard currency, were willing to sell their most precious masterpieces. Rembrandts, Gainsboroughs, and Turners crossed the Atlantic, with collectors paying record prices for the privilege of owning them. Those who couldn't afford paintings lapped up prints, engravings, and sketches. In 1916 German museum director Wilhelm von Bode warned that American collectors were using "enormous sums of money accumulated" from selling munitions to Europe to drain the continent of its masterpieces. Soon, he decried, America's museums would "equal or surpass the great museums of Europe."[17] "I'm terribly excited," Philadelphia collector Alfred C. Barnes wrote in a letter to a friend in 1920, "about a windfall brought about by the war. The Dutch government are evidently in bad straights [*sic*]. The thirteen finest Cezannes in existence—masterpieces of raw power—changed ownership today when I delivered ... my check."[18] U.S. collectors also sapped Europe's museums of future masterpieces. Dealers organized "European War Benefit Sales" to provide financial relief to overseas artists. The artists were only too happy to sell their work to eager and rich Americans.

After World War I and throughout the roaring 1920s, art collecting boomed, benefiting both dealers and museums. Art was seen as a desirable investment for those with excess cash even with the collapse of the stock market in 1929. The onset of the Great Depression and concurrent political turmoil in Europe led to further opportunities for collectors. In 1931 the Soviet government acquired cold cash by putting some of Russia's most treasured paintings on the market. Marjorie Merriweather Post, heir to the breakfast cereal fortune, bought Russian icons, porcelains, and silver, which are now at Hillwood Estate, Museum and Gardens in Washington, D.C. Andrew Mellon purchased more than $5 million worth of paintings, including Raphael's exquisite *Alba Madonna*, for $1,166,400,

Economic troubles in Russia during the early part of the 20th century meant that Fabergé eggs such as this one could be purchased by American millionaires. **Gatchina Palace Egg, 1901, House of Fabergé, Peter Carl Fabergé (Russian, 1846–1920), and Mikhail Perkhin (Russian, 1860–1903).**
The Walters Art Museum (44.500)

setting a record price for a single painting. Mellon's purchases of Titians and Vermeers—sequestered in a safe in the Corcoran Gallery of Art—were great fodder for journalists.[19] While most citizens suffered from economic woes, the former U.S. treasurer was spending millions of dollars to indulge his muses. But the banker-turned-politician had a plan.

The *Alba Madonna*, ca. 1510, Raphael (Italian, 1483–1520).
Andrew W. Mellon Collection, National Gallery of Art (1937.1.24)

**Marjorie Merriweather Post, 1942, by C. M. Stieglitz.**
New York World-Telegram and the Sun Newspaper Photograph Collection, Library of Congress

In 1936 Mellon made an extraordinary gesture. He gave his treasures to the U.S. government along with an endowment to care for them and a building to house them. "Over the period of many years I have been acquiring important and rare paintings and sculpture with the idea that ultimately they would become the property of the people of the United States and be made available to them in a national art gallery," Mellon wrote to President Franklin Delano Roosevelt. "I have given . . . securities ample to erect a gallery building of sufficient size to house these works of art and to permit the indefinite growth of the collection."[20] The National Gallery of Art was born.

Established on the National Mall, the National Gallery of Art was a gift to the nation, destined to grow as other collectors came forward: Mellon's son Paul; five-and-dime tycoon Samuel Kress; department store heir Lessing Rosenwald; and, much to the chagrin of the Philadelphia Museum of Art, which had coveted his collection, Philadelphia collector Joseph Widener. Still, Mellon's magnificent gift was tinged with scandal. While overseeing the U.S. Treasury, Mellon had been charged with falsifying his personal income tax returns. He subsequently endured a series of humiliating public trials. Federal prosecutors intimated that

Mellon evaded conviction by using his art collection to curry favor with Congress and the American people.[21]

By the 1930s art patrons like Mellon exercised great influence over the kind of art the country's leading museums would acquire and exhibit. Some did more than collect works by long-dead European masters. Prominent socialites like Gertrude Vanderbilt Whitney and Peggy Guggenheim socialized with living artists, acting as modern-day Medicis. Whitney parlayed her fortune and collection into the Whitney Museum of American Art. Guggenheim eventually married surrealist painter Max Ernst, whom she helped escape the growing fascist movement in Europe.

Because they took risks, art patrons sometimes found themselves on the front lines of political battles. In 1932 Wilhelm Valentiner, the German-born director of the Detroit Institute of Arts (DIA), met Mexican muralist Diego Rivera and his wife Frida Kahlo at a tennis match in California. Valentiner was taken by this striking couple, especially Kahlo, whom he found "especially charming and typical of modern Mexico."[22] He hired Rivera, an avowed Marxist, to adorn the museum's courtyard with 27 frescoes depicting the spirit of industrial Detroit. The frescoes were financed

**Gertrude Vanderbilt Whitney, ca. 1909.**
Library of Congress.

**Max Ernst and Peggy Guggenheim, Surrealist Gallery, Art of This Century, ca. 1942.**
Courtesy of the Solomon R. Guggenheim Foundation, New York

by the decidedly not-Marxist Ford Motor Company, under the leadership of Henry Ford's son Edsel, a collector himself and head of the Detroit Arts Commission. The murals were controversial from the moment they were unveiled in 1933. The press complained that the subject—industrial might—was inappropriate for an art museum. Clergy railed against Rivera's use of nude models and accused him of pornography. Politicians demanded the frescoes be whitewashed. Ford rallied to Rivera's defense, and today the carefully conserved murals, considered to be among the artist's finest works, remain on display in Detroit. Frida Kahlo, too, came to be revered for her immense artistic talent. In 2015 DIA opened an exhibition that chronicled Frida and Diego's time in Detroit and included Kahlo's works from that time as well as Rivera's preparation sketches for the frescoes.

\*    \*    \*

The rich and powerful collect foreign things . . . [but] the day will soon come when many public museums will look upon the promotion of American art as one of their most important functions.

—JOHN COTTON DANA, 1917[23]

In the early 1920s, declaring that collecting oil paintings from Europe was a waste of time and money, John Cotton Dana began to build a collection of American art for the Newark Museum. He convinced department store magnate Carrie Bamberger Fuld to shift her collecting passion from the art of Italy to the art of New York City. It was a bold move. Prior to this time, most collectors considered American-made art to be

Diego Rivera's famous murals at the Detroit Institute were controversial when they were unveiled to the public. Detroit Industry (North Wall), 1932–1933, Diego Rivera (Mexican, 1886–1957).
Gift of Edsel B. Ford, Detroit Institute of Art (33.10.N)

"naïve" and "substandard." Only a few college campus museums, including those at Smith College and the Rhode Island School of Design, had bothered to acquire much in the way of artwork by Americans. Now, with thriving artists' colonies emerging in New York's Greenwich Village and all along the Eastern Seaboard, the collect-American movement began in earnest.

Fascinated by the notion of "homegrown genius," a few pioneering collectors worked with dealers in Philadelphia and New York to purchase works by artists like Quaker preacher Edward Hicks and Harlem Renaissance painter Horace Pippin. Taken with local sea and landscape painting, they set up small museums in artists' colonies like Montclair, N.J., and Ogunquit, ME. In 1924, the Museum of Fine Arts in Boston became one of the first art museums to acquire photography, accepting 27 photographs from Alfred Stieglitz, who insisted that they be framed and treated as works of art. It cannot be overemphasized just how radical this decision was; at the time photography was barred by most elites because it was too accessible, too popular, too technological.

Collectors and artists also looked westward. Intrigued by Native American aesthetics, they bought Cheyenne beadwork and Navajo weaving.[24] Infatuated with the myth of the "Old West," New York businessman Philip Cole amassed more than 600 paintings and bronzes evocative of the Old West, including work by Charles M. Russell and Frederic Remington. Then, in what has been called the "shrewdest acquisition of American art of the 20th century," Oklahoma oilman Thomas Gilcrease bought Cole's collection in its entirety and founded the Gilcrease Museum, now part of the University of Tulsa.[25]

By the 1930s two trends in collecting were in full swing. Like architectural movements of the day, one looked forward and the other back. In the first, newly founded museums of industry began to amass the latest machines. After the Century of Progress World's Fair of 1933, Chicago's Museum of Science and Industry became the repository for American-made hardware like electric generators, teletype machines, and tractors. Even art museums collected the nation's technological marvels. In 1935, with leadership from Jock

**Alfred Stieglitz, American, 1864–1946.** *The Hand of Man* **(Long Island City, N.Y.), 1902, was one of the first photographs to be accessioned as a work of art into an art museum in the United States.**
Courtesy of Museum of Fine Arts, Boston. Gift of Alfred Stieglitz, 24.1740. © 2020 Museum of Fine Arts, Boston

Whitney, an early investor in a three-color film process called Technicolor, MoMA founded a film library—the world's first archive to collect Hollywood movies.[26] The military also saw the value of preserving evidence of the nation's power. It donated surplus hardware from prior wars to museums such as the Smithsonian and a newly established Air Force Museum near Dayton, OH. Museums that document today's technological innovations, such as the Museum of Computer History in Mountain View, CA, and National Museum of Nuclear Science and History in Albuquerque, N.M., have their roots in these early-20th-century impulses to assemble collections of engineering marvels.

A second post–World War I collecting trend was more low-tech. With a nostalgia for the simpler world of yesteryear, the heirs of industrialists began to purchase handmade crafts. Both "collect-American" movements had advantages over museums' earlier collecting meth-

**Mother-and-child doll, 1870–1880, Seneca.**
The Metropolitan Museum of Art, Ralph T. Coe Collection; gift of Ralph T. Coe Foundation for the Arts, 2011 (2011.154.22)

*Meat's Not Meat till It's in the Pan*, 1915, by Charles Marion Russell (1864–1926) is one of the many important American paintings acquired by Thomas Gilcrease. It now resides in the Gilcrease Museum in Tulsa, OK.
Courtesy of Gilcrease Museum, Tulsa, Oklahoma (0137.2244)

ods. American-made items were more available and less expensive. They could serve as patriotic counterpoints to items from abroad and provide evidence of "native genius and sensibility." They were important symbols of the contributions the United States had made to the arts, industry, and world progress as well as the humble origins of the country's wealthiest citizens. By 1930 the term *Americana* was well established in the museum field. Collectors around the nation turned their efforts to hunting down beautiful objects made on U.S. soil.

Texas millionaires focused on a specialized branch called "Texacana." In Houston, Ima Hogg—contrary to rumor, she did not have a sister named Eura—daughter of a Texas governor and heir to an oil fortune, collected American and Texan furniture. "From the time I acquired my first Queen Anne armchair in 1920, I had an unaccountable compulsion to make an American collection for some Texas museum," stated Hogg, affectionately known as Miss Ima. Her pieces went to Bayou Bend, a 15-acre estate outside Houston. Today the stately mansion is part of the Museum of Fine Arts, Houston, and houses one of the largest collections of Americana in the nation.[27]

An even larger collection of Americana resides in tiny Delaware, at a 983-acre country estate known as Winterthur. Henry Francis du Pont, heir to his family's gunpowder and chemical fortunes, believed that items like finely crafted silver and furniture could offer the public a "new understanding and respect for the integrity of American craftsmanship." He amassed more than 85,000 objects, focusing on the decorative arts and later remarking that his only regret was not acquiring more.[28] In 1930 du Pont established Winterthur as a nonprofit educational foundation. It opened to the public as a museum in 1951.

Other family fortunes built Americana collections. In 1932, MoMA cofounder Abby Aldrich Rockefeller's collection was the centerpiece of MoMA's taste-setting exhibition, *American Folk Art: The Art of the Common Man in America, 1750–1900*. This was the first exhibition that elevated the status of folk art to fine art. MoMA trustee Stephen Clark, heir to the Singer Sewing Machine fortune, also had a penchant for the "plain people of yesterday." He toured rural areas, harvesting old spinning wheels, butter churns, and weathervanes. He put this massive collection in a stone dairy barn in Cooper-

**Portrait of Ima Hogg, ca. 1920. Artist: Wayman Adams, American, 1883. Oil on canvas.**

The Museum of Fine Arts, Houston, The Bayou Bend Collection, gift of Alice C. Simkins, B.79.292

**Vase, 1893–1896, designed by Louis Comfort Tiffany (American, New York, 1848–1933).**

The Metropolitan Museum of Art; gift of H. O. Havemeyer, 1896 (96.17.10). His daughter, Electra Havemeyer Webb, also collected American items and founded the Shelburne Museum in Vermont

stown, N.Y., and called it the Farmers' Museum. Soon it contained all manner of outmoded implements—plows, tools, ox carts—hauled in by "wise old farmers."[29] Another notable collector of Americana was Electra Havemeyer Webb, heir to a sugar fortune, wife of a Vanderbilt, and big-game hunter (a grizzly bear she shot in Alaska is still on display in Anchorage's airport). In 1947 her collection—including hatboxes, carousel horses, and more

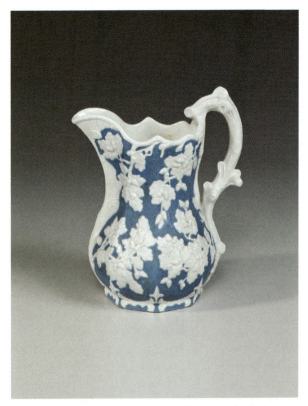

**United States Pottery Company. *Charter Oak* pitcher, ca. 1853–1858, parian ware, colored slip.**

Daisy Wade Bridges Collection. H1978.176.15. Collection of the Mint Museum, Charlotte, N.C. Courtesy of the Mint Museum

**This 1927 Rolls-Royce Phantom I Pall Mall phaeton S 123 PM was given to Winterthur Museum, Garden and Library in March 2019. It allows the institution to show how motoring guests of founder Henry Francis du Pont would have arrived on his estate in its heyday.**

Courtesy of Winterthur Museum, Garden & Library

than a thousand duck decoys—opened to the public as the Shelburne Museum in Vermont, dubbed by one admirer as a "collection of collections."[30]

* * *

A collection consists of much more than the objects within it. A collection reveals something significant about the collectors, their ideals, and society at large. In the years prior to World War II, a chief motive behind natural science collecting was Charles Darwin's theory of evolution. Social Darwinism, which sought to apply Darwin's theory of natural selection to human society, asserted that "inferior" species and civilizations were disappearing as more advanced societies were evolving. Collecting was seen as one way of rescuing our natural history from the march of progress. Whereas explorers once randomly plucked items from nature, they now worked with universities and museums in pursuit of a mission: to assemble a logical order of the world and evidence of biological evolution. They began, naturally enough, with the dinosaur.

Henry Fairfield Osborn, president of the American Museum of Natural History in New York from 1908 to 1933, played a leading role in instigating dinosaur expeditions. The son of a railway magnate and a nephew of J. P. Morgan, Osborn set up a vertebrate paleontology department at Columbia University for the museum's teaching and study purposes. Using his connections to New York's elite, he organized excavations of quarries in the West. Archaeologists and their students headed out on digs, and before long railway cars filled with fossils from the wilds of Wyoming and Montana began arriving in New York.

Osborn soon realized that dinosaurs could play a useful role outside of the classroom and laboratory. He created the nation's first public exhibits of rigged-up skeletons of such creatures as *Tyrannosaurus rex* and *Triceratops*.[31] Not to be outdone by New York society and fiercely competitive with J. P. Morgan, industrialist Andrew Carnegie financed a dinosaur expedition to "get one for Pittsburgh." The resulting dig in Wyoming uncovered "Dippy," an almost complete 10-ton *Diplodocus* for the Carnegie Museum. Carnegie "was so proud of this specimen, named carnegiei in his honor, that he presented 10 life-size replicas to 10 leading world museums," setting off the dinomania that is part of popular culture to the present day.[32]

All over the country natural history museums began to purchase casts and fossils from dealers, often

**Henry Fairfield Osborn and his wife, Marjorie, ca. 1915–1920.**
George Grantham Bain Collection, Library of Congress

**Roy Chapman Andrews, undated.**
George Grantham Bain Collection, Library of Congress

In September 1921, the American Museum of Natural History hosted the Second International Congress on Eugenics and published this photo of attendees in its annual report. Henry Fairfield Osborn is standing in the front with Major Leonard Darwin, a son of Charles Darwin.

trading with one another for just the right bone to complete a dinosaur skeleton. Those with access to funds organized their own digs. In 1906 an ambitious, freshly minted graduate of Wisconsin's Beloit College arrived on the doorstep of the American Museum of Natural History, determined to get a job there. Roy Chapman Andrews was hired to scrub the floors in the taxidermy department. Soon he talked his way onto collecting expeditions to Alaska and Japan. He also caught the eye of Osborn, who tapped Andrews for his most celebrated collecting expedition, a 1922 trip across the Gobi Desert, to find the legendary "missing link," that is, evidence that Asia, not Africa, was the birthplace of humankind. This distinction was important to Osborn, as we shall see. Yet, instead of the humanoid skeletons that Osborn coveted, Andrews unearthed troves of dinosaur fossils. One discovery—unhatched, fossilized dinosaur eggs—captured the public's heart. Crowds packed AMNH's halls to get a peek at them. Andrews catapulted to fame, and his portrait appeared on the cover of *Time*.

To finance future expeditions to China in the name of "American ideals, American science and the American flag,"[33] Andrews hatched a clever fundraising scheme: "The Great Dinosaur Egg Auction." When

the Chinese government got wind that a single egg was fetching up to $5,000, officials accused Andrews and his paleontologists of stealing China's treasures to sell for profit, scouting for oil and mineral deposits on behalf of the nation's industrialists, spying, and opium smuggling. Chinese officers arrested a team of Andrews's colleagues. In fact, the suspicions had merit. Andrews was involved in espionage and used his museum missions to gather data for the U.S. government on Chinese industry and military. Strained relations between the two countries prevented further expeditions. But Andrews's fame grew, and he is frequently cited as a model for Hollywood film icon Indiana Jones.

Osborn's own collecting activities generated a different kind of notoriety. Creationists opposed to the teaching of evolution had found a visible enemy in natural history museums and railed against the public displays that "poisoned the minds of little children with the foul miasma of evolution." In 1922, as the Scopes Monkey Trial loomed in Tennessee, Osborn debated prosecutor William Jennings Bryan in the press and on lecture platforms. Though he eloquently defended science against fundamentalist religion, the motives behind Osborn's collecting expeditions were indefensible. He fervently believed that the principles of "natural" selection applied to human beings. Horrified by the Italian, Jewish, and Greek immigrants and African Americans from the South streaming into northern U.S. cities, Osborn and his followers sought to use systematic arrangements of specimens to prove the "spiritual, intellectual, moral and physical" superiority of the "Nordic race." He named numerous invalid species simply to support his views of eugenics, and eventually his work and reputation were discredited. Today, Henry Fairfield Osborn is known as one of the worst taxonomists in the history of paleontology.[34]

After World War II the study of fossils became more scientifically rigorous, their collection and exhibition less influenced by social theory. Dinosaur digs continued, under the auspices of university paleontology departments and museums such as those at Montana State University, University of Utah, and Texas Tech University. The focus returned to teaching and research.

Today, natural history museums remain the venue by which most of us encounter the fossilized remnants of these giant creatures, often in surprising ways. In the 1980s the Museum of Science in Boston toured *Dinosaur Show*, six computer-operated models of fully fleshed-out beasts who bellowed and swished their tails. In the 1990s, with the first *Jurassic Park* movie drawing huge audiences, animatronic dinosaurs roared into museums across the country, including the Smithsonian.[35] Striving to meld our age-old fascination for dinosaurs with contemporary exhibition techniques and the teaching of evolutionary biology, the Philadelphia Academy of Natural Sciences, Denver Museum of Nature and Science, and others retooled their displays.[36] In 2004 the Indianapolis Children's Museum opened "Dinosphere," a huge, enclosed dome filled with the fossilized bones of juvenile dinosaurs. It includes a see-through fossil lab where visitors can touch real bones and talk with real paleontologists. In 2013, the Middle Tennessee Museum of Natural History (about 35 miles southeast of Nashville) cooked up an education program that pairs fossils and paleontologists with artisanal beer. The "Brews and Bones" craze spread across the country. In 2018, the Perot Museum of Nature and Science in Dallas joined in with its first daylong Dino Fest, a "celebration of all things dinosaur," complete with a paleo-lab and beer garden. For its Dino Fest, California Academy of Sciences added "cretaceous cocktails" and "mesozoic snacks" to the mix.

Discoveries of new fossils make headlines every year. But none has yet rivaled the 20th century's most spectacular dinosaur discovery. In 1990 an amateur fossil hunter named Sue Hendrickson stumbled on the most complete *T. Rex* ever in South Dakota. Press coverage of the 10-ton skeleton rivaled the hullaballoo surrounding Roy Andrews's Chinese dinosaur eggs decades before. After a legal battle between the Native American landowner, commercial fossil hunters, scientists, and the U.S. government, the *T. Rex*, now known worldwide as "Sue," was auctioned in 1997 for $8.36 million, a record price for a fossil. The buyer was Chicago's Field Museum in partnership with McDonald's Corporation and Walt Disney resorts. Although purists decried the commercialism of this price-spiking deal, visitors were wildly enthusiastic. Attendance at the Field spiked by 35 percent after Sue's debut.[37]

In 2017, the Field Museum dismantled its celebrity dinosaur, bone by bone. Reassembled according to the most current scientific information about dinosaur anatomy, Sue moved upstairs to new digs in the Griffith Hall of Evolving Planet, fashioned as a Late Cretaceous forest, complete with multimedia that recreates South Dakota 67 million years ago. Sue (no doubt with assistance from a human ally) even has a Twitter feed and wrote in early 2018: "Another change to note: since my original unveiling 18 years ago, scientific opinion on determining the sex of tyrannosaurs has lacked sufficient data. As such, I would like to state that my preferred pronouns are 'they/them' to refer to me in the third person. As in, 'SUE is a *T. rex*. They are a majestic murderbird, and Chicago is lucky they grace the city with their presence.'"[38]

Fossil collections continue to be lightning rods for religious fundamentalists. Sometimes visitors who hold their information on dinosaurs to be "biblically correct" have confronted museum workers. In 2005, the Museum of Earth in Ithaca, N.Y., responded by publishing guidelines for training docents to explain scientific method.[39] Still, according to a 2017 Pew Research Trust report, one-third of the nation's adults believe that dinosaurs and humans coexisted.[40] Thus, museums with "evolution" displays are often targets of complaints, sometimes even threats of funding cuts.[41]

Lack of funds wasn't a problem for recent renovations at the nation's two most-visited dinosaur halls. Another issue was. In 2014, self-proclaimed fossil lover David H. Koch underwrote renovations of the halls to the tune of $60 million, as long as they would bear his name. Koch made his fortune in the fossil fuel

**SUE's back and better than ever with scientific updates including placed gastralia, updated pose, and wishbone in a new suite.**
© 2018 Field Museum, photo by Martin Baumgaertner

**DinoFest 2018 at the Perot Museum of Nature and Science, Dallas.**
Photo by Lindsay Rapier/Perot Museum of Nature and Science

industry. Prominent scientists and educators criticized his motives, noting that Koch has given even larger grants to "anti-science" lobbying organizations that actively deny climate science and oppose clean energy.[42] Although Koch resigned from AMNH's board, the museum's David H. Koch Dinosaur Wing as well as the Smithsonian's David H. Koch Hall of Human Origins and David H. Koch Hall of Fossils are looming reminders of the uneasy relationships between a collection, its public display, and the name attached to it.[43]

\* \* \*

It's a question of only a few years when everything reminding us of America as it was at the time of its discovery will have perished.

—FRANZ BOAS, ANTHROPOLOGIST, 1898[44]

In the early 20th century, part of the dinosaur's allure was the mystery of its extinction. Wealthy citizens were becoming increasingly fascinated by vanishing worlds, intrigued not only by fossils but also by the nation's disappearing indigenous cultures and receding flora and fauna. This was a time of rapid industrialization and urbanization. Ranchers, cowboys, miners, settlers, speculators, and railroad

**Anthropologist Franz Boas in an Inuit Caribou garment.**
Courtesy of American Philosophical Society, Philadelphia

tycoons had pushed their way westward for nearly a half century. No one of the day paused to remark on the fact that industrialists had destroyed the land and way of life they now scrambled to preserve. Symbolic of the destruction were the immense herds of buffalo slaughtered to the point of extinction. Even more tragic was the systematic destruction of the American Indians and their way of life. By the early 20th century, the "Native American population was about 2 percent of what it had been [before the arrival of the Europeans]," notes James Nason, curator at the Burke Museum, University of Washington, and a member of the Comanche Nation. "Scientists said 'if we don't do something right now to study these people, we will have lost our chance. They will be gone.'"[45] Driven by a perceived urgency and perhaps by a mixture of guilt and nostalgia, Americans feverishly collected specimens, both at home and abroad. Museums gladly embraced the movement.

Explorers uprooted plants from the rainforests of South and Central America and the valleys of Alaska. They deposited the flora at museums and botanical gardens, where the plants were dried, pressed, and

**William Hornaday, a founder of the National Zoo, with a baby bison at the Smithsonian, 1886.**
Smithsonian Institutional Archives

transformed into "botanical specimens." To botanical gardens they brought live trees, shrubs, flowers, seeds, and bulbs that were propagated, hybridized, and transformed into glorious assemblages of "exotic species." From the mountains of Canada to the deserts of Africa, hunters "bagged and tagged" thousands of lions and tigers and bears. Scientists poached hundreds of thousands of bird eggs and nests or ventured to the wilds of Nebraska and Wyoming to "collect" the great buffalo. While taxidermists mounted buffalo hides for display, zoos tried to perpetuate the species in captivity. The founder of the Smithsonian's National Zoo, William Hornaday, envisioned the zoo as a "city of refuge for the vanishing species of the continent." An early champion of animal conservation, Hornaday organized the transport of bison from the Great Plains to Washington, D.C., and cofounded the American Bison Society to help preserve these great beasts of the American wild.[46] By the 1920s, the collecting of smaller specimens like plants, birds, insects, and snakes was so popular that museums distributed butterfly nets and "killing bottles" to eager children, as part of a growing educational movement called "Nature Study." "No youngster can borrow [a net] until he has learned 40 insects from the Museum collection," was the rule at the Brooklyn Children's Museum.[47]

The popularity of the emerging scientific field of anthropology furthered interest in "dying" civilizations. Sponsored by world's fairs and museums, anthropologists strived to collect as much as they could about so-called primitive and vanishing tribes—sometimes even, as we shall see, "collecting" the tribal members themselves. During the Civil War, the Army Medical Museum began to acquire human bones. First surgeons donated the limbs of amputees, preserved in formaldehyde. When wounded soldiers tried to reclaim their legs, the museum declared the appendages belonged to the U.S. government, part of the war effort.[48] Then the museum became a repository for the skulls of Native Americans killed in battle. The idea was to study their cranial capacity to prove that these peoples were subhuman and thus unfit to own or manage their lands.[49]

Museums also acquired Native American household, ceremonial, and sacred objects. They used a variety of methods. Sometimes Native Americans who needed money were persuaded to sell items at very low prices to dealers, collectors, and anthropologists. But often they were unwilling to part with objects. George Dorsey, an anthropologist who directed expeditions for the Field Museum, instructed one of his assistants: "When you go into an indian's house and you do not find the old man at home and there is something you want, you can do one of three things; go hunt up the old man and keep hunting until you find him; give the old woman such price for it . . . running the risk the old man will be offended; or steal it. I have tried all three plans and have no choice to recommend."[50] Sometimes looters, seeking to turn a quick profit, dug up unprotected areas. In one infamous example, they removed hundreds of sacred wooden statues guarding Zuni shrines in New Mexico and sold them to collectors and museums. They did this despite the fact that the Zuni believe that removal of the Ahayu:da war gods, meant to decay naturally in the outdoors, will lead to war, violence, and natural disaster.

In other cases tribal elders asked museums to safeguard sacred objects.[51] In the 1890s the Omaha Indians of Nebraska loaned sacred poles and medicine bundles to the Peabody Museum of Archaeology

In the 1980s, Omaha leaders asked the Peabody Museum of Archaeology and Ethnology to return their Sacred Pole, given to the institution for safekeeping a century earlier.
© President and Fellows of Harvard College, Peabody Museum of Archaeology and Ethnology, PM2004.24.32151A

**Maya. Human effigy cache vessel, 250–500 CE, earthenware, slip paint.**

Gift of Dr. and Mrs. Francis Robicsek. 2004.96. 1 A-B, collection of the Mint Museum, Charlotte, N.C. Courtesy of the Mint Museum

and Ethnology at Harvard University with the understanding that someday their tribe would reclaim and care for them. In many instances anthropologists simply took items, believing they were rescuing them from mistreatment or destruction by the primitive and uneducated peoples who had made them. An early AAM manual for museum workers unapologetically rationalized museums' rights to these items: "Most history museums require some anthropological material to represent the red man's part in the story of the white man."[52]

The 1906 federal Antiquities Act, signed into law by President Theodore Roosevelt, was the government's first attempt at historic preservation. Its goal was to protect historic and prehistoric sites on federal land, such as Chaco Canyon and Mesa Verde, which had been vandalized by grave robbers. It also expressly allowed the gathering of Native American artifacts and remains "for the benefit of and permanent preservation in public museums." Now archaeologists, working in tandem with museums, could legally unearth sacred graves and gather bones, relics, and funerary objects. And they did, by the thousands. Between 1906 and 1907 one archaeologist named Gerard Fowke unearthed hundreds of Comanche remains in central Missouri. These eventually were acquired by the Missouri Historical Society.[53]

The Antiquities Act was devastating to Native American culture. "Native American remains were no longer their own," said Nason. "The bodies of the dead became property like baskets or bowls in a collection."[54] Explorers and anthropologists went beyond the collecting of skeletons and shrunken heads. They also collected living people. In 1897 Arctic explorer Admiral Robert E. Peary gave the American Museum of Natural History "material" that included several barrels of human bones retrieved from a graveyard in Greenland and what he called six "faithful Eskimos." The captured people were relegated to the basement, where four of them, including a man named Qisuk, soon died of tuberculosis. For the benefit of Qisuk's son Minik, the museum staged a fake funeral. Its chief curator William Wallace adopted the young boy. In 1906, Minik learned that Qisuk's corpse had not really been buried. Wallace had skinned and processed it, putting the skeleton on display in the museum.[55]

In 1910 a "wild man" who would come to be called Ishi suddenly appeared in the town of Oroville, CA. His tribe, the Yahi-Yana, had been destroyed by disease and massacre. Alfred Kroeber, an anthropologist at the University of California in Berkeley, persuaded the Bureau of Indian Affairs to permit him to move Ishi into the university museum's basement. Ishi lived for years at the Phoebe A. Hearst Museum of Anthropology, working as a janitor to earn his keep in addition to serving as a living display, making arrowheads and spears that eventually became part of the museum's collection. He became a must-see sensation. After Ishi died of tuberculosis in 1916 his brain was removed, despite Kroeber's protests, and sent to the Smithsonian, where it was kept in a glass jar in storage, forgotten for almost a century.

Ishi, the only surviving member of the Yahi Yana tribe, demonstrating archery at the Phoebe A. Hearst Museum of Anthropology, 1914.
Courtesy of the Phoebe A. Hearst Museum of Anthropology, Berkeley, and the Regents of the University of California (15-6007)

## WORLD WAR II: A TURNING POINT

Before World War II, museums, whether dedicated to art or science, flora or fauna, were essentially in what museum scholar Stephen E. Weil has called the "salvage and warehouse business."[56] The war years profoundly impacted collectors' attitudes and practices, which became characterized by a heightened protectiveness of both their own belongings and those of others. Fearing an attack on U.S. shores, many museums squirreled away their most precious objects in basement vaults or far-off sites. The war's toll in Europe also would have dramatic consequences for museums in the United States.

The war years in Europe were a time of systematic, widespread, state-mandated theft. With the Nazis' rise to power, the movement of art across borders became frantic, in many cases the result of collectors' efforts to save human lives. In Switzerland in 1939, the Nazi Party auctioned off modern artwork from leading

German museums. The stated goal was to rid Germany of work by "degenerates," namely Bolsheviks, Jews, or anyone critical of the Reich. The real goal was to obtain foreign currency. Many American collectors boycotted the sales, but some participated, including publisher Joseph Pulitzer and Maurice Wertheim, a progressive Jewish philanthropist. In the words of Pulitzer, they acted to "save the art." At the same time, Hitler dreamed of establishing two museums: a "Museum of an Extinct Race" filled with Jewish relics and an art museum filled with European masterpieces. To raise more money and stockpile objects for Hitler's planned monuments to his greatness, the Nazis looted European museums. They stole artwork from Jewish collectors and dealers. They pilfered religious items from Jewish households. Works "vanished" into the hands of dubious owners.[57]

After World War II, American museum specialists traveled to Western Europe and Japan to assess the

Monuments Men (unidentified) finding Rembrandt's self-portrait stashed in a mine.
Monuments, Fine Arts, and Archives Program

war damage to monuments, art, and other cultural treasures. The Roberts Commission was a federal agency, headed by Supreme Court Justice Owen Roberts and housed at the National Gallery of Art. Many members would go on to run major museums around the nation, including the Toledo Art Museum, Baltimore Museum of Art, and the Isabella Stewart Gardner Museum. Also known as the Monuments Men, the group included women, such as Edith Standen, a member of the Women's Army Corps who later became tapestry curator at the Metropolitan Museum of Art in New York.[58]

With the horrors of World War II still fresh in their minds at the dawn of the nuclear age, museums became increasingly concerned about security.

Monuments Man Lt. Frank P. Albright; Polish Liaison Officer Maj. Karol Estreicher; Monuments Man Capt. Everett Parker Lesley; and Pfc. Joe D. Espinosa, guard with the 34th Field Artillery Battalion, pose with Leonard da Vinci's *Lady with an Ermine* upon its return to Poland in April 1946.
Monuments, Fine Arts, and Archives Program

Edith Standen, Monuments, Fine Arts, and Archives Section of the Office of Military Government, United States, 1946

The United Nations Educational, Scientific and Cultural Organization (UNESCO) published a guide that showed museums how to protect collections from nuclear annihilation, earnestly recommending the use of metal-slatted Venetian blinds to counter the light from an A-bomb explosion and "fairly thick cellophane tape" (duct tape had just become available to civilians) to seal windows and prevent the seepage of radiation. In 1951 the director of the Corcoran Gallery of Art went so far as to propose that because of the "threat of atomic missiles," museums should remove their entire contents to a "separate building located . . . well beyond the potential [enemy] target area." He suggested the so-called targeted museum buildings be used instead for public lectures or concerts. Presumably, in the event of a nuclear attack, audiences would just duck and cover, comforted by the fact that the museum's collections were safe from the threat of obliteration.[59]

Meanwhile, U.S. museums discovered that while European art prices were still relatively high, works from Asia were widely available. The art of Asia had first entered an American museum collection in the

Ernest Fenollosa sold this Edo period Japanese woodblock print (nishiki-e) by Katsushika Hokusai to William S. and John T. Spaulding in 1911, and they donated it to the Museum of Fine Arts, Boston, a decade later. It is titled *Surugadai in Edo* (Tōto sundai), from the series *Thirty-Six Views of Mount Fuji* (Fugaku sanjūrokkei). The Spaulding brothers were part of an early-20th-century group of Boston-based connoisseurs of Japanese art.
Museum of Fine Arts, Boston. William S. and John T. Spaulding Collection 21.6782. © 2020 Museum of Fine Arts, Boston

1880s when zoologist Edward Sylvester Morse acquired pottery during a scientific expedition to Japan and gave it to Boston's Museum of Fine Arts (MFA). At the same time, the MFA appointed the renowned scholar Ernest Francisco Fenollosa as its first curator of "Oriental arts." He curated the nation's first major exhibition of Chinese painting and befriended and advised other pioneering collectors of Asian artwork. One was Detroit railcar magnate Charles Lang Freer, who in 1906 bequeathed his collection to the eponymous Freer Gallery of Art in Washington, D.C. The stature of Asian art grew. Between the two world wars, flour executive Alfred Pillsbury donated Chinese jade and terra-cotta figurines to the Minneapolis Institute of Art. Harvard-trained scholar Laurence Sickman helped gather exceptional Chinese landscape paintings for the Nelson-Atkins Museum of Art in Kansas City.[60] In 1927, 40 children's and public museums, including the Indianapolis Children's Museum and the Charleston Museum, acquired beautiful Japanese "friendship" dolls, complete with elaborate kimonos and matching suitcases, as part of an international friendship campaign between U.S. and Japanese cities.

World War II changed attitudes toward Japan. During the war, friendship dolls were removed from public display. Some were burned and destroyed, while other items mysteriously disappeared.[61] After the war, museums reactivated their interest in Asia.[62] Sometimes GIs who had served in the Pacific presented their local museums with "souvenirs" from their tours of duty. Other museums sent curators to comb the black markets of Tokyo for bargains on lacquer items, jade, and statues. Curators at the Cleveland Museum of Art were advised to buy especially valuable objects, such as screens, as quietly as possible, lest the Japanese government declare them national treasures and prohibit exportation.[63]

At the same time European dealers and artists who had survived the war flooded into the United States, and the fine arts scene exploded. Galleries in Manhattan attracted a new generation of wealthy collectors whose fortunes were growing in the postwar economy.

**Japanese friendship doll Miss Shimane, ca. 1927.**
Children's Museum of Indianapolis. Daniel Schwem

Among those who caught the bug were Chicago's Mary Block and her husband Leigh, vice president of Inland Steel; Houston's John and Dominique de Menil, whose fortunes dovetailed with the Texas oil boom; New York's Barbara Duncan, wife of a chemical company executive; and Detroit's Lydia Kahn Winston, daughter of industrial architect Albert Kahn. The Blocks purchased Impressionist paintings that eventually went to the Art Institute of Chicago and Northwestern University in Evanston, IL. The de Menils were drawn to surrealism; they eventually founded an entire museum in Houston. Duncan, a major collector of Latin American art, later donated to the Blanton Museum of Art at the University of Texas, Austin. And Kahn became the first private collector to purchase a work by Jackson Pollock—for $275, in 1946.[64]

Homegrown artists such as Pollock and movements like Abstract Expressionism were a boon to private collecting. Dealers promoted art as risk-free financial investment; simply hang a canvas by an up-and-coming artist on your wall and watch it double in value before your eyes. Or befriend a museum director, let him advise you, unofficially of course; then promise the pieces to the museum, take a tax deduction, and hang them in your house until death do you part.[65]

In 1946 the San Francisco Museum of Modern Art opened the nation's first art rental gallery. Its goal was to promote collecting to an even wider field of potential art buyers: the growing middle class. Art collecting also was promoted in magazines like *Good Housekeeping* and by department stores. At the popular department store Sears and Roebuck, shoppers could come away from a single visit with new cookware, a modern couch, and, for an extra $300, a real Picasso lithograph to hang over it. Those who couldn't afford an original could purchase a "paint-by-number" kit and fashion their own Mona Lisa.

Postwar interest in the fine arts spread from suburban shoppers to artists' colonies (Provincetown, MA) to avant-garde college communities (Black Mountain, N.C.). Victor D'Amico, MoMA's head of education, surmised that the turn to aesthetics was related to a "spiritual hunger" that arose during the nuclear age: "One wonders whether there is not a relationship between the growing power of destructiveness on the part of our scientific genius, and that indescribable urge for creation on the part of the general public."[66]

Ironically, the Cold War had the opposite effect on museum acquisitions. Amid the explosive scientific discoveries and vibrant art scene of the 1950s, most museums abandoned voracious collecting. Gone was the obsession with swashbuckling dinosaur diggers and eccentric millionaire art collectors. It was time to protect and preserve.

### THE 1950s AND 1960s: PROTECT AND PRESERVE

By the mid-20th century, collections faced more tangible threats than Cold War paranoia. Museums were bursting at the seams. Many objects were in poor condition. Early explorers and science curators often yanked natural materials right from the ground. Once in museums, these items received little care beyond perhaps an application of a toxic pesticide like arsenic or a soaking in gasoline to kill any remaining larvae. Bringing priceless artwork from abroad to the United States was, in the words of one noted collector, "as simple as shipping a sack of potatoes."[67] But of course this meant that it frequently arrived in rotten condition—grimy, cracked, discolored. Thomas Gainsborough's famous *Blue Boy* wasn't even blue when the prized acquisition arrived from its voyage from London to the United States: thick coats of varnish had given the canvas a sickly greenish tinge. Once in a museum, objects were subject to even more damage from intensive day-lighting, forced heat, and cramped storage. As conservator Sheldon Keck observed, "We have learned from sad experience that [art and other precious objects are] subject to the ravages of time, climate, chemistry and microorganisms."[68] Not to mention the scourge of museum basements: vermin that happily nested among the treasures and chewed to their hearts' content.

Objects also had vague paper trails, even though a cataloging system of neatly filed blue index cards devised by librarian Henry Watson Kent had been in use since 1910. Directors and trustees made up an elite social network, using collections as private playthings. Cutting inside deals was common practice. There are tales of directors who would phone a director-pal at another museum and ask to borrow a rare European masterwork. The desired painting would be stuffed into the trunk of someone's car and driven to its new destiny, backed up by a handshake. In those years, museum vaults, supposedly established in the public trust, were largely unguarded from both the natural elements and human temptation.[69] As the middle class snuggled into a suburban lifestyle, museums also turned inward—toward the matters of conservation and documentation.

Operating in a world where collectors value their objects almost as much as life itself, the museum conservator is like a medical doctor, saving a damaged treasure through a proper treatment. In the 1920s museums adopted promising medical technologies to care for collections. Field Museum scientists used X-ray machines to examine mummies without unwrapping them. Art museums, cautious about an influx of counterfeit art, turned to X-rays and microscopes to help identify forgeries.[70] A pioneering laboratory for this work was housed at Harvard University's Fogg Art Museum, where Paul Sachs, an heir to the banking firm Goldman Sachs, trained students to learn the

**Paul J. Sachs teaching future museum directors and conservators in the Naumberg Room, Fogg Museum.**
Photograph by George S. Woodruff, 1944. Fogg History Photographs, International News Photos, folder 4. Harvard Art Museums Archives, Harvard University, Cambridge, MA.

In the 1950s, the Public Museum of Grand Rapids started sending collections artifacts—including the mounted animals pictured here—to schools throughout the region.
Courtesy of the Public Museum of Grand Rapids.

anatomy of a work of art—its materials, chemistry, application techniques, and the signature flourishes of important artists.[71]

In the 1950s two of Sachs's protégés, Carolyn Kohn Keck and Sheldon Keck, helped transform the art of restoration into the science of conservation. Whereas restorers altered works of art by applying and manipulating materials, conservators like the Kecks sought to repair objects and return them to their original state. In 1955 Carolyn taught the first painting conservation course at the New York State Historical Association in Cooperstown. In 1959 Sheldon opened the first training program for art conservators at New York University. With the emergence of trained conservators, larger universities and museums invested in fully stocked laboratories, while smaller museums relied on regional facilities, like the one founded at Oberlin College in 1952, to care for their works.[72]

As conservators learned more tricks of the trade, they founded the American Institute for Conservation of Historic and Artistic Works (1972) to develop new ways to deal with the chronic problem of treating, conserving, and preventing further deterioration of collections. Conservators asserted their voices, advising the field on systems such as climate control and ventilation. Conservators became "institutional gadflies," holistic practitioners dedicated to maintaining the health of collections. Put a humidifier next to that armoire or it will crack. Lower the light level on that engraving or it will fade. Don't serve dessert in that gallery unless you want ants crawling up your Renoir.[73]

If conservators took on the role of doctor, registrars became the accountants. Until World War II recordkeeping was primarily the responsibility of curators, often referred to as "keepers." Their job was to keep collections in some kind of order. But curators hadn't kept pace. They had other things to think about, such as acquiring more objects. In the 1950s a new kind of keeper—the professional registrar—emerged.[74] The registrar was charged with tracking collections and documenting their condition and provenance. Rising art values and the increased number of traveling exhibitions made this task a specialty. Insurance firms were entering the fine arts business and required accurate records, especially when art traveled between museums. In the 1960s registration became more specialized with the introduction of computerized databases.[75] Over the next 50 years, database systems would become increasingly sophisticated. As images of objects have been digitized for both in-house use and museums' websites, collections professionals' purviews widened to include overseeing "digital assets."[76]

The act of digitizing collections has been a magnificent gift to the public. For example, in 2008, the Walters Art Museum in Baltimore unveiled the powerful and groundbreaking Archimedes Palimpsest project. The Archimedes Palimpsest is a 13th-century prayer book whose pages contain two erased treatises by the ancient Greek mathematician that exist nowhere else. It arrived at the Walters severely faded, stained, and moldy, yet bearing traces of an alluring mystery. For 10 years, Walters's conservators and curators worked to reveal the hidden texts via a special X-ray imaging technique. The museum then released the treatises on the web. As curator William Noel explained on the project's website, "what was erased text, in terrible condition, impossible to access, and yet foundational to the history and science of the West, is now legible, and instantly available for free by clicking HERE."[77] No one has to travel further than the nearest computer screen to mine in detail a one-of-a-kind mathematical treasure.

Today, collections professionals' concerns have magnified. They include not only digital preservation and care but restoration of analog materials—like batteries and floppy disks—necessary for running historic computer equipment. As researchers and curious web surfers readily curate their own journeys through museums' collections databases, the question of how deeply digital technology will change the way institutions honor, protect, and preserve their collections' physical and intellectual properties is foremost in museum collections professionals' minds.

This illuminated manuscript titled "Evangelist Mark Seated in His Study" (ca. 1025–1050) was donated to the Walters Art Museum by Henry Walters in 1931. It was part of the museum's exhibition *Lost and Found: The Secrets of Archimedes* during 2011–2012.

## THE 1970s: RUMMAGING THROUGH CLOSETS

Other pressing concerns arose during the 1970s. Despite the dedication of collections professionals, most museum closets remained a mess, with a few secret hiding places long obscured from public view. In the early 1970s, as museums lobbied for federal monies and tax advantages, two insider practices emerged from the mothballs and into the headlines. The first involved museums disposing of collections they no longer wanted. The second involved museums holding on to objects they had no business owning: looted antiquities, sacred Native American entities, Nazi plunder.

Nearly every museum has sorted through its collections and at one time or another disposed of, traded, transferred, or sold unwanted things. In 1918, anticipating decluttering guru Marie Kondo by a more than a century, AAM warned museums that holding on to "worthless debris" would "clog up and impede their progress."[78] Getting rid of objects, a practice known as deaccessioning, is a sensible way to manage the vast quantity of stuff that sits in collection vaults.[79] For decades, staff and board alike have questioned the ethics as well as the finances of holding and caring for so many things that will never see the light of day in the face of other urgent needs, such as paying living wages to staff; charging a lower admission price to visitors; or, more recently, dealing with financial shocks like COVID-19.[80]

Deaccessioning, however, turns out to be tricky business.[81] There are the legalities attached to bequests and donors' stipulations. There are the politics of informing donors or their progeny without hurting feelings or financial loyalty. There are ethical questions about market manipulation. What if an organization is tempted to accession something to increase its value (by virtue of its association with a museum) only to later "flip it" for profit? This all leads to the matter of public perception. Is the authentic, original object so historically or artistically important that it must remain in the public trust forever—and therefore in a museum? How will a community react when it discovers that its public museum is privately selling off objects from the collection? Is every treasure priceless? Who says so?

In 1942 the Illinois State Museum's mounted elephant Charlie had become a "white elephant." The museum found Charlie a new home at the Decatur Illinois Republican Headquarters. No one bristled. That same year the Smithsonian unloaded a "number of cannon balls" for the nation's wartime metal salvage campaign. It seemed perfectly appropriate—even patriotic—to give another worthy cause first dibs on unwanted items.[82] But attitudes about deaccessioning have always been more touchy when it comes to artwork. In the 1950s, the Minneapolis Institute of Art drew ire when it sold 4,500 second-rate works. Suspecting that the director was in cahoots with the auction house and getting a cut of the proceeds, the Minneapolis trustees launched an investigation, leading to the director's resignation. They understood that collections sales must first and foremost benefit the museum, a recommendation now articulated in AAM's Code of Ethics.[83]

The stakes rose during the 1970s. Art sitting in storage had skyrocketed in value. Operating costs were rising. Inflation was high. It was increasingly expensive to run a museum, let alone maintain a collection. A scandal at a New York museum brought these issues to the fore.

In 1971 Thomas Hoving, the director of the Metropolitan Museum of Art, presided over the sale of art given to the museum by Adelaide Milton de Groot. According to Hoving, since the 1940s the Met's curators had considered de Groot a difficult personality and her paintings second-rate. Gradually, they transferred her collection to storage. But knowing that de Groot would eventually bestow a large cash gift to the museum, they cared for the works and courted their donor. When she died in 1967, the Met got its donation and more. Her paintings weren't second-rate; in fact, they were worth a fortune. De Groot's will stipulated that if the Met didn't want the paintings, they were to go to the Wadsworth Atheneum in Hartford, CT. Hoving was not about to send them to a rival museum. He wanted to use the de Groot "sludge," as he called it, to "raise a twenty million dollar war chest" for the Met. Through a series of undercover transactions between an international network of dealers (some of them disreputable), the Met sold one of the works, Henri Rousseau's *Tropics*. It landed in a private office in Tokyo. The next year, the Met secretly sold another donor's painting: Dorothy Bernhard's gift of Vincent van Gogh's *The Olive Pickers*.[84]

When these covert sales became public, art experts were outraged. They questioned why they were necessary (the Met was not hurting for money), how the prices were set, who profited, and the impact this would have on other museums. New York's attorney general launched an investigation. In a scathing article in *Art in America* titled "Should Hoving Be De-accessioned?" art historian John Rewald assailed the Met for arrogance: "Has it occurred to anyone at the Metropolitan that its high-minded practices can backfire and hurt other museums? . . . A fundraiser for at least one American museum has already been told by a prospective contributor: 'Why come to me if you need money? Do what Hoving does and sell some of your pictures.'"[85]

The scandal ended on a positive note. The Met's trustees adopted strict deaccessioning policies that became models for other museums. Museum associations revised their codes of ethics with such nonambiguous statements as "Funds obtained through disposal [of collections] must be used to replenish the collection."[86] Nonetheless, over the years, it has proven hard for some organizations to resist the temptation to sell valuable art to raise a "war chest."[87]

On July 18, 2013, a headline in the *New York Times* read "Billions in Debt; Detroit Tumbles into Bankruptcy." Because of municipal mismanagement and the ongoing loss of population and tax base, Detroit

**The deaccession of *The Olive Pickers* may have been scandalous, but this 1889 painting by Vincent van Gogh titled *Women Picking Olives* was donated to the Metropolitan Museum of Art by Walter H. and Leonore Annenberg, where it remains today.**
The Metropolitan Museum of Art, The Walter H. and Leonore Annenberg Collection, Gift of Walter H. and Leonore Annenberg, 1995, Bequest of Walter H. Annenberg, 2002 (1995.535)

was in dire straits. City officials cooked up a radical plan to raise money. Once again (as discussed in the prior chapter), the sacrificial lamb would be the Detroit Institute of Arts. This time, the city planned to sell DIA's prized Van Goghs, Cézannes, and Bruegels to stave off cuts to retired municipal workers' pensions. The museum pushed back. "I'm an old European socialist," said DIA's director Graham Beal. "I would do anything I could for pension-holders and their problems. But those problems have nothing to do with DIA."[88] The museum sought counsel. Working under great pressure, Judge Gerald Rosen sketched out a solution on the back of a legal pad. It came to be known as the "Grand Bargain," a complex set of negotiations whereby philanthropists agreed to help bail out Detroit's General Retirement Fund. In return, the art would forever remain in Detroit. The state of Michigan

and the courts agreed. Cashing out DIA's art wouldn't erase Detroit's chronic problems, but it would irreparably harm the museum and the city. "When faced with the question of pensions or paintings," writes legal scholar Maureen B. Collins, "Detroit and its supporters answered 'both' in a way that blazes a trail for other creative solutions to equally compelling dilemmas." In 2015, Judge Rosen's legal pad with its "historic doodle" was accessioned into DIA's collection, where it remains alongside the paintings that it helped to save from the auction house.[89]

## ILLICIT TRAFFICKING OF CULTURAL PROPERTY

A lintel from Thailand. A statue from Nigeria. Mosaics from Cyprus. Textiles from Peru. Museums have always been destinations for pilfered treasures from ancient monuments or archaeological sites. The illicit trafficking of cultural property and looting of antiquities in poor or war-torn countries for the benefit of museums and collectors in wealthier ones has been a significant problem probably even before Napoleon's war trophies went to the Louvre and Lord Elgin's Parthenon friezes entered the British Museum. Archaeologists, government officials, dealers, journalists, auction houses, the military, and even tourists are complicit. Before the 1970s, if the contraband happened to be an important antiquity or work of art (or a convincing fake), it stood a good chance of commanding a high price and then drifting into a museum collection, especially one in the United States.

Two international organizations—UNESCO and the International Council of Museums (ICOM), both founded in Paris in 1946—have long been concerned about the illicit international traffic of art and antiquities into U.S. museums. Beginning in the 1970s, delegates at international gatherings began to pose uncomfortable questions. By coveting antiquities from around the world and paying top dollar for them, were U.S. museums supporting the trafficking of plunder? Should they demand better documentation before accepting an object of dubious origin? What should they do about contraband that was already in their collections?

If the answers to these questions seemed clear to international agencies, discussions within museums were cloudy. Scholars frequently argued that antiquities were safer in a museum in an "advanced" country than buried underground in the "third world." Some directors went so far as to plead "cultural poverty," arguing that the United States was a relatively young nation and thus needed antiquities from "culturally rich" but "financially poor" nations.[90] In other words, antiquities' role in scholarship and public education was more important than the corrupt means by which they had been obtained.

The debate over one case changed the course of museum collecting. In 1947, as interest in pre-Columbian antiquities was growing worldwide, the Guatemalan government passed a law restricting their export, hoping to protect the country's cultural heritage. It did little good. During the 1950s and 1960s archaeologists at Harvard and the University of Pennsylvania set up large-scale projects to study Mayan relics and ruins throughout Mexico and Guatemala. They hired locals to clear-cut paths through dense jungles and do the heavy manual labor involved in excavation. Soon or-ganized groups of thieves (called "pothunters") began smuggling artifacts off the sites, now more accessible due to the paths the archaeologists had funded. Using power saws and other crude methods, the robbers hacked away at pyramids and temples. No site was immune; even national monuments were mutilated. Smugglers slipped fragments—sometimes as large as 10 by 30 feet—across borders and through airport customs. Dealers sold the goods on the international art market, asking as much as $500,000 for a single piece. Many were then given to museums.

Initially the universities sponsoring the digs did not intervene. But in 1969 Clemency Coggins, a doctoral student at Harvard University, published a detailed description of the systematic theft of Mayan relics in Guatemala and Mexico, complete with maps and photos. With her colleagues at Harvard's Peabody Museum, she documented 15 sites where vandals had sawn off or smashed to bits ancient stelae carved with "extraordinarily beautiful" Mayan hieroglyphics and masks. Risking her career, Coggins provided evidence that much of the plunder resided in U.S. museums. (Later she would receive a gold medal from Archaeological Institute of America for her courage.)[91] More researchers got involved. In an exposé titled *Plundered Past*, journalist Karl E. Meyer published an augmented list of looted South American sites.

By 1970, professionals had banded together to take action. ICOM issued an "Ethics of Acquisition," stating that before adding something to its collection, a museum was ethically bound to find out who had owned the object, where it had come from, and whether it was exported legally. In the United States, Froelich Rainey, director of the University of Pennsylvania Museum of Archaeology and Anthropology, condemned the "wholesale destruction of archaeological sites" and urged wealthy nations to introduce "more rigid import controls." In what is now known as the Philadelphia Declaration, the museum's curators pledged to "purchase no more art objects or antiquities for the Museum unless the objects were accompanied by a pedigree." Perhaps the most significant document that year was UNESCO's "Convention on the Means of Prohibiting and Preventing the Illicit Import, Export and Transfer of Ownership of Cultural Property." It called on museums to repudiate "theft, clandestine excavation and illicit export." In other words, a museum's duty is not only to safeguard its own objects but to safeguard cultural heritage in a broader, global sense.[92]

Mesoamerica, Guatemala, Department of the Petén, El Perú (also known as Waka'), Maya people (A.D. 250–900), Classic period (A.D. 200–1000), acquired by the Cleveland Museum of Art in 1967. El Perú was one of the sites studied by Clemency Coggins during her groundbreaking work on looting in Central America.

Some institutions remained defiant. In 1972, despite near certain knowledge that an ancient Greek terra cotta vase known as the Euphronios krater had been pilfered from an Etruscan site, the Metropolitan Museum of Art purchased it and put it on display.[93] Even after the UNESCO Convention was ratified by the U.S. Senate in 1983, the black market for looted antiquities prospered. With governments of source countries threatening legal action, the museum field worked to raise awareness of the problem to law officials, customs agents, and curators. In 2004 AAM and ICOM released a Red List of Latin-American Cultural Objects at Risk, an important step in curbing the illicit traffic in pre-Columbian and colonial-era objects from churches and archaeological sites.

Still, many museums, including the Met, continued to acquire suspicious pieces, sometimes even with the AAM's blessing.[94] "The world's cultural achievements belong to everyone," James Cuno, a museum director and defender of the right of museums to hold on to antiquities, argued. According to Cuno, "governmental efforts to retain works of art within a given jurisdiction as evidence of a pure, essentialized, state-based identity are contrary to the truth and history of [the fluidity of] culture."[95] In 2005, a scandal at the Getty Museum put the issue in a harsher light.

The Getty had a long history of shady transactions involving antiquities. In 1953, oil mega-tycoon J. Paul Getty opened a small museum in his oceanside villa near Los Angeles, largely as a tax shelter. As Mr. Getty's stocks soared in value, the museum's curators made grand plans to spend a fortune on the world's finest antiquities. Until the mid-1980s, when the *Los Angeles Times* and Internal Revenue Service began to investigate, Juri Frel, the Getty's curator of antiquities, did what he felt necessary to build such a collection. Frel forged documents, falsified records, bribed officials, hobnobbed with a network of crooked dealers, lied to trustees, and inflated the value of desired work to give donors ridiculously huge tax write-offs. He even did some small-time smuggling of his own, once stuffing an ancient Egyptian marble head into his wife's handbag to evade U.S. Customs. In 1986, after being confronted by museum officials, Frel quietly slipped out the country. His successor, Marion True, was not as fortunate.

True came to the Getty in the 1980s as a reformer. In her role as curator of antiquities, she flagged fakes

**Euphronios krater while it was on display at the Metropolitan Museum of Art.**
Photo by Tim Pendemon from Wikimedia Commons

in the collection and oversaw the return of confirmed loot to source countries. Yet that didn't stop her from helping the museum to procure an item that would forever alter her life: a limestone and marble sculpture of Aphrodite, thought to be looted from Sicily. This time, the Italian government took action. On April Fool's Day, 2005, True was ordered to stand trial in Rome for allegedly being part of a scheme to fake documentation for stolen antiquities.[96] She became the first U.S.-based curator to be criminally charged by a foreign government for trafficking in looted art. Her indictment and the subsequent press exposé of the shady underworld of the antiquities market were a "public relations catastrophe," noted Gary Vikan, former director of the Walters Art Museum.[97] Until the case was dismissed in 2010, True endured a humiliating legal battle. Many believe that she was "scapegoated," not only for the Getty's past deeds but for illicit acquisitions in museums everywhere. With the trial of Marion True, the field had hit a crossroad. Did curators now have to pay the price for the age-old way some museum collections had been attained? What did the Italian government's actions mean for objects in museum collections with questionable paper trails? As Peter Morrin, director of the Speed Art Museum (Louisville, KY) said, "You can make all the philosophical arguments you want about the value of universal museums, but you can't ignore the courts or public opinion."[98] It was time to return unlawfully attained antiquities.

In the early decades of the 21st century, museum workers carefully packed hundreds of bronze statues, marble busts, and ceramic urns—including the Euphronios krater—into crates bound for Greece and Italy. The Walters Art Museum returned a spectacular solid-gold monkey head to Peru (2011); the Denver Art Museum, a monumental sandstone sculpture to Cambodia (2016). Repatriating antiquities is a win-win proposition, according to *Los Angeles Times* journalists Jason Felch and Ralph Frammolino, authors of a detailed account of the Getty scandal. "Italian authorities have reported a marked decline in looting from archaeological sites. American museums have all but stopped purchasing recently looted Greek and Roman antiquities."[99] In return, some governments have even agreed to lend materials back to U.S. museums for the pleasure of audiences. Yet the question lingers: how do museums draw a line between honoring a request for repatriation and protecting previously stolen works from unstable nations or war zones?

Unfortunately, despite significant progress, the market for looted artifacts continues to thrive. ICOM's Red Lists of endangered or missing cultural treasures have grown in number, extending across Asia and especially the war-torn Middle East. But there is hope. Technologies like blockchain hold promise for tracking transactions between dealers, auction houses, collectors, and museums in order to ferret out questionable items. And most importantly, a new generation of museum professionals and ethical collectors is aware that ancient art is not a commodity to be stolen, traded, and sold for the benefit of those in wealthy countries. It is tangible evidence of human creation around the globe, part of the DNA of a landscape, a cultural identity, the evidence of ancestors.[100]

## THE NATIVE AMERICAN GRAVES PROTECTION AND REPATRIATION ACT (NAGPRA)

The forefathers shot the Indians or poisoned them with bad whisky . . . all that remains of them are the few tools and stone implements which they carried, and which we find in their graves.

—W. J. HOLLAND, DIRECTOR, CARNEGIE MUSEUM, 1902[101]

For Native America, NAGPRA provides a new sense of empowerment under which long-lost items can be repatriated, and it means that Native Americans can be active participants in the museum community.

—ROGER ECHO-HAWK (PAWNEE), 2002[102]

An even more contentious fight for repatriation has involved cultural materials excavated on U.S. soil. Enacted in 1990, the federal Native American Graves Protection and Repatriation Act (NAGPRA) requires museums that receive federal funds to inventory their collections of Native American sacred objects, human remains, and objects of cultural patrimony; send summaries of these inventories to Native tribes; and repatriate items if tribes with appropriate cultural affiliation to the objects request it. NAGPRA is the "single most important piece of national cultural property legislation ever adopted in the United States," wrote James Nason (Comanche). "[T]he passage of this legislation . . . was a stunning victory for Native American communities."[103]

The victory was long in coming. Since the massive late-19th-century anthropological collecting, museums and Native Americans endured what anthropologist James Clifford described as a "charged set of . . . asymmetrical power relationships."[104] Museums harbored many ancestral remains and sacred objects while Native Americans struggled to honor their ancestors and maintain their traditions. Inspired by the 1970 UNESCO convention and successful repatriations of aboriginal objects by Australian and Canadian museums, American tribes asserted their rights to their heritage. They questioned museums about displays that presented Native Americans as "savages." They asked for the return of pipes, medicine bundles, ceremonial masks, funerary objects, and human remains. Some museums responded callously, either ignoring the requests or refusing them outright. Tribal leaders persisted. A breakthrough came in 1978 when Congress passed the American Indian Religious Freedom Act (AIRFA), establishing Native Americans' rights to use and possess sacred objects necessary to ongoing religious practices. According to Nason, AIRFA "sent shockwaves through the museum community," which feared the day when tribes would come to them, law in hand.

Throughout the 1980s tribes pressured museums and saw partial success. Omaha leaders approached Harvard's Peabody Museum and declared that they were ready to take care of their sacred pole, loaned to the museum for safekeeping a century earlier. The Missouri Historical Society helped purchase land for the reburial of the Comanche remains unearthed after the Antiquities Act.[105] The board of the Denver Art Museum authorized the return of war gods to the Zuni and helped secure a shrine for the objects' placement. By 1989 several states had passed repatriation laws and many museums had quietly returned items to tribal communities. The federal government also ordered the Smithsonian to survey its Native American holdings, authorized the creation of the National Museum of the American Indian, and began to debate the passage of NAGPRA.

When museums became aware that repatriation could become federal law, they worried out loud. What do Native Americans know about proper care? How will tribes prove that an object is really sacred? How will they prove ownership? Won't they simply drain museum collections and then turn around and sell objects for profit to private collectors? And how will we pay for all the extra work this is going to create? They even went so far as to state that these objects were safer in a museum than anywhere else. In its 1988 annual report, the AAM boasted of "slowing the process on the Native American Museums Claim Commission Act." Similarly, the American Association of Anthropology argued for anthropologists' right of scientific inquiry and research. How could museums return skeletal re-

**The repatriation ceremony marking the return of the sacred pole to the Omaha people in the 1980s.**
© President and Fellows of Harvard College, Peabody Museum of Archaeology and Ethnology, PM2004.24.31958C

mains for reburial, when there is much to learn from their DNA? Attorney Walter Echo-Hawk (Pawnee) countered, "What Europeans want to do with their dead is their business. We have different values."

Eventually siding with Native Americans was the U.S. Congress. After all, families who had lost young men in wars were asking for their remains; why shouldn't Native Americans be granted this same basic right? Qisuk's skeleton still sat in a storeroom at the American Museum of Natural History, Ishi's brain in a glass jar on a shelf at the Smithsonian. Didn't rights regarding human remains supersede the right of scientific inquiry? Led by Arizona representatives Morris Udall and John McCain and Hawaiian Senator Daniel Inouye, and after heated negotiations between Native American activists and museums, NAGPRA passed. President George H. W. Bush signed it into law. "It is the hope and commitment of AAM and Native American leadership that, having dealt with this issue in the political arena, we can now, together turn to the much more exciting and important promise of establishing a new and dynamic relationship between Native Americans and museums," wrote AAM President Ellsworth Brown.

Museums scrambled to create inventories and decode NAGPRA's legal jargon. "The intent of the law was very good, but compliance turned out to be difficult," said Peter Tirrell, of the Sam Noble Museum of Natural History in Norman, OK, which held 4,500 sets of human remains and about a million Indian artifacts.[106] Museums found themselves entangled in tribal politics when more than one group claimed the same object or people belonging to the same tribe disagreed.

Museums also found that Native American spiritual beliefs conflicted with museum practice, especially when it came to hermetically sealed storage and object conservation. According to American Indian traditions, sacred objects are living entities that require special care. Some must not be handled by women. Others must be fed organic materials. These requirements baffled museum administrators, who still managed to hammer out compromises that allowed for private sacred ceremonies within collections areas.

Many objects collected in the field had been preserved with toxins, making them potentially harmful both to museum workers and the people to whom they were repatriated. In 1996 lawmakers added a clause to NAGPRA that required museums to disclose information on the chemical treatment of repatriated objects. By 2019, museums and federal agencies had completed over 2,500 inventories and repatriated over a quarter of a million funerary and sacred objects, with more in process.[107] As an indication of just how much material they had been hoarding, museums' fears about losing vast amounts of their collections turned out to be unfounded. Both Ishi and Qisuk finally were laid to rest in their homelands.

NAGPRA transformed museum practice on many levels. With government support, museums developed comprehensive inventories and trained staff, which benefited them far beyond the law's requirements. Others created programs, recorded oral histories, and learned the stories and significance of collection objects. In the 2010s, the growing field of "digital repatriation"—led by the National Museum of the American Indian—allowed museums to provide password-protected digital images and information on their holdings to tribal communities.[108]

Nonetheless, in the decades after NAGPRA's passing, some museums continued to hide behind the law's vague language, lack of funding, and scientists' claims to their right to conduct research on ancient human remains.[109] California tribal communities found themselves caught in the crosshairs of state university politics and bureaucracy, when they sought to rebury ancestors stored at the Phoebe A. Hearst Museum of Anthropology at the University of California, Berkeley. By 2013, Mark Macarro, tribal chair for the Pechanga Band of Luiseño Indians, claimed that the Hearst had only repatriated 3 percent of its vast holdings of skeletal remains, a "disgraceful violation of basic human dignity, decency and federal and state laws." California legislators took action. In 2018, Governor Jerry Brown signed a bill requiring the timely return of indigenous remains in all University of California museum collections to their respective tribes. "As long as these remains are out there and our people are in pieces in different institutions," Macarro explained, "the tribes have this sense that things are really out of balance."[110]

Beyond legal compliance, repatriating sacred Native American items has intangible benefits. In the 1980s, when George Horse Capture was curator at the Plains Indian Museum of the Buffalo Bill Historical Center in Cody, WY, Cheyenne representatives asked for the return of a Sacred Arrow bundle sitting in the museum's collection. Horse Capture was chosen to carry the item to the repatriation ceremony in Oklahoma. "The society leaders were there," he wrote, "and each man in turn addressed me, expressing his heart-felt feelings about the return of this object, how it was essential to their tribe. All involved were deeply serious and many wept. . . . Overcome by emotion, I presented them with the sacred object in the name of my museum. . . . Later, as I thought about the events, I felt . . . proud of my museum. I thought that perhaps . . . our museum could never do anything more beneficial than return this sacred object to its tribes. I believe this action to be one of the high points of my professional career—and the ultimate duty and privilege of a museum. What better contribution to a people can a museum provide than to help them survive?"[111]

## NAZI-ERA LOOT

These looted artworks are the remnants of a lost museum destroyed and scattered around the world by Hitler's murderous attempt at changing history.

—HECTOR FELICIANO, 1997[112]

As with the cases of illicit antiquities and Native American remains, it took a few intrepid individuals, eventually backed up by professional associations and the courts, to call for the return of Nazi-era loot to its rightful owners. After the fall of Communism in Europe in 1989, researchers finally had access to sealed records. Lynn H. Nicholas pieced together the first account of how and why the Nazis had hijacked art, publishing the details in her award-winning book *The Rape of Europa* (1994).[113] Nicholas, along with Paris-based journalist Hector Feliciano, confirmed that looted artwork was in U.S. museum collections, shocking many museum professionals. The acquisitions were technically legal. But inadequate documentation about previous ownership—i.e., an artwork's provenance—confused the situation.

Henri Bondi, nephew of deceased Viennese collector Lea Bondi Jaray, took up the charge. In 1997, he wrote to the Museum of Modern Art (MoMA), claiming that a painting on display there—Egon Schiele's *Portrait of Wally*—had been stolen from his aunt in 1939 and was rightfully his. MoMA refused to turn it over, stating it did not belong to the museum, but to the Leopold Foundation of Austria, which had loaned it for a traveling exhibition. The district attorney of Manhattan stepped in and seized the painting, unnerving the museum community. What did the seizure mean for future exhibitions? Would other collectors be reluctant to lend works with questionable pasts to museums? Within months MoMA's worst fears were realized when two lenders opted out of an upcoming Pierre Bonnard exhibition. Like much disputed work from the Nazi era, *Wally* had a convoluted history involving many unclear transactions. But one thing was clear. MoMA's legal obligation was to the lender, not Bondi. MoMA shipped the painting back to Austria. Even so, Bondi's fight had opened a door. (He eventually received a $19 million settlement from the Leopold Foundation.)

With the likelihood of more claims, President Bill Clinton formed an advisory commission in 1998, chaired by Edgar Bronfman, head of the World Jewish Congress. At a conference convened by the U.S. State Department and U.S. Holocaust Memorial Museum, museums chose to be proactive. They adopted a far-reaching plan called the *Washington Principles* for addressing Nazi plunder. Both the AAM and Association of Art Museum Directors issued guidelines. "Red flags" were placed around artworks with spotty paperwork from the war years and posted on the Internet by organizations like the International Foundation for Art Research (IFAR) and the Getty Information Institute. "The art world will never be the same," predicted Metropolitan Museum of Art director Philippe de Montebello, commenting on the gravity of so many agencies taking such a clear moral stance.[114]

In 1999, the Seattle Art Museum became the first museum in the United States to return a painting under the new principles: Henri Matisse's *Odalisque* to the family of French dealer Paul Rosenberg. Still, newspapers and heirs of Holocaust victims accused the field of not going far enough. In 2001, AAM published a methodology to help museums navigate the complicated process of researching suspect art and then unveiled the Nazi-Era Provenance Internet Portal, a gateway to digitized information about collections in U.S. museums. Museums could no longer rely on blissful ignorance or the passage of time when in late 2016, President Barack Obama signed the Holocaust Expropriated Art Recovery (HEAR) Act into law, eliminating the statute of limitations for claims related to Nazi looting. Two years later, the Virginia Museum of Fine Arts returned an early-16th-century painting to heirs of the Jewish Dutch art dealer Jacques Goudstikker. Like all Nazi plunder, it had a complicated history. At one point the notorious *Reichsmarshall* Hermann Goring had stashed this precious canvas in a secret repository to keep it safe for the planned (and thankfully never realized) *Fuhrermuseum*.[115]

As of 2020, an estimated 100,000 looted Nazi-era artworks remained unaccounted for. "We must all recommit to faithfully implementing the *Washington Principles* before Holocaust survivors breathe their last breath," wrote former state department official Stuart Eizenstat. "We owe it not only to those who lost so much in the Holocaust but also to our own sense of moral justice."[116]

### 1980s–2000s: WIDENING THE SCOPE

The bottom line begs the question, "Who owns history?" The answer must remain, "None of us and all of us."

—THOMAS LIVESAY, MUSEUM OF NEW MEXICO, 1996[117]

In the real world—including the real world of museums—not all lives matter equally, and it shows in our collections and in the stories we tell . . . every choice we make about what things we preserve and what stories we tell is a value judgment about whose lives matter.

—KEVIN JENNINGS, TENEMENT MUSEUM, 2018[118]

A costume worn by hip-hop artist Run DMC. An Atari 2600. A chair from the set of *The Oprah Winfrey Show*. Prince's *Purple Rain* suit. How have these objects, all

Minneapolis native Prince's iconic costume in *Purple Rain*, along with a ticket to his first concert and other memorabilia, are in the collections of the Minnesota Historical Society.

Courtesy of the Minnesota Historical Society

This hand-painted, rainbow-colored Puerto Rican flag was collected by Orange County Regional History Center staff from one of the temporary memorials less than two weeks after the Pulse nightclub shooting on June 12, 2016. This one artifact, of more than 10,000, not only represents the love and outpouring of support from, and for, the Orlando community, but also the intersectionality of the individuals impacted.

Image by Melissa Procko; courtesy of Orange County Regional History Center, Florida; caption by Pamela Schwartz connected to popular culture, come to be collected alongside Renaissance paintings and Victorian-era porcelain?

Slave shackles. Armbands emblazoned with the Star of David. The door from Martin Luther King Jr.'s cell in the Birmingham, AL, jail. An ad with racist drawings of Chinese immigrants. A briefcase found in the 9/11 rubble of the World Trade Center. A rainbow flag left at the Pulse nightclub in Orlando, FL, after one of the deadliest mass shootings in American history.[119] How did these objects, evidence of struggle and tragedy, come to be collected alongside works celebrating the best of humankind?

The drive to collect objects that reflect the full range of human experience grew out of 1960s social activism. In 1967 G. Ellis Burcaw, director of the University Museum of Idaho, observed that the nation's museum collections were limited in scope. He implored museums to tell a fuller story, to begin "actively collecting [objects of] the poor, the working classes, the minority groups,"[120] instead of passively cataloging whatever collectors chose to bring in the doors. The protective bubble around museum collections was slowly dissolving, as curators and collectors adjusted to political and social change. Rejecting the idea of a "melting pot" where different traditions and generations merged into a single identity, they saw the nation as a mosaic of distinct traditions and cultures. How would recognizing these increasingly diverse viewpoints influence museums? How could collections more effectively serve all of society? Museums took a daring step. They strove to document the lives of all peoples, not just the wealthy.

The nation's museums began to amass two new types of collections. The first focused on documenting contemporary times and the rise of mass-media culture. The second reflected the country's changing racial, ethnic, religious, and social character, as well as evidence of past acts of oppression.

Art museums were the first to collect contemporary items and, by the 1970s, the collecting of art by living artists was in full swing. Contemporary art collecting allowed art museums to grow. First- or even third-rate works by the Old Masters were increasingly scarce—"endangered species," as one museum director said. Contemporary art was in continual production.

During this period the National Endowment for the Arts (NEA) Museum Purchase Plan, launched in 1968, enabled more than 50 smaller regional museums—including the Arkansas Arts Center in Little Rock, the Speed Art Museum in Louisville, KY, and the Amarillo Art Center in Texas—to buy works by living artists.[121]

American artist Alice Neel's painting *Priscilla Johnson* (oil on canvas, 1966) at the Speed Art Museum in Louisville, KY, is an example of an art purchase made possible by funds from the National Endowment for the Arts.
Collection of the Speed Art Museum, Louisville

During this time, collectors also began to buy work by contemporary Hispanic artists—although museum departments devoted to that genre wouldn't come into their own until the Museum of Fine Arts, Houston, led the way in the 1990s.[122]

Contemporary art collecting faced a new challenge —the transformed nature of artworks. Unlike the art of the past, easily mounted on pedestals or stretched onto frames, contemporary art adopted a bewildering number of guises. Some works were so enormous or heavy or reliant on electronic technology they warranted special rooms, entrances, and floors. Others existed only as sounds, and still others as ideas. Many were constructed from materials that decayed easily or were meant to erode. Others occurred as performance, involving the audience and spaces outside the museum. Yet while artworks dramatically changed, the nature of collecting them did not. Art curators persuaded collectors to make donations. They purchased work through dealers, galleries, auctions, and later, art fairs and biennales.[123] They commissioned artists to produce new works. They read journals and listened to the opinions of critics and experts. As they had since World War I, they operated in a well-honed marketplace, set up for the buying and selling of art.[124]

Outside art museums, collecting methods were different. In universities, the new field of social history was looking away from "great men and great deeds" toward long cycles and day-to-day life. The new narratives of history stressed the emergence of new technologies, patterns of work, arrangements of domestic living, and interactions among social groups. Social historians argued that U.S. history must tell the stories of all, from rural laborers to the urban working classes, from slaves to immigrants.

With expansive motives but small budgets, social historians rummaged through the material culture of American society. Like raccoons, they raided attics, garbage dumps, and abandoned buildings. Like scavengers, they shopped everywhere—at flea markets, garage sales, and eventually online. Like peddlers, they knocked on doors, collecting oral histories, sifting through photo albums, and watching endless reels of old home movies to capture an aural and visual record of the extraordinary moments of ordinary life.

Curators felt a sense of urgency. Objects needed to be preserved now, before they reached the landfill. Collecting today would give present generations more control over the way curators of the future interpreted the 20th century. And thus, in the 1970s, American historians set their sights on documenting the popular culture of a generation obsessed with immortalizing themselves: baby boomers.

An icon of baby boomer culture sits in the Smithsonian's National Museum of American History (NMAH). In 1978 Edith and Archie Bunkers' easy chairs—along with a doily and two mock beer cans—from the set of the hit 1970s television show *All in the Family* joined the collections of "America's Attic."

**Archie and Edith Bunkers' chairs from the set of the 1970s television show *All in the Family***
Division of Cultural and Community Life, National Museum of American History, Smithsonian Institution

These $8 thrift-store chairs were acquired after the show's last filming, donated by the show's producer Norman Lear at the request of NMAH curator Ellen Roney Hughes. "On their own merit, the chairs—lacking in provenance, beauty or distinction—would never have been accepted," noted Hughes. "[We] acquired them because they were central props in a television show that was . . . revealing of common beliefs, values and behaviors in American life during the 1970s . . . a widely shared American cultural experience with passionate fans and detractors."[125]

NMAH elevated the junkyard chairs to museum quality, caring for them in keeping with the highest standards of registration and conservation. They went on display along with another prop of immense meaning to baby boomers: a pair of the ruby slippers Judy Garland wore in the 1939 movie *The Wizard of Oz*. As the Smithsonian added other iconic TV and movie props to its collections—the original set from chef Julia Child's cooking show; the original Cookie Monster puppet from *Sesame Street*—reactions flowed. Critics, including Smithsonian Secretary Robert McCormick Adams, slammed the museum for adding "trivial" artifacts to its august collections: "If the relics of T.V. are accepted as additions to permanent collections of museums," said Adams, "is there not a danger that we will contribute to the ongoing erosion of vital standards of judgment and performance in the society at large?"[126]

But the Bunkers' chairs resonated with most Americans. Nearly 25 percent of visitors specified that they had come to NMAH specifically to see them. As Hughes argued, "the forms of American popular culture—movies, television programming, country music . . . are products of American creativity with worldwide impact and recognition."[127] Thus emerged museums devoted solely to collecting and exhibiting mass-media culture, including the Museum of Television and Radio, founded in 1975 by CBS executive William S. Paley, the Museum of the Moving Image in Astoria, N.Y. (1981), and the World Video Game Hall of Fame in Rochester, N.Y. (2015).

Around the country, museums began to add objects of the moment to their collections vaults. They were curating time capsules for the future. In the 1980s Philadelphia's Please Touch (Children's) Museum worked with toy manufacturers to collect each year's top-selling items, along with accompanying advertising. Someday they would shed light on growing up in middle-class America during the age of Cabbage Patch kids, Transformers, and animatronic talking bears.

**A Cabbage Patch doll, named Hector Marc, from the 1980s.**
Image courtesy of the Children's Museum of Indianapolis

The beat of contemporary collecting picked up when museums became repositories for something near and dear to many hearts: popular music. The Country Music Hall of Fame and Museum in Nashville opened in 1967 and grew to include more than 200,000 recordings as well as associated ephemera, like Elvis Presley's Cadillac. The Smithsonian purchased items related to jazz great Duke Ellington and hip-hop pioneer Grand Master Flash. Documenting the history of rock 'n' roll, the Rock and Roll Hall of Fame and Museum in Cleveland (opened 1995) includes curiosities like Beatle John Lennon's granny glasses. Seattle's Experience Music Project (founded by Microsoft cofounder Paul Allen in 2000) dove into edgier tastes. Growing up as a shy and awkward kid in in the 1960s, Allen idolized rock and blues guitarist Jimi Hendrix. He amassed a 5,000-object collection of Hendrix memorabilia, once paying $50,000 for a shard from a Fender Stratocaster that the rock legend had smashed in concert.[128] In addition to these flashy museums, a chorus of smaller grassroots music museums continue to pop up around the country, playing to our love affair with music and celebrity.

Historical societies focused their efforts on documenting how local events and movements shaped their communities. In the 1970s and 1980s, the Oakland Museum of California gathered artifacts from

**Elvis Presley's Cadillac at the Country Music Hall of Fame in Nashville, TN.**
Photo by Bob Delevante; courtesy of the Country Music Hall of Fame and Museum

surfers, hippies, yuppies, and black power and gay rights activists—examples of late-20th-century youth and political culture in California. Along with the objects, the museum took another radical step: collecting the owners' stories. "I have sometimes loosely referred to this phenomenon as collecting the people along with their objects," noted Oakland's pioneering history curator L. Thomas Frye. "While it is possible to conduct the collecting of objects and documentation as a close-ended process, it is equally possible to continue the relationship to be open-ended, with a continuing dialogue between the source person and the museum."[129] Contemporary collecting thus wasn't only about documenting materials from the recent past. It was about building relationships with people—in the present tense.

A leader in collecting the material culture of Generation X, millennials, and Generation Z has been the Strong Museum in Rochester, N.Y., originally a repository for Margaret Woodbury Strong's immense collection of 19th- and early-20th-century toys. The

**Mother Maybelle Carter's Gibson L-5 guitar is featured in the Country Music Hall of Fame's core exhibit,** *Sing Me Back Home: A Journey through Country Music.*
Courtesy of the Country Music Hall of Fame and Museum

museum's painted tops, pull toys, and porcelain dolls were charming, but so staid that visitors stayed away. In the 1990s the museum sought to broaden its appeal by adding Barbie dolls and G.I. Joes, a *Star Wars* Halloween costume, and an Atari 2600, possibly the first video game console to enter a museum collection. Curator Scott Eberle and director G. Rollie Adams explained their reasoning: "Outside the museum's walls, American culture was making room for body piercing. Could we blame our visitors for thinking of us as detached, fussy, or unspontaneous? Could we blame them for staying home?"[130] While broadening its collection, the Strong also refined its purpose. In 2006, it rebranded itself as the National Museum of Play, a museum about the history, impact, and importance of play.[131]

Children's play was transforming in the United States with record sales of video game consoles. The Strong's vice president for exhibitions and social historian Jon-Paul C. Dyson saw an opportunity to build the most comprehensive collection of video games and related archival materials in the world, eventually founding the World Video Game Hall of Fame (2015), housed at the Strong. It collects not only vintage games (like *The Legend of Zelda* and *World of Warcraft*) that occupied many hours of millennials' childhoods, but the papers of famous game designers like Will Wright (*The Sims*) and Ed Logg (*Asteroids*). "I believe firmly that video games are the most important medium of the 21st century," said Dyson. Acknowledging the potential for the same level of skepticism the Smithsonian faced with its Archie Bunker chairs, Dyson added, "[e]very time a new form of media has become popular, it has been greeted with suspicion, hostility and fear. For example, when the novel became popular . . . people worried it would corrupt young people. The same was true of . . . comic books and rock 'n' roll after World War II, and . . . movies and television throughout the 20th century . . . but [video games] need to be understood within a broad historical context that relates to other aspects of the human historical experience."[132] The museum also collects materials that document activists' fears that video games promote violence and other antisocial behaviors, as well as controversies like #gamergate about gamer world misogyny.[133]

\* \* \*

Exploring contemporary history in [museums] is a dark, bloody, and contested ground, not for the faint of heart.

—LONNIE BUNCH, 1995[134]

Modern-day collecting is a practice in storytelling. Institutions need to ask themselves what are the stories we want to collect around? What are the dynamic compelling narratives of our time? Which stories lost over time do we want to lift up?

—MASS Action, 2019[135]

In more than a century of frenzied collecting, few people had thought to save items that represented the nation's ugly side. "Why would anyone save artifacts from such humiliating experiences like the Chinese Exclusion Act?" asked John Kuo Tchen, describing his difficulties in finding materials about Chinese immigration for the Museum of Chinese in the Americas in New York.[136] Social historians and curators such as Tchen argued that collecting these experiences was important to opening up a dialogue about the nation's history. Part of a museum's purpose should be to pre-

This "coaching book," used to prepare individuals for interrogation at California's immigration center in Angel Island, includes questions like "How many times has your father gone back to China? When did he return [to the States]?" and "Who are your classmates? Who's your teacher?"
Museum of Chinese in America (MOCA) Collection

serve and present evidence of a community's travails. Edward T. Linenthal, author of a history of the U.S. Holocaust Memorial Museum, calls this kind of collecting a "vibrant form of memory work."

The first museum to collect the experiences of non-English immigrants was founded one year after Congress passed the restrictive Immigration Act of 1924. The Norwegian-American Historical Association, housed at St. Olaf College in Minnesota, not only collected nostalgic items from the old country but also documented the "tangled problems involved in the adjustment of [Norwegian pioneers] to their new environment." (The collection has since been transferred to the Vesterheim Norwegian-American Heritage Center and Museum in Decorah, IA.) During the years leading to World War II, churches and synagogues engaged in analogous efforts. Chicago's Polish Roman Catholic Union preserved archives and objects related to Polish immigration and founded a Polish American Museum in 1937. New York's Jewish Theological Semi-

nary and the Hebrew Union College in Cincinnati collected Jewish ceremonial objects to "illustrate the life of the people" and "counteract . . . prejudice against Jews." Both sets of collections grew for ominous reasons. When Poland was invaded by the Nazis, the Polish American Museum purchased significant artworks that were in Chicago on loan from the Polish government. The goal was that they remain safe in the United States. Likewise, the Theological Seminary purchased objects from European synagogues. Their goal was to finance Jewish emigration to safer countries. This collection formed the basis for the Jewish Museum, which opened in Manhattan in 1947.[137]

It wasn't until the 1960s that other marginalized communities began to found museums that documented their cultural heritage, as well as their hardships. Native American tribal members wanting to pass on traditions to new generations organized the Cherokee Heritage Center (Tahlequah, OK, 1963) and A:shiwi A:wan (Zuni, N.M., 1965). Latino activism

During the 1920s, the descendants of Norwegian immigrants to the midwestern United States were the first to found a museum that documented the history of struggles of a minority group in the United States.
Courtesy of the Vesterheim Norwegian-American Museum, Decorah, Iowa

birthed the Mexican Museum (1965) and El Museo del Barrio (East Harlem, N.Y., 1969); Asian American activists founded the Wing Luke Asian Museum (International District, Seattle, 1966); the Museum of Chinese in the Americas (Chinatown, N.Y., 1980); and the Japanese American National Museum (Little Tokyo, Los Angeles, 1982).[138]

The collecting of the history of one group—African Americans—illustrates how difficult and fraught with emotion memory work is. Beginning in the 1960s African American collections grew in two ways. First, mainstream museums worked with social historians to incorporate black history and culture into their collections. Second, black community leaders started their own institutions as part of the wave of American ethnic museums.

The first collection of African Americana, however, had been organized decades earlier by Puerto Rican intellectual Arturo Alfonso Schomburg. In the 1910s Schomburg moved to New York and began to collect books, art, and other materials with the goal of affirming Africans' role in the making of world civilization and disproving the myths of racial inferiority espoused by people like Henry Fairfield Osborn. Too challenging for a museum at that time, the Schomburg collection was acquired by the New York Public Library, where it has since grown to more than one million records and objects. Likewise, in the late 1920s, working under the supervision of anthropologist Franz Boas, novelist Zora Neale Hurston compiled extensive collections of Southern "Negro folk expression," including songs, children's games, "hoodoo spells," and "black magic." They are now part of the Library of Congress.

There had long been talk about a "National Negro Memorial and Museum" on the National Mall, but it was not until well after the civil rights movement that traditional museums collected black history in the context of the nation's culture.[139] In the 1970s the Smithsonian gathered material from the movement, including buttons, tapes of speeches, and eventually the "Whites Only" Woolworth's lunch counter from Greensboro, N.C. The task was relatively easy. The movement was only a few years old, with many participants still alive and willing to contribute mementos and stories.

But collecting the physical evidence that had led to the need for a movement in the first place—objects related to slavery and Jim Crow—proved to be more difficult. Out of fear and a desire to forget, these materials had largely been destroyed, save for a rare item of clothing or escaped slave's diary hidden in an attic.

**Zora Hurston beating the hountar, or mama drum, 1937.**
New York World-Telegram and the Sun Newspaper Photograph Collection, Library of Congress

Stories had been passed down orally. With successes like the 1977 TV miniseries *Roots: The Saga of an American Family* and the growth of African American studies in universities, historic houses found that visitors were often more interested in the daily lives of enslaved workers than the wealthy homeowners.[140]

In 1979—to the dismay of nervous tour guides—social historians at Colonial Williamsburg declared that it was time to acknowledge who had really worked the fields and kitchens at Williamsburg during the colonial era. Museum leaders agreed to expand the narrative, but there was a major impediment. In all its rooms of carefully restored pieces, Williamsburg had

Lonnie G. Bunch moderates a panel on the "Heroes of the Civil Rights Movement: Views from the Front Line" at the Civil Rights Summit at the LBJ Presidential Library in Austin, Texas. In 2019, Bunch was named secretary of the Smithsonian.
Photo by Lauren Gerson

preserved no objects related to the enslaved people who lived there. Thus the museum's first programs on slavery relied on actors and inventive theater techniques rather than on physical artifacts. In 1994 Colonial Williamsburg reenacted a slave auction, complete with a reconstructed slave block. It was the brainchild of Christy Coleman, CW's director of African American interpretation. The NAACP protested, calling the staged event "traumatic" and "trivializing." Taking such a professional risk, Coleman later recalled, "was a gut-wrenching experience . . . but after it was all said and done, people were . . . glad that it happened. And it was a sea change for museums. The word was, 'if Williamsburg can depict [a slave auction], certainly we can talk about [slavery] at our sites and on our tours.'"[141]

Following the slave auction reenactment, other sites in Virginia, including Thomas Jefferson's Monticello and James and Dolley Madison's Montpelier, also created interpretative programs about the enslaved people who had toiled there. Virginia was not the only state where museums began to confront the material evidence of slavery. In the mid-1970s, archaeologists started to dig around 11 former slave dwellings on the grounds of the Hermitage, Andrew Jackson's Tennessee home. Meat bones, religious charms, coins, and weapons led to conclusions about slaves' diets, beliefs, economy, and power relations with plantation owners. Around the nation, historical societies slowly dug out slave auction flyers, bills of sale, flyers offering bounty for captured escapees, and other archival evidence of slavery buried deep in storage.

Of course, some African Americans didn't trust mainstream museums to collect and interpret their history, especially given the prominence of museums that still interpreted Civil War– and Jim Crow–era artifacts to tell stories that honored the Confederacy. How could a collection assembled by the families of Confederate soldiers or even well-meaning but detached professionals and academics tell a community's true stories? Shouldn't African Americans take charge of how their history was being collected and interpreted? Activists initiated a black museum movement. In 1961 Margaret Burroughs founded the Ebony Museum (now DuSable Museum of African American

History) in Chicago and in 1965 Charles Wright followed with a museum in the basement of his Detroit obstetrics practice. To gather artifacts, Wright asked Detroit residents to look in their attics or basements for maps, letters, or pictures that would "unravel the mysteries of the American negro."[142]

In the Anacostia neighborhood of Washington, D.C., and in New York City's Harlem, black leaders began to work with their communities to develop art and cultural exhibits to advance black pride. Soon other cities—Dallas (1974), Philadelphia (1976), and Los Angeles (1979)—had organized museums of black culture and history.[143] The goal, according to Mabel O. Wilson, author of *Negro Building: Black Americans in the World of Fairs and Museums*, was to assemble "historical evidence that blacks had been vital contributors to the nation's prosperity [and] . . . to detail the legacy of forced servitude under enslavement and the untenable costs of racial oppression."[144]

Like the earliest museums in the United States, these institutions often were founded before they had buildings or collections. Community members operated under a sense of scarcity and duty that echoed the urgency of 19th-century collectors. In 1982 Byron Rushing, then-director of the Museum of Afro-American History in Boston, called on black Americans to start collecting their heritage right away: "Collecting black material culture is . . . not a game or a hobby. It is part of a life-and-death struggle . . . to control what is collected about us [and] to take a step closer to independent interpretations of our historical condition."[145]

Curators from black-run museums searched local churches, barbershops, and other businesses. They asked for objects like scrapbooks, quilts, photographs, and baseball uniforms. To get what you need, Rushing suggested, "Invite yourself, get invited, to look through attics and cellars. Call people when you hear they're moving. Read obituaries. Let lawyers, ministers, undertakers know you are collecting." In addition to gathering what they could about family and community life, activists saved important buildings and burial grounds. In 1981 a coalition lobbied to save the Lorraine Motel in Memphis, site of Martin Luther King Jr.'s assassination, from demolition and turn it into a museum. Citizens in Henning, TN, founded the Alex Haley Museum, preserving the *Roots* author's boyhood home and porch, where he listened to his grandparents tell the stories that inspired his masterpiece.

The 1990s witnessed a surge of African American collections and the founding of institutions, such as the National Voting Rights Museum in Selma, AL (1991); the National Civil Rights Museum alongside the restored Lorraine Motel (1991); Birmingham Civil Rights Institute (1992); an expanded Charles H. Wright Museum of African American History in Detroit (1997–1998); and, most significantly, the founding of the National Museum of African American History and Culture on the National Mall (2003). African American archaeology projects spread to historic museums in northern and midwestern towns that had been active in the Underground Railroad movement.

Yet artifacts were still extremely rare, and museums competed fiercely for them. In 2001 an online auction website announced that the Montgomery, AL, bus on which Rosa Parks had launched the famous boycott was for sale. For years the bus sat in an Alabama field, storing rusty tools; now its owner wanted to cash in. Bidding was fierce. The Henry Ford Museum and Greenfield Village in Dearborn, MI, won out to the tune of $492,000, plus the costs of restoration. Steven Hamp, the museum's director, declared the prize acquisition to be the single most important artifact of the civil rights movement.

Not possessing the Ford Museum's budget, other museums relied on grassroots connections to acquire artifacts. At the Birmingham Institute an amateur col-

**Rosa Parks refused to sit in the back of this Montgomery, AL, public bus in 1955, helping to launch the civil rights movement in the United States. It is on display at the Henry Ford Museum in Michigan.**
Photo from Wikimedia Commons

A display of buttons recovered in archaeological excavations of sites at James Madison's Montpelier in Virginia, where enslaved families lived, is meant to reinforce the idea of the individuality and unique identities of members of the enslaved community.
Photo: Chris Danemayer; courtesy of the Montpelier Foundation; caption: Elizabeth Chew

lector donated shards of glass he had gathered off the street after the 1960s racist attack at the 16th Street Baptist Church that killed four young girls. In 2002 the Tennessee Legislature granted the Civil Rights Museum in Memphis the right to display unsealed police evidence from King's assassination. Items such

The South Yard, located adjacent to the Madison House, contained three slave quarters, two smokehouses, and a kitchen. As of 2020, all six buildings were being reconstructed based on intensive archaeological investigations.
Photo: Terry Brock; courtesy of the Montpelier Foundation; caption: Elizabeth Chew

as a bullet found in King's body and a gun seized from assassin James Earl Ray packed an emotional wallop.

Perhaps the most gut-wrenching civil rights–era artifact to enter a museum collection was donated by a family whose tragedy helped to ignite the movement. In 1955, Emmett Till, an innocent 14-year-old African American boy, was murdered by an angry white mob in a small town in Mississippi. A jury acquitted the killers. In 2005, the case was reopened. Till's body was exhumed in order to gather more evidence. It was at this point that the family made a stunning decision: to donate Till's original casket—made famous in photos and media coverage of the tragedy—to the National Museum of African American History and Culture. "It's going to speak louder than pictures," explained Till's cousin Simeon Wright. "I hope it's going to make people think 'If I had been there in 1955, I would have done all I could to help that family.' If it could just evoke just that one thought in someone, it would be enough, because then they would go out and help their fellow man, their community and the church and the school, wherever. . . . That's all I want."[146]

The difficulties of piecing together objects that documented past injustices only underscored museums'

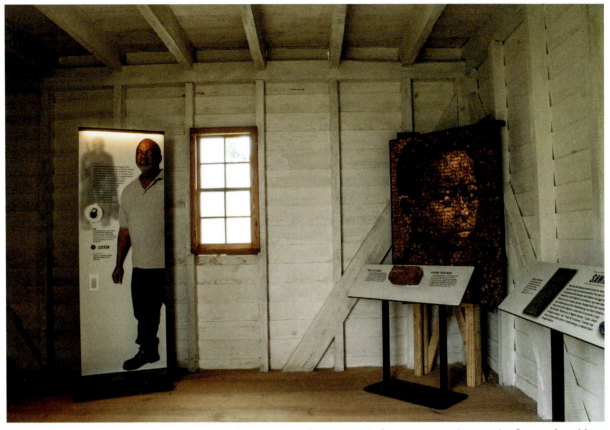

This reconstructed slave dwelling at James Madison's Montpelier in Virginia features a mosaic portrait of an enslaved boy, made from archaeologically recovered brick fragments. Bricks at Montpelier were made by enslaved women and children and often retain the fingerprints of their makers, as the one on the panel in front of the mosaic does.
Mosaic: E Pluribus Unum by Rebecca Warde, 2017; photo: Chris Danemayer; courtesy of the Montpelier Foundation; caption: Elizabeth Chew

resolve to be more proactive in the collecting of pivotal historical events. Alongside the efforts of African American historians and activists to document their community's history, in 1978 a group of Holocaust survivors and politicians announced plans for a museum about the Holocaust in Washington, D.C. They worked with the same sense of urgency that spurred other collectors. In the wake of a rising movement of Holocaust deniers, they realized the need to show people evidence of what had happened.

Researchers traveled to Europe to visit concentration camps and ghetto sites. They saw that the camps, now state museums in Poland, possessed horrific evidence: bags of human hair, victims' suitcases, and leftover canisters of Zyklon-B gas. The Majdanek Camp had hundreds of thousands of shoes that had been ripped off the feet of victims, so they asked for

4,000. It was important that items be donated, not purchased. No one wanted to create a market for the evidence of evil.

Caring for such objects was "overwhelmingly painful" to museum staff. "Professionally, I had been used to dealing with beautiful things," said Registrar Emily Dyer. "We [the collections staff] had to try to steel ourselves from becoming emotionally involved, but of course that was not always possible." There were also delicate conservation challenges. Artifacts often arrived battered and dirty, but it was not appropriate to restore them to their former pristine condition. For example, the museum acquired an encrusted milk can in which archives had been buried so they would survive the war. Conservator Steven Weintraub developed a special process to preserve the mud that clung to the can, since the poor condition was important to its story.

The U.S. Holocaust Memorial Museum displays a few of the many hundreds of thousands of shoes that the Nazi concentration camps removed from victims' feet before sending them to the gas chambers.

In 1985, San Francisco's GLBT Historical Society began to archive materials pertaining to "San Francisco's vast Queer past."[147] These included historic underground publications, letters, recordings, archives related to the AIDS crisis, and ephemera including clothing once worn by the assassinated politician Harvey Milk, the first openly gay official elected in California. GLBTHS showed these collections at Pride parades and public libraries, and in 2011 opened a permanent exhibition space at the edge of San Francisco's famed Castro District.

As historian Edward Linenthal has observed, "No longer is there a lengthy period between events and the urge to memorialize."[148] Potent memory work in the form of museum collecting began to take place in the immediate aftermath of calamities. In 2001, within hours of the September 11 terrorist attack, the Library of Congress began to collect blogs commenting on the event; a day later, staff launched a project to collect oral histories. New York museums immediately began to archive the experience with makeshift exhibitions of photographs. Within days, with the support of New York Port Authority, curators went to the Fresh Kills landfill in Staten Island, where World Trade Cen-

ter debris was being piled. They tagged melted steel, ash-covered computer disks, carbonized furniture—anything they felt worthy of being preserved as a "tactile, three-dimensional expression of the unspeakable scale" of the disaster.

As the *New York Times* stated, "curators began the physically and intellectually exhausting work [of collecting] even as the firefighters were still battling fires. . . . Relying on a mixture of professional experience, aesthetic judgment and a strong dose of gut reaction, they picked out objects from amid the 1.4 million tons of debris to save . . . items that are valuable by virtue of their connection to cultural history, like Judy Garland's ruby-red 'Wizard of Oz' slippers at the Smithsonian."

It may seem hard-hearted to compare rummaging through the September 11 landfill (or other sites of disaster) to collecting popular culture. But the *Times* had a point. So many people experienced the terror attacks through the lens of mass media. Many turned to museums to help make sense of these events. Museum collections had entered a new era. They were now expected to document the full spectrum of the human experience, from the sublime to the tragic—and to do so almost instantly.

In 1994, former camp prisoners, their families, and volunteers reassembled a barracks from the Heart Mountain War Relocation Center in WY (pictured here) inside the Japanese American National Museum in Los Angeles.
Japanese American National Museum (Gift of Mori Shimada, 92.10.2DE)

Visitors learn about Queer history through artifacts and stories displayed by the GLBT Historical Society in San Francisco.
Photo: Gerard Koskovich, GLBT Historical Society, 2019

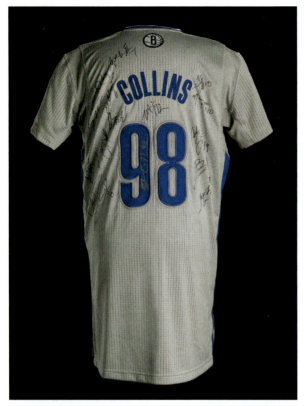

In 2013, Jason Collins became the first openly gay athlete to play in any of the four major American pro sports leagues. The next year, his number 98 jersey—with a number he chose to honor Matthew Shepard, a gay college student beaten to death in 1998—became a top-seller on NBA.com.

Collection of the Smithsonian National Museum of African American History and Culture, Gift of Jason Collins

\* \* \*

A finished Museum is a dead Museum, and a dead Museum is a useless Museum.

—G. BROWN GOODE, 1891[149]

What shall museums collect? First of all, ideas.

—JOHN COTTON DANA, 1917[150]

By the early 21st century, as museum collections continued to grow, stretch, and emerge in new digital formats, many questions remained. But one thing was clear. Museums had gained an immense amount of cultural knowledge in their century of collecting. They had learned that one museum's white elephant is another's treasure; and vice versa. They had learned that possession is not nine-tenths of the law. And, like a child advancing into a new stage of development, they had learned the beauty of being open to figuring out new

ways to share their treasures with all the people who cared about them. "Not meaning to denigrate the immense importance of museum objects and their care," wrote museum theorist Elaine Gurian in 1999, "they, like props in a brilliant play, are necessary but alone are not sufficient."[151] Museums' value to society had fundamentally shifted from amassing, housing, and caring for collections to serving as places that use collections to gather people, tell stories, and spark ideas. Accessibility, education, empathy, and exhibition were the way to keep objects and those ideas alive and meaningful.

Perhaps most importantly, museums had learned that an object's meaning is like a prism: it changes with time and according to the perspective of who is looking at it and from which angle. This leads to the questions that museums continue to debate. Which objects belong in museums? Which don't? Should museums categorize objects as art, scientific specimens, and historical evidence in order to keep track of them? Should there be museums focused solely on marginalized populations and their untold stories? Or should the items we collect be woven together to tell new, more complex and nuanced stories about the United States and the world? Which stories and myths do we keep intact while we decolonize museum collections? What kind of encyclopedia of the world should museums preserve for future generations?

In 2018, collectors and curators at the Baltimore Museum of Art attempted to answer these questions through what its director, Christopher Bedford, called "an unusual and radical act." The issue at hand was BMA's relevance to its populace. In a city whose population is two-thirds African American, the museum lacked significant work by artists of color. Baltimore native Amy Sherald had painted First Lady Michelle Obama's portrait, on view in the National Portrait Gallery, but prices for her works (as well as those of other star artists) were so high that Baltimore couldn't afford them. Previous tax incentives for collectors to purchase and donate the works were long gone.[152] Thus, to raise the funds, BMA deaccessioned and sold seven works by "blue chip" white male artists to build a "war chest to acquire work by contemporary women and artists of color." Amy Elias, a BMA board member whose donated Andy Warhol was among the paintings sold, offered an apt reflection on the field's new direction. "Visions change," she said. "Just because you looked at things one way years ago, doesn't mean you look at them the same way now."[153]

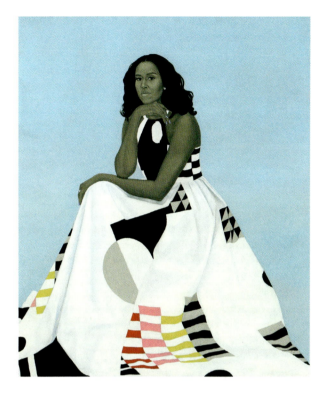

The Baltimore Museum of Art deaccessioned artwork in order to build its collection of pieces by contemporary African American artists like Amy Sherald, famous for painting the portrait of First Lady Michelle Obama. Michelle LaVaughn Robinson Obama, by Amy Sherald, oil on linen, 2018.

**Interior of the Baltimore Museum of Art**
© Michael Ventura

## NOTES

1. J. Paul Getty, quoted in Jason Felch and Ralph Frammolino, *Chasing Aphrodite: The Hunt for Looted Antiquities at the World's Richest Museum* (Boston: Houghton Mifflin, 2011), 17.

2. Roberta Conner, "Tamastslikt Cultural Institute," in Gail Anderson, *Mission Matters: Relevance and Museums in the 21st Century* (Lanham, MD: Rowman & Littlefield, 2019), 120.

3. S. Dillon Ripley, *The Sacred Grove* (Washington, D.C.: Smithsonian Institution Press, 1969), 23.

4. Institute of Museum and Library Sciences, *Collecting to Collections: A Report to the Nation* (2010), 2. AAM's 1994 publication *Museums Count* defines a collection as "discrete items such as a painting, a mounted bald eagle, or a locomotive. Lots/taxa are groups of small objects counted as a group, e.g., insects. Archival materials are documentary materials such as a correspondence found in a historic house, or a scientist's field notes. Books are different from archival materials. They are defined as printed, bound materials that are part of a collection. Finally [are] sites, structures, and acres of land that are used for educational purposes, such as a historic farmstead, a house designed by a famous architect of a botanical garden." The aggregate rate of collection growth is discussed in Stephen E. Weil, ed., *A Deaccession Reader* (Washington, D.C.: American Association of Museums, 1997), 2–3.

5. Trevor Jones, Plenary Session, Iowa Museum Association, October 6, 2015, accessed November 1, 2019, http://www.activecollections.org/thought-pieces/2015/10/23/active-collections-rethinking-the-role-of-collections-in-your-museum.

6. Charles Eliot Norton, quoted in Steven Conn, *Museums and American Intellectual Life, 1876–1926* (Chicago: University of Chicago Press, 1998), 43.

7. Another influential dealer was the late-19th-century French art dealer Paul Durand-Ruel, who foresaw that Impressionist painting would have a ready audience of willing American buyers. Sometimes called the "man who invented Impressionism," in 1886, working with the American Art Association, Durand-Ruel exhibited some 300 Impressionist works by then-unknown artists like Monet and Renoir in New York, helping to develop significant private collections that eventually ended up in major U.S. museums. See "Documenting the Gilded Art: New York City Art Exhibitions at the Turn of the 20th Century," New York Art Resources Consortium, https://gildedage2.omeka.net/exhibits/show/highlights/galleries/durandruel.

8. This account was synthesized from many sources, including S. H. Behrman, *Duveen* (New York: Random House, 1952); Meryle Secrest, *Duveen: A Life in Art* (New York: Knopf, 2004); Philipp Blom, *To Have and to Hold: An Intimate History of Collectors and Collecting* (Woodstock, N.Y.: Overlook Press, 2002), 124–36; Nathaniel Burt, *Palaces for the People: A Social History of the American Art Museum* (Boston: Little, Brown and Company, 1977); Aline B. Saarinen, *The Proud Possessors* (New York: Conde Nast, 1958); Edward Samuels, *Bernard Berenson: The Making of a Legend* (Cambridge, MA: Belknap Press, 1987), 195; and Richard Wollheim, "Berenson," *Spectator*, March 25, 1960, 435.

9. David Edward Finley, *A Standard of Excellence: Andrew W. Mellon Founds the National Gallery of Art* (Washington, D.C.: Smithsonian Institution Press, 1973), 21. Finley directed the National Gallery of Art from 1938 to 1956.

10. For a history of art thefts in museums, see Simon Houpt, *Museum of the Missing: A History of Art Theft* (New York: Sterling, 2006). Houpt notes that the Gardner Museum was so concerned that the condition of the works be kept pristine (in the hopes that they would someday be returned) that they issued a press release on the 15th anniversary of the theft, pleading with whoever had the paintings that they be stored in proper temperature and humidity conditions (p. 73).

11. John Anderson, *Art Held Hostage: The Battle over the Barnes Collection* (New York: W. W. Norton & Company, 2003); Jason Felch and Ralph Frammolino, *Chasing Aphrodite: The Hunt for Looted Antiquities at the World's Richest Museum* (New York: Houghton Mifflin, 2011); Dorothy Kosinski, "This Art Museum Was Founded in Response to a Pandemic Death. It Has Much to Teach Us Now," *ARTnews*, April 3, 2020; and Grayson Harris Lane, "Duncan Phillips and the Phillips Memorial Gallery: A Patron and Museum in Formation, 1918–1940" (doctoral dissertation, Boston University, 2002).

12. Douglas and Elizabeth Rigby, *Lock, Stock and Barrel: The Story of Collecting* (Philadelphia: J. B. Lippincott, 1944), 286–87; Deborah Franklin, "When One Man's Castle Was His Home," *Via* (January/February 2003): 39; Blom, *To Have and to Hold*, 133; Victoria Kastner, *Castle: The Biography of a Country Home* (New York: Harry N. Abrams, 2000); and David Nasaw, *The Chief: The Life of William Randolph Hearst* (Boston: Houghton Mifflin, 2000).

13. David Goodrich, *Art Fakes in America* (New York: Viking Press, 1973), 81.

14. Saarinen, *Proud Possessors*, 61.

15. For an analysis of early art tariff laws and their impact on art collecting, see Kimberly Orcutt, "Buy American? The Debate over the Art Tariff," *American Art* 16, no. 3 (Fall 2002).

16. Calvin Tompkins, *Merchants and Masterpieces: The Story of the Metropolitan Museum of Art* (New York: E. P. Dutton & Co., 1970), 296. Newspaper quotes taken from "Art Note," *New York Times*, March 23, 2013.

17. Wilhelm von Bode, quoted in Samuels, *Bernard Berenson*, 195.

18. Albert C. Barnes, letter to John Dewey, quoted in George E. Hein, *Progressive Museum Practice: John Dewey and Democracy* (Walnut Creek, CA: Left Coast Press, 2012), 104.

19. Behrman, *Duveen*, 28; "Mellon & Madonna," *Time* (March 4, 1935): 32.

20. Andrew Mellon, letter to Franklin D. Roosevelt, December 22, 1936, in Finley, *Standard of Excellence*, 47.

21. There are many versions of the story behind Mellon's collecting and tax scandals. A sympathetic one is relayed by his son Paul in *Reflections in a Silver Spoon* (New York: William Morrow & Co., 1992).

22. Valentiner described Rivera as a "strange looking heavyset man, wearing a black serape and a large Mexican hat" and Kahlo as wearing a "large reboso, a white veil over her forehead, a red rose in her hair." Quoted in Margaret Stern, *The Passionate Eye* (Detroit: Wayne State University Press, 1980), 189.

23. John Cotton Dana, *The New Museum: Selected Writings by John Cotton Dana*, ed. William A. Peniston (Washington, D.C.: American Association of Museums, 1999), 47.

24. Other prominent early collectors of Native American art included Milford Chandler; David T. Vernon (Colter Bay Visitor Center in Grand Teton National Park, WY); Adelph Spohr (Buffalo Bill Historical Center, Cody, WY); Florence Rand Lang (Montclair Art Museum, N.J.); Charles Fletcher Lummis (Southwest Museum, Los Angeles, now under the auspices of the Autry National Center); Mary Cabot Wheelwright (Santa Fe, N.M.); and George Gustav Heye (National Museum of the American Indian, New York, N.Y.), who perhaps assembled the largest early collection of both artwork and archaeological specimens. This research was conducted by Adam Lovell in 2003. See also E. Shepard Krech III and Barbara A. Hall, *Collecting Native America 1870–1960* (Washington, D.C.: Smithsonian Institution Press, 1999). Tulsa's Thomas Gilcrease, an enrolled member of the Creek Nation, was likely the first patron of Native American artists helping to establish the careers of Acee Blue Eagle (Creek/Pawnee), Woody Crumbo (Potawatomi), and Willard Stone (part Cherokee). See Carole Klein, "Patron, Friend, and Collector," in *Thomas Gilcrease* (Tulsa, OK: Gilcrease Museum and the University of Tulsa, 2009), 100.

25. Carol Haralson, ed., *Thomas Gilcrease* (Tulsa, OK: Gilcrease Museum and the University of Tulsa, 2009), 10.

26. Mary Lea Bandy, "Nothing Sacred: Jock Whitney Snares Antiques for Museum," in *The Museum of Modern Art at Mid-Century* (New York: Museum of Modern Art, 1995), 75–103.

27. Texas wasn't alone in this regard; records at the de Young Museum in San Francisco suggest that in the 1920s California collectors coined the term *Californiana* for objects associated with the state's missions and pioneers. Information on Bayou Bend updated on January 16, 2019, from https://www.mfah.org/visit/bayou-bend-collection-and-gardens/.

28. Shirley Moskow, "Henry Francis du Pont: Brief Life of a Passionate Connoisseur: 1880–1969," *Harvard Magazine* (July–August 2003): 40.

29. Louis C. Jones, *The Farmers' Museum* (Cooperstown: New York State Historical Association, 1948).

30. Wendy Moonan, "A Discoverer of Folk Art [Electra Havemeyer Webb]," *New York Times*, January 3, 2003, B43.

31. Osborn's displays were also notable for their colorful mural backdrops of fully fleshed creatures fashioned by an imaginative young artist named Charles R. Knight. Knight would go on to paint dinosaur murals at natural history museums around the country.

32. Carnegie is discussed in Charles Gallenkamp, *Dragon Hunter: Roy Chapman Andrews and the Central Asiatic Expeditions* (New York: Viking, 2001), 38–39; M. Graham Netting, "The Carnegie Museum," *Museum News* (April 1959): 10; and Charlotte M. Porter, "Natural History in the 20th Century: An Oxymoron?" in *Natural History Museums*, eds. Paisley S. Cato and Clyde Jones (Lubbock: Texas Tech University Press, 1991).

33. Roy Chapman Andrews, quoted in Gallenkamp, *Dragon Hunter*, 184. See also James L. Clark, *Good Hunting: Fifty Years of Collecting and Preparing Habitat Groups for the American Museum* (Norman: University of Oklahoma Press, 1966), 89–95. Andrews's handwritten journals available in the library of the American Museum of Natural History begin with his rules for his crew members: "No cussing the weather. No insinuations if there is sand in the soup. No profanity unless of picturesque variety. All male members must share in the pumping of tires."

34. John Roach Stratton, quoted in Constance A. Clark, "The Museum in Modern Babylon" (chapter 2), in *God or Gorilla: Images of Evolution in the Jazz Age* (Baltimore, MD: Johns Hopkins University Press, 2008). This chapter offers a fascinating account of Osborn's use of the museum as a vehicle to communicate his strident positions on eugenics. See also Larry A. Witham, "Museums and Sanctuaries," in *Where Darwin Meets the Bible: Creationists and Evolutionists in America* (London: Oxford University Press, 2002). To read more on Osborn's views, see Edward P. Alexander, *The Museum in America: Innovators and Pioneers* (Walnut Creek, CA: AltaMira Press, 1997), 27; Claudia Roth Pierpont, "The Measure of America," *New Yorker* (March 8, 2004): 48–63; and Charlotte M. Porter, "The Rise of Parnassus: Henry Fairfield Osborn and the Hall of the Age of Man," *Museum Studies Journal* (Spring 1983): 26–34.

35. Kim Masters, "Smithsonian to Charge Fee for Animated Dinosaur Show," *Washington Post*, April 4, 1990, A1, A18.

36. For a detailed discussion on how museums use dinosaur exhibitions to teach evolutionary science, see Judy Diamond and Judy Scotchmoor, "Exhibiting Evolution,"

*Museums and Social Issues: A Journal of Reflective Discourse* 1, no. 1 (Spring 2006): 21–48.

37. See Steve Fiffer, *Tyrannosaurus Sue: The Extraordinary Saga of the Largest, Most Fought over T. Rex Ever* (New York: W. H. Freeman & Co., 2000); Lauren Grant and Marie Malaro, "Disputed Bones: The Case of a Dinosaur Named Sue," ALI-ABA Course of Study Materials (Philadelphia: March 1993), 121–57; and Tessa Gunawan-Gonzalez, unpublished research paper on the Sue controversy (Museum History and Theory Graduate Seminar, John F. Kennedy University, 2002).

38. See Steve Johnson, "With a Skeleton and Megaplanters, the Field Museum Fleshes Out Its Main Hall," *Chicago Tribune*, June 26, 2018, https://www.chicagotribune.com/entertainment/museums/ct-ent-field-museum-makeover-complete-0627-story.html; and Steve Johnson and Phil Geib, "The Dismantling of Sue," *Chicago Tribune*, February 5, 2018, https://www.chicagotribune.com/entertainment/museums/ct-ae-0205-sue-trex-take-down-htmlstory.html. For Sue's original blog post, see "I (SUE the T. rex) am moving to my own place and all y'all are invited," Field Museum, January 30, 2018, accessed January 21, 2019, https://www.fieldmuseum.org/about/press/i-sue-t-rex-am-moving-my-own-place-and-all-yall-are-invited.

39. Warren Allmon, *Evolution and Creationism: A Guide for Museum Docents* (Ithaca, N.Y.: Museum of the Earth, 2005), accessed January 7, 2019, https://www.priweb.org/downloads/education/Docent%20Guide.pdf.

40. David Masci, "For Darwin Day, 6 Facts about the Evolution Debate," Pew Research Center, February 11, 2019, accessed January 20, 2019, http://www.pewresearch.org/fact-tank/2017/02/10/darwin-day/.

41. See Witham, "Museums and Sanctuaries."

42. Kate Sheppard, "Inside Koch's Climate Denial Machine," *Mother Jones* (April 1, 2010), accessed January 11, 2019, https://www.motherjones.com/politics/2010/04/inside-kochs-climate-denial-machine/. See also "Open Letter from Scientists to the American Museum of Natural History," Natural History Museum, January 25, 2018, http://thenaturalhistorymuseum.org/open-letter-from-scientists-to-the-american-museum-of-natural-history/.

43. Sarah Kaplan, "The Smithsonian's Renewed Fossil Hall Sends a Forceful Message about Climate Change," *Washington Post*, May 26, 2019, https://www.washingtonpost.com/national/health-science/the-smithsonians-renewed-fossil-hall-sends-a-forceful-message-about-climate-change/2019/05/25/bc896212-78d2-11e9-b3f5-5673edf2d127_story.html.

44. Franz Boas, quoted in nceds.ucsb.edu, accessed December 29, 2002.

45. James Nason, quoted in Nancy Joseph, "Heading Home: The Burke Museum Returns Artifacts to Northwest Tribes," *Arts and Sciences Perspectives* (October 2001), https://artsci.washington.edu/news/2001-10/heading-home.

46. David Hancocks, *A Different Nature: The Paradoxical World of Zoos and Their Uncertain Future* (Berkeley: University of California Press, 2001), 92.

47. "Take the Child Outdoors," *Museum News Letter* (American Association of Museums) 1, no. 3 (November 1917): 1–2.

48. Martin Gammon, *Deaccessioning and Its Discontents: A Critical History* (Cambridge, MA: MIT Press, 2018), 125, 279.

49. Dan Monroe, "Native American Repatriation: History, Requirements, and Outlook," *Western Museums Conference Newsletter* (Winter 1990/1991): 3.

50. George Dorsey, quoted in Stephen E. Nash and Gary M. Feinman, eds., "Curators, Collections and Contexts: Anthropology at the Field Museum, 1893–2002," *Anthropology*, no. 36 (September 2003): 89.

51. Allyson Lazar, "Repatriating More than You May Know: The Problem of Native American Objects and Past Museum Conservation Practices" (master's project, John F. Kennedy University, 2000), 39.

52. Laurence Vail Coleman, *The Museum in America* (Washington, D.C.: American Association of Museums, 1939), 60.

53. Francis P. McManamon, "The Antiquities Act: Setting Basic Preservation Policies," *Cultural Resources Management* (Washington, D.C.: National Park Service, 1996).

54. Nason, quoted in Joseph, "Heading Home."

55. Kenn Harper, *Give Me My Father's Body: The Life of Minik, the New York Eskimo* (South Royalton, VT: Steerforth Press, 2000). See also Geoffrey Hellman, *Bankers, Bones and Beetles: The First Century of the American Museum of Natural History* (New York: Natural History Press, 1968), 89.

56. Stephen E. Weil, "From Being about Something to Being about Somebody: The Ongoing Transformation of the American Museum," *Daedalus* (Summer 1999): 229.

57. Lynn H. Nicholas, *The Rape of Europa* (New York: Alfred A. Knopf, 1994), 3–5.

58. Other appointed specialists to the Roberts Commission/Monuments Men were David Edward Finley (director, National Gallery of Art); Horace Jayne (curator, Metropolitan Museum of Art); George L. Stout (conservator, Fogg Art Museum); Paul Sachs (Harvard University); Francis Henry Taylor (director, Metropolitan Museum of Art); and John Walker (chief curator, National Gallery of Art). A semifictional film about this era titled *Monuments Men* was released in 2014.

59. A. Noblecourt, *Protection of Cultural Property in the Event of an Armed Conflict* (Paris: UNESCO, 1956), 125; and Hermann Warner Williams Jr. (director, Corcoran Gallery of Art), "The Museums' New Dilemma," *Museum News* (March 1, 1951): 7.

60. For a deeper (and fascinating) account of the collecting of Chinese art in the United States, see Karl Meyer and Shareen Blair Brysac, *The China Collectors: America's Century-Long Hunt for Asian Art Treasures* (New York: St. Martin's Press, 2015).

61. See "The True Story of Miss Kyoto," Boston Children's Museum, accessed April 10, 2019, http://japanesehouse.bostonchildrensmuseum.org/sites/default/files/resource-pdfs/True%20Story%20of%20Miss%20Kyoto.pdf.

62. Beginning in the early 1950s, the number of exhibitions of Japanese art in U.S. museums increased dramatically. See Yoshiaki Shimizu, "Japan in American Museums: But Which Japan?" *Art Bulletin* 83, no. 1 (2001): 123–34, doi:10.2307/3177193.

63. Carl Wittke, *The First Fifty Years: The Cleveland Museum of Art 1916–1966* (Cleveland, OH: Cleveland Museum of Art, 1966), 114. Analogous art collecting efforts in Latin America also arose as a result of World War II, fueled by American businesses desiring a presence in Central and South America. See Suzanne B. Reiss, *Art, Artists, Museums and the San Francisco Museum of Art: Oral Interview of Grace L. McCann Morley* (Berkeley: Regional Cultural History Project, University of California, 1960), 42.

64. Francine du Plessix, "Collectors: Mary and Leigh Block," *Art in America* 54 (September 1966): 64–65. See Pamela G. Smart, "Sacred Modern: An Ethnography of an Art Museum" (doctoral dissertation, Rice University, 1997), for the history of the de Menil collection. See also Sylvia Hochfield, "Lydia Winston Malbin: A Futurist Eye," *ARTnews* (April 1988): 91–92.

65. Discussed in Sophy Burnham, *The Art Crowd* (New York: David McKay Company, 1973); Daniel M. Fox, *Engines of Culture: Philanthropy and Art Museums* (Madison: State Historical Society of Wisconsin, 1963); and Peter B. Trippi, *Association of Art Museum Directors: A Review of Its First 75 Years: 1916–1991* (New York: Association of Art Museum Directors, 1992), 10–11.

66. Victor D'Amico, quoted in Carol Morgan, "From Modernist Utopia to Cold War Reality," in *The Museum of Modern Art at Mid-Century: Continuity and Change*, ed. John Elderfield (New York: Museum of Modern Art, 1995), 158.

67. Henry Huntington, quoted in James Thorpe, *Henry Edwards Huntington: A Biography* (Berkeley: University of California Press, 1994), 438.

68. Sheldon Keck, *Museum News* (September 1964): 13.

69. "Ethics and Professionalism," *Museum News* (November/December 1988): 41. Marjorie Cohn, curator of prints at the Fogg Art Museum, shares Paul Sachs's "phone a director-pal" story in Janet Tassel, "Reverence for the Object," *Harvard Magazine* (September/October 2002): 54.

70. Marion Todd, "Solving the Problems of Art by X-ray," *American Magazine of Art* 17, no. 11 (November 1926): 578–81. The world of art fakes has inspired its share of legends and intrigues. For example, in 1923, the Met's curators purchased what they believed to be a small bronze horse from 5th century, B.C., Greece. In 1967, addressing an audience of 800 art experts at a seminar on art forgery, Joseph Veach Noble, the Met's vice director for administration, reported that while he was fond of the work, it was a fraud. The speech caused a great stir—Met director Thomas Hoving likened the horse to a cheating spouse—and removed it from view. The accusations of cuckoldry turned out to be false. In 1972, competing specialists had conducted meticulous scientific experiments and declared that the horse was authentic.

71. Caroline K. Keck, *A Handbook on the Care of Paintings* (Nashville, TN: American Association for State and Local History, 1965), 27; and Todd, "Solving the Problems."

72. The lab at Oberlin College founded by conservator Richard D. Buck was preceded by one at the University of Delaware, founded in 1951 by historian Charles Montgomery. During the 1950s, Oberlin was the site of the Intermuseums Conservation Association, jointly sponsored by museums in Buffalo, N.Y.; Columbus and Toledo, OH; Indianapolis; and Davenport, IA. As stated on pages 29–31 of the college's fall 1952 *Bulletin*, the lab's goal was to (1) embrace the idea of conservation, a long-term plan for the maintenance of the structure and artistic integrity of museum objects, and (2) provide these services as a professional rather than a commercial enterprise.

73. Arthur Beale, "A National Strategy for the Conservation of Collections," *Collections* 2, no. 1 (August 2005): 11–28.

74. Dorothy H. Dudley and Irma Bezold, *Museum Registration Methods* (Washington, D.C.: American Association of Museums, 1958).

75. A. L. Freundlich, "Museum Registration by Computer," *Museum News* (February 1966).

76. Jonathan Walters, "Tracking Advances: As Technological Advances in Conservation Occur, Conservators Are Developing a New Approach in Their Museum Role," *Museum News* (January/February 1989).

77. See "The Archimedes Palimpsest Project," Archimedes Palimpsest, accessed August 25, 2019, http://www.archimedespalimpsest.org.

78. *Museum News Letter* (AAM) 1, no. 7 (March 1918): 1.

79. As Stephen E. Weil explains in "Deaccession Practices in American Museums," *Museum News* (February 1987): 44–50:

> The logic [of deaccessioning] appears inescapable. For those museums that collect in "open" fields, i.e., those in

which new objects are constantly created—history, technology, and contemporary art are all examples—the only alternatives to deaccessioning are to accept the expense of continually increasing storage facilities, maintenance budgets, and staff, or else to cease collecting entirely. The first may be impractical. The second would be irresponsible. By contrast, the adoption of a soundly based deaccession policy is both practical and responsible.

80. Michael O'Hare, "Museums Can Change—Will They?" *Democracy: A Journal of Ideas* (Spring 2015), accessed November 9, 2019, https://democracyjournal.org/magazine/36/museums-can-changewill-they/.

81. Martha Morris, "Deaccessioning," in *The New Museum Registration Methods*, eds. Rebecca Buck and Jean Gilmore (Washington, D.C.: American Association of Museums, 1998), 167.

82. Charlie the Elephant is mentioned in the *Museum News* (June 15, 1942): 4. See also "Smithsonian Gives Its Cannon," *Museum News* (November 1, 1942): 4.

83. See "Direct Care of Collections: Ethics, Guidelines and Recommendations," AAM, updated March 2019, https://www.aam-us.org/programs/ethics-standards-and-professional-practices/direct-care-of-collections/.

84. Tompkins, *Merchants and Masterpieces*, 332; Thomas Hoving, *Making Mummies Dance: Inside the Metropolitan Museum of Art* (New York: Simon & Schuster, 1994), 290–306.

85. John Rewald, "Should Hoving Be De-accessioned," reprinted in Weil, *A Deaccession Reader*, 34.

86. Trippi, 62. See also Marie Malaro, "Deaccessioning—The American Perspective," in Weil, *A Deaccession Reader*, 49; and Steven Miller, "The Pitfalls and Promises of Deaccessioning," in *AAM 1991 Conference Sourcebook* (Washington, D.C.: American Association of Museums, 1991), 23–30.

87. To read about other late-20th-century deaccessioning scandals, see Andrew Decker, "Museums under Scrutiny," in *Museum News* (November/December 1988): 28–29; and Kevin M. Guthrie, *The New York Historical Society: Lessons from One Nonprofit's Long Struggle for Survival* (San Francisco: Jossey-Bass, 1996). For a more recent and very thorough investigation of the history of deaccessioning, see Martin Gammon, *Deaccessioning and Its Discontents: A Critical History* (Cambridge, MA: MIT Press, 2018).

88. Graham Beale, quoted in Randy Kennedy, "The Agony of Suspense in Detroit," *New York Times*, October 2, 2013, accessed November 1, 2019, https://www.nytimes.com/2013/10/03/arts/design/detroit-institute-of-arts-copes-with-threat-of-art-selloff.html.

89. Maureen B. Collins, "Pensions or Paintings? The Detroit Institute of Arts from Bankruptcy to Grand Bargain," *University of Miami Business Law Review* 24, no. 1 (2015), http://repository.law.miami.edu/umblr/vol24/iss1/3.

90. Joseph Veach Noble, "Report of the AAM Policy Committee," *Museum News* (May 1971): 22–23.

91. In 1997, Boston's Museum of Fine Arts put jades, pottery, and burial urns on display from one of the looted Mayan sites Coggins had documented. The objects had been obtained by a trustee before laws had been enacted prohibiting their import. Technically, the antiquities did not *belong* to the MFA; they were on loan. And, as then-director Alan Shestack pointed out, it was awkward to question a trustee's integrity: "You cook your own goose very quickly if you tell a museum member or board member that you will not accept their gifts on quasi-legal or ethical grounds."

92. There are many excellent sources on the discussions that led to the 1970 UNESCO Convention on Illicit Traffic. Those consulted by this author for this section include Allison Akbay, "Collecting Cultural Property: Art Museums and Pre-Columbian Artwork" (master's project, John F. Kennedy University, 2003); Clemency Coggins, "Illicit Traffic of Pre-Columbian Antiquities," *Art Journal* 29, no. 1 (1969): 94–98; Curators of the University Museum of Pennsylvania, "The Philadelphia Declaration," *Antiquity* 44 (April 1970): 171; Laura Green, "Guatemala and the Museum of Fine Arts, Boston: Law, Ethics and Cultural Patrimony" (unpublished paper that won the Marie Malaro Excellence in Research and Teaching Award at the George Washington University, Spring 2000); Marie Papageorge Kouroupas and Ann J. Guthrie, "The Culture Property Act: What It Means for Museums," *Museum News* (June 1985): 47; P. M. Messenger, *The Ethics of Collecting Cultural Property*, 2nd ed. (Albuquerque: University of New Mexico Press, 1999); Karl E. Meyer, *The Plundered Past* (New York: Atheneum Press, 1973); Patrick J. O'Keefe, *Commentary on the UNESCO 1970 Convention on Illicit Traffic* (Leicester, U.K.: Institute of Art and Law, 2000); Linda F. Pinkerton, "Word to the Wise: Scrutinize Objects of Questionable Origin," *Museum News* (November/December 1989): 28–31; and Colin Renfrew, *Loot, Legitimacy and Ownership* (London: Duckworth, 2000).

93. See Felch and Frammolino, *Chasing Aphrodite*, 18–19; and Thomas Hoving, "Super Art Gems of New York City," *Artnet*, 2001, accessed January 19, 2019, http://www.artnet.com/magazine/features/hoving/hoving6-29-01.asp.

94. As Marilyn Phelan discusses in her chapter "Legal and Ethical Considerations in Museum Acquisitions," in *Museum Philosophy for the Twenty-First Century*, ed. Hugh H. Genoways (Lanham, MD: Rowman & Littlefield, 2006), 30,

> In 1999, AAM submitted an amicus curiae brief supporting an art collector [who was also a benefactor of the New York Metropolitan Museum of Art] in importing into the United States a looted third century B.C. Phiale . . . [on the ground that disallowing the import

would] threaten the ability of U.S. museums to collect … and make available for public exhibition objects from around the world.

95. James Cuno, *Museums Matter: In Praise of the Encyclopedic Museum* (Chicago: University of Chicago Press, 2011), 76–77, 97. For others who argue on behalf of museums' rights to keep antiquities, see Tiffany Jenkins, *Keeping Their Marbles: How the Treasures of the Past Ended Up in Museums and Why They Should Stay There* (Oxford: Oxford University Press, 2016).

96. Felch and Frammolino, *Chasing Aphrodite*, 325.

97. Gary Vikan, *Sacred and Stolen: Confessions of a Museum Director* (New York: SelectBooks, 2016), 268. See also Max Anderson, quoted in Geoff Edgers, "One of the World's Most Respected Curators Vanished from the Art World. Now She Wants to Tell Her Story," *Washington Post*, August 22, 2015.

98. Peter Morrin, quoted in Felch and Frammolino, *Chasing Aphrodite*, 301.

99. Felch and Frammolino, *Chasing Aphrodite*, 11.

100. Frank Howarth, "Decolonizing the Museum Mind," *AAM Center for the Future of Museums Blog*, October 8, 2018, accessed January 17, 2019, aam-us.org.

101. W. J. Holland, quoted in David R. Waters, "W. J. Holland's Speech at the International Congress of Americanists, 13th Session, in 1902," *Annals of the Carnegie Museum* 71, no. 2 (May 28, 2002): 132.

102. Roger Echo-Hawk, *Keepers of Culture: Repatriating Cultural Items under the Native American Graves Protection and Repatriation Act* (Denver: Denver Art Museum, 2002), 176.

103. James D. Nason, "Native American Intellectual Property Rights," in *Borrowed Power: Essays on Cultural Appropriation*, eds. Bruce Ziff and Pratima V. Rao (New Brunswick, N.J.: Rutgers University Press, 1997), 240. For a more detailed analysis of NAGPRA, see Echo-Hawk, *Keepers of Culture*; and Christina F. Kreps, *Liberating Culture: Cross Cultural Perspectives on Museums, Curation and Heritage Preservation* (London: Routledge, 2003). See also the memorandum of December 26, 1990, published in *AAM 1991 Conference Sourcebook*, 75.

104. James Clifford, "Museums as Contact Zones," in *Routes: Travel and Translation in the Late Twentieth Century* (Cambridge, MA: Harvard University Press, 1997), 188–99.

105. Robert Archibald, personal interview, February 19, 2004. For a personal reflection on the Missouri Historical Society's Commanche collection, see Robert Archibald, *A Place to Remember* (Walnut Creek, CA: AltaMira Press, 1999), 56–58.

106. Personal correspondence.

107. James Pepper Henry, quoted in "20 Years and Counting: James Pepper Henry's Multifaceted View of NAGPRA," *Museum News* (November/December 2010); and "By the Numbers: Decolonizing the US Museums," *Museum* (July/August 2019): 6.

108. For an insightful discussion of the impact of digital repatriation on Native knowledge, see Aaron Glass, "Indigenous Ontologies, Digital Futures: Plural Provenances and the Kwakwaka'wakw Collection in Berlin and Beyond," in *Museum as Process: Translating Local and Global Knowledges*, ed. Raymond Silverman (London: Routledge, 2015), 19–44.

109. See Kim Turner, "Improving Cal NAGPRA: Honoring Native American Rights" (master's project, University of San Francisco, 2016), accessed April 6, 2019, https://repository.usfca.edu/capstone/442; and Carl Zimmer, "Tribes' Win in Fight for La Jolla Bones Clouds Hopes for DNA Studies," *New York Times*, January 29, 2016. For a fuller discussion of scientists' counterarguments about repatriation of human remains, see Jenkins, *Keeping Their Marbles*, 303–8.

110. Ethan Coston, "Governor Brown Signs Bill Supporting Repatriation of Indigenous Remains at UC Campuses," *Triton*, October 18, 2018, accessed April 5, 2019, http://triton.news/2018/10/governor-brown-signs-bill-supporting-repatriation-indigenous-remains-uc-campuses/. See also Felicia Mello, "Native American Tribes Clash with UC over Bones of Their Ancestors," *Cal Matters*, July 10, 2018, https://calmatters.org/articles/native-american-tribes-clash-with-uc-over-bones-of-their-ancestors/.

111. George P. Horse Capture, "Survival of Culture," *Museum News* (January/February 1991): 51.

112. Hector Feliciano, *The Lost Museum: The Nazi Conspiracy to Steal the World's Greatest Works of Art* (New York: Basic Books, 1997).

113. Lynn H. Nicholas, *The Rape of Europa* (New York: Alfred A. Knopf, 1994).

114. Stuart E. Eizenstat, "Art Stolen by the Nazis Is Still Missing. Here's How We Can Recover It," *Washington Post*, January 2, 2019, accessed April 4, 2019, https://www.washingtonpost.com/opinions/no-one-should-trade-in-or-possess-art-stolen-by-the-nazis/2019/01/02/01990232-0ed3-11e9-831f-3aa2c2be4cbd_story.html?utm_term=.2c5128adee69.

115. "VMFA Board of Trustees Votes to Return Nazi-Looted Painting," VMFA, October 10, 2018, https://www.vmfa.museum/pressroom/news/vmfa-board-trustees-votes-return-nazi-looted-painting/.

116. Eizenstat, "Art Stolen."

117. Thomas A. Livesay, "A Final Word," *History News* 51, no. 3 (Summer 1996): 32.

118. Kevin Jennings, quoted in Ericka Huggins and Kevin Jennings, "Who Will Tell My Story," *Museum* (March/April 2018): 14.

119. Emilie S. Arnold, "The Wound Is Fresh: Exhibiting Orlando's LGBTQ History in the Shadow of the Pulse

Nightclub Massacre," *Exhibition* 36, no. 2 (Fall 2017): 26–35.

120. G. Ellis Burcaw, "Active Collecting in History Museums," *Museum News* (March 1967): 21. Burcaw's sentiments were echoed in a seminal and widely discussed article by Duncan Cameron of the Brooklyn Museum that appeared five years later: Duncan Cameron, "The Museum: A Temple or the Forum," *Journal of World History*, no. 1 (1972). Cameron argues for the representation of "popular culture, folk art and the life style of . . . the working classes."

121. See Thomas W. Leavitt, "There's Hope for Montclair, NJ," *Museum News* (June 1972); and National Endowment for the Arts, *A Legacy of Leadership: Investing in America's Living Cultural Heritage since 1965* (Washington, D.C.: National Endowment for the Arts, September 2000). The Museum Purchase Plan awarded grants to commission or purchase work from living American artists. Other museums to build collections from this program included the Utah Museum of Fine Arts, the Walker Art Center, and the North Carolina Museum of Art.

122. Mari Carmen Ramirez and Theresa Papanikolas, eds., *Collecting Latin American Art for the 21st Century* (Houston: Museum of Fine Arts, 2002).

123. See John Zarobell, *Art and the Global Economy* (Berkeley: University of California Press, 2017).

124. Art museum curators were also aware of social historians' fascination with the everyday. In 1971, the Art Galleries at the University of California, Santa Barbara, exhibited political posters, stating, "Let this [exhibition] be regarded as a signpost of our politically and culturally self-conscious times, rather than as a work of 'instant history.'" In 1972–1973, curators at the Wichita Art Museum organized a traveling exhibition on "kitsch," featuring "commercial objects, generally shoddy, gawdy, and tawdry" such as plastic ferns, a night-light in the shape of an astronaut, and a pink-plumed ballpoint pen. See Jan von Adlemann, "The Grotesque around Us," *Museum News* (May 1973): 19; and a review of UC Santa Barbara's exhibit catalog in *Museum News* (May 1971): 44.

125. Ellen Roney Hughes, "The Unstifled Muse," in *Exhibiting Dilemmas: Issues of Representation at the Smithsonian*, eds. Amy Henderson and Adrienne L. Kaeppler (Washington, D.C.: Smithsonian Institution Press, 1997), 156–57.

126. Robert McCormick Adams, quoted in Hughes, "Unstifled Muse," 169.

127. Hughes, "Unstifled Muse," 172.

128. Laura Rich, *The Accidental Zillionaire: Demystifying Paul Allen* (Hoboken, N.J.: John Wiley & Sons, 2003), 163–64.

129. L. Thomas Frye, "Museum Collecting for the Twenty-First Century," in *A Common Agenda for History Museums*, ed. Lonn W. Taylor (Nashville, TN: American Association of State and Local Histories, 1987), 9. See also Frye's article, "The Recent Past Is Prologue," *Museum News* (November 1974): 24–27.

130. Scott Eberle and G. Rollie Adams, "Making Room for Big Bird," *History News* (Autumn 1996): 23–24.

131. Juilee Decker, *Museums in Motion*, 3rd ed. (Lanham, MD: Rowman & Littlefield, 2017), 185.

132. Jon-Paul C. Dyson, "Collecting, Preserving, and Interpreting the History of Electronic Games, An Interview with Jon-Paul C. Dyson," *American Journal of Play* 10, no. 1 (Fall 2017), http://www.journalofplay.org/sites/www.journalofplay.org/files/pdf-articles/10-1-interview-dyson.pdf.

133. The Strong Museum was not the only museum to recognize the impact of electronic games on the American psyche. In 2017, the Bullock Museum in Austin, Tex., opened *Pong to Pokemon: The Evolution of Electronic Gaming*. It featured such historic items as a *Space Invaders* arcade cabinet and hand-drawn sketches for the first release of *DOOM Bible*.

134. Lonnie G. Bunch, "Fighting the Good Fight: Museums in an Age of Uncertainty," *Museum News* (March/April 1995): 60.

135. Joy Bivens, Ben Garcia, Porchia Moore, Nikhil Trivedi, and Aletheia Wittman, "Collections: How We Hold the Stuff We Hold in Trust," accessed on #MassActionReadingGroup: Chapter 7, *The Incluseum* (July 2019), 134, https://incluseum.com/2019/07/08/massactionreadinggroup-chapter-7/.

136. John Kuo Wei Tchen, "Creating a Dialogic Museum," in *Museums and Communities: The Politics of Public Culture*, eds. Ivan Karp, Christine Mullen Kreamer, and Steven D. Lavine (Washington, D.C.: Smithsonian Institution Press, 1992), 289.

137. Walter Muir Whitehill, *Independent Historical Societies* (Boston: Harvard University Press, 1962), 404; and Grace Cohen Grossman, *Jewish Museums of the World* (New York: Hugh Lauter Levin Associates, 2003), 30–32, 241–315. See also Rachel M. Howse, "A History of Jewish Archives 1947–Present," *Collections* 2, no. 1 (August 2005): 47–62.

138. Other notable "ethnic museums" of this period include Mexican Fine Arts Center Museum (Pilsen District, Chicago, 1982); the Mexic-Arte Museum (Austin, TX, 1983); and the National Hispanic Cultural Center (Albuquerque, N.M., 1985).

139. Mabel O. Wilson, *Negro Building: Black Americans in the World of Fairs and Museums* (Berkeley: University of California Press, 2012), 297.

140. For a discussion of the relationship between the "*Roots* phenomenon" and the building of museums, see Wilson, *Negro Building*, 297–302.

141. See Christy Coleman, quoted in Chandelis R. Duster, "Meet the Black Woman Reclaiming the Narrative

of the Civil War," NBC News, July 12, 2017, accessed April 10, 2019, https://www.nbcnews.com/news/nbc blk/meet-black-woman-reclaiming-narrative-civil -war-n782006; and Tamara Jones, "Living History or Undying Racism? Colonial Williamsburg Slave Auction Draws Protest, Support," *Washington Post*, October 11, 1994.

142. Wilson, *Negro Building*, 272.

143. Christy S. Coleman, "African American Museums in the Twenty-First Century," in *Museum Philosophy for the Twenty-First Century*, ed. Hugh H. Genoways (Lanham, MD: Rowman & Littlefield, 2006), 151–60.

144. Wilson, *Negro Building*, 297.

145. Byron Rushing, "Afro-Americana: Defining It; Finding It; Collecting It," *Museum News* (January/February 1982): 33–40.

146. See Abbie Callard, "Emmett Till's Casket Goes to the Smithsonian," *Smithsonian* (November 2009), accessed April 10, 2019, https://www.smithsonianmag .com/arts-culture/emmett-tills-casket-goes-to-the -smithsonian-144696940/#XvKu5EbLslbFz26O.99.

147. See GLBT Historical Society, accessed January 6, 2019, https://www.glbthistory.org; and Gerard Koskovich, "Displaying the Queer Past: Purposes, Publics, and Possibilities at the GLBT History Museum," *QED: A Journal in GLBTQ Worldmaking* 1, no. 2 (2014): 61–78.

148. Edward T. Linenthal, "Oklahoma City, September 11 and the 'Lessons' of History," *History News* (Winter 2002): 15.

149. G. Brown Goode, *The Museum of the Future* (Washington, D.C.: Government Printing Office, 1891), 445.

150. Dana, *New Museum*, 40.

151. Elaine Gurian, "The Many Meanings of Objects in Museums," *Daedalus* 128, no. 3, (1999): 165.

152. In 2006, the U.S. Congress eliminated a loophole called "fractional giving," which allowed collectors to donate works to a museum over multiple years in order to claim maximum deductions. For a discussion of contemporary tax incentives for donating art to a museum, see Alicia C. Beyer, "Gone but Not Forgotten: The End of Fractional Giving and the Search for Alternatives," *Columbia Journal of Law and the Arts* 6, no. 3 (2013): 459–89.

153. See "The Baltimore Museum of Art Announces Second Round of Contemporary Art Acquisitions Made with Auction Proceeds," Baltimore Museum of Art, https://artbma.org/documents/press/New_Acquisi tions_Release_final.pdf; and Julia Halperin, "The Baltimore Museum Sold Art to Acquire Work by Underrepresented Artists. Here's What It Bought—and Why It's Only the Beginning," *Artnet*, June 26, 2018, accessed March 22, 2019, https://news.artnet.com/art-world/baltimore-deaccessioning-proceeds-1309481.

# CHAPTER 4

# *The Exhibition*

## From Cases to Spaces

> Nothing is easier than aweing people with vast accumulations ... of knowledge and things. Much harder is conveying information in visible forms that everyone can understand.
>
> —J. G. WOOD, 1887[1]

> Museum exhibitions empower objects, language, settings and artistry to spark the endlessly generative process of making meaning, making story and understanding time.
>
> —LESLIE BEDFORD, 2014[2]

IN 1888, ON A FINE SPRING DAY, A 22-YEAR-OLD banker set out on a lunchtime stroll that would help change the course of museum history. As Frank Chapman ambled past fashionably dressed Manhattanites, he couldn't help but notice the feathers adorning their opulent hats. Egrets. Pelicans. Ostriches. He started to compile a list. By the time Chapman's hat count had reached 700, he had documented the plumage of more than 40 kinds of birds. "In most cases," he later recalled, "mutilation rendered identification impossible." Why

were so many beautiful birds being slaughtered for the sake of an urban fashion trend? Something had to be done. Chapman quit his day job, joined the staff of American Museum of Natural History, and devoted the rest of his life to ornithology and species conservation. In 1903, he completed a magnificent set of exhibitions, some of which can still be seen today. AMNH's Hall of North American Birds was part of Chapman's strategy to sway public opinion about the "feather wars" the fashion industry was waging against birds and their habitats. By showcasing birds in a setting that mimicked their natural environs and calling attention to their endangerment, Chapman's work influenced Theodore Roosevelt to establish the nation's first federally protected bird sanctuary, leading to the National Wildlife Refuge System and the Migratory Bird Treaty Act.[3] Chapman saw that museums' missions extended far beyond collecting, counting, and

**Hat, ca. 1890, Mlle. Louise. Use of woven bast fiber in this hat evokes a bird's nest. The design illustrates the popularity of using real birds as millinery trim in the late 19th century.**
Brooklyn Museum Costume Collections at the Metropolitan Museum of Art, Gift of the Brooklyn Museum, 2009, Gift of Pratt Institute, 1943

**View of the Cuthbert Rookery Diorama at the American Museum of Natural History in New York, ca. 1930**
Courtesy of the American Museum of Natural History Library

categorizing objects. Meaningful public exhibitions could help transform the ways visitors think about their lives, their values, and the world. To this day, the Audubon Society, which Chapman helped to found while he was at the AMNH, fights antienvironmentalists' efforts to weaken these acts.

Since their beginnings, museums have strived to move their audiences toward deeper understandings of the world around them. The most successful curators, designers, and educators have understood the exhibition as a three-dimensional medium with the power to communicate knowledge and stir emotions. Their techniques and ideas changed alongside the advent of new communications technologies and philosophies about the meaning and purpose of displaying objects.

By the late 19th century, curators were already starting to acknowledge that museums were "intolerably dull" places that only appealed to small circles of scholars and collectors, most of them obsessed with arcane details. The average visitor, one curator lamented, "stroll[ed] listlessly . . . painfully wearied by the monotony of long rows of . . . [cases of] bones and stones."[4] If museums' purpose was to educate and enlighten, how could systematic and cluttered displays compete with dynamic new public destinations like department stores and Wild West shows? In the 1880s, taxidermists, anthropologists, and curators responded by re-creating the environments from which collections had been removed in order to provide a context for understanding them. The result was the field's first significant innovation: habitat dioramas, life groups, and period rooms. More innovations would come as the decades unfolded.

## HABITAT DIORAMAS AND LIFE GROUPS: RECONSTRUCTED ENVIRONMENTS

Before the advent of color cinema and other modern media, habitat dioramas and life groups exposed urban dwellers to exotic worlds. These revolutionary mini-environments—many of them fantasies derived from their creators' imaginations—have their roots in late-19th-century world's fairs.

In 1876, at the Philadelphia Centennial Exposition, Americans experienced strange new tastes, sounds, and sights. A fleshy fruit called the "banana." A newfangled device called the "telephone." And straight from its debut in Paris, Jules Verreaux's rendition of two fierce lions attacking a courier and his terrified camel. Verreaux's masterpiece impressed the Carnegie Natural History Museum so much that its curators paid $50 to transport it to Pittsburgh. It remains on display there to this day.

Until this time, taxidermy was a crude art form. Animal hides were stuffed with straw or lumpy rags. Legs were fashioned from wooden rods. The resulting creations stood at attention in lifeless poses. Verreaux had done something radical: he combined taxidermy with theatrics in order to illustrate a story. His technique influenced a new generation of taxidermists. One was a 22-year-old adventurer named Carl Akeley, who is often called the "father of modern taxidermy."

In 1886, after achieving fame for preserving the skin of Jumbo, P. T. Barnum's beloved elephant, Akeley quit a commercial studio job in upstate New York for a post at the Milwaukee Public Museum. Like Verreaux, Akeley wanted to create dramatic displays. But as a lover of the outdoors, he also wanted to instruct an increasingly urbanized public about the natural world. His encounters with a semiaquatic rodent would inspire him to do just that. Akeley began to study local muskrats. He dissected them. He sketched their anatomy. He sculpted them in realistic poses. Then he carefully attached hides to the clay models. Akeley was interested in the artistic as well as the scientific. By serendipity, Milwaukee was home to a pre-movie form of entertainment called the cyclorama. This was a public theater with an enormous circular canvas that, when accompanied by sound and light, illustrated a story, usually a war battle. Cyclorama painters moonlighted at the museum, where they shared ideas with Akeley. In 1890 Akeley fit a miniaturized version of the cyclorama's curved backdrop into a wood-framed case; the canvas depicted a river bending into the horizon. In front of the river, he placed his anatomically correct muskrat models in various poses—swimming, eating, sleeping. Most ingeniously, Akeley used the case's glass front to "slice" the river, showing the interior construction of the lodge, the water's surface, and a subsurface view of the animals' watery habitat. Thus, instead of freezing one dramatic event as Verreaux had, Akeley created an entire story that condensed many moments of a muskrat's day into one physical space. Still on view today, *Muskrat Group* became the prototype for what would be known as the "Milwaukee style" of exhibit design.

**Jules Verreaux's stuffed Barbary lions attacking an Arab courier and his camel, 1887, on display at the Carnegie Museum in Pittsburgh.**
Photo by Melinda McNaugher; courtesy of the Carnegie Museum of Natural History

**Exhibition hall at the California Academy of Sciences, 1895**
Courtesy of a Private Collector, OpenSFHistory / wnp27.3682

**Carl Akeley is often called the father of modern taxidermy.**
Courtesy of American Museum of Natural History Library

**Delia Akeley, Carl's wife, was also an accomplished taxidermist and once saved her husband's life when he was charged by a bull elephant.**
National Park Service, YOSE 4838

**The *Muskrat Group*, America's first museum habitat diorama, 1890.**
Courtesy of the Milwaukee Public Museum

A related innovation was taking place 90 miles to the south, in the city of Chicago. This one involved posing models of human figures into stories about "primitive" life, a practice related to the early paternalistic attitudes of anthropologists that were discussed in the prior chapter. World's fairs regularly "displayed" live native peoples in "faithful environments" of their villages, attracting crowds of spectators.[5] At Chicago's 1893 Columbian Exposition, sculptors attempted to make these popular temporary exhibitions more permanent. They borrowed life-casting techniques from Scandinavian ethnology and British wax museums and, using live people as their models, created mannequins. These were dressed in the clothing, hairstyles, and ornamentation specific to different tribes. The mannequins were then positioned in lifelike poses, performing daily activities such as cooking. The scene was encased in glass, allowing visitors to walk around the display, as if they were visiting actual villages.

Smithsonian curator William Henry Holmes, one of the innovators of "life groups," explained their practical advantage. Mannequins, he pointed out with implacable logic and no touch of irony, didn't need to be fed and housed. They could live on in perpetuity to "form a permanent exhibit, which, when set up in the museum, continues to please and instruct for generations."[6] Life-group sculptors paid faithful attention to detail but also trusted their imaginations. Artistic license often led to mistaken or intentional stereotypes about indigenous cultures. In 1901, for example, at the Pan-American Exposition in Buffalo, Holmes unveiled 12 dioramas of people from the Arctic to the Antarctic. The best known of the Buffalo life groups featured an Inuit family from Greenland, laughing as they harpoon a seal. Calling his creation *The Happy Eskimos*, Holmes's idea was to portray "Eskimos . . . [as] the most cheerful and mirth-loving people you ever saw." *The Happy Eskimos* played to the fantasies of a public fascinated by Arctic exploration. It was

*Arctic Region* life group, anthropology exhibit, U.S. National Museum, ca. 1915.
2002-10659-000002 National Museum of Natural History

transferred to the Smithsonian, where it remained on display for more than 80 years.[7]

Anthropologist Franz Boas of New York's American Museum of Natural History (AMNH) took a more literal approach to life groups. In 1899, as Boas organized AMNH's North Pacific Coast Hall, he insisted that clothing, ornaments, and tools be displayed "correctly" and with reference to their actual use based on his field research. Boas's best-known life group depicted the Kwakiutl people of northern Vancouver, with whom the anthropologist had lived and studied. In the end, Boas was disappointed with the displays. It was weird to fill a classical building with mock indigenous villages. "It is an avowed object of a large [life] group to transport the visitor into foreign surroundings," he wrote, "[but] the surroundings of a Museum are not favorable to an impression of this sort. The cases, the walls, the contents of other cases, the columns, the stairways, all remind us that we are not viewing an actual village . . . and spoil the whole effect."[8]

Life groups and habitat dioramas spread to museums across the nation. In part through innovators like Akeley, Holmes, and Boas, interest in taxidermy and anthropology was growing. Curators exchanged information about the new exhibits at professional meetings. University and art college students actively sought museum apprenticeships, hoping to join collecting expeditions sponsored by wealthy patrons. This influx of talent led to larger and more complicated displays. In 1910 AMNH suspended a 64.5-foot Haida canoe from the ceiling of the North Pacific Coast Hall and filled it with mannequins of a Chilkat (Tlingit) chief and dancers in ceremonial dress, being rowed to a Potlatch feast. A highlight of school field trips, the scene was memorably described by J. D. Salinger in his classic midcentury novel *The Catcher in the Rye* as

**Anthropologist Franz Boas insisted that his life-group displays be based on original research.**
Courtesy of American Museum of Natural History Library

"this long, long Indian war [sic] canoe, about as long as three goddam Cadillacs in a row, with about twenty Indians in it, some of them paddling, some of them looking tough."[9]

In 1914 the State Museum of New York in Albany unveiled six depictions of local Iroquois daily life, designed by Arthur C. Parker, an archaeologist of Seneca descent whose aim was to educate the public about living Native American cultures. Parker added theatrical lighting, darkening the hall and illuminating each case from within. The effect must have been as astonishing for visitors as entering a movie palace, one of the nation's nascent forms of entertainment.

Habitat diorama designers also took cues from the movies, envisioning large halls with high curved ceilings, theatrical lighting, and elaborate landscape paintings that served as backdrops for dramatic scenes of animal life. Advances in transportation allowed hunters to venture afar. New rifle technologies helped them gun down the perfect specimens to play starring roles in their elaborate sets.[10] Although these so-called research expeditions were "essentially glorified hunts for sportsmen and trustees," they resulted in some of the nation's most enduring dioramas.[11] These include Carl Akeley's crowning masterpiece, the Hall of African Mammals, still on display at AMNH. Akeley and his wife Delia's African escapades are legendary. Carl was once pinned by bull elephants; his porters fled in terror while Delia came to his rescue. Another time, with his bare hands, Carl killed a charging leopard. Finally, in 1926, he lost his life to disease while researching the finishing touches for AMNH's gorilla diorama, now named in his honor.

By the 1930s, Franklin Delano Roosevelt's Works Progress Administration was sponsoring diorama makers to create mini-scenes for National Park Service

**An exhibit of klipspringers and baboons at the Akeley Hall of African Mammals in the American Museum of Natural History.**
By Ryan Somma—Flickr: Klipspringer, CC BY-SA 2.0, https://commons.wikimedia.org/w/index.php?curid=15336818

nature centers as well as larger sets for urban museums across the country. Although their artistry was acknowledged, by the end of the century, both life groups and dioramas fell out of favor.[12] They were expensive to build and maintain. They took up a lot of gallery space. Mounted animals shed, sometimes to the point of disintegration, unless treated with poisons that posed dangers to staff. But most importantly, just as life groups perpetuated cultural and racist stereotypes, habitat dioramas perpetuated bad science, sometimes positioning animals into "completely bogus nuclear families," such as a momma and poppa grizzly bear working in unison to raise their progeny when in fact momma bear would have been working extra hard to prevent poppa from eating his own cubs.[13] Most museums have since dismantled the early life groups. Habitat dioramas, on the other hand, still have passionate defenders. At one time, these detailed sets were at the forefront of important environmental legislation. One could argue that those that remain today stand as important cultural artifacts and compelling works of art.[14]

## PERIOD ROOMS: PATRIOTISM, COMMERCIALISM, AND EDUCATION[15]

Period rooms were the domestic version of the habitat diorama. Whereas habitat groups played to museum-goers' fantasies of what lay beyond civilization, period rooms fed their illusions about the indoor lives of the rich and famous. The people who fashioned these displays had a variety of motives. Some were out to make money. Others wanted to patriotically celebrate the country's earliest heroes. And still others approached period rooms as exceptional educational environments that could stir visitors' emotions.

Curators of the earliest American period rooms took their cues from two movements: historic house preservation and world's fairs. In 1854, the Mount Vernon Ladies' Association, led by Ann Pamela Cunningham, initiated the historic house movement. Cunningham and her team of "lady regents" restored George Washington's Virginia mansion with intense attention to re-creating it exactly as they imagined it had been when George and Martha lived there. Their goal was patriotic, a "labor of love, in redeeming from

**Founding members of the Mount Vernon Ladies Association, 1848, the first historic preservation organization in the United States.**
Courtesy of Mount Vernon Ladies' Association

**Re-created bedroom in George Washington's Mount Vernon mansion**
Courtesy of Mount Vernon Ladies' Association

oblivion and sure decay the home of . . . the immortal Washington . . . including its old 'servants' hall' [sic] and kitchen."[16] Concurrently, world's fair planners recreated colonial New England kitchens staffed with cooks who sold "ye olden tyme" pudding, stew, and baked beans. Their goal was to turn a profit.

Education was the goal behind the earliest museum-based colonial kitchens—at Memorial Hall in Deerfield, MA (1891); the deYoung Museum in San Francisco (1896); the Hull House Museum in Chicago (1900); and the Oakland Museum (1910). To furnish these so-called ancient kitchens, curators cobbled together objects from many sources. Charles P. Wilcomb, designer of the San Francisco and Oakland kitchens, raided his New Hampshire aunt's pewter collection, as well as "forsaken corners of attics, cellars and barns" all over New England to compose his vision of Yankee thriftiness. The centerpiece was a fireplace from which hung strings of dried fruit and drip wax candles. Plates, pitchers, and ladles were arranged in cupboards. Beside a rocking chair sat a spinning wheel, indicating that kitchens served a variety of functions in colonial times. Chicago's Hull House colonial kitchen served as a backdrop for a modern kitchen in which settlement workers taught American-style cooking classes to recent immigrants. Colonial kitchens must have seemed strange to young

people during the early 20th century. The rooms lacked sinks and iceboxes, by now fixtures in most kitchens. Their rudimentary implements demonstrated how far the country had come materially.

Museums also devised colonial bedrooms—usually furnished with a dresser, hook rugs, and canopy bed properly made up with a snow-white coverlet. These bedrooms were so tidy that they had a decidedly unlived-in quality. Visitors must have wondered at the starched lives of their phantom inhabitants. As historian James Deetz has observed, colonial period rooms gave the "impression that all Americans sprang into existence at the age of twenty-one and were very neat."[17]

In 1907 in Salem, MA, George Francis Dow crafted a 17th-century bedroom, parlor, and kitchen for the Essex Institute. Dow's aims differed from prior efforts. He did not want to create a background exhibit to sell "ye olden tyme" meals or inspire immigrants to cook American-style. Dow wanted to stir his visitors' emotions and appreciation for the lives of past occupants. Thus, he designed his period rooms to look like they were inhabited by real people. Knitting needles dangled from an in-process stocking. A pair of eyeglasses sat atop an opened newspaper. Dow trained three women, dressed in home-spun period attire, to greet visitors and show them around the house. This

**The first colonial kitchen exhibition, fondly called the "ancient kitchen" by today's museum staff.**
Courtesy of Pocumtuck Valley's Memorial Association Memorial Hall Museum, Deerfield, MA.

**Elvis Presley's boyhood kitchen, ca. 1940, is preserved at the Elvis Presley Birthplace and Museum in Tupelo, MS.**
Courtesy Michael Ventura Photography

practice of using costumed actors to animate a historic re-creation would become known as "living history."

While museums stuck to frugal kitchens and bedrooms, wealthy individuals went on shopping sprees in Europe, buying up extravagant rooms that had once belonged to the nobility or successful merchants. They not only acquired paintings and furniture; they also bought the walls, ceilings, and floors. The purchases made headlines. The rooms eventually made it to museums. In 1904, railway magnate Charles Lang Freer bought the *Peacock Room*, a 19th-century English dining room that had belonged to a shipping magnate. Designed by James McNeill Whistler as a "fantasy view of the 'Orient,'" the fabled room was festooned with blue and gold peacocks. The *Peacock Room* was bequeathed to the Freer Gallery of Art in 1923. It inspired more peacock rooms, including the one in Elvis Presley's Graceland mansion in Memphis.[18]

With the growing market for Americana, curators in U.S. art museums developed period rooms to, in the words of historian Gary Kulik, "invest early American objects with the aura of art." Paintings and sculpture were coordinated with furniture that reflected the revival of a colonial American style. In

1924, the Metropolitan Museum of Art opened its American Wing, 17 elegant rooms of decorative arts and furniture. Designer Richard Halsey arranged the rooms in chronological order, from a 17th-century Haverhill, MA, parlor to an early-19th-century Baltimore dining room. Halsey, a stockbroker by trade, believed that the Met's period rooms would serve as "tastemakers" for the public, who then would exhibit their own "good taste" by purchasing reproductions in department stores.

Throughout the 1920s, art museum curators went on a period room mania. In Saint Louis, they studied pictures in books and re-created what they saw; in Philadelphia, they stripped homes slated for demolition and arranged restored parts into cohesive rooms. Most museums didn't go to such lengths; they simply purchased wholly furnished rooms from dealers. From 1918 to 1929, the Brooklyn Museum installed 21 such rooms from various parts of the country. When Brooklyn snapped up the entire first floor interior of Edenton, N.C.'s Cupola House, concerned locals formed their own museum association to prevent further losses. In the 1960s, preservationists copied the Cupola rooms that resided in Brooklyn

**Designed by James McNeill Whistler, the peacock motifs in this room at the Freer Gallery of Art in Washington, D.C., inspired other peacock rooms, including one at Elvis Presley's Graceland.**
Slowking4, Creative Commons, April 29, 2014

and put the imitations back into the historic house in North Carolina. Finally, an interesting technique was to re-create an artist's studio as part of a museum. In 1930, the Charles M. Russell Memorial Museum in Great Falls, MT, featured the famous "cowboy artist's" log cabin studio.

The period room plunged underground in 1933, with the Chicago Museum of Science and Industry (MSI)'s famous *Coal Mine*. MSI founder Julius Rosenwald had seen an exhibition about mining extraction at Munich's Deutschesmuseum and wanted one for Chicago. Museum staff came upon a defunct coal operation in Johnson City, IL. The company was only too happy to unload its equipment at a bargain basement price.

With extensive input from retired miners, MSI painted a room in its basement to resemble a mine's interior. It scented the space with perfume, specially formulated to mimic a mine's distinct odor. On the first floor, in what is likely the first-ever museum ride, visitors boarded a Johnson City elevator cage. It

creaked down rollers, plunging visitors down a shaft, cleverly fashioned with canvas walls. Once inside the semidarkened "mine," visitors watched machines extract "seven tons of coal," as water trickled in through ditches. Enthusiastic former miners donned gear and staffed the exhibit, becoming the museum's most popular tour guides. MSI even added taxidermy: an ersatz canary-in-the-coalmine, which miners traditionally observed to monitor oxygen levels. "Real?" bragged MSI's proud director Waldemar Kaempfert. "It is impossible to distinguish reality from illusion here." Even so, *Coal Mine* failed to mention real issues such as union-management conflicts and miner safety. *Coal Mine* was built as a patriotic ode to technological progress and, as its original catalog states, to inspire an appreciation for how coal will "lead to the end of social ills . . . [to] national wealth, cheap goods, [and] domination of world markets."[19]

Although popular with audiences, simulated environments like *Coal Mine* were almost immediately

Parlor from James Duncan Jr. House, Haverhill, MA, on display in American Wing, Metropolitan Museum of Art.

Rogers Fund 1912, #12121, Metropolitan Museum of Art

Hall, the Cupola House, ca. 1725, reinstalled at the Brooklyn Museum, Robert B. Woodward Memorial Fund.

*Coal Mine* offered everything associated with a "real" mining experience, including authentic workers.
© Museum of Science and Industry, Chicago, USA/Bridgeman Images

questioned by scholars. Artificial settings and dramatic vignettes cheapened what Princeton University art historian Frank Jewett Mather called an object's "museum values," that is, its aesthetic and spiritual qualities.[20] Re-creations froze objects in the past instead of relating them to the present day. As Alexander Dorner, who directed the museum at the Rhode Island School of Design in the 1940s, said, "[A] museum that tries to separate the past from the present is indeed like a head without a body or a body without a head."[21]

Outside the museum's walls, art and science were becoming more abstract. The roaring 1920s had introduced jazz music, surrealism, broadcast radio, and Einstein's Theory of Relativity. Thanks to expanded public education, the nation's literacy rates had risen. In 1880, 20 percent of the U.S. population was unable to read or write in any language. By 1930, 95 percent of the nation was literate. Curators could now convey information through abstract arrangements supplemented with text rather than stage set. It was time for museums to reflect the language of modern times.

## MODERN DESIGN: WHITE WALLS AND THE MYTH OF NEUTRALITY

The impetus for the "neutral" modernized spaces that came to be called "white cubes" came from Germany's Bauhaus. Founded shortly after World War I, the Bauhaus school believed that society should be more egalitarian and open-minded. As one of its founders

explained, "we were more than an art institute; we were seeking to find a new way of life."[22] This could be achieved through efficient designs for products and buildings. In the 1920s, teams of Bauhaus artists developed a streamlined approach to exhibitions using sleek new industrial materials such as cellophane and wire netting and creating linear pathways for visitors to follow.

Profoundly influenced by these ideas, four interconnected visionaries reshaped museum exhibition design in the United States: social activist Katherine Sophie Dreier and wunderkind museum directors Alexander Dorner, Everett "Chick" Austin, and Alfred H. Barr Jr. The Brooklyn-born daughter of German immigrants, Dreier often traveled to Europe during the 1920s. There, she socialized with avant-garde artists, who inspired her to organize the first modern art installation in a U.S. museum. For nine weeks in 1926, *International Exhibition of Modern Art* presented more than 300 works from 23 countries at the Brooklyn Museum. It attracted 52,000 visitors and generated provocative reviews in the national press.

Dreier wanted to promote the aesthetic of modernism. Standard practice at the time was to cover the walls with richly brocaded wallpaper and then stack every inch of space with art. Dreier, however, positioned her paintings against plain walls, leaving blank spaces between the works. In a nod to the museum's period rooms, but mindful of the modernists' emphasis on the present, she displayed four domestic rooms with purchases from a local department store. Her aim was to promote modern art as an essential item for the modern home. The Brooklyn show also featured a scale model of a "television room," consisting of a "small dark room" where visitors would "turn a button" to rotate European masterworks onto a screen. "Someday, all the important museums will have their own real television rooms," Dreier predicted. The visionary Dreier was also, as one right-wing U.S. congressman later described her, an "active left-winger."[23] She deliberately promoted the artwork of refugees, often coming to blows with more conservative forces that wanted to privilege the work of "patriotic" Americans over "suspicious" foreigners. She was also an active suffragist and organized one of the nation's first shows devoted to contemporary woman artists (1934). She eventually donated her early modern art collection to Yale University, where it remains today.[24]

Alexander Dorner, the pioneering director of the Museum of Art, Rhode Island School of Design (RISD), also had roots in Germany. In 1927, while director of the Landesmuseum in Hanover, Germany, Dorner commissioned artist El Lissitsky to create *Abstract Cabinet*, a modular room for the display of modern paintings. To view the art contained in the cabinet, visitors rotated differently sized cases and panels made of corrugated tin and other shimmering industrial materials. The installation changed constantly, depending on how visitors arranged the art inside. *Abstract Cabinet* created an international buzz, and several U.S. art museum directors sailed to Hanover to see it. Nazis destroyed the cabinet in 1936, but with help from his U.S. colleagues, Dorner was able to flee Europe. Eventually landing in Rhode Island, he continued his experiments with modern installation techniques, experimenting with wall colors,[25] window screens, and even a push-button device that allowed visitors to turn selected objects on their sides.[26]

Dreier and Dorner's experiments in modern exhibition design attracted the attention of two classmates in Harvard University's legendary museum training course, Everett "Chick" Austin and Alfred Barr Jr. Austin was a prodigy who "did things sooner and more brilliantly than anyone," Barr once said. In 1927, the 26-year-old Austin moved to Hartford, CT, to take over the directorship of the staunchly traditionalist Wadsworth Atheneum. There he staged risky exhibitions and programs, deliberately choosing *Distinguished Works of Art* as the title of his first show

**Installation view of *Distinguished Works of Art*, January 18–February 1, 1928.**
RG9_1_F3270, photograph collection, Wadsworth Atheneum Museum of Art Archives, Hartford, CT.

because, he said, only a few of the Wadsworth's works were "distinguished." He believed a good curator should not cram the galleries with second-rate works but separate quality from mediocrity and choose only the art with the greatest aesthetic value. Austin had a penchant for costume balls, opening galas, and magic shows, which he liked to perform at the museum. For *Distinguished Works*, he placed a velvet curtain at the center of the exhibition. At a choice moment on opening night, he dramatically pulled back the curtain to reveal the museum's new acquisition, a prized painting by Tintoretto. Austin went on to organize the nation's first exhibition of surrealist art in 1931 and its first Picasso retrospective in 1934.[27]

Credit for institutionalizing modern exhibition design, however, goes to Alfred Barr Jr., founding director of New York's MoMA.[28] Like Dreier and Dorner, Barr favored a modern and flexible aesthetic using contemporary materials. Like Austin, he believed in spare displays of outstanding pieces. Only "distinguished" works should be shown regularly, with less significant ones left in storage. These techniques have become so standard that today most visitors don't even notice them.

In the 1930s, as MoMA was erecting its first building, Barr called for interior galleries to be open and loft-like. As exhibitions changed, movable partitions could be inserted to reshape room sizes and patterns of circulation. Barr also thought about how to explain art to visitors. Until this time, museum labels provided minimal information; a work's title, the artist's name, and perhaps the medium were typeset or handwritten on a small label centered in the bottom of a frame. Barr pioneered a different approach: lengthy text, with information on country of origin, the artist's biography, and how the work related to others in the room, typewritten onto labels and thumbtacked to walls. Conveying information in what we now call the "interpretative label" allowed an increasingly literate public to wander through museums at their own pace, rather than follow the scripted tour of a docent.

To enhance the viewer's experience, Barr searched for a "neutral" wall color that would create minimal distraction. He experimented with various shades and textures of beige cloth. He then turned to the famous Bauhaus credo, "white, everything must be white." White was the color the Bauhaus disciples associated with hygiene, purity, and sun-bleached Mediterranean architecture. It evoked both the classical past and new beginnings. White paint became the standard background for exhibitions, and gallery spaces came to be called "white cubes." They were heralded by the art world as a glorious innovation. "The development of the pristine, placeless white cube is one of modernism's triumphs—a development commercial, esthetic and technological," art critic Brian O'Doherty wrote later. "In an extraordinary strip-tease, the art within bares itself more and more."[29]

MoMA's stripped-down galleries freed both artists and curators. Visitors no longer were distracted by fussy wallpaper. Throughout the ensuing decades curators would mount a wide range of adventurous shows on the ubiquitous white walls: cubist, Dada, and surrealist paintings; African masks, East Indian textiles, and pre-Columbian carvings; and Americana and household items elevated to high design.

Three of Barr's closest collaborators at MoMA disagreed with the "white cube" approach. Architect Philip Johnson felt that Barr's original wall color choice of beige was far better than white. "Never, never use white," he said. "Then your frame is much brighter than your picture."[30] Longtime MoMA curator Dorothy Miller also believed in creating displays that showed artwork at its best. As a leading tastemaker who introduced New Yorkers to some of the most promising contemporary artists of the day—Jackson Pollock, Mark Rothko, Ellsworth Kelly—she favored symphonic arrangements: "what you look for and what you try to achieve are climaxes—introduction, surprise, going around the corner and seeing something unexpected, perhaps several climaxes with very dramatic things, then a quiet tapering off with something to let you out alive."[31] Finally, curator and future MoMA director Rene d'Harnoncourt believed that exhibition design could never be neutral. It was integral to the meaning of the work. For his landmark show *Indian Art of the United States* (1939) he used modern design to elevate the status of Native American culture in the eyes of museumgoers. As an antidote to natural history museums' life-group displays, d'Harnoncourt invited contemporary Hopi and Navajo artists—for example, Fred Kabotie and Dooley Shorty—to create artwork in front of visitors in MoMA's galleries. To today's eyes, this installation, with well-dressed patrons gazing down at Navajo artists, looks like an extension—not an antidote—of what was going on at world's fairs. But the idea was innovative by virtue of its setting in a modern art museum. Also innovative was d'Harnoncourt's use of color to show off the work's aesthetic qualities; the walls were painted sky blue and colorful textiles were displayed on bright orange platforms.[32]

**Navajo artists executing sand painting during the MoMA exhibition *Indian Art of the United States*, March 1941.**
Digital image © the Museum of Modern Art Licensed by SCALA/Art Resource NY

Nonetheless, the white cube method predominated. There were pragmatic reasons for simplifying exhibition design. A standardized style of presentation was ideal for traveling exhibitions. In 1932 MoMA established a Department of Circulating Exhibitions, the first museum department dedicated to developing shows that would tour to other institutions. 1939 saw a marked rise in frequently changing installations in large urban museums as these institutions competed for audiences with other attractions. The AAM advocated that the most practical way to accommodate a constant stream of changing exhibitions was to have a "neutral setting for exhibits without decorative effects of any kind."[33]

Modern design caught on beyond art museums. Anthropology and science museum curators found that industrial materials and "neutral" backgrounds could help convey intellectual theories, especially about scientific progress, human control of the natural world, and racial hierarchy. Carlos Cummings of

the Buffalo Museum of Science compared exhibitions to how textbooks narrated history in a crisp, logical order: "The [museum's] individual rooms . . . are regarded as chapters; and the individual exhibits, carefully selected to complete the narrative, are considered as paragraphs or pages."[34] In 1937 the Milwaukee Public Museum rearranged a collection of 3,328 birds' eggs. Breaking with Akeley's "Milwaukee style," curators grouped the eggs onto geometric cylinders, sorted by color and size into six equally spaced rows in a classical wooden case. The result looked more like a cabinet in a grocery store than nests in the wild. In 1941, the National Park Service went so far as to advise nature centers to avoid mimicking the great outdoors: "Attention is drawn more by the method of display than by the inherent beauty or attractiveness of the object itself. A rusty nail, common cinder or any other object may be so displayed and lighted that it will attract attention quicker than the rarest and most valuable gem."[35]

**Goss Egg Collection display at the Milwaukee Public Museum as it looked in 1937.**
Courtesy of the Milwaukee Public Museum

***Races of Mankind***, an unscientific and overtly racist comparison of the races of the world, went on display at the Field Museum of Natural History in Chicago as the Nazis were gaining power in Germany.
Photo by Charles Carpenter. CSA77747, © Field Museum

In 1933, Chicago's Field Museum departed from its tradition of life groups in an apocryphal "modern" anthropological exhibition: *Races of Mankind*. Its aim was to use modern design to allow visitors to systematically compare racial features from around the world. The Field commissioned Malvina Hoffman—a student of French sculptor Auguste Rodin—to model 98 different "racial stocks" in bronze. Rather than organizing the sculptures into life groups, Hoffman reconfigured the Field's long hall of Greek cornices with partitions and screens. She arranged the sculptures to progress from "Neanderthal to Nordic" on pedestals set into lighted niches. For this "avenue of man," she chose "pale golden beige" for the walls and modern linoleum for the floor. A side gallery featured charts of different kinds of eyes, hair, and skin and a map of "racial stocks." In the same year that the Nazis seized power in Germany, such racial categorization could hardly have been neutral. In fact, consultants on the exhibition included Eugen Fischer, who would later become Hitler's foremost advisor on "race hygiene."[36]

This unscientific science exhibition endured until 1969 when a letter-writing campaign by civil rights activists convinced the museum to dismantle it. (In 2016 the Field conserved, reinstalled, and reinterpreted 50 of Hoffman's sculptures in *Looking at Ourselves: Rethinking the Sculptures of Malvina Hoffman*. This exhibit confronted in an honest way the original intentions behind the display.)[37]

During World War II, designers realized that maps, charts, and globes were useful visual devices for explaining national security and military strategy to an increasingly nervous public. The 1941 exhibition *Can America Be Bombed?* featured a globe flanked by large bombs, with a missile aimed at the southeastern United States. The show was designed by Works Progress Administration artists and traveled throughout the country.

After the United States entered the war, "map and globe" exhibitions became popular. In 1943, the Newark Museum used designs by renowned engineer R. Buckminster Fuller to build *Dymaxion World*, a

*Can America Be Bombed*, a pre–World War II exhibition that appeared on the front page of AAM's *Museum Newsletter* one week before Pearl Harbor was bombed.
Courtesy of Cleveland Museum of Art

**Close-up of the Globe in MoMA's *Airways to Peace*, 1943.**
Gottscho-Schleisner Collection, Library of Congress, Prints and Photographs Division

geodesic globe-like structure designed to show how the war was impeding the flow of "vitally important drug plants" into the United States. That same year, maps were a prominent feature of MoMA's *Airways to Peace: An Exhibition of Geography for the Future*. Bauhaus typographer Herbert Bayer took MoMA's visitors on a cartographic journey through the new kinds of mapping being employed in military campaigns. *Airways'* main feature was a giant transparent globe, surrounded by charts, maps, Mercator projectors, and aerial photographs. Accompanying text was written by Wendell Willkie, a former presidential candidate and prominent opponent of American isolationism.[38]

The internationalist approach that dominated the war years soon was overtaken by Cold War paranoia. Wisconsin Sen. Joseph McCarthy achieved national attention with his anticommunist "witch hunt" against artists and intellectuals. Even the most innocent exhibition theme could infuriate McCarthy's followers. In 1956, for example, the self-anointed "Dallas County Patriotic Council" demanded that that Dallas Museum of Art cancel a *Sports Illustrated*–sponsored art exhibition celebrating sports because of four works that had been painted by blacklisted artists.[39] (We will learn more about that political battle in the next chapter.)

Other less "subversive" exhibitions were far more popular. Key among them were the Museum of Modern Art's *Family of Man* (1955)[40] and *The Farmer's Year*, which opened at the Farmers' Museum in Cooperstown, N.Y. (1958).[41]

*Family of Man* remains the most visited photography exhibition of all time, and in the words of historian Eric Sandeen, "one of the most significant cultural productions of 1950s America."[42] Its iconic catalog is still in print. Scholars and artists continue to debate its merits. Was it art, schmaltz, or propaganda? In 2018, photo historians Shamoon Zamir and Gerd Hurm suggested that *Family of Man* was, in fact, an antiwar exhibition. It depicted "not the horror of war but what is lost in war—what in fact would be irretrievably lost in a third, nuclear war."[43]

The show's curator, 76-year-old Edward Steichen, had been chief photographer for *Vogue*. In 1952, intrigued by a photojournalism series about the human experience published in *Ladies' Home Journal*, Steichen issued a worldwide call for photographs that documented the "gamut of life from birth to death." From more than 4 million submissions, Steichen and his assistants selected 503 photos by 257 photographers from 68 countries. He divided the photos into "universal" themes—lovers caressing, couples arguing,

children playing, mourners praying—and asked his brother-in-law, the famed Chicago poet Carl Sandburg, to write a prologue in the catalog to pull the photos together with one central focus. "A camera testament," Sandburg wrote, "a drama of the grand canyon of humanity, an epic of fun, mystery, and holiness—here is the Family of Man."

The exhibition was also noteworthy for its revolutionary design by architect Paul Rudolph. At the entrance a new transparent material called Lucite® displayed the photographs so that they seemed to float in the air. Rudolph grouped them according to Steichen's vision of the human life cycle and painted the walls different colors to emphasize a progression from birth to death. Photos of women giving birth were hung in a white-curtained, womb-like "pregnancy temple." The show's only controversial image (banned in the catalog) came near the exit: a giant color photo of an A-bomb exploding, juxtaposed with photos of children from around the world, playing ring-around-the-rosy. In the 1950s and 1960s, *Family of Man* traveled the

Jack Delano's photograph *Tobacco Farmers near Windsor Locks, CT, 1940* was shown in MoMA's iconic *Family of Man* exhibition.

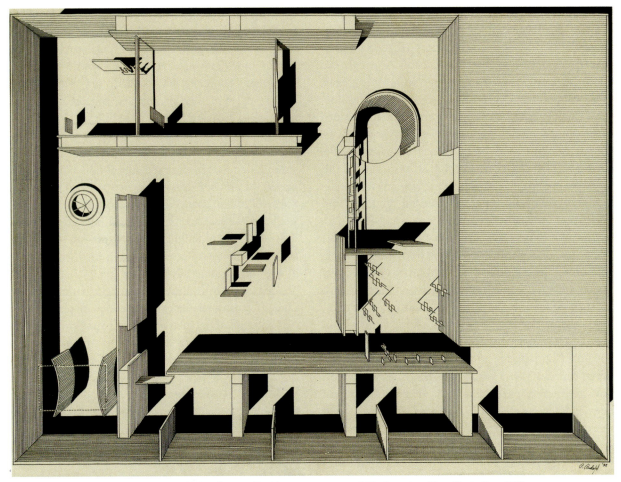

**Architect Paul Rudolph's floor plan design for *Family of Man*, Museum of Modern Art, New York City, 1952.**
Paul Rudolph Archive, Library of Congress Prints and Photographs Division, LC-DIG-ppmsca-03530

world, setting attendance records from Pittsburgh to Paris, from Minneapolis to Moscow. Today it is on permanent display in Luxembourg, Steichen's birthplace.

The rural counterpart to *Family of Man* was *The Farmer's Year* at the Farmers' Museum in Cooperstown, N.Y. Like *Family of Man*, it employed an easy-to-follow storyline flavored with Cold War–era rhetoric about universal values: in this case, hard work and pragmatism. Director Louis C. Jones was a pioneer in the field of public history and an accomplished folklorist, perhaps best known for his compilation of ghost stories titled *Things That Go Bump in the Night*. He was aware that with the passage of time, the museum's jumbled collection of agricultural bric-a-brac was becoming increasingly uninteresting. He engineered a far more eye-catching idea: leading visitors through a year in the life of a 19th-century farmer using the design format of a picture calendar. Twelve earth-toned panels, each titled with the name of a month, contained short captions written in a conversational style. Below each panel, a few carefully chosen objects

illustrated that month's theme. In "Fixing and Sharpening Tools," for example, five sentences explained how in February the thrifty farmer prepares tools for the coming spring. Six different kinds of sharpening devices illustrated this point. The museum had areas where children could use old-fashioned tools. "From a knowledge of the resourcefulness," wrote Jones, "the ingenuity, the courage and laughter of our people comes a lift of the chin, a confidence in our hearts that we too shall solve our problems and look forward to the tomorrow of our children's children."

*The Farmer's Year* organized history according to chronology set within themes, as opposed to period rooms or cases of objects. On view from 1958 to 1982, it had an enormous impact on the first generation of public history graduate students, especially those enrolled in the museum studies program at Cooperstown.[44] Throughout the next decades, history museums built on Jones's approach, adding more layers of information in the form of lengthy text (sometimes called the "book on a wall" approach).[45] *The Farmer's*

During the Cold War, American values like rugged individualism and ingenuity were incorporated into exhibitions like the groundbreaking *The Farmer's Year* (1958) at the Farmers' Museum in Cooperstown, N.Y. It was modeled on the picture calendars that were popular at the time.

Courtesy of the Farmer's Museum

*Year* was popular with tourists who visited Cooperstown for the Baseball Hall of Fame and locals who wanted their children to see what farm life used to be like. Perhaps its concept of the cycle of time was reassuring to a public puzzled by a steady stream of postwar lifestyle innovations.

## A NEW CUBE: MUSEUMS IN THE AGE OF TELEVISION

In the 1950s, broadcast television mesmerized the nation. Restaurants, movie theaters, and libraries all reported diminished business.[46] Museum attendance continued to rise, but curators were concerned about the impact this luminous new medium would have on visitors. Exhibitions that once seemed daring suddenly looked mundane when compared to the marvels of viewing moving pictures at home. Worried that television would erode their appeal, museums responded by producing their own shows and adding new technol-

ogy into their galleries. These visionary efforts were forerunners to the YouTube channels, podcasts, cellphone tours, and other 21st-century digital technologies museums now embrace.

In 1951, the same year *I Love Lucy* premiered on TV, families could also tune their black-and-white sets to the game show *What in the World*. Hosted by the University of Pennsylvania's Museum of Archaeology and Anthropology, it featured guest panels of dapper American and European curators. Accompanied by eerie space-age music, a "mysterious" museum artifact would appear before them. Was it a petrified gourd? A paleolithic reptile tooth? A primitive sword covering? And most importantly: which curator possessed sufficient "museum mentalities" to figure out "what in the world" it was?[47]

Throughout the decade, museums across the nation sponsored weekly shows on local networks, achieving minor celebrity status for their directors and curators.

A 1951 game show called *What in the World* featured curators using their "remarkable museum mentalities" to identify "mysterious" artifacts.
Courtesy of Penn Museum (neg # 139460)

Brothers Zach and Noah Kaufman become news anchors in Chicago Children's Museum's 1991 *Newsroom* exhibition.
Courtesy of Marjorie Schwarzer

Indianapolis Children's Museum hosted a children's hour. California Academy of Sciences' show featured "friendly scientists" conducting experiments in a "museum lab." Museums had been broadcasting lectures on radio since the 1920s, but the visual nature of television held greater promise for replicating the exhibition experience. Television could "tell the museum story with immediacy, dramatic focus, high interest and broad appeal," wrote Robert Dierbeck, who served as the Milwaukee Public Museum's television coordinator during the 1950s. Some scholars, however, were appalled at the thought of condensing their life's work into TV sound bites. One museum director lamented, "The day is not too far away when . . . museum personnel will have to be actors as well as scientists."[48]

Other museums embraced this new form of communication. Curators even tried to make connections between artwork and popular television shows, including Saturday morning cartoons. In 1955, the Boston Museum of Fine Arts put a full-scale cutout of the Disney cartoon version of Davy Crockett, King of the Wild Frontier next to a rare 19th-century painted portrait of the real Mr. Crockett.[49] Around the same time Chicago's new educational television station, WTTW, established its fledgling operations at the Museum of Science and Industry. The broadcast studio doubled as a public exhibition where visitors could watch television production in action, years before interactive TV studios would become popular exhibitions in other museums.

Museums adjusted their exhibitions in other ways. Twenty years after the Muzak Corporation began to pipe music into retail environments, art museums added sound to their galleries. In 1942, with its curators leaving to join the war effort, the Saint Paul Art Gallery in Minnesota recorded lectures onto vinyl records and provided record players so that a visitor could "help himself to a gallery tour." In 1957 a company called Acoustiguide introduced a reel-to-reel tape recorder, hooked to a thick leather strap that visitors could tote through galleries. According to an early Acoustiguide ad, simply by pushing a button museumgoers could listen to experts "present authoritative information exactly as the director wants to have it presented."[50]

Science museums produced exhibits that surpassed the limitations of a small black-and-white screen. Some focused on the public's fascination with human bodies and advancing medical technology. In the late 1940s, the Cleveland Health Education Museum (now part of the Cleveland Museum of Natural History) unveiled

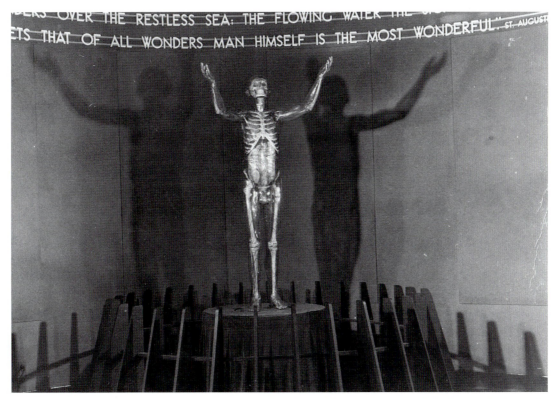

**To compete with television, science museums focused on the public's fascination with the human body. At the Cleveland Health Education Museum in the late 1940s, visitors could gaze at a giant transparent woman. Later, sound was added.**
Courtesy of Cleveland Museum of Natural History

**Updated *The Giant Heart* exhibition at the Franklin Institute, Philadelphia, as of 2019.**
By Superx308—Own work, CC BY-SA 4.0, https://commons.wikimedia.org/w/index.php?curid=81178914

Juno, a giant transparent woman based on Der Glae-serne Mensch in Dresden, Germany.[51] Visitors could gaze upon Juno's organs, veins, and teeth—everything but her soul. Juno and her Teutonic counterpart traveled the country, popularizing the use of transparent mannequins to teach human biology, long before the colorful and popular *Body Worlds* exhibitions of plasticized human bodies.

Combining transparency with size and movement, Chicago's Museum of Science and Industry in 1952 and Philadelphia's Franklin Institute in 1954 constructed multistory plaster hearts that visitors could step into, early versions of the gigantic human jaws and other blown-up body organs seen in science museums around the world today. One doesn't know whether scientists were amused or aghast when one young visitor to the Franklin Institute commented, "Thank you for the Heart exhibit. I learned so much. I never knew my heart had stairs in it."[52]

Still, most museums were content to rely on more traditional exhibition techniques. "Everyone is familiar with the neglected museum, with its badly lit, inadequately labeled and jammed exhibition cases," Lothar Witteborg, chief of exhibitions at AMNH, wrote in 1958. "Many museums were and still are being designed and the exhibits installed according to traditions established before our Industrial Revolution."[53] Of course, old-fashioned exhibitions triggered fond memories for devout museumgoers. "You could go [to the museum] a hundred thousand times, and nothing would have changed," wrote novelist J. D. Salinger. "The only thing that would be different would be you."[54] But exhibition designers understood that the nation's museums needed to move beyond nostalgia in order to keep pace with a changing nation.

## THE HANDS-ON MOVEMENT

As the 1960s began, the nation was about to experience radical change. Postwar affluence coupled with the communicative powers of mass media contributed to a new era marked by a "vast and surprisingly broad degree of dissidence." Within this social climate, avant-garde artists, educators, civil rights activists, and market-savvy directors questioned the purpose of museums. Did the public get anything out of exhibitions that relied on the passive viewing of objects? Activists wanted exhibitions to engage the public and become more relevant to people's daily lives. In the words of famed designer Alexander Girard, it was time for shows that were a "joyous spectacle, a dance."[55]

Avant-garde artists led the way. In the early 1960s, influenced by experiments in European galleries, they began to rebel against what artist Allan Kaprow called the "shhh—don't touch" atmosphere of art museums.[56] White cubes were too institutional; artist Robert Smithson declared that they "murdered and entombed art," separating it from life, much the way prisons or hospitals separated inmates and the ill from humanity. Furthermore, artists believed that the white cube approach brought out the worst in curators. They selected and arranged works according to their own predetermined categories and then spouted "intellectual rubbish" about their choices.[57] Charged with hanging as few paintings as possible, curators acted more like power mongers than art lovers. For example, at one Wadsworth Atheneum show, the mischievous Chick Austin hung five abstract paintings sideways, declaring that it made the exhibition "much better, and I knew only one or two persons would know the difference."[58]

Artists revolted by staging their own installations in galleries, which they called "happenings." They encouraged visitors to become part of the art-making by writing on the walls or even stomping on artwork.[59] In 1965, for example, Yoyoi Kusama created a participatory kaleidoscope chamber that she called *Infinity Mirror Room—Phalli's Field*. Provocatively, fabric sculptures of white phalluses covered with red dots rose up from the floor of her mirrored room, creating what art historian Jo Applin has called a "psychologically charged mode of encounter."[60]

By the end of the 1960s, adventurous curators brought the spirit of "happenings" to museums. In 1969 Chicago's Museum of Contemporary Art hired environmental artists Christo and Jeanne-Claude to wrap its building, inside and out, using cloth, plastic, and twine. Only the white walls of the interior were left bare.[61] At the Whitney Museum of Art, curators Marcia Tucker and James Monte organized *Anti-Illusion: Procedures/Materials* in which artists parodied the shape, size, and proportions of white rooms. Sculptor Robert Morris, for example, placed large L-beams at odd angles in the museum, forcing visitors to weave their path through the works and experience a cube-shaped room in an entirely new way. That same year, at RISD's museum, Andy Warhol created *Raid the Icebox*, a pun on the term *white cube*. Warhol pulled eclectic items—parasols, shoes, jars—from the museum's storage vaults and arranged them according to personal whim.[62]

Like Dreier and Dorner's modern art exhibition experiments, these experimental shows set the stage for new kinds of installations that have influenced artists to this day. Avant-garde art, however, attracted small audiences. And sometimes curators paid the price for pushing art museum culture farther than it was ready to go. In 1971, for example, the Guggenheim fired its curator for commissioning Hans Haacke's piece, "Shapolsky et al. Manhattan Real Estate Holdings," a critique of museum trustees' real-estate dealings.

It was left to the educators at science centers and children's and neighborhood museums to introduce participatory exhibitions to the broader public. These staff members, concerned about the state of math and science education in the post-Sputnik era, sought to challenge traditional ways of teaching. They turned to educational psychologists and education reformers, whose research had found that people learn and retain more when they touch and manipulate objects. Maybe there was a way to convert this research into new kinds of museum exhibitions.

Los Angeles–based designers Ray and Charles Eames were among those who proposed a solution. The revolutionary wife-husband team already was famous for using modern design to bring sophisticated ideas to a mass audience. They had produced a best-selling reclining chair that graced both art museum exhibitions and middle-class homes, and films that communicated difficult scientific concepts in entertaining ways. At the California Museum of Science and Industry in Los Angeles (now the California Science Center) in 1961, the couple created *Mathematica: The World of Numbers and Beyond*. Their vision was that visitors would not follow a strict linear pathway but would weave their way randomly through the infinite pleasures of mathematics.

In a shiny industrial space of stainless steel, fiberglass, and blinking light bulbs, visitors could press buttons, pull levers, and turn cranks that set various phenomena in motion. To discover the laws of probability, they could trigger a 12-foot-high machine to drop 30,000 plastic balls through a maze of pegs to form a bell curve. To learn how surfaces form, they could pull wires from a giant vat of detergent that stretched into bubbles. The beauty of mathematics was illustrated through natural phenomena: cracked mud, veins on a leaf, an egg. "'Mathematica' had a reassuring quality," recalls former California Science Center

***Raid the Icebox***, curated by Andy Warhol, Museum of Art, Rhode Island School of Design, Providence, April 23–June 30, 1970.
Courtesy of the RISD Museum, Providence, R.I.

**Ray and Charles Eames.**
© Eames Office, LLC (eamesoffice.com)

curator Jay Rounds, "communicating that, through mathematics—no matter how crazy things may seem—there is an underlying order to the world's chaos." Expanded versions of *Mathematica*, including the contributions of women, people of color, and other mathematicians who were unrecognized in the original exhibit, can be seen today in many science museums.[63]

The Eameses were part of a circle of designers and educators interested in participatory experiences that made learning fun. One of their admirers was Frank Oppenheimer, a University of Colorado physics professor. Oppenheimer had achieved notoriety in the 1940s, when he and his brother J. Robert helped develop the atomic bomb in Los Alamos, N.M. During the McCarthy era, the brothers were blacklisted for speaking out against nuclear weapons. Oppenheimer felt it was essential to understand and not fear science. He envisioned a "refreshing and stimulating" place that would connect young people to the joys of science: an "exploration center [with a] laboratory atmosphere." This center's exhibits would have "aesthetic appeal, as well as pedagogical purpose . . . designed to make things clearer rather than to cultivate obscuran-

tism or science fiction." In 1969, Oppenheimer realized his dream when he opened the Exploratorium in an abandoned airplane hangar near San Francisco's Golden Gate Bridge. Over the ensuing decades, its staff and alumni would revolutionize science exhibits around the globe.[64]

Oppenheimer dispensed with the formal trappings of museums like glass cases and discrete walled-off galleries. Instead he augmented a few castaway exhibits from the National Aeronautics and Space Administration (NASA) with cheap materials like scrap wood and dishwashing liquid. "We view a science museum as a collection of props that constitute an inter-locking web of mini-curricula that can be used . . . at all levels, by . . . children, their friends or their parents or by our own staff when they use the place for learning or for teaching classes," he stated. "We are continually filling in and adding on to these interlocking 'curriculitos.'"

Exploratorium exhibits sought to increase visitors' understanding of natural phenomena, like optics, vibration, and motion. These exhibits transformed as visitors manipulated them. For example, one of Oppenheimer's first exhibits consisted of a rope separat-

**Exploratorium founder Frank Oppenheimer using one of his infinitely fascinating exhibits.**
© Exploratorium, www.exploratorium.edu

**The Exploratorium as it looked in the 1970s, complete with a "tactile dome" exhibition.**
© Exploratorium, www.exploratorium.edu

ing two seemingly identical white rectangles. When visitors removed the rope, suddenly both sides appeared as different shades of gray. A handwritten label explained the science behind the optical illusion of "The Gray Steps."

Throughout the Exploratorium, visitors were encouraged to create their own experiences, rather than simply read and look. Oppenheimer was more interested in what people did in an exhibition than in having them memorize facts. "Nobody flunks museum" was his famous mantra.

To encourage visitors to learn by doing, he put the Exploratorium's carpentry shop in full public view. Staff fixed, built, and tested things right in front of visitors. To encourage creativity, he founded an artists-in-residence program, where artists and scientists collaborated on pieces that featured prisms, swirling mist, and mirrors. The museum eventually produced more than 600 exhibits that traveled to museums around the world. Oppenheimer also imported an idea from the Palais de la Découverte in Paris and trained high school students to demonstrate processes, such as dissecting a cow's eye, and then explain the science to visitors. A product of San Francisco's era of psychedelia and flower children, the Exploratorium was loud, confusing, and joyous. In 2013, as San Francisco became a city of technology start-up gurus, the Exploratorium moved to a larger space near San Francisco's Embarcadero and expanded its digital footprint with a large array of research and training programs aimed at engaging even more people in science.

While Oppenheimer was building the Exploratorium in San Francisco, a museum director in Boston was redefining an institution half a century old. The Boston Children's Museum had been founded in 1913 by teachers who wanted to use natural history specimens with their students. Its initial exhibitions consisted of wooden cases filled with the requisite rocks, shells, and stuffed birds. Fifty years later not much had changed.

But in 1962 BCM hired the son of world-famous pediatrician Benjamin Spock to direct the museum. Michael Spock had much in common with Frank Oppenheimer. They had both grown up in New York, frequenting the city's museums and, coincidentally, attending the same private grammar school, whose curriculum was based on John Dewey's philosophy of experiential learning. But unlike the academically precocious Oppenheimer, Spock was dyslexic and did poorly in school. He found himself drawn to museums as places of learning where teachers wouldn't judge his performance, and spent long hours during his childhood at MoMA, where he felt more comfortable than at school.[65]

Spock joined BCM at an ideal time. First, there were lots of school-age children around. Public schools were at peak capacity due to the postwar baby boom. Second, Congress was keenly interested in education reform, passing such legislation as Project Head Start (1964) and the Elementary and Secondary Education Act (1965). Third, with its plethora of universities and think tanks, Boston was a magnet for educational research. Spock believed that museums could aid education reform through a new approach to exhibitions. Thus began the hands-on exhibition movement, where children were encouraged not only to look at objects, but manipulate them. Museums had long sponsored supervised "children's hours" where young visitors could touch specimens or partake in an art activity. Spock believed that handling objects shouldn't be confined to occasional programs. Rather, it was a core part of the museum visit. Kids needed to create something related to an exhibition's theme, to join in, to interact, in effect, to become scientists and artists.

In 1963, Michael Sand, a graduate of RISD who had worked for the Eameses, joined BCM's staff. For their first collaboration, *What's Inside* (1964), Spock and Sand cut open a range of objects—a baseball, a car, a toilet—so children could examine the insides. Children could even crawl through a manhole and see the innards of Boston's sewer system. It was an immediate success. For *How Movies Move*, the museum's next hit, kids were encouraged to spin zoetropes made out of hatboxes to make their own mini-movies. "We had to coach the parents," recalls Sand, "and tell them—it's okay, your kids can touch and handle things even though we're a museum."

By 1969 BCM had transformed its galleries into an interactive exhibit center where collections were supplemented with hands-on activities. Most of these activities used store-bought objects, but BCM also experimented with hard-to-find technologies. Spock recalls one station where children could operate four Wang calculators, "which was a big deal at the time," and possibly the first use of computers in a public gallery space.

Hands-on exhibitions and activity spaces soon made their way to mainstream museums. The Salt Lake City Art Center and North Carolina Museum of Art opened galleries of touchable work for audiences with visual impairments in the mid-1960s. A few years later the Bell Museum of Natural History in

Some of the breakthrough exhibits at the Boston Children's Museum encouraged children not just to look at objects but to handle them. *What's Inside* allowed young visitors to examine the insides of various objects.

Courtesy of the Boston Children's Museum

Minneapolis and Florida State Museum in Tallahassee created rooms with touchable activities for children.

Staff at Boston Children's Museum continued to test new approaches. In 1971, BCM built a carpeted Plexiglas playpen to accommodate babies while parents and older siblings enjoyed the rest of the museum. Staff noticed that older children were fascinated with the babies. In response, the museum developed *Before You Were Three*, about what it is like to be a baby. When staff discovered that adults were sharing parenting experiences in the space, they added a private area for nursing and changing babies, a first in a museum. In 1974 BCM educator Judith White took this idea to the Smithsonian and created an "alternative space . . . halfway between the exhibits in glass cases and the actual collections."[66] The Smithsonian Discovery Room had seating, touchable objects like mammoth molars and barnacles, and a steady presence of staff and volunteers—all the more innovative because of its placement in an adult-oriented institution. Four years later BCM inaugurated *PlaySpace*, a secure indoor exhibition with activities (including a play castle and slide) designed for very young children. One of the first exhibits in the country to serve both toddlers and their parents, *PlaySpace* has been refined and replicated for museums, airports, shopping malls, and other public spaces around the world.[67]

Although some traditional curators and scholars were critical of the hands-on movement, educators and social activists charged ahead, viewing museums as public spaces and exhibitions as vehicles for communicating ideas. The civil rights movements of the 1960s had raised questions about whether exhibitions could resonate beyond the white upper and middle classes who were the majority of museum visitors. An exhibition at the Smithsonian's Anacostia Neighborhood Museum helped to answer that question. The museum buzzed with neighborhood kids who were primarily from low-income African American families. Noticing the children's terrified reaction to two pet rats in the museum's petting zoo, museum education director Zora Martin Felton decided to address the issue of vermin in Anacostia. *The Rat: Man's Invited Affliction* (1969) featured a reconstructed, trashed-out backyard containing live urban rats. Visitors viewed the yard through peepholes as they learned about the history of rat infestation in cities and obtained sociological, scientific, and medical information on dealing with vermin. This memorable exhibition would later inspire museum professionals interested in socially relevant issues that would resonate with real issues in people's lives.[68]

The same year *The Rat* opened, the Metropolitan Museum of Art in New York decided that it too would reach out to African American neighborhoods. The

**Organized by the Anacostia Museum in 1969, *The Rat* was one of the first exhibitions devoted to socially relevant issues—in this case, the health problems caused by rats in an urban neighborhood.**
Smithsonian Archives, Record Unit 378, Box 6, #2005-63004

*Harlem on My Mind: Cultural Capital of Black America 1900–1968*, Metropolitan Museum of Art, 1969.
Image copyright © The Metropolitan Museum of Art, Image source: Art Resource, NY

result was an epic disaster. *Harlem on My Mind: The Cultural Capital of Black America* was envisioned to "chronicle the creativity of the downtrodden blacks, and, at the same time, encourage them to come to the museum." But as curator Allon Schoener later recounted, "reaching out to the black community was entirely new and unfamiliar for white cultural institutions. They had plenty of experience excluding blacks, but not many ground rules for inclusion."

*Harlem on My Mind* consisted of 15 galleries of enlarged photographs that Harvard University professor Henry Louis Gates later called "one of the richest and most comprehensive records of the history of the African-American in the 20th century." Yet when the show opened, African American visitors were dismayed. They expected to see paintings by black artists, long excluded from the Met. What they got was historic photographs, taken mostly by white photographers.

The situation deteriorated further when the show's catalog rolled off the presses. It opened with Met director Thomas Hoving's essay describing his wealthy white childhood, complete with a black "maid of sunny disposition" named Bessie. Hoving waxed on, earnestly explaining how, as a child, he believed that "Negroes were people. But they were happy, foot-twitching, smiling." Another essay by Harlem high-school senior Candice Van Ellison addressed the tensions between Jews and blacks in Harlem. "[P]sychologically, blacks may find that anti-Jewish sentiments place them, for once, within a majority," Ellison wrote. "Thus, our contempt for the Jew makes us feel more completely American in sharing a national prejudice."

The Jewish Defense League and Black Emergency Cultural Coalition picketed the museum. Protesters slashed eight paintings and etched the letter *H* (for Hoving) into a Rembrandt. The mayor threatened to slash the Met's funding. The museum was forced to withdraw the catalog, close the exhibition, and increase security.[69] *Harlem on My Mind*'s spectacular failure was a wake-up call for museums. They had a lot to learn if they wanted more communities to feel welcome inside. New approaches were needed if ivory-tower museums were to take on street-level issues.

In 1971, a few dozen blocks away, Joseph Veach Noble, a former Met executive now in charge of the Museum of the City of New York, had another socially relevant issue on his mind: the epidemic of drug overdoses. Thus arose the groundbreaking exhibition *Drug Scene*. Its entrance featured three caskets and a cutout of addicts shooting up heroin. The museum did not hire models to pose for photos; it showed real addicts. Nor did it put placebo drugs on display; curators convinced the New York State Narcotic Addiction Control Commission that real drugs were needed. "[Getting samples of genuine illegal] heroin, LSD, marijuana, amphetamines, and barbiturates became priority number one [as opening day neared]," Noble explained. The show also included morgue pictures and a soundtrack featuring popular singers who had died of overdoses. Recovering addicts were hired as staff, sporting "ask me" buttons and dialing an Addiction Control Center hotline for visitors requesting help. This happened about once a day, according to Noble.[70]

*Drug Scene* broke attendance records at the museum, then toured the state, setting even more records. No matter how uncomfortable a topic, if an exhibition was carefully researched and presented with authentic voices, museums were learning that they could be a positive force for educating and attracting visitors.

### 1976: THE BIRTH OF THE BLOCKBUSTER

Since the 1900s, lines of people have wrapped around city blocks for museum exhibits. In 1907, they queued up for a public health show on tuberculosis at the American Museum of Natural History in New York City. AMNH had to remain open 13 hours a day and hire 50 extra guards to accommodate the crowds. In the 1930s, they stood for hours at the San Francisco Museum of Art (now SFMOMA) to see Picasso's *Guernica*. On the show's last day, visitors staged a sit-in to convince the museum to extend its hours.[71] In 1969, they waited patiently outside the Smithsonian to gaze at the most expensive geological specimen ever acquired—an authentic moon rock, freshly transported to earth by the Apollo 11 astronauts.[72] But one event stands above all others in defining the museum blockbuster: *Treasures of Tutankhamun*, known colloquially as "King Tut."[73]

From 1976 to 1979, more people lined up to see the ancient boy king, his solid gold funerary mask, and 55 glittering treasures from his tomb than ever before in museum history. "In Chicago the faithful queued up outside the Field Museum at ten o'clock the night before—rain or shine," noted *ARTnews*. In New Orleans they collapsed after a nine-hour wait in the blazing sun. In Los Angeles they camped outside for up to two days. Thousands were turned away. In venues around the country "King Tut" drew so many people—8.25 million to be exact—that it led to audience-control innovations such as stanchions, timed tickets, and advance sales that are standard today.

In 1969, people stood in line for hours to see this two-pound moon rock sample, collected by Apollo 11 astronauts (left to right) Edwin E. "Buzz" Aldrin Jr. and Neil A. Armstrong, and presented to Frank Taylor, then-director general of museums at the Smithsonian Institution.

National Aeronautics and Space Administration (NASA), NASM-NASA-MSFC-6903159

The "King Tut" extravaganza was the result of a fortuitous confluence of events: diplomatic feats by U.S. and Egyptian government officials; the 1974 Arts and Artifacts Indemnity Act through which the federal government guarantees insurance coverage of certain art objects; and the United States bicentennial celebration. The bitter rivalry between J. Carter Brown, director of the National Gallery of Art (NGA), and Thomas Hoving, director of the Metropolitan Museum of Art, raised the stakes. Both men competed fiercely for their institution's right to premiere the show, throwing more and more incentives to officials in order to curry favor.[74]

The NGA won. In 1976, Brown presided over a high-profile press opening in Washington, D.C. Hoving retaliated with another high-profile tactic. He negotiated with Egyptian authorities to make molds of the show's jewelry and sculpture, which were cast into merchandise and sold in an "official Tut Store" when the show came to New York. The Met spun off even more products: scarves, posters, all the logo merchandise now commonly found in museum shops. Other "Tut" products—everything from towels to tote bags, even toilet seats—appeared in department stores. Tut even appeared on New York's *Saturday Night Live* when, in 1978, comedian Steve Martin performed his "Funky Tut" routine: "Now if I'd known / They'd line up just to see him / I'd've bought me a museum / King Tut."

In most televised events, Brown took the credit for wooing the exhibition to the United States. Yet for his marketing prowess, Hoving earned himself the unofficial title "King of the Museum Blockbuster." The term *blockbuster* had recently been coined in Hollywood after the success of the movie *Jaws*. No matter who we have to thank, one thing is clear: "King Tut" altered the course of museum exhibition history. Seeing dollar signs, museums began to focus on producing spectacles rather than developing long-term installations.

But what of the show itself? Was it worth the hype? It was for those drawn to the mesmerizing story of Tutankhamun's short and mysterious reign. Or for those titillated by rumors; a death curse reportedly haunted those who came too close to the objects. Organized into an Antechamber, Burial Chamber, Treasury, and Annex that corresponded to the tomb, ancient Egyptian objects—gigantic, beautiful, strange—unfolded across the galleries, culminating in the sight of Tut's iconic solid gold mask, with a cobra and vulture springing from his forehead. Interestingly, surveys showed that visitors took their time in the exhibition. They tended to read most of the information that was presented in labels and were overwhelmingly positive about their experience. By the 1980s the number of temporary

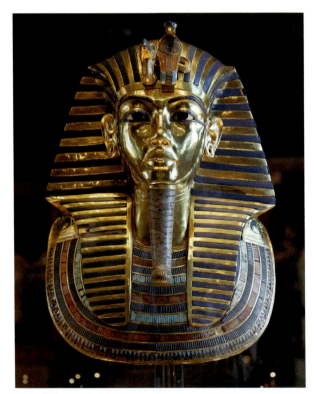

The gold mask of King Tutankhamun helped to launch the era of the blockbuster.

J. Carter Brown, director of the National Gallery of Art, competed intensely with Thomas Hoving for blockbuster shows. To Carter's right is the painting *Saint Peter*, studio of Sir Peter Paul Rubens, ca. 1616/1620.

Photo by Michael Geissinger, 1989; Library of Congress Prints and Photographs Division

THE FINE ARTS MUSEUMS OF SAN FRANCISCO

# TREASURES OF TUTANKHAMUN
## JUNE 1 – SEPTEMBER 30, 1979

M. H. DE YOUNG MEMORIAL MUSEUM,
GOLDEN GATE PARK,
SAN FRANCISCO, CA 94118

SPONSORED BY THE EMPORIUM AND THE MUSEUM SOCIETY

The solid gold portrait mask, encrusted with semi-precious stones, found in the tomb of the 14th Century B.C. Egyptian Pharaoh, Tutankhamun, is one of fifty-five spectacular objects on display in the exhibition.

Entrance ticket to *Treasures of Tutankhamun*, Fine Arts Museums of San Francisco, 1979.

Courtesy of Marjorie Schwarzer

exhibitions at a typical urban art museum had jumped by more than 50 percent. Not all had long lines of visitors, but they led critics to complain about the "blockbuster mentality" with its lackluster scholarship, glossy ads, and chintzy knock-off products.

Still, blockbusters have exposed large numbers of people to outstanding collections and artists. Successful blockbusters can quickly erase a deficit, put a stop to budget cuts from local elected officials, and provide operating support for more intellectually adventurous shows. In 1982 the Met ran a $2.1 million deficit. In 1983, after hosting *The Vatican Collection: The Papacy and Art*, it was $263,000 in the black.[75] In 1995 city officials pondered cuts to the Philadelphia Museum of Art. They changed their minds after the museum's Cézanne exhibition boosted city coffers with hotel and restaurant revenues. Three years later, the bottom line of the Museum of Fine Arts, Boston, was buoyed by *Monet in the 20th Century*. Cynics nicknamed it "Money in the 20th Century." Blockbusters also helped many science museums reach new audiences; in the 2000s, families stood in line at science museums in Philadelphia, Seattle, and Chicago to come face-to-face with Lord Voldemort's flowing black wardrobe and other iconic *Harry Potter* movie sets and props.

Not all blockbusters are moneymakers. Many (including sequels to "Tut") have proven to be too logistically complex and expensive for most museums to host. Nonetheless, a well-marketed blockbuster can attract crowds. In recent years, social media has helped. In the 2010s, Yayoi Kusama's twinkling infinity mirrors attracted a following, thanks to visitors who realized they were perfect backdrops for selfies.[76] Between 2017 and 2018, buoyed by hashtags on Instagram, Twitter, and Facebook, Kusama's ethereal installations were hits at the Mattress Factory (Pittsburgh), the Broad (Los Angeles), and the High Museum of Art (Atlanta). After installing work by Kusama, the Cleveland Art Museum's visitation jumped by 31 percent.

Social media also boosted audiences for the Met's Costume Institute shows, especially *Heavenly Bodies: Fashion and the Catholic Imagination* (2018).[77] Consisting of forty elaborate papal robes and other Vatican treasures displayed alongside medieval art, *Heavenly Bodies* was not planned as a blockbuster. But then on May 7, 2018, multiple A-list celebrities showed up at the Met's Costume Institute gala in glamorous pope-inspired attire. Images of R&B singer Rihanna in a lavish pearl- and crystal-studded papal outfit complete with miter and tiara went viral. *Heavenly Bodies* became an instant must-see. Over 1.6 million people

**Yayoi Kusama, *Repetitive Vision* (1996), at the Mattress Factory in Pittsburgh (formica, adhesive dots, mannequins, mirrors).**
© Michael Ventura Photography

**Exhibitions from the collection of Metropolitan Museum of Art's Costume Institute became blockbusters during the 2010s.**
Metropolitan Museum of Art Costume Institute, Gift of James R. Creel IV and Mr. and Mrs. Lawrence G. Creel, 1992. 1992.31.2a–c

visited during the five-month run, of what is, as of 2019, the most visited show in the Met's history. Beyond the celebrity hype, curator Andrew Bolton surmised that the show's popularity was due to its theatrical staging; it was an "experiential moment for people, with the fashion and art mixing together in a procession-like way . . . like a pilgrimage."[78]

## 1980s: EDUCATIONAL TRANSFORMATION

While art museums perfected the blockbuster, children's museums and science centers focused on the needs of children and their caregivers in a changing world. These museums valued a hands-on approach to educating youth and were fortified by the theories of John Dewey (learning through experience) as well as other educational reformers like Lev Vygotsky (learning through social interaction), Maria Montessori (learning through self-directed activity in a thoughtfully prepared environment), and Howard Gardner (learning in multiple ways).[79] They banded together to create alternative community environments that could supplement the education of the nation's children.

The Exploratorium assisted by creating low-tech traveling science exhibitions—for example, *Anti-Gravity Mirrors* and *Bernouli Blowers*—complete with instruction manuals called "Exploratorium Cookbooks."[80] With access to do-it-yourself packages, new organizations were able to replicate Exploratorium-type exhibitions cheaply and easily. Features at other youth museums like "PlaySpaces," child-size grocery stores, and bubble-blowing vats were also copied around the country. Some professionals cringed. Would all science centers and children's museums start to look and feel alike? Was the art of exhibition-making being reduced to a paint-by-numbers formula? But audiences didn't seem to care. They were delighted to have reliable, educationally sound hands-on exhibitions close by.

Furthermore, influenced by exhibitions like *The Rat* and *Drug Scene*, children's museums were eager to tackle topics that schools were afraid to touch, including disabilities, mortality, and racism. They explained those issues in honest ways that made sense to children. In 1975, Boston Children's Museum created *What If You Couldn't*, a response to children's curiosity and anxiety about disabilities. Janet Kamien, a 27-year-old former special needs teacher, led the charge, developing spaces where children of all levels and abilities could use tools like wheelchairs, prostheses, and Braille. Her idea was to demystify these objects while promoting empathy for people who use them.

In 1983, Kamien took on another sensitive topic: mortality. *Endings: An Exhibit about Death and Loss* included a diorama of a funeral parlor, a casket, bottles of embalming liquid, and a time-lapsed video of a dead mouse being devoured by maggots. Recognizing the potency of experiences like grief, loss, and mourning, Kamien set up a "talkback board"—a cork bulletin board on which visitors could thumbtack opinions, reactions, or questions written on small sheets of paper. *Death and Loss* ushered in a visitor-oriented process of creating exhibitions. Kamien was not a subject-matter expert nor was she a curator in charge of a collection. She had envisioned both *What If You Couldn't* and *Death and Loss* as dialogues between the museum and its audience. She solicited visitors' opinions about what they wanted to learn and then worked with teams of experts to figure out how to do it.[81]

By the mid-1980s teamwork and educational theory had inched their way into more traditional museums. They were influenced not only by children's museums, but by business developments like customer surveys and cross-functional teams. Previously, museums had relied on one or two experts—what one director has called the "priestly voice of absolute authority"—to decide what should go on the gallery floor.[82] Now survey data showed that this approach wasn't working. Most people did not walk from object to object in the order in which curators intended. They usually didn't read labels, especially long ones. Once again, museums were lagging behind other nascent entertainments that were capturing the public's imagination: video game consoles, portable music (the "Walkman"), and unfiltered television content (C-SPAN).

Activist-scholars spoke up about other issues museums were ignoring. They urged natural history museums to talk about global biodiversity, cultural diversity, and the fragile relationship between people and the natural environment. Anthropologists and Native American activists took on the stereotypes portrayed in life groups. Feminist art historians showed that art museums largely bypassed the works of women and artists of color. Social historians pointed out that most history museums still focused on "great white men" and disregarded other stories. These conversations convinced many curators, especially those new to the field, that museums needed to change not only their methods, but the stories their exhibitions were telling.

The new ways of thinking helped bring the venerable diorama back into the museum field's good graces, as natural history museums set about transforming their dioramas from frozen vignettes into

*Wolves and Humans* opened at the Science Museum of Minnesota in 1983 at a time of debate about the gray wolves' fate. The design helped to reinvigorate the habitat diorama and its role in discussions about species conservation.
Courtesy of International Wolf Center, Ely, MN.

action stories about fragile ecosystems. An influential example is the Science Museum of Minnesota's *Wolves and Humans: Coexistence, Competition, and Conflict* (1983). The exhibit opened at a time when the gray wolf's fate was hotly debated in Minnesota. *Wolves and Humans* presented a diversity of human attitudes about wolves. It featured a diorama of a wolf pack, including an alpha wolf killing a deer; piped-in sounds of howling; and a computer game that allowed visitors to play the part of wolves on a deer hunt. A video loop presented a range of opinions on reintroducing wolves to the wild, from ranchers and hunters to environmentalists and biologists. *Wolves and Humans* toured sites in 18 states, including Yellowstone National Park, and is now on permanent display at the International Wolf Center in Ely, MN.[83]

The American Museum of Natural History sought to bring Franz Boas's early-century life groups into modern times. In 1988, the exhibition *Chiefly Feasts: The Enduring Kwakiutl Potlatch* opened. While in the past, anthropologist-curators had referred to field notes, this time they worked directly with Kwakiutl

people, who identified important cultural themes, contributed personal stories, shared family albums, and explained the significance of different objects. "As a result of working on this exhibition, I have undergone a transformation of both mind and soul," wrote the show's chief curator, Aldona Jonaitis. "Working with the Kwakiutl has . . . taught me something important about the meaning of scholarship. Often as academics, we address . . . a small coterie of fellow scholars . . . [but] I have learned that we bear a profound responsibility in trying to communicate to the public the culture of Kwakiutl . . . they are not anonymous descendants of a once-great culture, but real people with a rich ceremonial life."[84]

Most significantly, Native Americans began to establish their own tribal museums across the country, developing narratives that reflected their own cultures in their own ways. The National Museum of the American Indian (NMAI), which opened in 2004 on the National Mall, can be seen as a national forum for presenting diverse American Indian perspectives to a wide audience. One of its most powerful displays shows the history of treaties between the federal government and Indian tribes, documenting decades of broken promises and mistrust, as well as healing and resilience.[85]

Elsewhere a new kind of period room reflected the field of social history. Developed with the input of former residents, in 1988, New York's Lower East Side Tenement Museum opened in a restored mid-19th-century tenement building. Tiny three-room apartments—complete with rickety furniture and rusty pots—reveal how immigrant families eked out a living when they arrived. Tours led by educators engage visitors in fuller stories—where the residents came from, how large families slept and performed garment industry work in such cramped spaces, and what they did for entertainment. These period rooms were designed to spark discussions among modern-day families about the immigrant experience, both in the past and today. The Tenement Museum inspired other institutions to exhibit stories of immigrant laborers.

In the early 2000s, Ron Chew, director of the Wing Luke Museum of the Asian Pacific Experience in Seattle, worked with 15 former sweatshop workers (including his own relatives) on *If Tired Hands Could Talk: Stories of Asian Pacific American Garment Workers*. In 2003, the museum acquired the East Kong Yick Building, a former residence and social center for Seattle's Chinese, Filipino, and Japanese laborers. Refurbished into educational spaces supplemented with oral histories about who built, clothed, and fed Seattle, this space now serves as a reminder of Seattle's working-class history in a rapidly gentrifying neighborhood.[86]

Mining exhibitions also changed to reflect a heightened awareness of labor issues. When the Washington State Historical Society in Tacoma opened *Roslyn Coalmine* in 1996, it focused on the poor ventilation, long workdays, and low paychecks miners endured. A mining shaft, for example, includes a mannequin of a

**The Tenement Museum gives visitors a glimpse of the past lives of working-class immigrants on Manhattan's Lower East Side.**
Photo by Carol M. Highsmith—Library of Congress Catalog, public domain

The ship *Balclutha* at San Francisco Maritime National Historical Park features an exhibit on *Chinatown*. This was where cannery workers—mostly Chinese, Japanese, and Filipino migrants—lived in exploitative conditions as ships like *Balclutha* transported them to Alaskan salmon canneries in the early 1900s.
Photo by Sabrina Oliveros

In 2017, the Tenement Museum in New York City re-created a 1980s garment factory that is part of a larger exhibition accessible by guided tour about the conditions under which Chinese and other immigrants worked.
Photo courtesy of Potion Design

worker trapped in rubble. The exhibition ends with a display of historic union pamphlets.

Meanwhile, art museums began to turn white cubes into less icy environments. The Denver Art Museum (DAM) was among the first to augment its galleries with books, catalogs, and comfortable couches for leisurely reading. The idea, said DAM's Dean of Education Patterson Williams, was to create spaces that were "more emotional, warmer, more embracing, more stimulating." In the 1980s, DAM's educators went a step further and rewrote labels. They aimed to purge "academic and stuffy" art historical jargon and use fresh language that was more accessible and appealing.[87] They hoped that presenting different viewpoints in clear prose would build visitors' confidence to make up their own minds about the artworks on display. By the late 1990s, other art museums—notably those in the Bronx, Dallas, and San Jose, CA—were inviting community members to write labels in their own words.[88] Some experts felt their authority was undermined; these kinds of techniques "dumbed down" and cheapened exhibition content. But evaluations showed visitors tended to stay longer in those exhibitions and to read more labels. Museums also began to experiment with bilingual labels, in English and Spanish, to better serve the nation's growing immigrant population. Welcome improvements to the museum's physical space were brought about by the 1990 Americans with Disabilities Act, which compelled such changes as canting labels so people in wheelchairs could read them and creating audio and touch tours for people with visual impairments.[89] There was no question that by the end of the 20th century, museums of all kinds were transforming their exhibition spaces in order to be of service to a wider public. Nancy Villa Bryk, a curator at the Henry Ford Museum and Greenfield Village, reflected on what these changes meant for the curatorial profession: "It was not about 'us'—the curators. It was about 'them'—our visitors. While the challenges curators faced at the museum seemed daunting and at times painful, those feelings diminished as we embraced new perspectives, learned new skills, and adjusted to new ways of working with others."[90]

## 1990s–2000s: EXPOSING PAINFUL TRUTHS

Museums had been collecting items that were evidence of historical injustices for decades. But it wasn't until the late 1980s that they began to interpret and exhibit those objects for contemporary audiences. Through the forces of social history and technology, museums became platforms for exhibits about traumas like imprisonment, genocide, migration, and racism. To get their messages across, curators and designers moved away from text-heavy "books on a wall" toward juxtaposing powerful objects with personal accounts and emotional storylines. Eyewitnesses came forward to share their experiences. Artists took on the racist codes of museum display. Between 1987 and 1993, four exemplars of this new way of exposing history premiered, three in Washington, D.C., and one in nearby Baltimore.[91]

In 1987, *A More Perfect Union: Japanese Americans and U.S. Constitution* debuted at the Smithsonian's National Museum of American History (NMAH) on the National Mall. Presenting the story of Japanese American internment during World War II, the innovative exhibit featured not only objects, but interviews with eight Japanese American former prisoners on two video monitors. The use of oral testimony in a museum exhibition was startling to many. Once considered inferior to other kinds of archival documents because it was imprecise and overly anecdotal, oral history was just starting to be appreciated as a necessary way to capture memories and infuse them with personality and heartfulness. "We wanted to create a document that was incontestable," said filmmaker Selma Thomas, who produced the oral histories, "so that even museum visitors who were strangers to the story would have to accept it as true. If you believe in the power of historical record, this is it. But the oral history also gives it a humanity that is often lacking in other kinds of documents."

In 1993, the nearby U.S. Holocaust Memorial Museum opened. It too paired historical artifacts with eyewitness accounts and video interviews, walking visitors through the events of the Holocaust and providing spaces for contemplation and reflection.[92] According to USHMM founding director Jeshajahu Weinberg, formerly of Tel Aviv's Cameri Theater, the layout was intended to work "like the three acts of a drama. . . . The mechanism is the same as with any good novel or film or play . . . [with] the potential of evoking psychological identification." Designer Ralph Appelbaum enhanced the drama through floor and wall coverings that change from light to dark as visitors progress through the story. Appelbaum went on to use these same theatrical techniques to take visitors on emotional journeys through the birth of the American legal system, the horrors of war, and African American struggles and triumphs at museums like Philadelphia's National Constitution Museum (2003), Kansas City's National World War I Museum (2006), and the National Museum of African American History and Culture (2016).[93]

Appelbaum has described his design for the Holocaust Museum as a "controlled emotional encounter" where visitors are forced to walk through or around incriminating objects: for example, a cattle car that transported Jews to the death camps. A similar technique was used to powerful effect in *Field to Factory: Afro-American Migration 1915–1940*. It opened in 1987 at NMAH. Created by social historian Spencer Crew and designer James Syms, *Field to Factory* set a standard for civil rights and African American history exhibitions around the nation. The space takes visitors through the harrowing ordeal of the African Americans who, in search of a better future, moved from the rural South to the urban North between the two world wars. Visitors begin their journey at a re-created tenant farmhouse, learning about life in the South through artifacts ranging from agricultural tools to a Ku Klux Klan robe, then viewing a segregated train car, and ending up in the industrial North with its factory time clocks and black businesses and churches. As visitors proceed through this story, they suddenly confront a Jim Crow–era passageway with one door marked "colored," the other marked "white." Visitors must choose a door to walk through in order to continue.

In 1992, Fred Wilson, a New York artist of Carib-African descent, chose the Maryland Historical Society in Baltimore as the site for his landmark exhibition about race and power in the United States. Wilson's installation differed from those on the National Mall. He used the museum not as a gallery space, but as a canvas. His idea was to challenge museums' historical attitudes toward people of color through exposing their "language"—that is, what they had in their collections and how they chose to arrange those items. He elected to work with MHS because, he later recalled, "I was really uncomfortable there."

Wilson called his installation *Mining the Museum*, a triple pun on the word *mining*: digging something up, blowing something up, and making something mine. The artist juxtaposed items from the collections in rooms that he painted gray and titled "grim historical truths." He arranged Chippendale dining-room chairs around a crude wooden whipping post from the Baltimore City Jail. He altered the spotlighting on an antebellum painting to reveal an enslaved black youth in a metal collar crouching behind his young white owner. On an audio loop next to the painting, a timid voice asks, "Am I your brother? Am I your friend? Am I your pet?" Another display featured fancy silver juxtaposed with slave shackles. "Actually they had a lot to do with one another," the artist said. "The production of one was made possible by the subjugation enforced by the other." *Mining the Museum* was timed to be up during the 1992 AAM convention in Baltimore, where thousands of museum workers were gathered. It sent shockwaves through the profession. As researcher Randi Korn later recalled, people who visited it were "dazed by the heartfelt questions it raised about history, truth, values, ownership."[94]

Professionals from all parts of the field were energized by the possibilities these experiments had opened. "It was a significant moment," says Elizabeth Chew, who was working as an art historian at a traditional museum when these shows opened. She would go on to supervise the 2017 award-winning exhibition *A Mere Distinction of Colour*, at James and Dolley Madison's Montpelier in Virginia—a frank exploration of the ongoing legacy of slavery told through the stories of its descendants. "[*Field to Factory* and *Mining the Museum*] fundamentally changed my life," adds Chris Taylor, who visited Washington, D.C., on a fellowship when he was in college. "I remember standing in front of the Jim Crow doors. I remember seeing the KKK hood. At that moment, I started to understand the power of using objects to elevate hidden narratives . . . I thought that if you can show objects like this in a museum, wow." Taylor would go on to work at the Minnesota Historical Society, leading many of its MHS's pioneering diversity and inclusion programs before becoming chief inclusion officer for the State of Minnesota.[95]

Minnesota Historical Society was a hotbed of experimentation during the 1990s, turning its focus away from heroic storylines to more impressionistic shows about the random moments in people's daily lives. Its influential 1992 show *Minnesota A to Z*, for example, took a novel take on the state's history. Curators arranged historical moments not by chronology, but according to the alphabet, from *A* for Minnesota's amazing animals, all the way to *Z*, for zero-degree winter days. Next to each of the 26 letters were artifacts and stories from diverse Minnesotans supporting the themes.[96] The "alphabet" technique spread to other history museums. A year later, influenced by firework festivals, rock concerts, and science centers, MHS used a technique called "object theater" to develop its *Homeplace Minnesota* exhibition.

The term *object theater* had been coined in the 1970s by Ontario Science Center designer Taiso Miyaki, who saw that a combination of light, objects, and narrative provided a powerful theatrical medium for holding

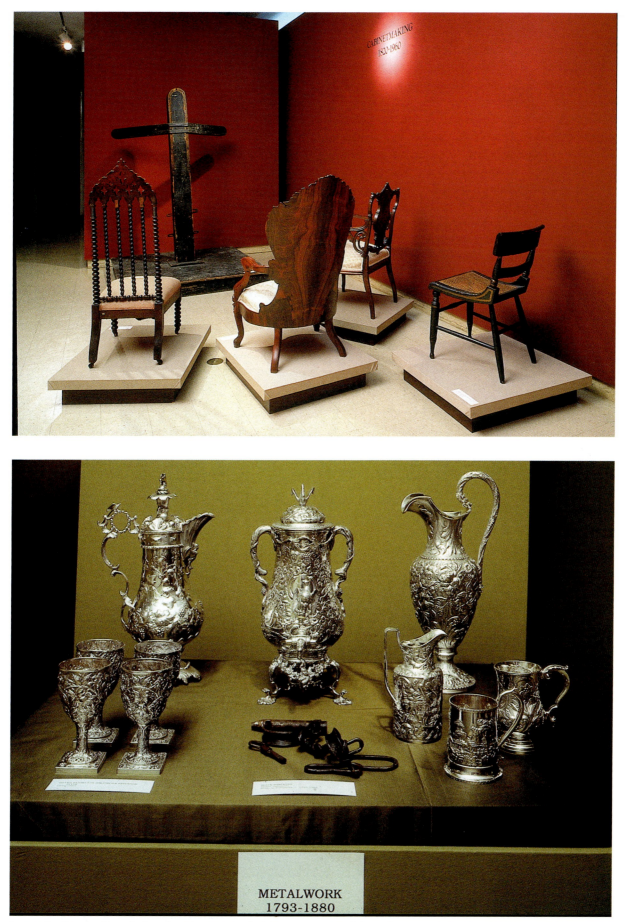

In search of "grim historical truths," in 1992 Fred Wilson manipulated the collections of the Maryland Historical Society to group objects like fancy silver items and slave shackles and finely carved chairs next to a crude wooden whipping post from the Baltimore City Jail. From *Mining the Museum*.

Courtesy of Maryland Historical Society

an audience's attention. In this spirit, *Homeplace* combined artifacts and narration to evoke a "feeling" for the state's history. Visitors entered a darkened space and sat in front of a stage that rumbled with light and sound. Flashes of light illuminated different objects. Recorded narration played excerpts from famous Minnesota literature and oral histories from the museum's archives.[97]

Like the alphabet technique, object theater spread to other history museums that applied it to such themes as culinary traditions (1998, Chippewa Valley Museum, Eau Claire, WI) and the Boston Massacre (2001, Bostonian Society). In 2004 the Mill City Museum, a branch of the Minnesota Historical Society, expanded the idea of object theater with *Flour Tower*. The museum used workers' voices, flashes of sound and light, and a ride through a flour silo to tell retired flour millers' stories. *Flour Tower*, explained the exhibit's developer Daniel

Spock, is a "very conscious homage to the Museum of Science and Industry coalmine."[98]

Another transformational MHS exhibition of this period was *Open House: If These Walls Could Talk*. In 2006, historian Benjamin Filene curated the rooms in an unremarkable house from Saint Paul's East Side to stitch together the stories of the ethnically diverse families (from German to African American to Hmong) who had inhabited it over the century. He aimed to show how a city's interior worlds—the places where ordinary people sleep and live—adapt to human dislocation and migration.

Not everyone bought in to the new direction exhibitions were taking. Politicians and conservative commentators accused curators of succumbing to a "liberal agenda" and "political correctness," arguments that fueled the period's "culture wars," the often-bitter

**Mill City Museum in Minneapolis. Its *Flour Tower* exhibition was designed partly as an homage to the Chicago Museum of Science and Industry's *Coal Mine*.**
By Runner1928—Own work, CC BY-SA 4.0, https://commons.wikimedia.org/w/index.php?cur id=57497579

debates about the right to exhibit potentially controversial perspectives.

Art museums took the brunt of these politically motivated attacks, as we will see in the next chapter. However, one contentious art museum exhibition bears discussion here: *The West as America: Reinterpreting Images of the Frontier, 1820–1920*. It opened at the Smithsonian's National Museum of American Art in 1991. *West as America* presented a "revisionist" perspective of the relationship between American landscape art and the Manifest Destiny. Although not the first exhibition to expose the colonialist and exploitative undertones of this genre of art, *West as America* was the most controversial. This is because of the hard-hitting language the curators used in the labels. Imagine politicians' reactions, for example, to this label: "Wishful Thinking I: Doomed Indians . . . these grim artistic metaphors of death also convey a guilty

longing that resilient Indians might really vanish." In comment books at the exhibition's exit, some visitors praised the labels as "eye-opening" and "courageous." But others condemned them as "socialist claptrap." Former Librarian of Congress Daniel Boorstin called the exhibit's tone "perverse, historically inaccurate, destructive." Yet, as often happens, the negative publicity benefited the museum. It had to extend the show's run by two weeks to accommodate curious crowds.[99]

Museums were realizing that they could trust their publics to respond positively to exhibitions that were honest and forthright. In 1990, Boston Children's Museum opened the exhibition *Kids Bridge*. It was the first in the nation to explore how racism impacts children. *Kids Bridge* was originally envisioned to celebrate multicultural Boston: the diverse foods, games, and festivals one can enjoy there. But in reflecting on her own experiences as a biracial child, codeveloper

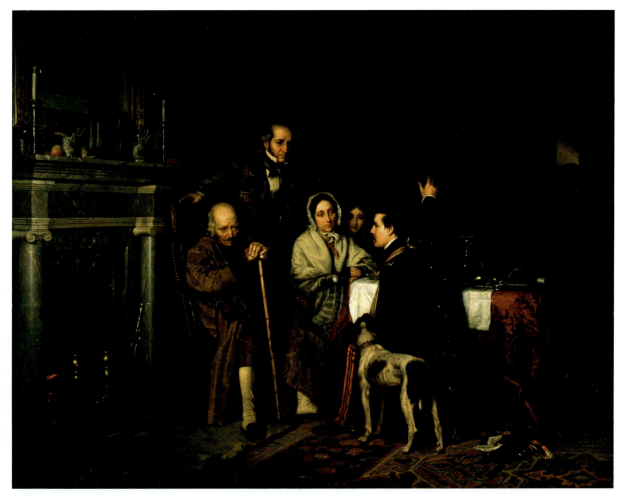

**Richard Caton Woodville's *Old '76 and Young '48*, ca. 1849, was part of the controversial 1991 *West as America* exhibition that was a focal point for the era's culture wars. The label accompanying this painting called out the "status" of the black servants in the background. At the time, these kinds of reinterpretations of art were shocking to many scholars and critics, although by and large the public responded well to the show.**
Courtesy of Walters Art Gallery

Joanne Rizzi-Jones realized that a celebratory approach wouldn't engage children of color. "We could not espouse the virtues of living in a multicultural society without talking about racism," she wrote (along with codeveloper Aylette Jenness) on the exhibition's introductory panel. BCM created an interactive video game about bullying and name-calling that was a key part of the exhibition. In one story, Tanisha is called a racial slur while on the school bus. Confused, angry, and hurt, she doesn't know what to do. Users could select potential reactions: ignore the insults, fight back, talk to an adult. Working on this component was tough, Jones-Rizzi later recalled; it was painful to face this subject. But children responded positively.

*Kids Bridge* traveled to numerous cities, influencing other youth museums to delve deeper. For example, Chicago Children's Museum staff interviewed hundreds of children about their experiences with racism, listening to the heartbreaking stories about name-calling and bullying. The result was its 1995 exhibition *Face to Face: Dealing with Discrimination*. CCM moved the name-calling off the video screen and into a mock school bus and Peace Diner, where children could role-play productive ways to deal with it. Staff developed related school curriculum on how the roots of bigotry influences our lives today. "Children's museums take seriously their unique opportunity—and responsibility—in promoting positive attitudes about diversity," said Carol Enseki, president of the Brooklyn Children's Museum.[100] Both *Kids Bridge* and *Face to Face* are now part of the KidsBridge Tolerance Center in Ewing, N.J.[101]

The soul-searching work of the 1990s emboldened museums of all disciplines to delve further into institutional racism. In 2005, New-York Historical Society mounted *Slavery in New York*, telling the previously unspoken story about enslaved people in northern states. Inspired by *Mining the Museum*, the museum juxtaposed archival materials such as legal records documenting merchants' buying and selling of slaves, with videos and reconstructed environments like the parlor of a slave-owning New York merchant.[102] Two years later, Minnesota Science Center opened *RACE: Are We So Different*, in collaboration with the

A young visitor (Adam Rose) listens to oral history in the exhibition *Grandparents: Learning Family History* at Chicago Children's Museum, 1995.
Courtesy of Marjorie Schwarzer

*Landscape of Slavery: The Plantation in American Art* exhibition, 2008, Gibbes Museum of Art, Charleston, S.C.
Image courtesy of the Gibbes Museum of Art

*Foundation*, 2004, by Juan Logan (American, b. 1946); Cast ductile iron; Collection of the artist; from the *Landscape of Slavery: The Plantation in American Art* exhibition, 2008, Gibbes Museum of Art, Charleston, S.C.
Image courtesy of the Gibbes Museum of Art

At James Madison's Montpelier, the exhibition *The Mere Distinction of Colour* documents the stories of the enslaved individuals who lived at the plantation.
Courtesy James Madison's Montpelier

American Anthropological Association. It exposed how race is a social construction that has oppressed and divided people. *RACE* was aimed not only at students, but also adult decision-makers: policy analysts, educators, doctors, lawyers. And in 2008, the Gibbes Museum of Art in Charleston, S.C., opened *Landscape of Slavery: The Plantation in American Art*. Acknowledging how *West in America* had deepened our understanding of how some 19th-century landscape paintings romanticized oppression, *Landscape of Slavery* looked at the heritage of plantation art. "Beautiful hills and fields" are "inseparable from brutality and violence" in southern states, stated the catalog. All of these shows attracted large audiences. *Slavery in New York* was extended, remounted, and remains online today. *RACE* toured the nation and was updated for permanent display; *Landscape of Slavery* was the most attended exhibition in the Gibbes's history, the beginning of a process in Charleston's museums, says Gibbes director Angela Mack, to tell more honest stories about local African American history.[103]

As educators and curators around the nation attempted to create more meaningful exhibitions and politicians debated controversial shows, artists poked holes at the whole system. "Institutional critique," the dissection and manipulation of museums' exhibition techniques epitomized by Fred Wilson's incisive work in Maryland, became an art form in and of itself. The Museum of Contemporary Art in La Jolla, CA, exhibited a habitat diorama of urban raccoons preying on heaps of human garbage, created by artist Mark Dion. At the Gibbes Museum of Art, Christian Boltanski deconstructed the period room in *Inventory of Objects Belonging to a Young Woman in Charleston*, reassembling her furnishings with labels identifying such objects as "mop" and "colander." In an even more satirical piece titled *Museum Highlights: A Gallery Tour*, performance artist Andrea Fraser spoofed docent tours at the Philadelphia Museum of Art. The number of artists using museums as palettes was so large that in the late 1990s MoMA presented a collection of such works in *The Museum as Muse: Artists Reflect*. Museum techniques had become so ubiquitous that it was now possible to create exhibitions about exhibitions.

Entire museums repackaged themselves as art installations. The Museum of Jurassic Technology, founded by performance artist David Wilson at an unspecified date and time, claims that it is "dedicated to the advancement of knowledge and the public appreciation of the lower Jurassic . . . through a hands-on experience of life in the Jurassic." A visitor to MJT in Culver City, CA, is treated to a series of eclectic, possibly contrived, exhibits of scientific phenomena, seemingly historical events that may never have happened and works that may or may not be art. On display are such items as a solid piece of lead in which (supposedly) a South American bat is trapped and a microscopic portrait of Ernest Hemingway sketched onto an apple seed. Art critic Ralph Rugoff compares MJT to a mockumentary, calling it a "modern meta-museum—a museum about museology . . . that uses falsehoods as a way of conveying a type of experiential truth that escapes analytical approaches."[104]

## INTO THE 21ST CENTURY: SHARING POWER

"Good Lord, another blog." So begins one of the early 21st century's most influential museum blogsites: Nina Simon's Museum 2.0. In 2006, the 25-year-old experience development specialist at the International Spy Museum in Washington, D.C., found museum exhibitions to be one-sided; they relied too heavily on what Simon called "tightly-closed feedback loops" between experts. Perhaps the nascent phenomenon of the "participatory Web" could help advance museum practice. Wikipedia had been around for about five years; YouTube had just celebrated its first anniversary. Participatory sites like these, Simon believed, improve as more and more people contribute content and ideas. Could museums create better exhibitions if they crowd-sourced ideas? Continually prototyped, beta-tested, and adjusted exhibit components? Built networks of diverse individuals who could work together to radically transform institutions? These ideas had been around since the 1960s hands-on movement. But Simon pushed them forward by translating them into the millennial language of the Internet. Her blog attracted a wide following of a new generation of museum workers, and her subsequent 2010 book *The Participatory Museum* became an instant classic.[105] In 2011, Simon became executive director at the Museum of Art and History (MAH) in Santa Cruz, CA. In this small city of surfers, college students, organic farmers, and Internet geeks, she embarked on a set of experiments to put her ideas about bringing diverse groups of people to cocreate exhibitions into practice.

At the same time, about 70 miles to the north, at San Francisco State University, activist social worker Jamie Lee Evans and a small team of former foster youth were wrestling with how to write a curriculum to help child welfare supervisors and frontline workers. The need was urgent. The majority of children in their care suffered serious neglect, or worse. When they aged out of the system, things often devolved into homelessness or incarceration. What did caseworkers need to know in order to work more effectively with young people experiencing so much trauma in their lives? Evans, a survivor herself of foster care and homelessness, realized that objects could evoke empathy more powerfully than an instruction manual or lecture series. One by one, former foster youth came forward with material that epitomized their experiences: the sole letter received from an incarcerated parent; the only toy they had ever been given; a college diploma earned while living on the streets. The Foster Youth Museum was born. As more former foster youth came forward with stories and objects, the museum developed pop-up–style exhibitions with the themes of "lost childhood," "healing," and "intentional families" for social worker trainings, alternative art spaces, and churches.[106]

In 2017, Evans and curator/photographer Ray Bussolari teamed up with Simon and her staff at MAH for a community-curated exhibition called *Lost Childhoods: Voices from Santa Cruz County Foster Youth and the Foster Youth Museum*. Using a participatory process that involved foster youth, educators, artists, and youth advocates, *Lost Childhoods* juxtaposed photos of former foster youth with precious objects that illustrated their stories. Visitors could take home "action cards" with suggestions of small actions they could take to help. The exhibition was attended by people who could make an even larger impact: judges, caseworkers, elected officials. As Simon later noted, the "co-creation involved was deep and hard and important. The resulting exhibition told stories that had never been told, coming from voices that had often been silenced. And it encouraged visitors not just to participate, but to take action to help foster youth, and by doing so, make our community stronger." *Lost Childhoods* was not the first museum exhibition to lay bare the pain and resilience of invisible communities—the incarcerated, the homeless, the isolated elderly, undocumented immigrants. Nor would it be the last.

Since the 1880s, museums have experimented with creating environments that bring new ideas and ways of thinking to the forefront of society. In the 1920s, they looked to the cyclorama and world's fairs;

*Lost Childhoods: Voices from Santa Cruz County Foster Youth and the Foster Youth Museum*, installation photo, Summer 2018
© Ray Bussolari

the goal was contextual environments, like habitat dioramas and period rooms. From the 1930s to the 1950s, they looked to Bauhaus and new fields like industrial design and photojournalism to invent the white cube. The goal was neutral environments that ordered the world according to textbook precision. During the 1960s and 1970s, they looked to educational psychology and political activism to shape active learning spaces. The goal was connection and social relevance. In the 1980s and 1990s, they looked to emerging digital technologies, business team models, and people's lived experiences. The goal was multisensory environments that could convey multiple perspectives. Or as hands-on education pioneer Michael Spock put it, "organizing the learning experience" was no longer the "exclusive responsibility of the museum; it [was] shared with the visitor."[107]

"Truth-telling," "participation," "decolonization," and "empathy" have been the expectations in the early decades of the 21st century. Whether through highly polished art extravaganzas, emotionally charged walks through history, inventive combina-

**Captain, a former foster youth from Northern California, whose story of being forced to wear a hospital gown every day while institutionalized is told by the Foster Youth Museum**
© Ray Bussolari

tions of materials, or community-developed displays that connect us to other people's lives, museums' stock-in-trade is powerful exhibitions. As Penny Jennings, president of the National Association for Museum Exhibition, says, "Museum exhibitions can break open your understanding and let in a perspective you've never before considered."[108]

## NOTES

1. J. G. Wood, "The Dullness of Museums," *Library Magazine* 3, no. 61 (April 13, 1887): 30–40.

2. Leslie Bedford, *The Art of Museum Exhibitions: How Story and Imagination Create Aesthetic Experiences* (Walnut Creek, CA: Left Coast Press, 2014), 133.

3. Theodore Roosevelt, quoted in Julie Leibach, "Theodore Roosevelt: A Conservationist's Legacy Lives On," *Audubon*, September 16, 2009, https://www.audubon.org/news/theodore-roosevelt-conservationists-legacy-lives. For more on the extraordinary story of Frank Chapman's pioneering environmental advocacy see Laura Allen, "The Price of a Feather," National Parks Conservation Association, Summer 2015, accessed May 26, 2019, https://www.npca.org/articles/918-the-price-of-a-feather; Victoria Shearer, *It Happened in the Florida Keys* (Guilford, CT: Globe Pequot Press, 2008); and Francois Vuilleumier, "Dean of American Ornithologists: The Multiple Legacies of Frank M. Chapman of the American Museum of Natural History," *Auk* 122, no. 2 (April, 2005): 389–402.

4. Wood, "Dullness of Museums," 30–40.

5. At times native peoples were persuaded to participate so they could perform dances, songs, and other rituals that had been banned in their homelands due to colonization. See "Collection, Colonialism and Collaboration: A Dialogue," edited transcript of a conversation between Aaron Glass and Corrine Hunt, recorded in New York City on August 9, 2018, https://www.bgc.bard.edu/gallery/exhibitions/88/the-story-box/.

6. Holmes, quoted in William Fitzhugh, "Ambassadors in Sealskins: Exhibiting Eskimos at the Smithsonian," in *Exhibiting Dilemmas: Issues of Representation at the Smithsonian*, eds. Amy Henderson and Adrienne L. Kaeppler (Washington, D.C.: Smithsonian Institution Press, 1997), 213–14. For more information on Holmes's work as an ethnographer, curator, and artist, see Curtis M. Hinsley Jr., *Savages and Scientists: the Smithsonian Institution and the Development of American Anthropology, 1840–1910* (Washington, D.C.: Smithsonian Institution Press, 1981), 100–109.

7. Another influential life group of this period was *Hopi Snake Dance Group*, created by Theodore A. Mills in 1901 for the Carnegie Museum of Natural History. Mills had never witnessed a snake dance, nor did he comprehend its sacred context. Instead, he worked from photographs, dressing mannequins in real ceremonial clothing pur-chased from an Arizona trader. He then composed a scene featuring a curling serpent slithering through the mouth of one dancer, as others "charm" it with feathers. (In the mid-1990s, after NAGPRA passed, Carnegie dismantled *Hopi Snake Dance Group* and collaborated with American Indian advisors on more accurate exhibitions of Indian life and traditions.)

8. Franz Boas, quoted in Ira Jacknis, "Franz Boas and Exhibits," in *Objects and Others: Essays on Museums and Material Culture*, ed. George W. Stocking Jr. (Madison: University of Wisconsin Press, 1985), 101. For more information on the history of life groups, see Kevin Coffee, "The Restoration of the Haida Canoe Life Group," *Curator* 34, no. 1 (1991): 31–48; Fitzhugh, "Ambassadors in Sealskins"; Jacknis, "Franz Boas and Exhibits"; Barbara Kirshenblatt-Gimblett, *Destination Culture: Tourism, Museums and Heritage* (Berkeley: University of California Press, 1998); Richard Kurin, *Reflections of a Culture Broker* (Washington, D.C.: Smithsonian Institution Press, 1997), 84–93.

9. J. D. Salinger, *The Catcher in the Rye* (Boston: Little, Brown and Company, 1951), 120–21.

10. There are numerous fascinating accounts of the personalities behind the development of habitat dioramas in U.S. museums. See Edward Alexander, "Carl Ethan Akeley," *The Museum in America* (Walnut Creek, CA: AltaMira Press, 1997), 33–49; Stephen T. Asma, *Stuffed Animals and Pickled Heads: The Culture and Evolution of Natural History Museums* (New York: Oxford University Press, 2001); Lara Bjork, "Wildlife Dioramas and Natural History Museums in Theory and Practice" (master's project, John F. Kennedy University, 2000); Victoria Cain, "Nature under Glass: Popular Science, Professional Illusion and the Transformation of American Natural History Museums, 1870–1940" (doctoral dissertation, Columbia University, 2007); James L. Clark, *Good Hunting: Fifty Years of Collecting and Preparing Habitat Groups for the American Museum* (Norman: University of Oklahoma Press, 1966); Donna Haraway, "Teddy Bear Patriarchy: Taxidermy in the Garden of Eden, 1908–1936," *Social Text* 11 (Winter 1984–1985); "The Illusionary Art of Background Painting in Habitat Dioramas," *Curator* 33, no. 2 (June 1990), 90–116; Stephen Christopher Quinn, *Windows on Nature: The Great Habitat Dioramas of the American Museum of Natural History* (New York: Abrams, 2006); Karen A. Rader and Victoria E. M. Cain, *Life on Display: Revolutionizing U.S. Museums of Science and Natural History in the Twentieth Century* (Chicago: University of Chicago Press, 2014); Marjorie Schwarzer, "Butterflies in the Basement: Requiem for the Snow Museum of Natural History," in *The Marvelous Museum*, ed. Andrew Leland (San Francisco: Chronicle Books, 2010); Marjorie Schwarzer, "Shotgun Wedding: The New California Academy of Sciences

African Hall," *Exhibitionist* 28, no. 1 (2009); Marjorie Schwarzer and Mary Jo Sutton, "Diorama Literature Review," Oakland Museum of California, 2009, http://museumca.org/files/gallery-documentation/Diorama-Lit-Review_Schwarzer_Sutton.pdf; and Karen Wonders, "Exhibiting Fauna—From Spectacle to Habitat Group," *Curator* 32, no. 2 (June 1989): 131–56.

11. Karen Rader and Victoria Cain, "From Natural History to Science: Display and the Transformation of American Museums of Science and Nature," *Museum and Society* 6, no. 2 (July 2008): 155.

12. Willard L. Boyd, "Museums as Centers of Controversy," *Daedalus* 128, no. 3 (summer 1999): 212.

13. Asma, *Stuffed Animals*, 34; and Haraway, "Teddy Bear Patriarchy."

14. Andrea DenHoed, "The Making of the American Museum of Natural History's Wildlife Dioramas," *New Yorker*, February 15, 2016, accessed May 16, 2019, https://www.newyorker.com/culture/photo-booth/the-making-of-the-american-museum-of-natural-historys-wildlife-dioramas.

15. This account of period rooms comes from the archives of the Fine Arts Museums of San Francisco and Oakland Museum of California, as well as the following literature: Edward Alexander, *Museums in Motion* (Nashville, TN: American Association of State and Local History, 1979), 185; Karen Cushman, "Jane Addams and the Labor Museum at Hull House," *Museum Studies Journal* (Spring 1983): 20–25; James Deetz, "A Sense of Another World: History Museums and Cultural Change," *Museum News* (May/June 1980); Melissa Young Frye, "The Beginnings of the Period Room in American Museums: Charles P. Wilcomb's Colonial Kitchens, 1896, 1906, 1910," in *The Colonial Revival in America*, ed. Alan Axelrod (New York: W. W. Norton & Company, 1985), 217–40; Edward N. Kaufman, "The Architectural Museum from World's Fair to Restoration Village," reprinted in *Museum Studies: An Anthology of Contexts*, ed. Bettina Messias Carbonell (Malden, MA: Blackwell, 2004), 273–88; Elizabeth Kennedy, "Interpreting the Artist's Studio Memorial: An Exhibition Strategy of Museums of Western Art" (doctoral dissertation, University of Pennsylvania, Philadelphia, 2003); Gary Kulik, "Designing the Past," in *History Museums in the United States: A Critical Assessment*, eds. Warren Leon and Roy Rosenzweig (Urbana: University of Illinois Press, 1989), 12–17; Warren Leon and Margaret Platt, "Living-History Museums," in *History Museums in the United States: A Critical Assessment*, eds. Warren Leon and Roy Rosenzweig (Urbana: University of Illinois Press, 1989), 64–97; Amelia Peck, *Period Rooms in the Metropolitan Museum of Art* (New York: Abrams, 1996); Rodris Roth, "The New England, or 'Olden Tyme,' Kitchen Exhibit at Nineteenth-Century World's Fairs," in *The Co-*

*lonial Revival in America*, ed. Alan Axelrod (New York: W. W. Norton & Company, 1985), 159–83; and Patricia West, "'The New Social History' and Historic House Museums: The Lindenwald Example," *Museum Studies Journal* 2, no. 3 (Fall 1986).

16. *The Mount Vernon Ladies' Association of the Union: Annual Reports: 1858–1895* (Baltimore, MD: Press of the Friedenwald Co., 1896). Quotes from 1886 annual report, page 3, and 1872 annual report, page 5.

17. James Deetz, quoted in West, "'New Social History,'" 23.

18. Linda Merrill, *The Peacock Room: A Cultural Biography* (New Haven, CT: Yale University Press, 1998).

19. Waldemar Kaempffert, *From Cave-Man to Engineer* (Chicago: Museum of Science and Industry, 1933), 13–21. For more information, see Herman Kogan, *A Continuing Marvel: The Story of the Museum of Science and Industry* (New York: Doubleday and Company, 1973); and Jay Pridmore, *Inventive Genius: History of the Museum of Science and Industry* (Chicago: Museum of Science and Industry, 1996). By the 1990s, MSI's original miner-docents had long been replaced by college students parroting memorized scripts. The canary in the coalmine had long been replaced by more advanced smoke detectors. MSI updated its mine, emphasizing new safety measures.

20. Frank Jewett Mather, quoted in Steven Conn, *Museums and American Intellectual Life, 1876–1926* (Chicago: University of Chicago Press, 1998), 228–29.

21. Quoted in Samuel Cauman, *The Living Museum: Experience of an Art Historian and Museum Director: Alexander Dorner* (New York: New York University Press, 1958), 144–48.

22. Walter Gropius, quoted in John Burchard and Albert Bush-Brown, *The Architecture of America: A Social and Cultural History* (Boston: Atlantic Monthly Press, 1966), 355.

23. George Dondero, "Modern Art Shackled to Communism," greg.org, April 17, 2017, accessed July 10, 2019, https://greg.org/archive/2017/04/17/better-read-013-modern-art-shackled-to-communism-by-congressman-george-dondero.html.

24. Robert L. Herbert et al., *The Societe Anonyme and the Dreier Bequest at Yale University: A Catalogue Raisonne* (New Haven, CT: Yale University Press, 1984). A photo of the Brooklyn exhibition appears on page 10. See also Mary Anne Staniskewski, *The Power of Display: A History of Exhibition Installations at the Museum of Modern Art* (Cambridge, MA: MIT Press, 1998), 317.

25. For example, a room displaying Dutch Baroque pictures was painted cool gray; next door, a room with Rococo art was done up in a "symphony of pink, gold and oyster white," and in yet another room Impressionist paintings hung from near white walls, to bring out the light in the works' brushstrokes. To Dorner, his chosen wall colors

were "factors in visual communication" that helped contemporary people relate to art from the past.

26. For more on Dorner's contributions to exhibition design, see Judith Berry, "Dissenting Spaces," in *Thinking about Exhibitions*, eds. Reesa Greenberg et al. (London: Routledge, 1995), 307–11, for a theoretical comparison of El Lissitsky's *Cabinet* with Akeley's gorilla diorama; Cauman, *Living Museum*; Alexander Dorner, *The Way beyond "Art"* (New York: New York University Press, 1958), 144–48 (foreword by John Dewey); Curt P. Germundson, "Alexander Dorner's Atmosphere Rooms: The Museum as Experience," unpublished paper presented at the College Art Association Conference, March 2004; and Dietrich Helms, "The 1920s in Hannover," *Art Journal* (Spring 1963): 144. It is worth noting one legendary connection between Dorner and Alfred Barr: when Barr visited Hanover in the shadow of Nazism, Dorner tucked two canvases by Kazimir Malevich into an umbrella for Barr to smuggle out of Germany. Many years later MoMA returned the paintings to the artist's heirs in Russia. See Sybil Gordon Kantor, *Alfred H. Barr, Jr. and the Intellectual Origins of the Museum of Modern Art* (Cambridge, MA: MIT Press, 2002), 181–83.

27. Eugene R. Gaddis, *Magician of the Modern: Chick Austin and the Transformation of the Arts in America* (New York: Alfred A. Knopf, 2000), 5. Austin would go on to become director of the Ringling Museum in Sarasota.

28. See Staniskewski, *Power of Display*. Alfred Barr's thoughts on design are discussed page 61.

29. Brian O'Doherty, "Inside the White Cube," *Artforum* (November 1976): 42–43.

30. Philip Johnson, quoted in Staniskewski, *Power of Display*, 64.

31. Dorothy C. Miller, quoted in Audrey M. Clark, "Museums, Feminism and Social Impact" (master's thesis, State University of New York College at Buffalo, May 2019), 50. See also "Dorothy C. Miller Papers in the Museum of Modern Art Archives," accessed June 1, 2019, https://www.moma.org/research-and-learning/archives/finding-aids/dcmillerf. During her 35-year career at MoMA (1934–1969), Miller produced trend-setting American art exhibitions, propelling the careers of young unknown artists like Mark Rothko, Jasper Johns, and Frank Stella.

32. Staniskewski, *Power of Display*, 91–97.

33. Laurence Vail Coleman, *The Museum in America: A Critical Study* (Washington, D.C.: American Association of Museums, 1939), 208–209; and Victor J. Danilov, *Traveling Exhibitions* (Washington, D.C.: Association of Science and Technology Centers, 1978). Danilov documents the following organizations as early providers of traveling exhibitions to museums: American Federation of Art (1909); Western Association of Art Museums (1921); Museum of Modern Art (1932); American Institute of Graphic Arts (1937); Oak Ridge Associated Universities Museum Division Traveling Programs (1949—under contract from the U.S. Atomic Energy Commission); Smithsonian Institution Traveling Exhibition Services (SITES) (1952); International House of Photography at George Eastman House (1961).

34. Carlos Emmons Cummings, *East Is East and West Is West* (Buffalo, N.Y.: Buffalo Society of Natural Sciences, 1940), 114–15.

35. Ned J. Burns, *Field Manual for Museums* (Washington, D.C.: U.S. Government Printing Office, 1941), 63.

36. Lucia Procopio, "Curating Racism: Understanding Field Museum Anthropology from 1893 to 1969," *Museum Scholar* 2 (July 8, 2019), www.museumscholar.org. The author wishes to thank Procopio for her analysis of this exhibition, in research conducted while she was a student at Northwestern University.

37. Sources on *Races of Mankind* include Willard L. Boyd, "Museums as Centers," 213–14; Marianne B. Kinkel, "Circulating Race: Malvina Hoffman and the Field Museum's Races of Mankind Sculptures" (doctoral dissertation, University of Texas at Austin, 2001), especially pages 140–46; and Tracy Lang Teslow, "Representing Race to the Public: Physical Anthropology in Interwar American Natural History Museums" (doctoral dissertation, University of Chicago, 2002).

38. Staniskewski, *Power of Display*, 227–35.

39. "Dallas Armistice," *Time* (March 12, 1956): 70.

40. Sources include John Anderson, "*The Family of Man*: Rudolph's Setting for a Photography Show," *Interiors* (April 1955): 114–17; Leon Anthony Arkus, "The Family of Man," *Carnegie Magazine* (November 1956): 297; Jacob Deschin, "Mankind in Pictures," *New York Times*, September 21, 1952; Jacob Deschin, "Steichen Reports," *New York Times*, December 14, 1952; Jacob Deschin, "Pictures Wanted," *New York Times*, January 31, 1954; Jacob Deschin, "Panoramic Show Opens at Modern Museum," *New York Times*, January 30, 1955; Jacob Deschin, "Family's Last Day," *New York Times*, May 8, 1955; *The Family of Man* (New York: Museum of Modern Art, 1955), exhibition catalog; Dorothy Grafly, "The Weathervane—Camera, Friend or Foe?" *American Artist* (May 1955): 32; Aline Saarinen, "The Camera Versus the Artist," *New York Times*, February 6, 1955; Eric Sandeen, *Picturing an Exhibition: The Family of Man and 1950s America* (Albuquerque: University of New Mexico Press, 1995); Ben Shahn, "Art versus the Camera," *New York Times*, February 13, 1955; and Jonathan Weinberg, "The Family of Stieglitz and Steichen," *Art in America* (September 2001): n.p.

41. Terry Zeller, "From National Service to Social Protest: American Museums in the 1940s, '50s, '60s, and '70s," *Museum News* (March/April 1996): 52.

42. Eric Sandeen, *Picturing an Exhibition: The Family of Man and 1950s America* (Albuquerque: University of New Mexico Press, 1995), 39.

43. Shamoon Zamir and Gerd Hurm, introduction, in The Family of Man *Revisited: Photography in a Global Age*,

eds. Gerd Hurm, Anke Reitz, and Shamoon Zamir (London: I. B. Tauris & Co., 2018), 8.

44. Maria Quinlan Leiby, email exchange, 2004. See also Maria Quinlan Leiby, "Museums in the Rearview Mirror: Exhibits and Institutional Identity in Michigan Museums, 1930–1995" (doctoral dissertation, Michigan State University, 2000), 33.

45. The "book on a wall" idea can be traced to Smithsonian curator George Brown Goode, who in the 1890s argued that a truly educational museum should arrange labels (accompanied by specimens) systematically because objects could not be expected to speak for themselves.

46. David Halberstam, *The Fifties* (New York: Villard Books, 1993), 185.

47. John Crosby, "What in the World," *New York Herald Tribune*, June 20, 1952. University of Pennsylvania has uploaded several episodes of "What in the World" to its YouTube channel: https://www.youtube.com/watch?v=lJFK-oAwQUA.

48. Robert Dierback, "Television and the Museum," *Curator* 1, no. 2 (1958): 34–44.

49. "Davy in Beantown," *Time* 66, no. 6 (August 8, 1955): 59.

50. "Recorded Gallery Tours Succeed at St. Paul," *Museum News* (February 15, 1942): 1. "Acoustiguide will never take the place of a well-trained docent," full-page ad on page 10 of *Museum News*, September 1963.

51. Bruno Gebhard, "Art and Science in a Health Museum," *Bulletin of the Medical Library Association* 33, no. 1 (January 1945): 39–49. See also "The Development of the Health Museum," *Museum News* 43, no. 6 (1965).

52. Joel Bloom (former director, Franklin Institute) and Ann Mintz, personal communication, spring 2004.

53. Lothar P. Witteborg, "Design Standard in Museum Exhibitions," *Curator* 1, no. 1 (January 1958): 29.

54. J. D. Salinger, *The Catcher in the Rye* (Boston: Little, Brown and Company, 1951), 155–58.

55. Alexander Girard, quoted in Henry H. Glassie, *The Spirit of Folk Art: The Girard Collection* (New York: Henry N. Abrams, 1995), 17. On their honeymoon in Mexico in the 1930s, Girard and his wife, Susan, began to collect folk art. Girard went on to become a designer for the furniture company Herman Miller, Inc. He is also known for his design of the lobby of Eero Saarinen's John Deere building in Moline, IA, where he arranged farm tools, invoices, and old gloves into a clever modern montage. He conceived of MoMA's first exhibition on East Indian textiles (1954), called *Textiles and Ornamental Arts of India*. In the 1950s, he and Susan moved to Santa Fe and eventually donated their extensive collection to the International Museum of Folk Art. The display he designed for this vast collection of pottery, rugs, toys, baskets, and puppets still stands today.

56. Allan Kaprow, quoted in Charles Harrison and Paul Wood, eds., *Art in Theory, 1900–2000* (Malden, MA: Blackwell, 2003), 718.

57. Robert Smithson, "Cultural Containment," reprinted in *Art in Theory, 1900–2000*, eds. Charles Harrison and Paul Wood (Malden, MA: Blackwell, 2003), 970–71.

58. Chick Austin, quoted in Eugene R. Gaddis, *Magician of the Modern: Chick Austin and the Transformation of the Arts in America* (New York: Alfred A. Knopf, 2000), 335–36.

59. For a discussion of other influential art curators during this period and how their work anticipated the participatory impulses of social media, see Valerie Wainwright, "Social Media and the Democratization of American Museums" (master's project, University of San Francisco, 2019), 898.

60. Jo Applin, *Yayoi Kusama: Infinity Mirror Room—Phalli's Field* (Cambridge, MA: MIT Press, 2012), 3. See also Jessica Kubala, "Glass Box" (master's thesis, University of Houston, 2018); and Mika Yoshitake, ed., *Yayoi Kusama Infinity Mirrors* (New York: Hirshhorn Museum and Sculpture Garden and Prestel, 2017).

61. Brian O'Doherty, "The Gallery as Gesture," in *Thinking about Exhibitions*, eds. Reesa Greenberg et al. (London: Routledge, 1995), 334–40. O'Doherty discusses the political dimensions of the Christo installation, including its appearance shortly after the 1968 Democratic Convention in Chicago.

62. Maurice Berger, *Fred Wilson: Objects and Installation* (Baltimore, MD: Center for Art and Visual Culture, 2001), 22.

63. Sources for this discussion of *Mathematica* include Joseph Giovanni, "Flawed Equation," *Architecture* 87, no. 4 (April 1998): 59; Bob Reardon and Jack Lambie, "Mathematics on Exhibition," *Museum News* (June 1961): 14–17; and Jay Rounds, personal interview, March 2004. In Giovanni's article, he criticizes the California Science Center for discontinuing *Mathematica* in 1998.

64. Sources for this section include copies of grants and news articles in the Exploratorium's archives and in-person interviews conducted by Jessica Strick in fall 2003. Profound thanks to Strick for her painstaking research and interviews with Exploratorium staff members Ron Hipschman, Kathleen McLean, Peter Richards, and Larry Shaw. Written sources include *The Exploratorium*, Special Issue (March 1985) (dedicated to the memory of Frank Oppenheimer); Elaine Heumann Gurian, "Noodling Around with Exhibition Opportunities," in *Exhibiting Cultures: The Poetics and Politics of Museum Display*, eds. Ivan Karp and Steven Lavine (Washington, D.C.: Smithsonian Institution Press, 1991), 179; Frank Oppenheimer, "A Rationale for a Science Museum," *Curator* (November 1968); and Frank Oppenheimer, "Exhibit Conception and Design," presented in Monterey, Mexico, 1980, at the International Commission on Science Museums.

65. Sources for this section include Herminia Weishin Din, "A History of Children's Museums in the U.S.,

1899–1997: Implications for Art Education and Museum Education in Art Museums" (PhD dissertation, Ohio State University, 1998); Donald Garfield, "Interview with Michael Spock," *Museum News* 72, no. 6 (1993): 34–35, 58–60; Jeri Robinson and Patricia Quinn, *PLAYSPACE: Creating Family Spaces in Public Places* (Boston: Boston Children's Museum, 1984); and Vanessa Anne Van Orden, "Blazing New Trails: Community, Cultural and Age Issues in Children's Museums, 1968 to the Present" (undergraduate thesis, Wellesley College, 2000); as well as this author's conversations with Leslie Bedford, Kenneth Brecher, Elaine Gurian, Signe Hanson, Janet Kamien, Michael Sand, Dan Spock, and Michael Spock, and her experiences during her years of employment there from 1986 to 1991. For more information on the evolution of the Boston Children's Museum, see "Boston Stories," Boston Children's Museum, accessed June 1, 2019, http://www.bcmstories.com.

66. Caryl Marsh, quoted in Wendy Pollock, "Discovery Rooms: An Alternative Experience of the Museum," *ASTC Dimensions* (November/December 1999): 9–11.

67. See Robinson and Quinn, *PLAYSPACE*.

68. Sources for this section include John R. Kinard, "The Neighborhood Museum as a Catalyst for Social Change," *Museum* 37, no. 4 (1985): 217–21; and John R. Kinard and Esther Nighbert, "The Anacostia Neighborhood Museum," *Museum* 24, no. 2 (1972): 102–109. For a fuller discussion of the Anacostia Museum's early years, see Joy Gabriella Kinard, "John R. Kinard and the Legacy of African American Leadership" (PhD dissertation, Howard University, 2009); and Michele Gates Moresi, "Exhibiting Race, Creating Nation: Representations of Black History and Culture at the Smithsonian Institution, 1895–1976" (PhD dissertation, the George Washington University, 2003).

69. Sources include Steven C. Dubin, *Displays of Power: Memory and Amnesia in the American Museum* (New York: New York University Press, 1999), 18–63; Thomas Hoving, *Making Mummies Dance* (New York: Simon & Schuster, 1993), 164–65; and Allon Schoener, ed., *Harlem on My Mind: Cultural Capital of Black America* (New York: New Press, 1993). In regard to Ellison's provocative essay, it should be noted that she was citing a sociological study by two white scholars, Nathan Glazer and Daniel Patrick Moynihan; the citation had been removed by exhibition organizer Allon Schoener.

70. Joseph Veach Noble, "Drug Scene in New York," *Museum News* (November 1971): 10–15. See also Joseph Veach Noble, "Controversial Exhibitions and Censorship," *Curator* 38, no. 2 (1995): 75–77.

71. Katherine Church Holland, introduction, in *San Francisco Museum of Modern Art: The Painting and Sculpture Collection*, by Diana C. duPont, Katherine Church Holland, Garna Garren Miller, and Laura Sueoka (New York: Hudson Hills Press, 1985), 18. Holland notes that part of the painting's popularity stemmed from its negative reviews by critics who dubbed it a "monstrosity."

72. "See the Moon Rock, See Mr. Nixon," *San Francisco Chronicle*, October 5, 1969, 3.

73. Sources include "Dummies for Mummies," *ARTnews* (November 1978); Sylvia Hochfield, "Egytomania in New York," *ARTnews* (December 1978): 45–49; Hoving, *Making Mummies Dance*, 401–14; *Treasures of Tutankhamun* (Metropolitan Museum of Art, 1976), exhibition catalog; as well as the author's own recollections of standing in line to see this exhibition twice during her teenage years.

74. For an extended discussion of the rivalry between J. Carter Brown and Thomas Hoving, see Neil Harris, *Capital Culture: J. Carter Brown, the National Gallery of Art, and the Reinvention of the Museum Experience* (Chicago: University of Chicago Press, 2013).

75. Sponsored by Philip Morris, Inc., *The Vatican Collection: the Papacy and Art* featured 237 works of art including rare 13th-century frescoes and tapestries created by Raphael for the Sistine Chapel, and a "complete set of pontifical vestments," described by director Phillippe de Montebello as "some of the highest moments of human artistic achievement." Source: *The Metropolitan Museum of Art: The Vatican Collections: The Papacy and Art* (New York: Harry N. Abrams, 1982), 8.

76. Kubala, "Glass Box," 32.

77. See "1,659,647 Visitors to Costume Institute's Heavenly Bodies Show at Met Fifth Avenue and Met Cloisters Make It the Most Visited Exhibition in The Met's History," *The Met*, October 11, 2018, accessed September 15, 2019, https://www.metmuseum.org/press/news/2018/heavenly-bodies-most-visited-exhibition.

78. Andrew Bolton, quoted in Helen Stoilas and Nancy Kenney, "Heavenly Figures: How Two Met Shows Topped the Art Newspaper's Attendance Survey," *Art Newspaper*, March 26, 2019, accessed June 1, 2019, https://www.theartnewspaper.com/news/heavenly-figures-met-shows-top-the-art-newspaper-s-attendance-survey.

79. For more on educational theorists whose work influenced the transformation of museum exhibitions in the 1970s and 1980s, see Jerome Bruner, *Actual Minds, Possible Worlds* (Cambridge, MA: Harvard University Press, 1984); Mihaly Csikszentmihalyi, *Flow: The Psychology of Optimal Experience* (New York: Perennial Books, 1991); Jessica Davis and Howard Gardner, "Open Windows, Open Doors," in *The Educational Role of the Museum*, 2nd ed., ed. Eilean Hooper-Greenhill (London: Routledge, 1999), 99–104; John Falk and Lynn Dierking, *The Museum Experience* (Washington, D.C.: Whalesback Books, 1992); Howard Gardner, *Frames of Mind: The Theory of Multiple Intelligences* (New York: Basic Books, 1983); George Hein, *Learning in the Museum* (London: Routledge, 1998); and Lois Silverman,

"Visitor Meaning-Making in Museums for a New Age," *Curator* 38, no. 3 (1995): 161–70.

80. Ron Hipschman, "Square Wheels," in *Exploratorium Cookbook III: A Construction Manual for Exploratorium Exhibits*, 2002, http://www.exploratorium.edu/texnet/exhibits/motion/square_wheels/media/square_cbk.pdf

81. Janet Kamien, "In the Eye of the Beholder," *Transforming Practice*, eds. J. Hirsch and Lois Silverman (Washington, D.C.: Museum Education Roundtable, 2000), 126–31.

82. Graham W. J. Beal, quoted in Gail Gregg, "Your Labels Make Me Feel Stupid," *ARTnews*, July 1, 2010, accessed June 2, 2019, http://www.artnews.com/2010/07/01/your-labels-make-me-feel-stupid/.

83. *Wolves and Humans* was developed by taxidermist Curt Hadland and a team that included former theater designer Dick Leerhoff.

84. Aldona Jonaitis, "Chiefly Feasts: The Creation of an Exhibition," in *The Enduring Kwakiutl Potach*, ed. Aldona Jonaitis (Seattle: University of Washington, 1991), 21–23.

85. See "Nation to Nation: Treaties between the United States and American Indian Nations," National Museum of the American Indian, accessed June 26, 2019, https://americanindian.si.edu/explore/exhibitions/item?id=934.

86. Ron Chew, personal correspondence, June 2019.

87. Gregg, "Your Labels."

88. Early experiments with visitor-written labels occurred at the Bronx Museum of Art (1996); the Florence Griswold Museum of Art in Lyme, Conn. (2000); the Dallas Museum of Art (2000); and San Jose Museum of Art (2002). See Salwa Mikdadi Nashashibi, "Visitor-Written Labels in U.S. Art Museums" (master's project, John F. Kennedy University, 2002).

89. See *The Accessible Museum: Model Programs of Accessibility for Disabled and Older People* (Washington, D.C.: American Association of Museums, 1993); Elana Kalisher, "Reexamining Diversity: A Look at the Deaf Community in Museums," *Curator* 41, no. 1 (March 1998): 13–35; and Janice Majewski, *Part of Your General Public Is Disabled: A Handbook for Guides in Museums, Zoos, and Historic Houses* (Washington, D.C.: Smithsonian Institution Press, 1987).

90. Nancy Villa Bryk, "Reports of Our Death Have Been Greatly Exaggerated: Reconsidering the Curator," *Museum News* (March/April 2001): 40.

91. Kym Snyder Rice analyzes two additional noteworthy exhibitions of these years in Richmond, VA, that reframed American history in light of narratives that were ignored at the time: *In Bondage and Freedom: Antebellum Black Life in Richmond*, which opened at the Valentine Museum in 1988, and *Before Freedom Came: American Life in the Antebellum South* at the Museum of the Confederacy in 1992. See Kym Snyder Rice, "Slavery on Exhibition: Display Practices in Selected Modern American Museums" (PhD dissertation, George Washington University, 2015).

92. The same year (1993) the Simon Wiesenthal Center's Museum of Tolerance opened in Los Angeles. It also used immersive exhibition techniques to walk visitors through the harrowing experience of the Holocaust.

93. Ralph Appelbaum, "Designing an 'Architecture of Information'—The United States Holocaust Memorial Museum," *Curator* 38, no. 2 (1995): 87–94; and Jeshahahu Weinberg, quoted in John Strand, "Jeshahahu Weinberg of the U.S. Holocaust Memorial Museum," *Museum News* (March/April 1993): 43.

94. Randi Korn, quoted in Ken Yellis, "Fred Wilson, PTSD, and Me: Reflections on the History Wars," *Curator* 52, no. 4 (October 2009): 353. See also Melissa Rachleff, "Peering behind the Curtain: Artists and Questioning Historical Authority," in *Letting Go? Sharing Historical Authority in a User-Generated World*, eds. Bill Adair, Benjamin Filene, and Laura Koloski (Philadelphia: Pew Center for Arts and Heritage, 2011), 208–29; and Fred Wilson, Paula Marincola, and Marjorie Schwarzer, "*Mining the Museum* Revisited: A Conversation," in *Letting Go? Sharing Historical Authority in a User-Generated World*, eds. Bill Adair, Benjamin Filene, and Laura Koloski (Philadelphia: Pew Center for Arts and Heritage, 2011), 230–41.

95. Personal interview, January 2019.

96. Barbara Franco, "What's New in Exhibits?" *Cultural Resources Management* 23, no. 5 (2000): 46.

97. The author is indebted to Paul Martin and Daniel Spock for their help with this section.

98. Benjamin Filene, "Make Yourself at Home—Welcoming Voices in Open House: If These Walls Could Talk," in *Letting Go? Sharing Historical Authority in a User-Generated World*, eds. Bill Adair, Benjamin Filene, and Laura Koloski (Philadelphia: Pew Center for Arts and Heritage, 2011), 138–55.

99. See Dubin, *Displays of Power*, 152–85; Paul Mattick Jr., "At the Waterhole," *Arts Magazine* (October 1991), 20–23; Mary Panzer, "Panning 'The West as America': or, Why One Exhibition Did Not Strike Gold," *Radical History Review* (Winter 1992): 105–22; B. Byron Price, "Field Notes: 'Cutting for Sign': Museums and Western Revisionism," *Western Historical Quarterly* (May 1993): 230–34; "Showdown at 'The West as America' Exhibition," *American Art* 5, no. 3 (Summer 1991): 2–11; Alice Thorson, "Myths Made Manifest," *New Art Examiner* (October 1991): 16–19; Alan Trachtenberg, "Contesting the West," *Art in America* (September 1991): 118–23, 152; Alan Wallach, *Exhibiting Contradiction* (Amherst: University of Massachusetts Press, 1998), 105–17; and Brian Wallis, "Senators Attack Smithsonian Show," *Art in America* (July 1991): 27.

100. Carol Enseki, quoted in "Letter to the Editor: Children Will Lead," *Museum News* (May/June 2002): 7.

101. Stephanie Shapiro, "Exhibition Helps Children Explore Identity, Racism," *Baltimore Sun*, October 6, 1992, https://www.baltimoresun.com/news/bs-xpm-1992-10-06-1992280047-story.html; *Handprint* (Chicago Children's Museum, November/December 1995); Joanne-Jones Rizzi, personal correspondence, June 27, 2019. The author worked on the exhibition teams for both *Kids Bridge* and *Face to Face*.

102. Richard Ravinowitz, "Eavesdropping at the Well: Interpretative Media in the *Slavery in New York* Exhibition," *Public Historian* 35, no. 3 (August 2013): 8–45, accessed August 20, 2019, https://www.americanhistoryworkshop.com/wp-content/uploads/2014/07/Eavesdropping-essay-TPH.pdf.

103. Robert Garfinkle and Alan Goodman, "A Conversation about the Exhibit RACE: Art We So Different?" *Museums and Social Issues: A Journal of Reflective Discourse* 2, no. 1 (Spring 2007): 117–31; Angela D. Mack and Stephen G. Hoffius, eds., *Landscape of Slavery: The Plantation in American Art* (Charleston: University of South Carolina Press, 2008); Angela D. Mack, phone interview, June 24, 2019; Tariro Mezezewa, "Enslaved People Lived Here. These Museums Want You to Know," *New York Times*, June 26, 2019, accessed July 2, 2019, https://www.nytimes.com/2019/06/26/travel/house-tours-charleston-savannah.html.

104. See Ralph Rugoff, "Beyond Belief: The Museum as Metaphor," in *40 Possible City Surfaces for the Museum of Jurassic Technology*, eds. Robert Manguria and Mary-Ann Ray (San Francisco: William Stout, 1999), 99–103; Lawrence Wechsler, *Mr. Wilson's Cabinet of Wonder* (New York: Pantheon Books, 1995); and Fred Wilson and David Wilson, "Museum Freefall," in *Remix: Changing Conversations in Museum of the Americas*, eds. Selma Holo and Mari-Tere Alvarez (Berkeley: University of California Press, 2016), 134–39.

105. Nina Simon, *The Participatory Museum* (Santa Cruz, CA: Museum 2.0, 2010). See also Museum 2.0, https://museumtwo.blogspot.com.

106. Nina Simon, *The Art of Relevance* (Santa Cruz, CA: Museum 2.0, 2016), 147–50; Geoffrey Dunn, "How Nina Simon Reinvented Santa Cruz Art," *Good Times*, June 4, 2019, accessed June 19, 2019, https://goodtimes.sc/cover-stories/nina-simon-reinvented-art-santa-cruz/; Nina Simon, email correspondence, June 20, 2019; "Lost Childhoods," Santa Cruz Museum of Art and History, https://santacruzmah.org/exhibitions/lost-childhoods; Lauren Benetua, Stacey Marie Garcia, and Nina Simon, "Community Issue Exhibition Toolkit," Santa Cruz Museum of Art and History, September 2018; Jamie Lee Evans and Ray Bussolari, personal interviews between 2015 and 2019; and this author's experience as a member of the advisory board for the Foster Youth Museum.

107. Michael Spock, foreword, in John H. Falk and Lynn D. Dierking, *Learning from Museums: Visitor Experiences and the Making of Meaning* (Walnut Creek, CA: AltaMira Press, 2000), viii.

108. Penny Jennings, personal interview, June 27, 2019.

# CHAPTER 5

# *People, Politics, and Money*

## Making Sense of Museums

> Museum professionals and patrons alike must consider whether their specific, personal, artistic, professional and economic interests . . . are consistent with their interests as citizens of an open and democratic society.
>
> —ANDREA FRASER, ARTIST, 2018[1]

> Persistence helps. When you hit a roadblock (which I have repeatedly), back up a few steps and . . . know which principles you need to uphold.
>
> —MARVIN PINKERT, DIRECTOR, JEWISH MUSEUM OF MARYLAND, 2019[2]

MEMBERS OF THE CHARLESTON, S.C., CITY COUNCIL could relax at last. They'd just appointed the new director of the Charleston Museum, a 39-year-old "bluestocking" educator named Laura Bragg. The date was August 6, 1920, and the council was optimistic about the institution's future. It was, after all, the oldest museum in the United States—an oasis of gentility in a city that just a year prior had endured its worst racial violence since the Civil War. Bragg had museum experience and was college-educated, a rarity in those days. She could provide the kind of devotion and stability that was needed. But Charleston was in for a surprise: Bragg's tenure would give the city's power-brokers more headaches than joy.

Despite her qualifications on paper, Bragg turned out to be an unusual choice for the director's post. Unlike most women working in museums at the time, she had few personal financial resources. She suffered from a

**Exhibition in the Museum of American Finance, New York**
By Elsa Ruiz—Own work, CC BY-SA 3.0, curid=24348650

**Laura Bragg is pictured second from the left in this 1923 photograph titled "Women Directors of Museums at Charleston Meeting of the A.A.M." No other women are identified in the photo.**

Charleston Museum Archives, Laura Bragg Photography Album, 1978.78.1

disability—severe hearing loss. She was—in the parlance of the times—a "Boston spinster," that is, a lesbian. And, most shockingly to 1920s Charleston society, she believed in racial equality. One of her early actions was to defy the city's Jim Crow laws and open the museum's doors to African Americans.

The city overturned her efforts, passing a decree that the "Museum and its use is for white citizens of Charleston." But Bragg did not give up. Determined to "end ignorance" by introducing the wonders of the museum to everyone, she developed traveling kits, later called "Bragg Boxes." She distributed these kits for free to "schools for negro children." The city council cut off funds, but Bragg persisted. In 1928, the museum sent Bragg Boxes to every school in the Charleston area.[3]

Laura Bragg's professional travails were not unique. Nor was her persistence. Since the inception of museums in the nation, their leaders have stood up to political and economic threats while seeking higher ground.

U.S. museums may be known for their buildings, collections, and exhibitions, but it is the intertwining of people, politics, and money that ultimately shapes them. Museums reflect the aspirations and values of people—founders, collectors, workers, politicians, benefactors, and ultimately the public. These relationships have played out in dramatic ways as museums have professionalized: first in 1906 with the founding of the American Association (now Alliance) of Museums, and then in subsequent decades as they navigated political and budgetary storms while seeking to endear themselves to the public. In this chapter we learn about some of the gutsy individuals and collective actions that have helped museums not only open up to more diverse communities but also survive as institutions.

## PROFESSIONALIZING MUSEUMS: IRASCIBLE GENTLEMEN AND RADICAL WOMEN

In May 1906, 2 women and 69 men posed on the steps of the American Museum of Natural History in New York City for a group shot. No doubt they knew it was a historic moment. The photograph would document the birth of the AAM, the culmination of more than a quarter century of industrious museum growth.[4] Other like-minded workers—librarians, historians, doctors—had already formed professional associations. Now the time had come for those people working in museums to establish their own professional organization to identify common goals and needs. Until AAM's founding, collectors had focused on building up their own treasure troves, not a collective movement. Most museums were still essentially private storage rooms. Facilities were often grimy and poorly lit. Ventilation was poor. Arrangements of collections could be overpowering, and lectures mind-numbing. Museums needed to up their game if they wanted to establish their worth to society. But experienced workers were in short supply. To staff their

fledgling institutions, many founders resorted to the time-honored hiring methods of nepotism and luck. At some museums, "wayward" nephews and "spinster" daughters suddenly found themselves with the title of "director," charged with tasks like uncrating collections and fitting them into cases and then turning on the lights when visitors arrived.

Despite their lack of training, early museum staff readily embraced their work, taking advantage of the lack of rules and protocols to create a new kind of institution. Some even doubled as benefactors, donating their own collections and inheritances to keep the enterprise afloat. These individuals understood that the museum was a unique kind of outpost, one that needed to acquire and exhibit as much as possible in order to keep pace with the aspirations of a growing nation. In 1891, Smithsonian curator G. Brown Goode called this awareness "museum sense."[5]

**Curators at work in a museum office, ca. 1910.**
Courtesy of the Grand Rapids Public Museum, Michigan

Who possessed "museum sense"? Influential collector J. P. Morgan believed it was someone with "gentlemanly qualities" and a burning desire to build an empire of collections.[6] Fitting the bill perfectly was the Metropolitan Museum of Art's first director, Italian-born antiquities dealer Colonel Emanuele Pietro Paolo Maria Luigi Palma di Cesnola. The debonair Cesnola sold the Met his own collections of antiquities, many at a profit, some allegedly fake. The Milwaukee Public Museum's first director, Civil War veteran Carl Doerflinger, was also an affable gentleman who turned out to be a shrewd negotiator. This self-described "amateur archaeologist" took advantage of the financial misfortunes of a famed New York dealer and paid a pittance for an important natural history collection. Eventually the dealer's son, Henry L. Ward, moved to Milwaukee to direct the museum that held his father's beloved collection—the only way he could get close to it. "In those times," former AAM board chair Thomas W. Leavitt has explained, "directors were riding high, hobnobbing with the very rich, seldom challenged by scholars, much less by a public which never felt completely at home in [museum] palaces."[7]

AAM, on the other hand, promoted the careers of individuals who favored public service over collections empires. Once hired into a museum post, their first tasks needed to go beyond sorting through "collections of relics and rubbish ... monument[s] of confusion and mosaic[s] of conceit," wrote one such trailblazer, the archaeologist Arthur C. Parker, director of what is now the Rochester Museum and Science Center. Parker was born in 1881 on the Cattaraugus Indian reservation in western New York and descended from a prominent Seneca family. Dedicated to educating the public about the values and humanity of Native American culture, Parker's museum career spanned from 1903 to the end of World War II. His motto was that museums should "begin with people first ... by showing an interest in human beings [they will] bring a more appreciative interest in what the museum does and has to show."[8]

Putting people first was the mantra of another influential leader whom we met in previous chapters, John Cotton Dana, founder of New Jersey's Newark Museum. Described by his colleagues as provocative and irascible, Dana came from a wealthy Vermont family. His interest in public service began when, at the age of 32, he took a job at the Denver Public Library, where he developed the nation's first children's reading room. Moving to Newark, Dana pioneered the open-stack system at the city's public library, and in

This terra-cotta lamp (accession # 74.51.2364) dates to the end of the 6th century BCE and is said to be from Rizokarpasso, Karpasia, Cyprus. It was sold to the Metropolitan Museum of Art by its first director, Luigi Cesnola, ca. 1874. The Met's Cesnola Collection of Cypriote Antiquities was established well before the field adopted codes of ethics about financial transactions between a museum and its director.
Metropolitan Museum of Art creative commons

1909 he persuaded local collectors to display their art and specimens in its halls. Dana then talked city officials into turning part of the library into a community museum, with exhibitions and programs for the growing population of African Americans and immigrant factory workers. Like Laura Bragg in South Carolina and Arthur Parker in upstate New York, Dana believed that museums must open their doors to everyone.

Dana also believed that women were the keys to providing better services to the public. While most "gentlemen" viewed the museum as an acceptable

*Art Lovers* **(1863–1869), Honore Daumier, gray and black wash, charcoal, and graphite, with watercolor.**
Courtesy of the Cleveland Museum of Art Museum Open Access; Dudley P. Allen Fund 1927.208

**Beatrice Winser (left) succeeded John Cotton Dana (seated, at right) as director for both the Newark Public Library and Newark Museum and worked alongside Dana for much of his career at both institutions.**

Courtesy of the Newark Museum Archives; caption courtesy of the Newark Public Library hobby for the "genteel lady," Dana encouraged women to think of museums in terms of a career. Yet one could hardly call Dana an early feminist. Women should run museums, he believed, because they could be paid less to do more work: "[Male] collectors, experts and ultra-enthusiastic hobby-riders do not make good managers. They find irksome the attention to details which the proper conduct of such an office imposes. A director should have common sense, enthusiasm for education in all its forms, and an eagerness to learn of the good work a museum can do. . . . In almost every community, large or small today, it will be easier to find a woman than a man who is fitted to the director's task and is willing to take it."[9]

Women had contributed to the museum world since the late 19th century. Even though they didn't have the right to vote, speak at public meetings, or hold bank accounts in their own names, they built significant art collections, preserved historic buildings, and ran institutions. Some like Jane Addams and Ellen Gates Starr were social reformers. In 1889, these labor rights activists cofounded the Hull House Labor Museum in the heart of a poor immigrant enclave in Chicago. Their aim was to "provide comfort and pleasure" through social hours, displays of art, and opportunities to learn together in classes on everything from cooking to bookbinding.

Women were also accomplished naturalists, playing leading roles at early natural science museums such as the Worcester Natural History Society (now EcoTarium) in Massachusetts (1884) and the Museum of Vertebrate Paleontology at the University of California, Berkeley (1908). Some of these pioneering female scientists literally risked their lives for the sake of their museums. Within hours of San Francisco's 1906 earthquake, for example, botanist Alice Eastwood braved

The handwritten label for this botanical specimen, collected in 1887 by Alice Eastwood, shows marks from her daring rescue during the fires that engulfed the California Academy of Sciences from the 1906 Great Earthquake in San Francisco.
Courtesy of the United States National Herbarium, Smithsonian Institution Specimen ID: 02034902.3766; special thanks to Alice Fornari

The Fairbanks Museum and Planetarium in St. Johnsbury, VT, looks almost the same today as it did when Delia Griffin and her largely female staff of naturalists ran it in the early 1900s.
By Daderot

raging fires at the California Academy of Sciences, running up six flights of stairs to rescue its prized botany collection, using her petticoat to transport the specimens to safety. An even larger number kept their institutions afloat through financial sacrifices and clever schemes. In Texas, during the 1920s, ornithologist Ellen Schulz Quillin helped organize San Antonio's Witte Museum. Her annual salary was one dollar. Quillin later raised funds by creating a Reptile Garden where visitors could learn about desert wildlife while they munched on fried rattlesnake.[10]

Perhaps the most prickly place for the field's early female workforce was the art museum. The Whitney Museum of American Art's founding director, Julianna Force, endured insults about her appearance, including the nickname "Ugly Duchess." Her counterpart at the Guggenheim, Hilla Rebay, fared no better; newspapers derided her as a "buxom hausfrau." A notable battle between the sexes took place between Alfred Barr Jr., MoMA's first director, and Adelyn Breeskin, director of the Baltimore Museum of Art and a divorced mother raising three children. During the 1930s Barr frequently traveled to Balti-

more to court a collection of works owned by two wealthy sisters, Claribel and Etta Cone. The masterpieces included canvases by Matisse and Picasso that, Barr claimed, were too exquisite to remain in the backwater of Baltimore. But Breeskin held tough and scored the donation for the people of her city, where it remains today.[11]

Given their longtime influence on museums, it is interesting that only two women were photographed at AAM's first meeting, demonstrating how hard it was for women to assert their visibility in the professional world. Like the pioneers discussed above, both were noteworthy. They argued for the museum as a place of education at a time when other AAM founders mostly shared tips for properly dusting and mounting specimens. One was Anna Billings Gallup, a Mayflower descendant and one of the first women to graduate from the Massachusetts Institute of Technology. In 1902, she joined the world's first museum expressly dedicated to youth education: the Brooklyn Children's Museum. She quickly ascended to the role of director. In this era of child labor abuses and a lack of compulsory schooling, Gallup used her pulpit at several AAM meetings to advocate for the nation's youth. She called for "cheerful, sunny, attractive museums rich in natural objects, artistically displayed where children are sure to find a sympathetic welcome."[12]

The other prominent woman was Delia Griffin. She directed the Fairbanks Museum (and now Planetarium) in St. Johnsbury, VT, a museum that was largely staffed by women. Griffin's educational work at this small rural museum impressed Gallup, who repeatedly praised the Fairbanks Museum in her lectures and writings. She no doubt influenced her colleague's decision to take her ideas about object-based education to a larger stage. In 1913, Griffin become the founding director of the Boston Children's Museum.

Museums would not be where they are today without their first generation of trailblazers, seeking to bridge collections and ideas for the public. By 1916 AAM president Paul Rea (one of Bragg's mentors in South Carolina) acknowledged and chided them in the same breath: "museum development is not yet an

**Paul Rea (left) conversing with an unidentified colleague at an event at the 1923 AAM annual meeting. Rea directed the Charleston Museum from 1906 to 1920. He subsequently led some of the first data-gathering and research reports on museums across the nation for the AAM.**

Courtesy Charleston Museum Archives, Laura Bragg Photography Album, Object ID 1978.78.50

organized national movement; it is a series of isolated endeavors on the part of enthusiastic pioneers. The present need of American museums is . . . improvement and extension . . . and for education of public opinions concerning the value of such museums."[13] Nonetheless, these scattered accomplishments provided a foundation for what was to come.

### 1920s: FOUNDATIONS AND A COLLECTIVE SPIRIT

In the roaring 1920s new economic forces began to break the control wealthy collectors exerted over museums. Middle-class citizens banded into "friends" groups, pooling money to purchase objects and collectively influence the contents of a museum's collection. This occurred simultaneously at such places as the Cleveland Museum of Art, Montclair Art Museum (N.J.), and Cincinnati Art Museum. Objects with smaller price tags (such as decorative arts or unattributed artwork) now joined the masterworks acquired by lead collectors. By supporting these purchases, the middle class now had a modicum of influence in what the public could see in museums.[14]

At the same time, a new form of the philanthropic organization was starting to exert its influence on the nation's culture. In the spirit of Andrew Carnegie's famous "gospel of wealth," prosperous families began to create charitable foundations to support civic projects. The first was the Carnegie Corporation (1911); the second was the Rockefeller Foundation, founded in 1913, the same year Congress passed the federal income tax act. Although they pledged to do good, charitable foundations were not without their critics. Skeptics accused the foundations of manipulating the country's educational and social structure and wealthy people of dodging taxes by financing ventures—i.e., libraries, parks, and museums—that the government eventually would have to maintain.[15] Museums were especially vulnerable to this criticism, since municipalities already had donated land and, in some cases, buildings and local tax revenues to what a Carnegie-funded study described as "sterile salons of self-sufficient cliques."[16]

In the face of such doubts, those in charge of foundations agreed with AAM: museums needed to do a better job of promoting their societal value. It was critical at this pivotal juncture in museum history to nurture an independent network of trained museum workers who truly were dedicated to working for the public benefit.

In 1923, AAM received its first-ever grant, thanks to a branch of the Rockefeller Foundation. The money allowed AAM to expand its four-page national journal

*A Bishop Saint with a Donor (possibly Saint Louis of Toulouse)* is an early-15th-century tempera painting with raised and gilded gesso on wood from Catalonia, Spain, in the collection of the Cleveland Museum of Art. It is an example of the extraordinary kinds of works friends groups have raised the funds to purchase for museums since the 1920s.

and write the field's first code of ethics. AAM members used the newsletter to share information about their innovations, everything from "things you can touch" tables at the Natural History Museum in Providence, R.I., to the staging of Wagnerian opera at the Toledo Art Museum—apparently so entertaining that children stood on tiptoe throughout the entire performance. The two-page 1925 AAM Code of Ethics promoted a standard of professional behavior and, among other things, encouraged museum staff to refrain from "jealous acts, gossip, inquisitiveness, sarcasm [and] practical jokes."[17]

# Museum News Letter

Vol. I.  MAY, 1918.  No. 9.

### MUSEUM NEWS LETTER
Published monthly from October to June inclusive by The American Association of Museums. Free to members of the Association, to others fifty cents a year. Entered as second-class matter June 15, 1917, at the Post Office at Providence, R. I., under the act of August 24, 1912.

**Editor:** Harold L. Madison, Park Museum, Providence, R. I.; **Associate Editors: Science—** Mr. Frederick L. Lewton, Smithsonian Institution, Washington, D. C.; **Art—**Mrs. Margaret T. Jackson Rowe, 281 Benefit St., Providence, R. I.; **History—**Dr. Frank H. Severance, Buffalo Historical Society, Buffalo, N. Y.

**OFFICERS:** President—Dr. Henry R. Howland; Vice-President—Newton H. Carpenter; Secretary—Harold L. Madison; Treasurer—Dr. W. P. Wilson. **COUNCILLORS:** Benjamin Ives Gilman, Herbert E. Sargent, Dr. Oliver C. Farrington, Harold L. Madison, Roy W. Miner, Miss Anna B. Gallup.

Committees appointed by the American Association of Museums at its Annual Meeting, May 21-23, 1917: 1. On Compendium of Methods of Museum Administration: Newton H. Carpenter, L. Earle Rowe, G. H. Sherwood. 2. On Bibliography of Museum Literature: Dr. Nathaniel L. Britton, Henry W. Kent, Dr. Ralph W. Tower. 3. On Instruction in Museum Work: Fitz Roy Carrington, Henry L. Ward, Mrs. Margaret T. Jackson Rowe. 4. On Museum Buildings: Frederic A. Whiting, Dr. Oliver C. Farrington, Dr. A. R. Crook. 5. On Museum Co-operation: Frederic A. Whiting, Henry W. Kent, Harold L. Madison. 6. On Publication of Art Auction Sales: Raymond Wyer, Henry W. Kent, Miss Florence N. Levy.

### ASSOCIATION NOTES.

**Springfield Meeting, May 20, 21, 22, 1918.**

**Please Send Back the Yellow Card!**

For the knowledge of how many to expect at the Springfield meeting, and more especially that the secretary's membership records may be accurate, will you please fill out and mail the yellow preliminary registration card recently sent you?

**They Are Doing It.**

Not all, but some! In fact, the two "Recommendation to Membership" blanks sent each member of the Association were not sufficient for one man, but he improvised a third. Think of it! If each member were to add three new members our membership would number about 2,000. Think of it again and then do the right thing by your Association.

**Association Headquarters.**

Hotel Kimball, 140 Chestnut St., cor. Bridge St.
Without bath, single $2.25 up  double $3.50 up
With bath,  "  3.25 "  "  5.00 "
With shower,  "  2.75 "  "  4.00 "
Excellent accommodations also at Hotel Worthy and Hotel Victoria.

**How You May Know.**

That your Association dues are not paid in full to date. You will not possess a receipt from the treasurer.

11 active and associate members, and 1 sustaining member, have not paid for 1916-17, 1917-18.

17 active and associate members have not paid for 1917-18.

Let the News Letter help you "share up" your good things with other Museums.

### An Amendment to the Constitution.

The following amendment to the constitution of The American Association of Museums has been sent the Council for action by the Association at the Springfield Meeting:

Change the words "actively engaged" in the third paragraph of article three to the one word "interested."

The paragraph as amended will then read:

"Persons interested in the work of Museums may become Active Members on the payment of three dollars per annum, and may become Active Members for life upon the payment of thirty dollars at any one time."

As the Constitution now reads, only persons "actively engaged" in Museum work are eligible to Active Membership, and consequently have the privilege of voting and holding office. The amendment would give anyone "interested" in Museums these privileges.

The following reasons may be given in favor of the amendment:

1. The avowed aim of the Association (Const., Art. 3) "will be furthered not by professional exclusiveness, but by admitting those interested in the aims, even if not specialists in museum technique."

2. "Museums usually begin by the action of non-professionals. Where such a beginning is made, recognition by this organization would greatly expedite the establishment of such a museum on semi-professional and finally on professional lines."

3. "A thoroughly interested museum 'patron' may be more valuable as a member of the organization than even the most conscientious laborer at the clerical or installation work of the Museum. The membership now admitted is not chosen on professional grounds."

The following reasons may be given in favor of the Constitution as it now stands:

1. In the long run the avowed aims of the Association will be better furthered by confining their control to persons actively engaged in, and thereby responsible for some phase of museum work.

2. Under the present arrangement the non-professional is eligible to Associate membership and to Active membership as soon as he becomes actively engaged in museum work.

3. The present membership is based on museum responsibility and on that ground may be designated "professional". It is customary for a "thoroughly interested museum patron" to be a member of the museum's governing board and thereby eligible for active membership in the Association.

### SCIENCE.

**A Bird Chart.**

The Museum of Natural History at Springfield, Mass., has recently published a bird chart

Universal moral courage is the only desideratum which comes near to expressing what liberty implies.
—John Jay Chapman in "The Outlook."

*Museum News Letter*, May 1918. An item below the masthead on the front page reminds delegates to the annual meeting in Springfield, MA, to reserve their hotel rooms for the conference rate of $2.25 a night, $2.75 with a shower included.
Courtesy AAM and Marjorie Schwarzer

During the 1930s, Frederick Keppel, formerly a dean at Columbia University, became head of the Carnegie Corporation. No doubt influenced by his Columbia colleague, educational philosopher John Dewey, Keppel believed foundations could help museums and universities create formal training programs to expand the pool of qualified curators and directors.[18] Early on, some outspoken individuals had taken to the editorial pages of journals and newspapers to beseech industrialists to stop founding new museums until the nation could adequately train a workforce. Only then, wrote one, "[will] the public ... find that museums accomplish something more than the mere storing of private collections."[19] Keppel was able to steer Carnegie funds to the first serious museum training course in the country, established by Paul Sachs at Harvard University in 1922. Sachs, son of a founder of the financial firm Goldman Sachs, joined up with Edward Waldo Forbes, grandson of famed poet Ralph Waldo Emerson. Weaving financial acumen with poetic sensibility, they developed a rigorous curriculum that covered museum history, philosophy, management, and collections care.[20]

Museums also began to organize apprenticeship programs. In 1923 the Newark Museum launched a course in museum education that attracted young women from wealthy families; three of its graduates later established the curatorial and registration departments at the MoMA. Starting in 1929, with funds from the Rockefeller Foundation, the Buffalo Museum of Science trained designers and builders of dioramas. Graduates of Buffalo's program later influenced the development of museums in the national parks.

Newly trained workers shared practices with one another and organized regional support groups, beginning in 1927 with the Association of Midwest Museums.[21] Until this point the field's professional literature focused on the ins and outs of taxidermy, covering such appealing topics as "mounting an African Warthog" and "fluffing a vulture's feathers."[22] Now museum pamphlets, funded by Carnegie, began to talk about civic value, urging staff to abandon the "insidious decadence" of collectors and instead bridge the worlds of "high" and "low" culture for the public. Furthermore, Carnegie underwrote the first

**Frederick Keppel headed the Carnegie Corporation in the 1930s and helped to steer foundation monies toward important progressive educational studies and public classes in museums.**
Harris & Ewing Photograph Collection, Repository, Library of Congress Prints and Photographs Division

psychological studies of visitor behavior in the galleries. Between 1924 and 1928 Yale University professors Edward Stevens Robinson and Arthur Melton and their students documented the insidious condition known as "museum fatigue"—the exhaustion felt after even a few minutes of navigating interminable rows of displays, galleries, and flights of stairs.[23]

The combination of training and research gave museum workers the confidence to take action. As we saw in chapter 1, they developed experimental instructional programs. As we saw in chapter 2, they urged architects to design less confusing spaces. And likewise, as we saw in chapters 3 and 4, they shared practices for cataloging collections and uncluttering exhibitions. In these ways, museum workers began to collectively fashion museums that more readily benefited the public.

In the 1930s, again with funds from Carnegie, large urban museums established outposts in suburbs, designed to be less intimidating than the marble palaces in cities. Philadelphians, for example, could venture to a storefront branch of the Philadelphia Museum of Art in Upper Darby, PA. With window displays opening out to the street, the museum produced 17 exhibits in its first 12 months and stayed open until 10 p.m. every night, including Sunday. Supported by foundation monies, museums also sent exhibitions to the nation's black colleges, reaching out to students who had restricted access to traditional urban art museums.[24] Though these short-lived experiments ended during the Great Depression, they set the stage for later experimental practices that aimed to introduce museums to a broader cross-section of the population.

## FROM WORKS PROGRESS TO NATIONAL ENDOWMENT: MUSEUMS AND THE FEDERAL GOVERNMENT FROM 1935 TO 1965

With the stock market crash of 1929 and the onset of the Great Depression, the nation seemingly had little time to worry about museums. Yet museums' prior decades of creating new programs had paid off. Most surprising, benefactors who lost large fortunes in the

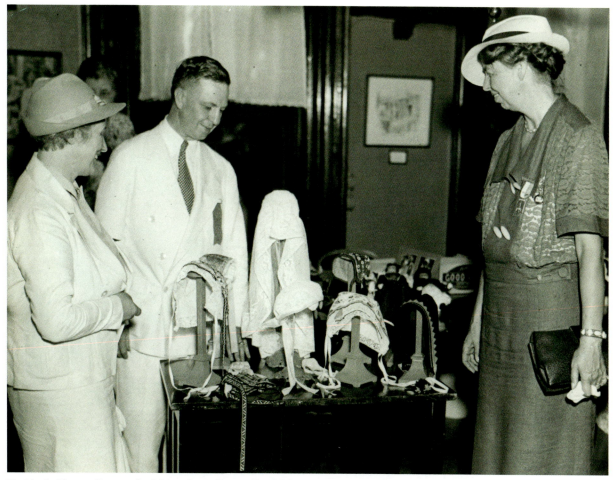

**First Lady Eleanor Roosevelt visiting the Indianapolis Children's Museum, 1940s**
Courtesy of Indianapolis Children's Museum

**Museum workers inspecting a WPA-era mini-diorama of a 19th-century cabinetmaking shop.**
Courtesy of Grand Rapids Public Museum, Michigan

**Holger Cahill, center right, national director, and Audrey McMahon, New York director of the Federal Arts Project, center left, at a 1938 gallery opening.**
Photo by Charles Eisenman, Archives of American Art, curid=16883324

crash donated more money to museums in the 1930s than they had during the roaring 1920s.[25] In Ohio, for example, the Toledo Art Museum's chief donor, Florence Scott Libbey, sacrificed her inherited interest in her husband's glass manufacturing fortune in order to finance the museum's construction, employing 2,500 construction workers who badly needed work. At the same time, Libbey paid for free public concerts for a community badly in need of uplift.

An essential boost came from the federal government. President Franklin Delano Roosevelt established a job creation program, the Works Progress Administration (WPA), in 1935. WPA funds led to an expansion of the National Park Service (NPS), including new museum-like nature centers along park trails around the country. At a centralized headquarters in Berkeley, CA, artists created relief maps and other exhibits for parks around the nation. In 1937, NPS inaugurated a museum division and chose Ned J. Burns as its first chief. Burns had begun his museum career at the age of 19, one of the first employees of New York's Staten Island Museum. Largely self-taught, Burns was fascinated with each and every aspect of museum work, from preserving mummies to mocking up miniature dioramas. By 1939, he was supervising hundreds of naturalists and artists working in 113 museums in federal parks. As the consummate museum cheerleader, Burns seized the day, urging them to create displays as "dynamic and fresh as today's newspaper."[26]

Another WPA program, the Federal Art Project (FAP), represented the largest infusion of federal cash the arts community had ever seen, and the first federal monies to go directly to the nation's museums. In 1935 Holger Cahill, a curator who had worked with John Cotton Dana to build the Newark Museum's American art collection, was asked to head the agency. "It'll be terrible," warned Cahill's friend Francis Henry Taylor, then-director of the Worcester Art Museum. "You'll have to say 'no' to so many people that you'll never

**Artists working with the Federal Art Project created the sea-themed murals, mosaics, and terrazzo floors at the present-day San Francisco Maritime Museum. The museum building was originally constructed by the WPA to house bathing facilities, restaurants, and lounges for the city's Aquatic Park.**
Photo by Sabrina Oliveros

have another friend as long as you live. Congressmen will have you up on the carpet every other minute, but of course you've got to take the job!"[27]

Under Cahill's leadership FAP employed almost 40,000 artists, many in museums. Their output was astonishing. They excavated and documented historic sites, organized and cataloged paintings and sculptures, repaired and cleaned specimens, and designed and installed exhibits. Among those who participated in this dynamic work program were artists who later catapulted to fame, including Jacob Lawrence, Lee Krasner, and Jackson Pollock. As silk-screen artist Anthony Velonis later quipped, the WPA "rescued a generation of artists to become productive citizens instead of cynical revolutionaries."[28]

The general public also benefited. Residents of small midwestern towns could now visit local history museums spruced up with new cases and furniture. City dwellers could see new wildlife dioramas at their local science academy and watch the construction of new buildings for local art museums. At new art centers around the nation, people could attend exhibitions organized by the WPA-sponsored Indian Arts and Crafts Board, take art classes, and learn new skills, from industrial design to home economics. No community was too large or too small. The exuberant activity during FAP years was, according to historian Howard Zinn, an "exciting flowering of arts for the people, such as had never happened before in American history, and which has not been duplicated since."[29]

Nonetheless, Francis Henry Taylor's warning to his friend Holger Cahill turned out to be prescient. Unlike the Park Service, identified with heroes like Theodore Roosevelt, the FAP was associated with African Americans, Native Americans, Jews, and radical New York artists. Redbaiting politicians claimed that a photography exhibition documenting housing squalor in Oklahoma City and similar projects were "tools of the Communist party designed to breed class hatred in the United States." Others disapproved of the program's racially integrated classes. Still others felt that with a war on the horizon, there would be plenty of work for everyone and the job-creation program no longer would be necessary.[30]

As the nation prepared for war, museums vanished from the federal radar. In this era of patriotic sacrifice, the U.S. government classified museums as recreational—that is, nonessential. That meant that museums did not merit special rations, such as gasoline or tires. Some were forced to suspend operations and shut their doors. A few were converted into temporary hospital wards or bomb shelters, with their collections stored off-site.

Some museum workers agreed. They felt that elite institutions didn't deserve special treatment while the world was in so much turmoil. Theodore Low of the Walters Art Gallery in Baltimore reminded his colleagues that government officials would not and should not "support a cultural Fort Knox."[31] Others, however, understood that museums could play an essential role during wartime. The staff at the Bishop Museum in Honolulu exemplified this commitment. In December 1941, as "dense columns of black smoke continued to rise from Pearl Harbor," the shell-shocked staff was in high gear, securing the museum. Within days they had arranged new exhibits and developed art classes for children unable to attend school. "I believe the museum is going to play a more important part than ever as a morale builder for the community," wrote the Bishop's director, Peter H. Buck.[32] This can-do attitude carried over to the mainland.

Two weeks after the attack several museum directors gathered for an emergency meeting at the Metropolitan Museum of Art. They resolved "to do their utmost in the service of the people in this country during the present conflict . . . and be sources of inspiration illuminating the past and vivifying the present [so] that they will fortify the spirit on which Victory depends." Within months hundreds of museums had launched programs to help people cope with the stresses of wartime, everything from the free children's classes to free movies, refreshments, and "smoking rooms" for soldiers on leave.[33]

Offering these services was both patriotic and practical. "Museums had to convince politicians and those who controlled the purse strings that they were contributing to economic recovery, to the fight against totalitarianism, and to winning the war," explains historian Terry Zeller.[34] The strategy worked. During the 1940s two-thirds of museums reported increased financial support from their municipalities; a few were even able to construct new facilities to accommodate expanded public use.

Michigan's Public Museum of Grand Rapids is an example of an organization that transformed itself during the war years. In 1939 its visionary new director, science teacher Frank "Dewey" DuMond, launched a campaign for a new building for the crumbling 84-year-old institution. "Our aim is . . . to give the taxpayers a lot for the little they invest," DuMond declared. During the war, the museum produced flyers on how to spot enemy planes and deaccessioned a

**Grand Rapids Public Museum director Frank DuMond believed that a museum should be as friendly as your next-door neighbor. In this photo, he tries on a 15th century suit of armor that had been donated to the museum.**
Courtesy of Grand Rapids Public Museum, Michigan

Spanish-American war cannon to be melted down for the "Salvage of Victory Clean-Up." After the war, the museum created a brochure titled "Servicemen: What of Those Souvenirs?" that encouraged the donation of war-related artifacts for its popular War Relics Hall. By 1947 the building project was a rousing success. The museum had expanded services, reached new audiences, and doubled its budget through "legitimate promotional stunts and publicity." It was, DuMond boasted, "accessible as a dime store and friendly as your next-door neighbor."[35]

Other directors realized that their institutions could serve as public relations tools—and not just for wartime concerns. Museums could be vital parts of the economy by helping businesses sell products. During the 1940s the director of the Museum of Science and Industry in Chicago brokered deals with companies for exhibits about consumer goods, such as a Com-

monwealth Edison display on the wonders of electrical appliances. At the same time, MoMA and other contemporary art museums worked with department stores to promote the purchase of modern furnishings, appliances, and utensils for the home.

Cold War politicians also appreciated how museums could communicate to the public. The federal government commissioned exhibitions that aimed to soothe people's fears about atomic testing and Soviet nuclear attack and opened the American Museum of Atomic Energy in Oak Ridge, TN, in 1949—the year it revealed that the city was a site of the atomic bomb-producing Manhattan Project. There, an exhibition called *Atoms for Peace* contained a diorama about mining uranium and bombastic prose about the promise of nuclear energy. The show toured the country.[36] In the early 1950s, to further put the nation at ease and promote the country's technological and

*Atoms for Peace* traveling exhibit from Oak Ridge, TN, 1957.
Photo by Edward Westcott

military superiority, the Smithsonian opened several exhibitions celebrating U.S. military history.

Behind the scenes curators and scientists, newly returned from the war, focused on their research, and paid little attention to the public. Directors—by now predominantly male—sank into a comfortable "old boys" network. "Museums are the last places where Captains of Industry can act with no government meddling," proclaimed an editorial in *Art News*. "This is the last area where Big Money, and in the older cities, Old Money, has its nineteenth-century prerogatives."[37] But the postwar political and economic climate was about to change.

The 1950s was a time of opportunity, thanks to the GI Bill and a booming economy. By 1953, the wealth gap between the nation's most monied citizens and others reached an all-time low, meaning that more American citizens than ever could buy into a middle-class lifestyle.[38] One result of this prosper-

ity was an expanded free labor force for museums: female volunteers. With their husbands at work, their children enrolled in high-quality public schools, and their leisure time increased due to labor-saving appliances, more and more women lent their energies to museums as volunteers. Women's committees became indispensable to day-to-day operations. At a time when exhibition improvements lagged due to a focus on collections care and conservation, energetic volunteers kept the museum connected to its public.

The white female volunteer transformed the U.S. museum and became the antidote to the stereotypical stern-faced uniformed male guard. She greeted visitors at the front door, cheerfully answered questions at the information desk, guided people through exhibitions, ran rental galleries, and invited middle-class patrons to afternoon teas organized by the women's committee. Finally the museum had a friendly face, and a rather fashionable one at that. Volunteering was considered so glamorous that the July 1952 issue of *Vogue* featured two fashionably attired women, posing in front of paintings at the Art Institute of Chicago.[39] That same year a young housewife named Mary Naquin Sharp wandered into the Baltimore Art Museum because "it was what everyone I knew was doing at the time." She remained an indispensable docent for more than 50 years. "We were doing everything," she recalls, "including lots of things that paid staff do now."[40]

At many museums, women volunteers outnumbered paid male staff two-to-one. In 1952 their numbers were so great that Sharp and others organized the American Association of Museum Volunteers, which was based at the Saint Louis Art Museum. Volunteers embraced their work and formed new friendships with each other. One of the outcomes was a natural inclination to influence the direction of museums in ways that can be viewed as both positive and negative.

One attempt to forward a political agenda took place in 1955 when a local women's luncheon club presented trustees of the Dallas Museum of Fine Arts (now the Dallas Museum of Art) with a list of "suspected communist sympathizers." They demanded that these artists' works be removed from display. The trustees refused to back down to a group of concerned "society ladies." Conversely, in 1962, 13 volunteers in a conservative community in Southern California banded together to found a new, more liberal institution: the Newport Harbor Art Museum, now part of the Orange County Museum of Art. That museum would play a vital role in standing up to right-wing politicians in defense of artists' rights

to free speech, as we will learn shortly. Children's museums also benefited from women's service organizations, notably Junior Leagues whose members launched scores of youth-oriented institutions during the latter part of the century.

With growing attendance and backed up by their volunteer corps, directors renewed calls for federal dollars. A government agency would become an important player in this regard. Museums were the furthest things from President Harry S. Truman's mind in 1950 when he signed legislation creating the National Science Foundation (NSF). Truman saw NSF as a way to support scientific research for national defense during the Cold War. Within the next few years, however, the agency would fund more than 200 research projects in natural history museums and botanical gardens. By the time of the space race toward the moon between the United States and Soviet Union, NSF and museums were sharing a mutual interest in educating the public about careers in science.

The government took a few more small steps toward supporting arts and culture museums. In 1954 President Dwight D. (Ike) Eisenhower signed the Excise Tax Reduction Act, which exempted museums from paying taxes on admission charges. Ike was an art lover and amateur painter; his treasury secretary, Douglas Dillon, was a collector and trustee of the Metropolitan Museum of Art. Though the president professed an interest in museums, he did not push for more systematic funding. Direct federal support was politically unfeasible, due to Cold War paranoia. In a vitriolic speech titled "Modern Art Shackled to Communism,"

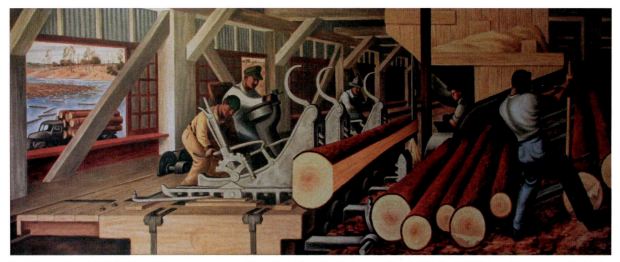

Jerry Bywaters painted this 1942 mural, *Lumber Manufacturing*, for the post office in Trinity, TX. He would go on to direct the Dallas Art Museum. During the 1950s he stood up to McCarthy-era censorship and later received special commendation from the Association of Art Museum Directors for his courage.
By Larry D. Moore—© 2015 Larry D. Moore, Public Domain, curid=39872277

**President Dwight D. Eisenhower was an amateur painter and art lover.**
Courtesy of Dwight D. Eisenhower Presidential Library, Museum and Boyhood Home

in 1949, Michigan Rep. George Dondero raged against art museums on the House floor. He described their directors as "aging but active left wingers" and "effeminates." Their museums exhibited artwork that was "anti-Christian, anti-sanity, anti-moral . . . trash" created by "evil" painters with "foreign names." Sen. Joseph McCarthy of Wisconsin took up the cause and blacklisted artists he believed were "un-American."[41]

Even though the U.S. Senate condemned McCarthy's tactics in 1954, the ripples of McCarthyism were strong. In 1956, once again community members in Dallas attempted to influence their museum. This time a larger citizens' group called the Dallas County Patriotic Council pressured the city to withdraw the Dallas Art Museum's maintenance funds because it had booked the traveling exhibition *Sport in Art*. Sponsored by *Sports Illustrated*, it contained works by four artists allegedly affiliated with "communist-front activities." The condemned images depicted such "unpatriotic" activities as ice skating and fishing. "The Reds are moving in upon us," warned the council. "Let those who would plant a red picture supplant it with the red, white, and blue. White for purity, blue for fidelity, as blue as our Texas bluebonnets."

Again, the trustees and the exhibit's local sponsor, department store magnate Stanley Marcus, held fast. "Museum says Reds can stay," announced the *Dallas Morning News*. *Sport in Art* opened as planned, its galleries flanked by armed guards. It drew larger than usual crowds and resulted in dozens of new memberships to the museum. The museum's director, noted Texas muralist Jerry Bywaters, later received a special commendation from the Association of Art Museum Directors for "withstanding the assault."[42]

The Cold War years also led to increased international showmanship. To highlight American ingenuity and democratic values, the United States Information Agency (USIA) toured exhibitions like MoMA's immensely popular *Family of Man* to Europe and Soviet Russia. (The USIA tour of *Sport in Art*, was canceled, however, because of its association with "subversive" elements.) In 1959 congressmen and senators began to advocate for funding the arts at home. The next year the nation elected John F. Kennedy, who promised to advance the values of progress, education, and social equality.

Strictly speaking, the arts and culture funding boom that followed JFK's election was the result of a confluence of astute lobbying, Cold War politics, economic good times, and complex negotiations regarding tax laws. Hearts, however, were won over through a public relations event. In December 1962 French Minister of Cultural Affairs André Malraux flew from Paris to Washington, D.C. His traveling companion was a small canvas with a big appeal—Leonardo da Vinci's *Mona Lisa*—which came to the United States on a two-and-a-half-month loan orchestrated by the Kennedy White House. Amid great fanfare, President and Mrs. Kennedy attended the opening at *Mona Lisa*'s first stop, the National Gallery of Art. For the next 26 days, 518,000 people waited in lines to glimpse the famous canvas, installed on a baffle draped in red velvet and guarded by Marines around the clock. The painting then traveled to the Metropolitan Museum of Art, where more than a million people paid homage to the woman with the enigmatic smile. *Mona Lisa*'s tri-

umphant tour helped the White House garner popular support for a federal arts and culture policy.

On the morning of November 22, 1963, the *New York Times* featured two long articles detailing JFK's plan to create an arts council of prominent cabinet officials to "bolster the cultural resources of the nation."[43] The elaborate scheme would never come to pass. That afternoon, in Dallas, the president was assassinated.

Vice President Lyndon Baines Johnson (LBJ) inherited a grieving nation on the brink of unrest. Civil rights issues loomed; there was a strong sense that the old order had to go. It was time to create, as LBJ called it, a "Great Society that . . . rests on abundance and liberty for all, where the city of man serves not only the needs of the body and the demands for commerce, but the desire for beauty and the hunger for community."[44] His vision included federal programs to bring the nation's arts and culture to all of its citizens.

**President John F. Kennedy, Marie-Madeleine Lioux, André Malraux, Jackie Kennedy, and Vice President Lyndon B. Johnson unveiling *Mona Lisa* at the National Gallery of Art, January 8, 1963.**

Working closely with Rhode Island Senator Claiborne Pell (Pell grants for college students are named in his honor), President Johnson invited museum directors to join arts luminaries like singer Marian Anderson, composer Leonard Bernstein, and photographer Ansel Adams on a National Council of Arts and Humanities. In 1965 LBJ signed the National Endowment for the Arts (NEA) and National Endowment for the Humanities (NEH) into existence. A year later, he signed the National Museum Act, designating funds for training and research to be administered by the Smithsonian. Foundations soon were required to make their records public and donate a set percentage of their annual earnings to bona fide charities, thanks to the 1969 Tax Reform Act. Businesses were making changes, too. In response to accusations that corpora-

**President Lyndon B. Johnson signing the Arts and Humanities Act in the White House Rose Garden and giving a bill-signing pen to photographer Ansel Adams, 1965.**
Courtesy of LBJ Presidential Library, image A1376-2a; photo by Yoichi Okamoto

tions abused labor, the environment, and consumers, corporate managers introduced the concept of "social responsibility." It made good business sense. From corporate executives' perspectives, a logical way to contribute to the welfare of communities and present the corporation's human side was to support that most human of activities, the arts.

In 1967 David Rockefeller, chair of Chase Manhattan Bank, founded the Business Committee for the Arts. Rockefeller's goal was to encourage more business leaders to give money to cultural organizations. "The emergence of the corporation as the controller of an enormous new medium of worldwide communications," said George Weissman, chair of Philip Morris, "the growing awareness of the corporation's potential and responsibility for enlightenment, the ever-widening scope of the corporation's horizons—these are the factors that will cement lasting relationships to the arts."[45]

With the opening of federal, foundation, and corporate coffers it seemed like museums' financial worries were finally over. Wealthy patrons were glad too; many had testified before Congress in support of the NEA. But there was another hurdle to clear. The Internal Revenue Service (IRS) still clung to its World War II classification, designating museums as recreational and "nonessential." As a result, they were denied the tax benefits and grants enjoyed by other nonprofits. Museums needed to organize if they hoped to truly benefit from the new funding opportunities.

And organize they did. In 1967, AAM convened a meeting of 12 directors from art and science museums, large and small, in Belmont, MD.[46] Led by E. Leland Webber, director of Chicago's Field Museum, they were joined by a rising star, Nancy Hanks, executive secretary for the Rockefeller Brothers Fund. The outcome was a landmark document known as *The Belmont Report*, a carefully crafted pitch for "substantial national aid." The report documented in detail the important work museums were accomplishing despite their scant budgets and crumbling buildings. It concluded by asserting that the "Federal Government has an obligation, as yet unmet, to assist in preserving, maintaining and wisely utilizing the national treasure in museums on behalf of all the American people."[47] Thanks in part to *The Belmont Report*, Congress was convinced that museums were educational organizations. With the 1969 Tax Reform Act, museums finally qualified for federal support and could bolster their organizations as never before. But were museums ready to take on so many new programs and initiatives? And to whom were they now beholden?

## 1970s: A DECADE OF ACTIVISM AND ADVOCACY

Federal funding required higher standards and accountability. Knowing that museums were still largely amateur operations, driven more by passion than professional standards, in 1970 AAM launched an accreditation program to improve their internal practices. Its founding chair, Tennessee historian William T. Alderson, shaped this program to encourage staff and trustees to work together to scrutinize museum operations and strive toward the highest standards of collections care, fiscal management, education, and exhibitions. To the typical museum visitor, however, the legislative victories and new administrative processes were barely noticeable. In the AAM accreditation program's initial years, less than 5 percent of applications were approved.[48] With few exceptions, museums looked and felt much the same as they had decades earlier. Outside on the streets, people were marching for civil rights, women's liberation, and peace. But inside, museums remained fusty ivory towers that looked down on the nation's turmoil.[49]

Public exhibits did not reflect the public's mood. In Chicago, the Field Museum's overtly racist exhibition *Races of Mankind* had remained unchanged since the 1930s. On the city's south side, the Museum of Science and Industry (MSI) developed an exhibition supporting the country's escalating military presence in Vietnam. It displayed a Huey helicopter with a machine gun pointing at a diorama of a Vietnamese village. Visitors could sit in the copter and electronically aim the weapon at a thatched hut, which presumably hid members of the Viet Cong. At New York's Whitney Museum, founded by two women, less than 3 percent of American artists showcased were female. In the language of the times, it is fair to say that at the close of the 1960s, museums were "the establishment": "out of touch" with the country's growing concerns about bigotry, the Vietnam War, and sexism. "Like the French nobility before the Revolution," stated one op-ed in AAM's *Museum News*, "the upper classes have repudiated their social obligations but not abdicated their privileges; they have retained the right to sit on boards and make policy decisions for the multitudes, who, increasingly, foot the bills."[50]

Idealistic young people began to push back, demanding change. Civil rights activists conducted a letter-writing campaign that persuaded the Field to dismantle *Races of Mankind*. That same year, war protesters swarmed MSI and forced the removal of the Huey helicopter. Activist artists marched on New York City's major art institutions, staging unruly actions

**The Circus World Museum in Baraboo, WI, was one of the first museums in the nation to earn accreditation from the AAM.**
By Carol M. Highsmith—Library of Congress Catalog, 2011630629

**Antiwar protest in front of the White House, 1968.**
Thomas J. O'Halloran—United States Library of Congress's Prints and Photographs division, digital ID ppmsca.24360

**Museum accreditation site visit to the Grand Rapids Public Museum, March 1970.**
Courtesy of Grand Rapids Public Museum, Michigan

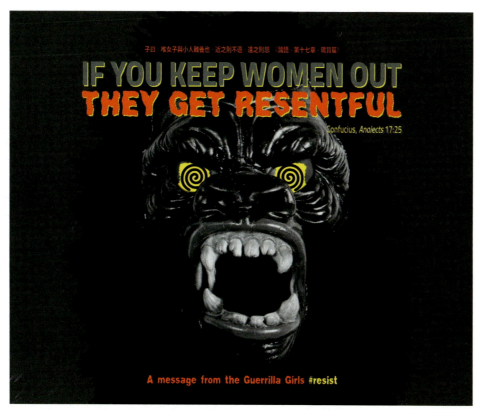

Since 1985, the feminist activists known as the Guerrilla Girls have stated that they have "attacked museums for their bad behavior and discriminatory practices toward women artists, including a 2015 stealth projection about income inequality and the super rich hijacking art on the facade of the Whitney Museum in New York."
© Guerrilla Girls; courtesy guerrillagirls.com

against the nation's powerbrokers and art-world elites. The Artists and Workers' Coalition unleashed cockroaches at a fancy gala at the Metropolitan Museum of Art. Women Artists in Revolution burst bags of cow blood on MoMA's floor while they shouted "rape."

Inside museum offices, staff also began to voice their concerns, optimistic that the new influx of government money would snuff out the old ways. "We were passionate about the Great Society and all the new possibilities that were opening up around us," recalled longtime museum leader Bonnie Pitman, who began her museum career in 1968. "We were not afraid of standing up and saying that things have to change."[51]

On June 1, 1970, the museum "establishment" and a new generation of political activists faced off. At the Waldorf Astoria Hotel in New York, elected officials and other luminaries had gathered to address AAM's annual convention about the new monies they had just secured for the field. Suddenly, 30 protesters stormed the halls. They bore signs with the words "Art Strike Against Racism, Sexism, Repression and War." Rafael Montanez Ortiz, director of New York's El Museo del Barrio, a museum founded a year prior by Puerto Rican activists, grabbed the mike. He spoke to the shocked audience and accused museums of "complicity with the atrocities of the times." The dialogue became loud and contentious. Half of the audience agreed with him. They began to pour out their frustrations about museums failing to confront the larger political issues of the day. The other half was furious, painting the protesters as "abrasive extremists." How dare they lash out at the government just as it was opening its coffers to museums?[52]

The protests at the 1970 AAM Meeting uncorked many pent-up feelings, from the unpopular war overseas to workplace conditions at home, especially hiring practices in museums. "[Discrimination in the museum field] certainly is prevalent," John Hightower, MoMA's director, admitted to the delegates. "Someone recently objected to a museum being referred to as racist. I replied that I knew the particular museum was not consciously anti-black or anti-Puerto Rican, only anti-Semitic. As far as the exploitation of women is concerned, the museum profession is notorious . . . museums hire bright, well-educated and talented women for extremely responsible jobs because it does not cost as much. This attitude is true throughout the country."[53]

Workers were now speaking out against their institutions in ways that would have been unthinkable in earlier decades. In an inflammatory editorial in *Art News*, Thomas B. Hess, a former curator at MoMA, laid bare the field's anti-Semitism, what he called the "most widely known, unspoken fact in the field." According to Hess, trustees were having a hard enough time dealing with American Jews inching their way onto boards and "brushing aside Jockey Club protocols." Hess's conclusion: "No Jew need apply" for a director job, "unless he has changed his name and religion."[54] In the grassroots journal *Ramparts*, critic Barry Schwartz launched an even more scathing exposé. No African American or Hispanic need apply for any museum job, other than guard or janitor. Schwartz took on the Oakland Museum, based in a California city that was 45 percent black and birthplace of the radical 1960s group the Black Panthers. The "lily-white museum commission" had recently fired the museum's director for hiring the wife of a local "black militant" in a professional position. Schwartz noted that there was hope through activism; the Oakland Black Caucus had called for a boycott of the museum.[55] Many decades later, the Oakland Museum would redress this turning point in its history. Its highly attended 2016 exhibition *All Power to the People: Black Panthers at 50* was funded by its women's board, no longer "lily-white."

Women, too, began to fight for equal pay and advancement opportunities.[56] In 1971, 20 female employees at the Metropolitan Museum of Art filed complaints of discrimination with the State of New York Civil Rights Bureau, with dozens more supporting their claims about a glass ceiling. John Cotton Dana's prophecy about women doing more work for less pay turned out to be right on the money. In 1975 Susan Stitt, later the first female director of the Historical Society of Pennsylvania, published data on the economic status of women in museums. She documented at least one case where a museum (illegally) offered pensions to men but not to women, as well as a salary gap of 30 percent.[57] The battle cry had been sounded.

It fell on deaf ears. By the late 2010s, the pay gap between genders had narrowed by only one penny (except in the case of female museum directors, for whom the gap with their male counterparts closed to "only" 18 percent). In her 2016 address at AAM's annual conference, Minneapolis Institute of Art director Kaywin Feldman attributed this dispiriting lack of progress to the fact that museum trustees of both genders still believed that women had no "gravitas."[58] For Feldman, speaking truth to power would pay off; in 2018 she made museum history when she became the first woman appointed to lead the National Gallery of Art. Likewise, Anne Ackerson and Joan Baldwin, two New York–based museum professionals who had come of age during the first wave of feminism, founded GEMM (Gender Equity in Museums Movement). With hundreds of active followers on social media, GEMM provides a forum and tools to encourage younger women and nonbinary professionals to keep up the fight. Its mission, in the spirit of 1970s activism, is to raise awareness, affect change, and champion transparency about gender equity in the museum workplace.[59]

One issue common to all museum workers, regardless of race or gender, is low pay. This issue also gained currency in the early 1970s. In 1971, PASTA/MOMA—the Professional and Administrative Staff of MoMA—organized what is likely the first museum worker strike. PASTA demanded fair pay, arguing that poorly paid staff were subsidizing the social status of wealthy patrons. The Teamsters took their side, refusing to cross PASTA's picket line to deliver food to MoMA's restaurant, leaving that task to volunteer "matrons in station wagons."[60] MoMA unionized, inspiring workers at other museums to organize. It should be noted, however, that MoMA's only African American female professional at the time, Howardena Pindell, did not feel she could take the risk to picket the institution. Many years later she reminded arts professionals that these early movements for labor equity were largely waged by women who had financial security in their lives and thus could afford to take risks: "The women's movement—basically, the white women—picketed. They called my office and said, 'You have to come down.' I said, 'Listen, no. I will get fired! You have a husband who supports you. I don't, so I'm the one who pays the bills.'"[61]

The struggles continued. In 1990, PASTA/MOMA strikers were back on the streets wearing decals saying "Modern Art, Ancient Wages" and handing out leaflets documenting unfair labor practices and an "appalling low" median wage of $28,000 a year. By the 2010s, strikes and union drives at museums around the nation were increasingly common, as museum worker dissent seemed to reach a boiling point. In 2015, at the AAM annual meeting in Atlanta, the group #MuseumWorkersSpeak organized an online forum for workers across institutions to discuss and confront the intersection of labor, access, privilege, and inclusion. More organized online efforts to document and analyze information about payscales and on-the-job work conditions followed as paying living wages remains an ongoing difficulty within the museum field.

In addition to spurring dialogues about workplace equity at all levels, perhaps the biggest changes of the turbulent 1970s were experienced by the public. If a museum visitor had fallen into a decade-long Rip Van Winkle–style nap circa 1969, she would have woken up into a radically changed environment. At a large urban art museum she would have witnessed crowds of tourists lining up to see treasures from abroad assembled into blockbuster shows. She would have been able to visit an array of historical sites newly renovated for the 1976 bicentennial celebration. Let's say she had traveled to San Francisco. She could have seen the first-ever museum exhibitions set up in an airport terminal, then visited a new "ethnic museum," such as the city's Mexican Museum, and perhaps ended up in the freewheeling atmosphere of a "hands-on science center," a far cry from the encased rows of specimens that probably lulled her to sleep in the first place.

Inside all of these bright new 1970s institutions she would probably read signs with words like "funded by the National Endowment for the Arts" or "made possible by Bank of America." She would have picked up a free glossy four-color brochure (an innovation at the time) filled with notices of educational events and festivals. Peeking inside offices, she would have spied workers frantically typing out grant proposals to fund even more programs. Perhaps she would have met a graduate student completing a summer internship as part of a new curriculum called "museum studies." She might even have spotted the museum's director jumping into a taxicab to head to the airport, on the way to a meeting at a funding agency in Washington, D.C., part of the plan for expanding the whole enterprise.

All over the country museums were exerting their influence on Capitol Hill. They were aided in their efforts by the first chair of the National Endowment for the Arts. Nancy Hanks had no museum experience to speak of, other than her participation in *The Belmont Report*. But she turned out to possess a remarkable "museum sense" and the impeccable political credentials needed in the corridors of power. Hanks was from a conservative Southern family, a distant relation of Abraham Lincoln and a close confidant of the governor of New York, Nelson Rockefeller. She was, by all accounts, charismatic, gracious, and a workaholic, making her a perfect candidate to get things done in Washington.

One of her first actions was to allocate NEA money in equal amounts to state arts councils (regardless of the state's population) to encourage the spread of arts and culture across the nation; that won her immediate allies across the Senate. Hanks then appointed as her deputy Michael Whitney Straight, a collector with family ties to the Whitney Museum of Art. That won her friends among the East Coast cognoscenti. (In an intriguing historical footnote, Straight later would admit that he was a former spy who had passed classified materials to the KGB.)[62] Hanks ensured that arts and humanities experts—rather than bureaucrats or politicians—reviewed funding requests, befriending her to the arts community. She also supported the idea that every federal dollar needed to be matched from another funding source, which encouraged corporations and foundations to donate more money to the arts. With Nancy Hanks at the helm, the great era of cultural democracy had received a huge boost.

The funding edifice in the nation's capital grew vigorously. In 1971, with a budget of just under $1 million, NEA distributed its first round of museum grants—103 in all, averaging about $3,000 each—to organizations ranging from the tiny Pacific Grove Natural History Museum in California to the behemoth Cleveland Museum of Art. That same year Congress passed the Museum Services Act, a bill to establish a separate federal agency devoted to shoring up museums' internal operations. By 1972 NEA's budget for museum projects had swelled from $927,000 to $4.4 million. These monies allowed museums to hire staff to create a vast array of new educational programs not only for their institutions but also for hospitals, prisons, rural elementary schools, and senior centers. Likewise, for the first time, the National Endowment for the Humanities (NEH) began to fund art and history museums.

Although the grant amounts were small, the hopes they engendered were large. As museums created new programs and exhibitions, they still faced severe staffing shortages, astronomical insurance premiums, and the rising costs of day-to-day operations. In 1973 Congress held a series of special hearings about museums' financial stresses. In testimony that transcribed into almost 800 single-spaced pages, director upon director informed Congress of their organizations' continued woes.[63]

Congress responded with a new program to reduce the costs of insuring international exhibitions. As the Nixon administration brokered diplomatic relations with the People's Republic of China, the government underwrote insurance for a traveling exhibition of ancient Chinese jade, porcelain, and statuary, meant to create goodwill between the two nations. It was so successful that in 1974 NEA inaugurated its Arts and Artifacts Indemnity Program, which reduced museums' insurance costs (some say by as much as $400,000

per show) for many of the international blockbusters of the 1970s, including *Treasures of Tutankhamun*, *The Splendors of Dresden*, and *Dead Sea Scrolls*.[64]

A native of Grand Rapids, MI, Nixon's successor, Gerald Ford, had warm memories of courting his wife Betty on dates at the Public Museum.[65] His vice president was Nelson Rockefeller, son of the founders of MoMA and Colonial Williamsburg. Under Presidents Nixon and Ford federal budgets for arts and culture soared, sometimes doubling in one year, sometimes "only" increasing by 25 percent, but always growing. Just in time for the nation's bicentennial celebration, President Ford proudly cut the ribbon at the National Museum of Air and Space on the National Mall, a showcase for iconic vehicles of flight and still one of the nation's most-visited museums. As Jimmy Carter entered office in 1977, Nancy Hanks ended her dynamic tenure at the NEA. Under her watch the number of applications for funding increased by a factor of nine and the agency's total budget grew at an even faster rate, from an initial $2 million to $115 million.

During the Carter administration support for museums continued to flourish. Joan Mondale, wife of Carter's Vice President Walter Mondale, became a leading spokesperson for all things cultural and artistic, earning the nickname "Joan of Art." Before becoming a political spouse Mrs. Mondale had worked at Boston's Museum of Fine Arts and the Minnesota Institute of the Arts. In 1977 she helped launch the Institute of Museum Services—whose legislation had been signed by Ford—at the Brooklyn Children's Museum. For the first time in history, the nation's museums had an agency devoted solely to them.[66]

An engineer by training, President Carter was committed to developing a more competitive workforce in the science professions and increased funding for the National Science Foundation (NSF). The directors of the Exploratorium and Franklin Institute traveled to Washington, D.C., and made the case that hands-on science centers could help. By 1978 NSF money was flowing to interactive exhibitions and related curriculum.

Museums of all disciplines, sizes, and locations had become part of a vast public process. Grants spilled forth from state and federal agencies. Still, federal money represented only a sliver of museums' overall budgets—an average of 3 percent—especially when compared to the sums other nations' governments devoted to their cultural institutions. At its peak in the late 1970s, NEA spent about $1.10 per citizen, whereas at the same time England spent $4 and France $10 per citizen in their respective nations.[67] Nonetheless, federal funds were an important catalyst for broad cultural development whose reverberations are still felt today. Museums now were able to fill "multiple responsibilities," said Nancy Hanks, "to the public, to their collections, to their staffs, to artists, scientists, and historians, and to the past, as well as the present and future."[68]

Along with federal dollars came federal reporting requirements that forced museums to clean up their sloppy business practices. Administrators had to implement financial audits, pay attention to employment laws, keep accurate records, and straighten out filing systems. The NEH required museums to consult with outside academic experts to enhance the content of their exhibitions. Curators and educators had often worked in isolation of other research institutions. Now they were exposed to ideas like social history and postmodernism that were sweeping college campuses. They began to incorporate these perspectives in exhibitions and programs.

Museum workers also began to share ideas with each other more freely, forming or revamping specialized professional committees and organizations devoted to their specific job functions, disciplines, and regions. These groups included the Association of Art Museum Directors (AAMD), Association of Science and Technology Centers (ASTC), and Association of Children's Museums (ACM), all active to this day.

Current and future museum professionals benefited from a fledgling university curriculum called "museum studies" that focused on museums as a career and not an afterthought. Others could enroll in workshops and purchase books that explained the intricacies of collections care, legal issues, and nonprofit administration.

Trained staff were joined by longtime volunteers and people who had wandered into museums through the proverbial back door. They came from the worlds of theater, journalism, and political activism, among other areas. Museums were attracting bright, enthusiastic staff who felt empowered to advocate for their own rights as employees while at the same time serve the public good. In the 1890s George Brown Goode had called on workers to possess a "museum sense." By 1980 Milwaukee Public Museum director Kenneth Starr reported that workers had "'a sense of profession,' an ever-heightening awareness of our common character and purposes, and an ever-greater understanding of who we are and what we are about."[69]

## KICKBACKS AND BACKLASH: NEW ETHICAL CHALLENGES

Growing professionalism and increased visibility led to deeper concerns about ethics. AAM's 1925 ethical code sat forgotten in the back of a file drawer. Meanwhile all kinds of dubious business activities—deaccessioning objects they didn't own, acquiring looted objects, partaking in insider transactions, tampering with wills, violating copyright law, circumventing employment laws—were landing museums in court. "In my first years as a [museum] director," stated the former head of the Field Museum, "I consulted a lawyer only a few times a year; by 1981 it seemed daily."[70] Understanding the letter of the law was becoming essential to leading a museum. Legal entanglements not only drained financial and staff resources, they threatened to erode public confidence at the very time museums were rising in visibility.

Two lawyers led the way for reform. In 1971 Marie Malaro became associate general counsel to the Smithsonian. As one of the first female attorneys to rise to prominence in the art world, she would go on to lead the museum studies graduate program at the George Washington University and write the standard legal primer for managing museum collections, still in use today. In 1974 Stephen E. Weil joined the Hirshhorn Museum and Sculpture Garden as its deputy director. Known for his quick wit, Weil penned dozens of influential essays on museum ethics and legal challenges. He would serve as AAM's councilor-at-large, vice president, and treasurer as well as scholar emeritus at the Smithsonian. Attorneys such as Weil and Malaro joined registrars, conservators, and others in instituting firmer ethical and legal guidelines for museums.

In 1978, after much haggling, AAM members finally agreed to a more substantial ethical code. The stakes were high. Even though "on matters of both substance and wording, [museums] were in total accord on few if any issues," the new code meant business.[71] It called museum workers "professionals" and sought their loyalty not only to their place of work but to the larger goal of preserving humankind's culture and heritage. Adherence to ethical principles would help determine whether a museum could receive accreditation from the AAM. Loyalty to the museum's mission was now more important than loyalty to a donor, a trustee, or even one's boss.

In less than two years the new code of ethics was put to the test. In the mid-1960s Jack Morris had been hired to direct the Greenville County Museum of Art in South Carolina, then a sleepy organization in an old house on the edge of town. By all accounts Morris had the "gentlemanly" knack of charming donors, collectors, and art dealers. By 1979 the Greenville museum was scarcely recognizable. Under Morris's leadership it had moved into a state-of-the-art building. Its display of Andrew Wyeth paintings drew crowds. It employed professional staff and proudly displayed the coveted AAM accreditation decal.

It turned out that Morris had pocketed kickbacks from dealers—$200,000, in fact—in return for helping the museum's leading patrons purchase the Wyeth works. In 1980 two employees questioned Morris's financial dealings, calling them a violation of the professional ethics that forbade museum employees from profiting on collections dealings. They further alleged that they had suffered reprisals for attempting to confront Morris directly. Distraught, they asked the museum's board to intervene. They also turned to AAM for help. Under the field's new ethical guidelines all museums were responsible for ensuring that their peer institutions operated solely to benefit the public trust.

Testifying in South Carolina before an investigative panel was H. J. Swinney, director of Rochester's Strong Museum and a member of AAM's board of directors. By accepting accreditation, Swinney stated, the Greenville board was "obligated to resolve the situation." Morris resigned, and the museum's board adopted a code of professional conduct.[72] It was becoming increasingly hard to do business the old way. The code of ethics would now be continually reviewed and revised.[73]

Ethical questions also were raised about the increased presence of corporate logos in exhibition galleries. With museum attendance growing, more corporations saw the benefits of associating their products with museums. They hired public relations firms to create exhibitions that then were packaged and offered for free to museums. From 1971 to 1977, for example, the Campbell Soup Company arranged a touring exhibition of antique soup tureens and other soup-related paraphernalia, covering all expenses for any museum that agreed to host the show. Many, including Kansas City's Nelson-Atkins and Buffalo's Albright-Knox accepted; after all, as famed psychologist Abraham Maslow once said, "a first-rate soup is more creative than a second-rate painting."[74]

Other kinds of arrangements, however, were even sketchier. Some curators and artists worried out loud that corporate managers cared more about product placement than scholarship and artistic integrity. In the mid-1970s, Hans Haacke created a series of biting artworks that critiqued corporate funding. To illustrate his point, Haacke used real corporate slogans such as an Allied Chemicals ad declaring, "The Road to Profits is Paved with Culture."[75] To complicate matters, profit wasn't the only motive behind some corporate sponsorships. Politics was. Industries with tarnished images began to associate themselves with museums in order to curry favor with policy makers and the public. For instance, in 1973, a South African mining company—directly linked to apartheid—sponsored *Gold Show* at the Metropolitan Museum of Art. Around the same time of the release of evidence linking smoking to lung cancer, cigarette manufacturer Philip Morris circulated the show *Two Hundred Years of American Indian Art*, tying beautiful baskets and beadwork to its core product, tobacco. "At Philip Morris," noted the exhibition catalog, "we have a great debt to repay to the North American Indians . . . who first cultivated tobacco and helped to found the oldest industry in the West."[76] Debates about such campaigns would pick up steam in the coming decades.

During the late 2010s, activists called on museums to remove from their walls (and boards of directors) the names of families whose companies were linked to denying climate change, perpetuating the opioid epidemic, financing drone warfare, and building private prisons.

The rallying cries of the 1970s and their many implications were hard to grasp at the time.[77] But one thing was certain. Museums no longer sat on the sidelines of society. As more and more groups of people worked to establish their role in the nation's story, and as staff tried to walk a fine line between speaking out and staying employed, museums found themselves at the heart of the debate over cultural politics.

## THE 1980s AND 1990s: GROWING POLITICAL PRESSURES

Soon after Ronald Reagan took office in 1981, the president announced 50 percent cutbacks to the NEA and NEH. His goal was to phase out both agencies because he saw federal support of the arts as unnecessary and even harmful. "The arts should do what they do best," the former actor said, "and leave the politics to the government."[78]

The Reagan administration's tax code revisions also removed incentives for donations of artwork. Decades of hard-fought gains seemed to vanish almost overnight.[79] To explore other avenues for funding cultural organizations, Reagan appointed leading actors,

In October 2019, as it prepared to reopen its expanded space, MoMA was still a site for protests. Here, protesters from Decolonize This Place called on one of MoMA's board members and the museum to speak with artists, community leaders, and immigrant rights organizations about their alleged connections to mass incarceration.
Photo courtesy of Decolonize This Place

musicians, and designers to a President's Council on the Arts and Humanities. The council would remain active until 2017, when its members unanimously resigned over Donald Trump's defense of white supremacist protesters in Charlottesville, VA.

Reagan-era politicians battled over the fate of the federal cultural agencies. To run the Institute for Museum Services (IMS), which provided valuable financial support for museum operations, Reagan appointed Lilla Tower, a former realtor and controversial wife of a Texas senator.[80] Tower spent the next three years

trying to shut her own agency down. Museums were protected by Rep. Sidney Yates of Illinois, who repeatedly took their side. Performing "minor miracles of political maneuvering," Yates saved the agency.[81] The Field Museum would later name a gallery in Yates's honor for his enduring support of museums in both Chicago and the nation.

To head the NEH, Reagan chose William Bennett, director of the North Carolina Humanities Council. In 1986 when Bennett was promoted to secretary of education, Lynne Cheney, wife of the future vice president

Dick Cheney, took the helm at NEH. As articulate, well-educated neoconservatives, Bennett and Cheney believed that museums' newfound interest in "multiculturalism" and social history diluted the intellectual and aesthetic standards of Western history. Both later testified in favor of eliminating the NEH.

Appointed as director of the NEA was Frank Hodsoll, a career foreign service officer. Although he professed to know nothing about art, Hodsoll proved to be a skillful negotiator who withstood repeated attempts to close the agency. In 1985, the Academy of Motion Pictures pitched in to help. They awarded the NEA's film preservation program, founded under Hodsoll's watch, an honorary Oscar much to the president's delight.[82] Hodsoll further convinced Reagan of the agency's worth by producing studies that showed how much museums contributed—in dollars and jobs—to their local regions. These kinds of economic reports live on to this day through arts advocacy organizations like Americans for the Arts. During his eight years as NEA chief Hodsoll finessed new programs focused on outreach, job training for minorities, and collections conservation. He also signed off on a grant that would later launch a thousand hate letters and several lawsuits. It was for an exhibition that included sexually explicit photographs taken by the controversial artist Robert Mapplethorpe that we will discuss later in this chapter.[83]

Science and children's museums fared better than their arts and culture counterparts during the Reagan years. At first, Reagan attempted to weaken them. Citing a controversy over the teaching of the theory of evolution, he tried to eliminate the science education division of the National Science Foundation (NSF). Congress responded by quadrupling the funds. This was because National Science Board research showed that schools were still failing to motivate students to pursue careers in science. Faced with a shortage of trained scientists and engineers, the nation was losing its competitive edge. Science centers were able to make a convincing case that their hands-on exhibits and teaching techniques inspired large audiences to take an active interest in science.[84]

Carefully navigating the political waters, science centers justified their funds with attendance figures and evaluation reports. As George Tressel, who was NSF's division head at that time, explained, "You can have the best exhibit or educational program in the world, but if there's no audience for it, as far as NSF was concerned, we hadn't bought anything."[85] The practice of measuring a program's success with data, engendered by the need to justify government grants, dovetailed with museums' shift toward other business practices, like customer service and marketing. With the need to attract more customers, for the first time museums of all types made a concerted effort to market their own institutions through paid advertising. In 1979 not a single U.S. museum had allocated a budget for advertising. By the mid-1980s more than half of the nation's museums were purchasing ads. And despite artists' critiques of their motives, corporations and wealthy individuals also stepped up their support of art museums. It could be argued that museumgoers benefited when the top strata of billionaires—who were the biggest beneficiaries of Reagan's tax policies—stepped up their involvement. Many invested in contemporary art production, capitalizing on the nation's creativity and cultural accomplishment.[86] As an ad for Chase Manhattan Bank explained during this trickle-down era, "With the government giving less for art and education, somebody's got to give and that somebody is America's corporations."[87] Throughout the 1980s the art of corporate sponsorship matured. When David Rockefeller had founded Business Committee for the Arts in 1967, private companies were donating about $22 million to the arts annually. By the mid-1980s that number had climbed to $700 million. Museum exhibitions were the top beneficiaries. Businesses made it clear that they wanted their names prominently displayed on credit panels and in ad campaigns—sometimes as large or even larger than the institution they were supporting. "There's not much P.R. potential in funding a shelter for abused women," admitted one executive. "You get the best visibility from art [exhibitions]."[88]

Soon museum walls were adorned with more corporate names than ever before, from the Omaha Steaks Room at the Joslyn Art Museum to the Altoids Curiously Strong collection at the New Museum of Contemporary Art in New York. Others harkened to past practices of linking shows to products. For example, the 1985 traveling exhibition *India!* promoted Bloomingdale's merchandise, and in 1988, Coors Beer sponsored the contemporary art show *Expresiones Hispanas 88/89*, at Los Angeles's Southwest Museum.[89]

Some schemes were over-the-top; for example, placing a new car in a museum lobby in exchange for a donation from an auto manufacturer. Or worse, science and children's museums displaying logos of companies that emitted pollutants into the environment or sold fast food that was fueling the childhood obesity epidemic. More than ever before, even though their institutions needed the money, museum professionals and the press began to question the line between corporate sponsorships and blatant advertising. Weren't museums supposed to be respites from corporate logos and advertising messages? Were dollars and cents replacing museum sense? "He who would ride the tiger may end up inside," warned J. Carter Brown, director of the National Gallery of Art.[90]

Meanwhile, art and history museums found themselves battling an even fiercer tiger. Conservative politicians and citizens' groups were again questioning the museum's role in society. Who determined whether an artist's creation was art, blasphemy, or pornography? How should museums present the nation's history? The central issue at stake was the appropriate use of taxpayers' funds. Elected officials argued that federally funded exhibitions and artworks should reflect traditional values, including those of rising conservative watchdog groups like the Moral Majority and the American Family Association (AFA), a right-wing membership organization dedicated to the "authority of God's Word at all times." Cultural historians and artists, on the other hand, believed that museums had an obligation to all Americans and operated in a gray area where objects have multiple and complex meanings. In the late-1980s, two defining episodes placed museums squarely on the front lines of these culture wars.

The first episode nearly destroyed the National Endowment for the Arts and almost landed a museum director in prison. In 1987, the Southeastern Center for Contemporary Art in Winston-Salem, N.C., received a $15,000 NEA grant for a traveling exhibition that included a work called *Piss Christ* by photographer Andres Serrano. *Piss Christ* was an image of a plastic crucifix submerged in urine, symbolizing the artist's ambivalence toward religion. It traveled to various sites with little notice, until it reached the Virginia Museum of Fine Arts in 1989. There, a visitor was outraged by the photograph and wrote a letter to the local paper, attracting the attention of Rev. Donald Wildmon, head of the AFA.

"The bias and bigotry against Christians which has dominated television and the movies has now moved over to art museums," Wildmon declared. He vowed to stop federal support of "anti-Christian" art.[91] He soon gained the support of an influential senator. Jesse Helms of North Carolina, who had long opposed the NEA, spoke out against Serrano on the Senate floor. Within days, 107 congressmen and 39 senators had signed a letter protesting the exhibit. Around the same time another NEA grantee, the University of Pennsylvania's Institute of Contemporary Art, was organizing *The Perfect Moment*, a retrospective of 175 photographs by Robert Mapplethorpe. The show featured formal compositions of flowers, portraits of children and adults, and what the photographer dubbed his "sex photos," which included graphic images of sadomasochism. Like the Serrano photo, the Mapplethorpe works were displayed without incident in their first venues.

That is, until another AFA mass mailing dubbed the show "child pornography" and Robert Dornan, a California congressman, denounced the show as well as Mapplethorpe's "homosexual lifestyle" on the floor of the House. Wary of the political fallout, the show's next venue, the Corcoran Gallery of Art in Washington, D.C., canceled it. Artists, gay rights activists, and even some museum advisory board members protested, attracting national attention to Mapplethorpe (who died from AIDS in 1989 at the age of 43), museums, and the NEA. The night before the show was to have opened at the Corcoran, protesters held a vigil outside and projected several Mapplethorpe photos, including his self-portrait, onto the building's façade. "The projection indicted the Corcoran's cancellation of 'The Perfect Moment,'" says art historian Richard Meyer, "by ironically simulating the museum's official function—the public display of art." The protest made national headlines. The Corcoran's director and other staff members quit, and the museum's membership plummeted.[92]

Under congressional pressure NEA withdrew two new grants from the Institute of Contemporary Art, the museum that had organized *The Perfect Moment*. During the 1990 Senate appropriation hearings Helms introduced an amendment to withhold federal funds from "obscene or indecent materials . . . including but not limited to depictions of sadomasochism, homoeroticism, the exploitation of children, or individuals engaged in sex acts." After much debate the amendment passed; all organizations receiving NEA grants would have to comply. President George H. W. Bush strongly supported the actions and, in deference to proponents of "family values," fired the NEA's chief, John Frohnmayer.[93]

One museum director refused to give in. The Mapplethorpe show was scheduled to open in April 1990 at the Contemporary Arts Center (CAC) in Cincinnati, a city that had banned adult bookstores and X-rated theaters. Harkening to the 1950s controversies in Dallas, a group called Citizens for Community Values demanded its cancellation, calling it the "kind of thing you expect to find in a porno shop in somebody else's

**Protest of the cancellation of** *Robert Mapplethorpe: The Perfect Moment,* **June 30, 1989, Washington, D.C.**
© Frank Herrera

town." CAC's director, Dennis Barrie, decided that the show must go on, a position that subjected his family to death threats and his museum to economic blackmail. Even before the show arrived, the "groups began a campaign of economic intimidation against our board," Barrie recalled. "The chairman eventually resigned from the board because the bank of which he was an officer was under tremendous pressure." On opening day, police evacuated the museum, shut it down, and led Barrie away in handcuffs as several hundred of his supporters chanted, "Gestapo go home." He was indicted on charges of pandering obscenity and child pornography, the first museum director prosecuted because of an exhibition's content.[94]

The controversy revealed, however, that the public had no desire to censor museums or artists. As Barrie's colleagues spoke out on his behalf, public sentiment also came out on the side of the museum. CAC's membership nearly doubled, Mapplethorpe's estate tripled in value and a jury acquitted Barrie, who went on to

work with the Rock and Roll Hall of Fame in Cleveland, the International Spy Museum in Washington, D.C., and the Mob Museum in Las Vegas.[95]

Despite the legal victory in Cincinnati, Helms's obscenity clause went into effect and most organizations receiving NEA funds complied. Fifteen grantees refused to sign the oath; of these, only two were museums—the Lehman College Art Gallery at the City University of New York and the Newport Harbor Art Museum (now Orange County Museum of Art) in Southern California, which took the strongest action of all. Located in the district of Robert Dornan, the congressman who had railed against Mapplethorpe, the museum—founded years earlier by proper society matrons—sued the NEA for violating the First and Fifth Amendments. The judge ruled in the field's favor, citing the obscenity clause's vagueness as well as its "chilling effect" on artistic expression.[96]

The culture wars raged on. Museums remained front and center in the larger national debate about the interpretation of history that was taking place across the country—on college campuses, among veterans' groups, in churches, and in the media. In 1991 Native American activists made headlines with a 16-day, 24-hour encampment at the Florida Museum of Natural History in Gainesville. They were protesting the absence of Native American perspectives in an NEH-funded exhibition celebrating the quincentennial of Christopher Columbus's voyage. When *First Encounters: Spanish Exploration in the Caribbean and U.S.: 1492–1570* traveled to the Science Museum of Minnesota, protesters threw a vial of blood on it to symbolize the legacy of Columbus's conquest. The museum responded by augmenting the exhibition with labels, a video, and a show about Native American resistance to colonial rule. Reacting to such controversies, former NEH chair Lynne Cheney accused museums of being "in the business of debunking greatness, Western society and even history itself" and advancing politically correct "anti-culture" values.

Veterans' groups also took issue with museum displays. In 1992 at the Visual Arts Center in Anchorage, Alaska, they complained to city officials about an installation by artist Dread Scott. The veterans said that *What Is the Proper Way to Display a U.S. Flag?* was unpatriotic because it featured an American flag spread out on the floor. An even larger group of veterans, the 180,000-member Air Force Association, took on the Smithsonian Institution over the display of one of the most profound military icons of the 20th century—the *Enola Gay*, the B-29 aircraft that dropped the world's first atomic bomb over Hiroshima, Japan. The controversy that ensued was a defining episode of the culture wars.

World War II veterans had raised funds to restore the plane, which sat disassembled in a storage facility. Looking ahead to the 50th-anniversary commemoration of the war's end, the vets proudly envisioned a mint-condition aircraft on display at the National Air and Space Museum (NASM). NASM Director Martin Harwit, a World War II veteran, and his curators saw a different role for the exhibition, which was to be called *The Last Act: The Atomic Bomb and the End of World War II.* "[We] worried that a massive, gleaming *Enola Gay* would give the impression that the museum was celebrating raw power," Harwit recalled. "To avoid this perception we needed to show that the bomb had caused unimaginable damage and suffering."

For five years the exhibition's curators wrestled with how to present a balanced story about the *Enola Gay* that described the events of 1945 but also questioned

It survived World War II only to be thrust into the culture wars of the 1990s. Left close-up view of the nose section of the Boeing B-29 Superfortress *Enola Gay* (s/n 44-86292, a/c no. 82, NASM A19500100000) while on exhibit in Gallery 103, National Air and Space Museum, Washington, D.C., June 20, 1995.
Photo by Carolyn Russo; courtesy of National Air and Space Museum, NASM-95-4624

the decision to drop the bomb. The Air Force Association accused the Smithsonian of political bias and political correctness. *Air Force Magazine* declared the proposed exhibit "unpatriotic" and "designed for shock value" rather than objective education. Eight thousand veterans signed a petition denouncing the show.

Because at the time the Smithsonian received 70 percent of its budget from federal appropriations, the veterans directed their concerns to Congress, which took up their cause. When the veterans and the curators were unable to reach a compromise, the Smithsonian aborted the show and Harwit resigned. The fuselage of the *Enola Gay* went on exhibit, on a smaller scale than had been envisioned, remaining on view until 1998. In 2003 the Smithsonian moved the restored plane to NASM's Udvar-Hazy annex in Virginia in an exhibition that focused on the aircraft's technology.

Politicians and historians used the *Enola Gay* controversy to voice their own points of view. "You are seeing ... a renewal of American civilization," said then-Speaker of the House Newt Gingrich. "The *Enola Gay* was a fight, in effect, over the reassertion by most Americans that they're sick and tired of being told by some cultural elite that they ought to be ashamed of their country." Hiroshima's mayor, on the other hand, called the cancellation "extremely regrettable" and noted that the people of his city "simply hoped to heighten public opinions toward the building of a world free of nuclear weapons." University of North Carolina historian Richard Kohn said the Smithsonian's decision was the "worst tragedy to befall the public presentation of history in the United States in this generation. In displaying the *Enola Gay* without analysis of the event that gave the airplane its significance, the Smithsonian Institution forfeited . . . an opportunity to educate a worldwide audience in the millions about one of this century's defining experiences." In the spirit of democracy and dialogue, newspapers around the country ran political cartoons and editorials that reflected all three perspectives.[97]

Although the public was visiting museums in higher numbers than ever, the *Enola Gay* and *Perfect Moment* controversies hurt the field's status on Capitol Hill. Politicians were questioning museum professional standards and, in some cases, threatening jobs and institutional budgets. Funding agencies survived, but in a weakened state. The events of the culture wars reverberate to this day. In 2019, students and alumni at the Corcoran School of the Arts and Design at the George Washington University created an exhibition of archival materials that retold for a new generation of visitors the trauma the institution experienced due to the Mapplethorpe cancellation. As director Sanjit Sethi said, "We can't as an educational institution move forward in a visionary capacity unless we confront major demons and ghosts in our past."[98]

When President Bill Clinton took office in 1992, his administration focused on reducing the federal deficit and balancing the budget rather than on restoring cultural funding. In 1997, under the leadership of Diane Frankel, founding director of the Bay Area Discovery Museum (Sausalito, CA), the Institute of Museum Services merged with the Institute of Library Services, to become "one efficient, centrally managed" agency: Institute of Museum and Library Services (IMLS). Likewise, NEA and NEH reshuffled their priorities. NEH funded exhibitions on "safe" topics like German Expressionist art and Japanese teenage life, two exhibitions that, ironically, would have been controversial during the World War II years.

Opponents of federal funding for arts and culture had won a key battle of the culture wars: lower budget appropriations. Yet in a larger sense, they lost the war. The troubles in Cincinnati became a lightning rod for activism over the next decades, especially LGBTQ+ rights, civil liberties, and freedom of expression. Museum professionals resolved to organize themselves more strategically. AAM and regional support organizations established annual advocacy days on Capitol Hill to make sure elected representatives remained aware of museums' value to their constituents. Foundations supported their case by underwriting more

studies that proved cultural institutions' economic worth to their communities.

During the George W. Bush administration, the federal agencies quietly rebuilt themselves. In 2003 NEA distributed $3.6 million—equivalent to the annual operating budget of one medium-size museum—to 91 museum projects carefully aligned to patriotic themes like *American Masterpieces: Three Centuries of Genius*. At the same time, IMLS quietly distributed thousands of grants for collections conservation and digitization, the improvement of museums of African American history and culture, and the Laura Bush 21st Century Library Program, honoring First Lady Laura Bush, a former children's librarian.[99]

The Barack Obama administration also bolstered federal museum support. Obama was a lifelong museumgoer who understood how important museums were to cultural identity and spending quality time with family.[100] In the spirit of First Lady Michelle Obama's advocacy for the nation's active-duty military personnel and their families, in 2010 NEA launched its Blue Star Museums program, which offers free admission to those families. In a rousing 2015 speech at the opening of the new Whitney Museum in New York City, Michelle Obama called on all museums to "open their doors as wide as possible, both to the artists they embrace and to the young people they seek to uplift."[101] Although conservative radio host Rush Limbaugh lambasted the First Lady's comments, the public joined the Obamas in embracing these values. First Lady Melania Trump agreed to be the honorary chair of the Blue Star Museums program in 2018, even while her husband's administration repeatedly tried to abolish the NEA, NEH, and IMLS. Congress and the American public fended the president off, thanks in part to the lessons learned during the culture wars.

Trump's policies also compelled museum associations, for the first time ever, to enter the political discourse beyond advocating for more federal funding. In 2019, the Association of Children's Museums, which represents the nation's youth museums, went on record opposing the administration's forced border separations of refugee children and parents. Around the nation, museums felt they too needed to take a stand on the administration's immigration policies since they ran so counter to the foundational philosophies of the museum field. The Tenement Museum expanded its programmatic offerings to help immigrants prepare to be naturalized as U.S.

Participants pose following a news conference launching Blue Star Museums at the Hampton Roads Naval Museum, in Norfolk, VA, May 26, 2016. Blue Star Museums is a collaboration among the National Endowment for the Arts, Blue Star Families, the Department of Defense, and more than 2,000 museums across America to offer free admission to the nation's active-duty military members and their families from Memorial Day through Labor Day.

Navy photo by Petty Officer 3rd Class Amy M. Ressler. The appearance of U.S. Department of Defense (DoD) visual information does not imply or constitute DoD endorsement.

An artwork made from recycled boxes by children in the Tornillo Children's Detention Camp at the Texas-Mexico border that was exhibited in Museo Urbano's *Uncaged Art*. As director Yolanda Chavez Leyva explains, "The children used a sign from one of the bathrooms as a base. 'UAC' means Unaccompanied Alien Children. They built a beautiful expression of faith on top of a sign that I find degrading and dehumanizing."

Photo by Justin Hamel, Frontera Studio; courtesy Museo Urbano, the University of Texas at El Paso

**Soccer field fashioned from pipe cleaners by children at the Tornillo Children's Detention Camp and displayed in the *Uncaged Art* exhibition at University of Texas, El Paso, 2019.**
Photo by Justin Hamel, Frontera Studio; courtesy Museo Urbano, the University of Texas at El Paso

citizens and refugees find legal support as part of its mission to "embrace and value the role of immigration in the evolving American identity."[102] In 2019, Museo Urbano in El Paso, TX, curated the exhibition *Uncaged Art: Tornillo Children's Detention Camp*, bringing to light the stories of individual teens being held in a tent city by the U.S. Department of Health and Human Services. *Uncaged Art* opened to acclaim at the Centennial Museum on the campus of University of Texas, El Paso. As museum director Daniel J. Carey-Whalen stated, "when the exhibit was offered, I did not think twice. My immediate thought was, 'the world needs to see this art!'"[103]

### EMBRACING ENTREPRENEURSHIP

Even before the culture wars, museums saw their safety net of dependable donors and generous federal grants dissolving. Only 25 percent of museums, mostly art institutions, had an endowment. Most existed year to year, or even month to month, with the ever-present possibility that one unforeseen disaster could put them out of business. During the late-1980s, money, always an issue, became the top concern.

Organizations were forced to make tough financial decisions that would impact not only their staff, but their visitors. For example, museums that had always been free of charge (such as the Museum of Science and Industry in Chicago, a beloved weekend hangout for neighborhood kids) found themselves charging admission fees for the first time in their history. At issue were ever-rising costs coupled with increased audience expectations. There was no easy way to balance the budget; even today the Association of Art Museum Directors estimates that, on average, museums would have to charge a ticket price of $55 just to cover the basic costs of doing business.[104]

How could museums spend less and make more? In this era of "social entrepreneurship," there was no shortage of ideas. Starting in the 1980s, museum professional literature shifted its tone, using businesslike jargon, previously unseen on the magazine's pages. Museums strove to be creative while optimizing every opportunity they could think of. Old-style ideas like "priceless treasure" and "NEA grant" were replaced with terms like *product development*, *special event rental space*, and *leveraged asset*. As Sherman

Lee, director of the Cleveland Museum of Art, observed, "Americans have never been happy with art, so they want to try to turn it into business, which they understand better."[105]

This was also the era of partnerships, whereby institutions strove to collaborate rather than compete with each other for grants, audiences, and even collections. For example, in the 1980s, museums in Boston pooled funds to purchase billboard ads with the catchy tagline "the only thing missing in the musem is 'u'" to build audiences for all the institutions in the region. In the 1990s, 13 children's museums formed the Youth Museum Exhibition Consortium, splitting the costs of creating high-quality touring shows.[106] Art museums cut costs by copurchasing artwork, an idea that had been floated many decades prior, but had repeatedly failed. Now the high price of artwork behooved organizations to avoid bidding against each other. In 2000, the San Francisco Museum of Modern Art, an early leader in these coownership agreements, finalized the copurchase of Matthew Barney's *Cremaster 2: The Drones' Exposition* with the Walker Art Center.

At the same time, museums' marketing and development departments grew in size and sophistication, hiring more staff with business and fundraising skills. Handwritten thank-you notes on embossed stationery gave way to mass mailings, databases, and other techniques that turned fundraising from a social art into a social science (and later, social media). Membership—a money-losing service that museums had offered since the late 19th century—now was viewed as a way to "capture" names and build a base of "supporters" who could be "cultivated" for larger donations. Museum members found themselves the targets of increasingly clever come-ons like tote bags, tickets to special events, gift-shop discounts, and one of the most coveted benefits, first dibs on enrollment in museum-led summer camps for their children, which, in turn, was another revenue source.

Museum marketers went even further in leveraging their institutions' public visibility. They courted hotel concierges, who could encourage cultural tourists and conventioneers to visit nearby museums. They placed promotional exhibitions in airports and restaurants. They advertised on supermarket bags, take-out containers, baseball caps, buses, banners, anywhere and everywhere.

To appeal to the growing population of single, educated adults, art museums added alcohol to the mix, beginning with the Asian Art Museum's 1999 "Sex, Sushi and Sake." By 2000, 80 percent of art museums were offering programming targeted to young adults, featuring after-hours "art"isanal cocktails, local brews, and DJs mixing live.[107] Others, like the Dallas Museum of Art, marketed to night owls, sponsoring a 33-hour marathon exhibition party, with a midnight jazz concert, 2 a.m. tours for insomniacs, and sunrise events for early risers. Historical house museums braved the scorn of traditionalists and capitalized on the seasonal allure of ghost stories, the occult, and 19th-century culture. They sponsored "haunted house" tours during Halloween season and "authentic" Victorian candlelight tours during the winter holidays.

Museums tried especially hard to appeal to shoppers. They hired retailing experts to develop profitable merchandise that went beyond the standard catalogs, reproductions, and educational toys typically offered. Art museums expanded into trendy accessories, refashioning bits of old exhibition banners into fashionable purses and commissioning unusual jewelry from local artists. Children's museums repackaged discarded industrial materials as recycled art supplies. Planetaria did a hot business in astronaut ice cream and moon cheese, science museums in polished rocks. Even elephants generously contributed to the zoo's bottom line: their dung was sold as garden fertilizer. And although the Witte Museum in San Antonio didn't revive Ellen Schulz Quillin's profitable fried rattlesnake appetizers, its store did sell rubber snakes, dinosaur chopsticks, and other tchotchkes. As they become more and more entrepreneurial, museums leveraged their most intangible and valuable quality: their allure, their trustworthiness, their reputation—the very word *museum*.

By the dawn of the 21st century, the museum had become a diversified economy with a formula for success: "great collections, great architecture, a great special exhibition, a great second exhibition, two shopping opportunities, two eating opportunities, a high-tech interface via the Internet, and economies of scale via a global network."[108] So stated the Guggenheim Museum's Thomas Krens, poster child for the fin-de-siécle entrepreneurial director. In 1998, with funding from BMW, Krens staged *The Art of the Motorcycle*, an ode to biker culture that broke box-office records by mixing the upscale biker crowd with the art-world elites. In an effort to replicate the Guggenheim's numbers, museums around the country assembled their own displays of vintage hot rods and stylish bikes. Three years later Krens turned the museum's iconic spiral ramp into a showcase for couture by Giorgio Armani, ushering in the era of high-ticket fashion exhibitions in museums around the nation: Vivienne Westwood,

Gianni Versace, Alexander McQueen. "Was this really art?" skeptics wondered. Did anyone really care as long as the crowds came? The answer was "no," at least until one museum crossed a line.

In 1999 the decades-old ethical debates about insider dealing, censorship, and blasphemy resurfaced at the Brooklyn Museum of Art, where entrepreneurial director Arnold Lehman presented *Sensation: Young British Artists from the Saatchi Collection*. Critics accused Charles Saatchi, a private dealer who helped finance the show, of having an implicit goal: to associate his collection with prestigious museums and increase the market value of the artworks he owned. But *Sensation* garnered even more attention due to a painting on display: Chris Ofili's *The Holy Virgin Mary* (1996), which was embellished with elephant dung. Many Roman Catholics were offended by the work, including then-Mayor Rudy Giuliani, who threatened to cut $7.2 million from the museum's budget and evict it from its city-leased space. In the end, Giuliani lost. The museum stayed, attendance boomed, and the art increased in value. It was a stunning example of how museums now occupied a high-profile position in the nation.[109] The stakes would become even higher as the new century unfolded.

## DIVERSITY, EQUITY, ACCESS, AND INCLUSION

As museums were fighting the culture wars, baby boomers—the very generation that had once dared museums to be more socially responsible—ascended to leadership positions. With a grander vision for museums than mere economic survival, they called on institutions to respond to societal change and circle back to AAM's foundational roots of education and public service. In 1992, AAM published a seminal report that reasserted these obligations: *Excellence and Equity: Education and the Public Dimension of Museums*. Museums, the report asserted, must "reflect society's pluralism in every aspect of their operations and programs" and work together to "create a sense of inclusive community that is often missing in our society." As Bonnie Pitman, chair of AAM's *Excellence and Equity* task force wrote, "the responsibility for effecting this change is ours."[110]

How could museums reflect the nation's pluralism and foster inclusive spaces? This was the right question for the times. With demographic shifts, the era's next generation would soon be the most racially and ethnically diverse population in the nation's history. But inside museums, senior staff did not even begin to

Organized on Thomas Krens's watch, *The Art of the Motorcycle* was controversial with critics but popular with both the leather crowd and the art effete. It featured vintage bikes such as this 1995 Aprilia Moto 6.5, which is in the collection of the Barber-Vintage Motorsports Museum, Birmingham, AL.
By Silosarg—Own work, CC BY-SA 3.0, https://commons.wikimedia.org/w/index.php?curid=23185427

In the early 1990s, Bonnie Pitman chaired the Excellence and Equity task force, whose report led to important changes in the museum field. After a decades-long career as director of several museums, including the Dallas Museum of Art, where she focused on visitor engagement with art collections, Pitman joined the University of Texas at Dallas in 2012. Her research there focuses on art and medicine and the power of observation. She engages medical professionals and others to incorporate the art of observation in their medical practices and to embrace a more humanistic understanding of health and well-being.
Photo by Roxanne Minnish; courtesy of University of Texas at Dallas

reflect this diversity: more than 97 percent were white. Clearly museums' soaring rhetoric was not in tune with the reality on the ground.

To find innovative ways to be relevant to a changing population, museums turned to their longtime partners, philanthropic foundations, whose bank accounts had swelled with the bullish stock market. In the closing years of the 20th century, foundations like Amoco, Mellon, W. K. Kellogg, and Ford underwrote research and training programs to help museums prepare for the nation's changing demographics.[111] Not everyone was pleased. Conservatives accused foundation officers of "philanthropical correctness"—that is, having a "liberal and multiculturalist agenda."[112] Inside museums, other skeptics complained that foundations had too much power and too little knowledge of how museums really worked. Yet the need for institutional reform was urgent.

In the early 1990s, museums began to invest in job-training programs to introduce young people from diverse communities to careers in the cultural sec-

tor. The hope was that some would appreciate the unique potential of museums to make a difference in people's lives. It would take a lot of hard work and open-mindedness. "I remember walking into the museum for my first interview," Angelica Velez, a participant in an early 1990s job-training program at Chicago Children's Museum (CCM), later recalled. "I was a pregnant teenager from 'the hood.' I looked around and then I looked at the museum staff, and I thought 'wow, I don't belong here.' But I needed a job, so when they offered it to me, I took it." Twenty-five years later, Velez was still at CCM serving as director of guest connections and charged with bringing other young people into the fold. "Looking back, I realize that what the museum was doing was very intentional. They were always about creating a community. They were serious in their belief that everyone belonged here, including me."[113] Although not everyone would find their niche the way Velez did, the many job-training programs for America's diverse youth that arose during the 1990s deepened the institution's understanding of the barriers as well as the considerable person-by-person effort it would take to recraft and diversify the institution. The genesis of one influential program in the Los Angeles area exemplifies the degree of seriousness with which museums pursued the goal of diversifying their workforce.

On April 30, 1992, around the same time as *Excellence and Equity* was released, eight-year-old Rebecca Horta and her siblings were huddled within the walls of a small apartment in Los Angeles's Koreatown district. They heard the shouts of rioters, as siren lights flashed through the windows. Rebecca's mother, an immigrant from Mexico, ordered the children to stay inside. On the other side of the city, Sanchita Balachandran was sitting in her high school chemistry class, smelling smoke and listening to police helicopters. She worried whether her mother, an immigrant from India, would be able to get home safely from her job in downtown LA.[114]

A day earlier, an all-white jury had ignored video evidence and acquitted four white police officers of torturing a black motorist named Rodney King. The city erupted in violence, despite the victim's appeal for calm: "can we all just get along?" As they watched the looting and mayhem on television, leaders at a posh Malibu museum also fretted. "We were still building the Getty Center . . . and we had been talking a lot about what our relationship with the city would be," recalled Deborah Marrow, then-director of the Getty Foundation. "[The riots] really accelerated our thinking and our urgency about making a difference."[115]

In the aftermath of the Los Angeles riots, the Getty Multicultural Undergraduate Internship Program (now the Getty Marrow Undergraduate Internships) was born.[116] Its goal was to bring young people from diverse backgrounds and parts of the city together in order to seed a new generation of museum professionals. The Getty funded museums all over Los Angeles to provide paid internships to people who otherwise would never have considered or been able to afford to apprentice at a museum, let alone consider museums as a career. The foundation supplemented the internships with training and ongoing opportunities to attend conferences and network.

**Rebecca Horta (left), an alumna of the Getty Multicultural Program, leads a training session at the Ontario Museum of History and Art with teen docents Jose Soto, Julissa Sota, and Ashley Espinoza. In 2020, Horta accepted a position at the Public Art Division of the Los Angeles Department of Cultural Affairs.**
Photo courtesy of Rebecca Horta and the Ontario Museum of History and Art, California

**Sanchita Balachandran, founder of Untold Stories, was one of thousands of museum professionals who benefited from the Getty Multicultural Internship program that began in the 1990s.**
Photo credit: James T. Van Rensselaer; courtesy of the Johns Hopkins Archaeological Museum

Rebecca Horta heard about the Getty program while, as a college student, she was looking for a summer job. Always drawn to art, she ended up helping with education programs at the American Museum of Ceramic Art in Pomona, eventually earning her master's degree in museum studies. She went on to serve as curator of education at the Ontario Museum of History and Art in Southern California.

Balachandran landed an internship working on an exhibition of landscape paintings at the Ruth Chandler Williamson Gallery at Scripps College. For her too, it was a life-changing experience, sparking a career path she had never before understood was even a possibility. Balachandran became an art conservator, eventually joining Johns Hopkins University as associate director of JHU's Archaeological Museum. She also founded Untold Stories, a nonprofit that serves a growing movement among conservators to expand their ethical framework to respond to current political and social needs and a "fuller spectrum of human cultural heritage."[117] All told, the Getty program has financed more than 3,200 internships at dozens of cultural organizations throughout Los Angeles. As

Balachandran shares, "The foundation chose to make a long-term investment in young people of color who didn't think they belonged in museums. I now believe that, despite the status quo, I absolutely belong in them and can use my training, experience, and perspective to make a difference."

### INTO THE 21ST CENTURY: MAKING SENSE OF WHAT MATTERS

Unfortunately, the surge of optimism brought forth by programs like the Getty's did little to quell museums' more immediate struggles. At museums small and large, from the Smithsonian to the Museum of Contemporary Art in Chicago, donors reneged on large gifts after clashes with directors over everything from curatorial content to accusations of financial mismanagement.[118] At the same time, with society's increasing reliance on the Internet, museums needed to make room in their budgets for full-time staff whose sole responsibility was to stay on top of new communications and technological trends. In addition to craving diverse perspectives and fresh voices, museums now needed leaders who could withstand the fiercest tempests.

After all, museums had become considerably more complex. In the new century, a leader needed to be an informed scholar, empathetic educator, astute fundraiser, financial whiz, community pillar, social butterfly, social media thought leader, and political animal; in short, a superhero. With such an impossible set of demands, burnout was rampant. Sometimes directors just up and quit. Often boards, worried about growing financial deficits or fearing too many radical ideas, dismissed them. Newspaper headlines about blowups between directors and boards replaced stories about controversial buildings and exhibitions.

Once a museum directorship had been seen as a lifelong post. By 2001, the average museum director's tenure shrank to four years. Half of those who left said they never wanted the job again. When some museums hired executives from the corporate world who presumably had more business acumen, that fueled even more discontent. It seemed that boards were abandoning decades of hard-fought gains in museum professional practice.[119]

The events of September 11, 2001, and concurrent burst of the first tech economic bubble brought additional woes. Museums struggled to recover. Tourism plummeted. Museum attendance dropped. City funding dried up. Corporate grants diminished due to mergers and weakening profits. Foundation endowments tumbled, triggering further declines. Layoffs were rampant, even at Krens's flashy Guggenheim. A 2004 Johns Hopkins University study found that 91 percent of the museums surveyed said they were in fiscal trouble, with more than one-quarter describing their situation as very severe.[120] The troubles became even more dire during the 2008–2009 recession. Real estate loan defaults ground the museum-building boom to a halt. Between 2009 and 2011, more than 20 museums—including the Fresno Metropolitan Museum of Art, Las Vegas Museum, and Gulf Coast Museum in Largo, FL—closed in communities hardest hit by the market plunge. Even relatively well-off areas were not immune. San Francisco's Asian Art Museum and the Brooklyn Historical Society nearly defaulted on bank loans. By 2009, almost every museum in the United States had cut budgets by between 5 and 20 percent, laid off or furloughed staff, canceled or scaled back exhibition plans, or delayed a capital project.

Still, museum professionals responded to difficult times with their characteristic generosity and humanity, setting aside financial and political worries for higher moral ground. Within minutes of the September 11, 2001, terrorist attacks, staff at the New York City Fire Museum, located a mile north of the World Trade Center, rushed to help with the rescue effort. Within hours, staff at other nearby museums were providing water and shelter. Within days, museums around the country were opening their doors free of charge to grief-stricken people seeking respite. Thousands unplugged from around-the-clock news coverage and poured into museums, seeking comfort and a place that would help them make sense of their world. "Hospitals are open. They're around to fix the body. We're here to fix the soul," Phillippe de Montebello, director of the Metropolitan Museum of Art in New York, stated after 8,200 visitors spontaneously streamed into the Met's galleries just two days after the attack.[121]

Within the months that followed, organizations as diverse as New York's South Street Seaport Museum and the Japanese American National Museum in Los Angeles were mounting exhibitions about the noble act of rescue and the even nobler act of tolerance. "As we gaze on the symbols of our shattered world we seek assurance in those things and values that bond us as members of the human family," Robert R. Macdonald, then-director of the Museum of the City of New York, wrote only a few days after the calamity, echoing the words of museum directors after the 1941 Pearl Harbor attacks.[122]

This spirit of community was confirmed almost four years later to the day, in September 2005, as Louisiana and Mississippi experienced the worst days of Hurricane Katrina. In New Orleans, staff at the Museum of Art and other museums remained on duty, heroically protecting the city's beloved collections from the ravaging floods. Within days, museum workers nationwide were organizing fundraising drives and expert assistance so that institutions in the devastated areas could reopen their doors as quickly as possible. And within the months and years that followed, they responded with similar selflessness to other environmental catastrophes around the globe: offering support to Japanese museum colleagues after the Tōhoku earthquake and tsunami (2011), opening their doors for free to grateful Northern California residents in the aftermath of the devastating Paradise fires (2018).

Museums found themselves responding to human tragedies in ways never previously imagined. On June 12, 2016, in Orlando, FL, Pamela Schwartz awoke to the news that a mass shooting had occurred at the Pulse nightclub, about a mile away from the Orange County Regional History Center where she worked as chief curator. "I immediately thought of all the mothers searching for their children," she said.